FRENCH COLONIAL DOCUMENTARY

FRENCH COLONIAL DOCUMENTARY

MYTHOLOGIES OF HUMANITARIANISM

PETER J. BLOOM

UNIVERSITY OF MINNESOTA PRESS / MINNEAPOLIS • LONDON

A previous version of chapter 3 was published as "Trans-Saharan Automotive Cinema: Citroën-, Renault-, and Peugeot-Sponsored Documentary Interwar Crossing Films," in *Virtual Voyages,* ed. Jeffrey Ruoff (Durham, N.C.: Duke University Press, 2006), 139–56; reprinted with permission of Duke University Press. Portions of a previous version of chapter 4 were published in "Hygienic Reform in the French Colonial Film Archive," *Journal of Film Preservation* 63, no. 1 (November 2001): 17–24; reprinted with permission. Portions of an earlier version of chapter 4 appeared as "Invisible Agents: Diagnosing French Colonial Interwar Cinema," in *(a): the journal of culture and the unconscious* 1, no. 2 (2000–2001): 76–92; reprinted with the permission of *(a)* and the California Psychoanalytic Circle.

Frontispiece: Reinhard Scheibner, *Mit Glans und Gloria,* 1995. From Reinhard Scheibner, *Lino-Métal: Compilation Gravures,* August–September 2001, Dernier Cri, Marseille, France. Courtesy of Reinhard Scheibner.

Published by the University of Minnesota Press
111 Third Avenue South, Suite 290
Minneapolis, MN 55401-2520
http://www.upress.umn.edu

Printed in the United States of America on acid-free paper

Library of Congress Cataloging-in-Publication Data

Bloom, Peter J.
    French colonial documentary : mythologies of humanitarianism / Peter J. Bloom.
        p. cm.
    Includes bibliographical references and index.
    ISBN-13: 978-0-8166-4628-9 (hc : alk. paper)
    ISBN-10: 0-8166-4628-7 (hc : alk. paper)
    ISBN-13: 978-0-8166-4629-6 (pb : alk. paper)
    ISBN-10: 0-8166-4629-5 (pb : alk. paper)
    1. Documentary films—France—History and criticism. 2. France—Colonies—History—20th century. I. Title.
    PN1995.9.D6B59 2008
    070.1'80944—dc22   2007043302

The University of Minnesota is an equal-opportunity educator and employer.

15 14 13 12 11 10 09 08   10 9 8 7 6 5 4 3 2 1

CONTENTS

INTRODUCTION

FRENCH COLONIAL DOCUMENTARY

Several themes present in this book crystallized unexpectedly when I attended a March 2006 lecture by Nicolas Torrenté, the U.S. executive director of Doctors without Borders (Médecins Sans Frontières, or MSF), at the University of California–Santa Barbara, where I currently teach. Torrenté presented a survey of humanitarian actions that MSF—winner of the 1999 Nobel Peace Prize and international humanitarian organization par excellence—undertakes in various regions of Africa, the Caribbean, South America, Asia, the Middle East, and beyond. A primary argument justifying the work of MSF is the need for a narrow humanitarianism that involves assisting communities in the throes of human catastrophes, including acts of nature and wars that affect various non-Western populations who cannot fend for themselves. These humanitarian disasters are rarely reported in the news media. MSF contends that most people in the West are simply unaware that they are occurring, and if better informed they could be led into action. Upon hearing these arguments and seeing an array of disturbing video clips as part of a PowerPoint presentation, I sensed the presence of French colonial humanitarianism as a specter in the lecture hall.

Footage of suffering people in the Congo, Sudan, Haiti, and elsewhere was reminiscent of the imagery used during the interwar period to justify French colonial humanitarian intervention. In fact, the images presented at this fund-raising event, masked as a lecture, had a powerful quality of abjection absent in most of the French colonial documentary footage and feature films discussed in the chapters that follow. In this book I argue that the power of the documentary image was intimately connected to the photographic construction of truth in the name of an evolutionary logic of civilization that was used to justify the imposition of French colonial authority. In other words, visual representations of an anarchic, pre-civilized state of being justified colonial intervention in the name of a biopolitics of civil and social rights. Further, photographic reconstructions of the primitive state of human civilization created a context for colonial interventionism as a scientifically constructed medical and hygienic discourse of social reform that projected a catoptrics of national, educational, and secular revival under the Third Republic (1870–1940) onto the colonies.

The rhetoric of a call to action by MSF in the name of unremitting humanitarian disasters around the globe repackages colonial humanitarian interventions. The high-protein, patent-pending plumpy'nut® food supplement, packaged for children who want to identify with astronauts but given to suffering adults alike, was featured as a sample of the new technologies used to save lives in disaster-stricken areas. Further, the MSF project mobilizes "technologies of disaster" in the name of an apolitical form of humanitarian action.[1] A crucial point, however, is the function of the endangered life as the justification for moral action, with victims depicted as existing in a state of exception, beyond the sovereignty of the state and without rights as citizens. It was in the name of global citizenry that the audience was rhetorically being hailed into a realm of "good works" in the name of humanity. Representing victimhood in this way refers to an important element in Giorgio Agamben's discussion of "bare life," where he writes: "He who will appear later as the bearer of rights and, according to a curious oxymoron, as the new sovereign subject . . . can only be constituted as such through the repetition of the sovereign exception and the isolation of *corpus,* bare life, in himself. . . . If one can speak . . . of 'law's desire to have a body,' democracy responds to this desire by compelling law to assume the care of this body."[2]

This "state of exception" transforms the human subject into "bare life" and contradicts the role of the body as subject to the laws of the sovereign, which in turn justifies a state of affairs that creates the law. An ultimate form of complicity between the infrastructure of structured global capital flows and self-administered antidotes attempts to regulate the conditions of disaster. When disaster strikes, it is often a matter of whether there are structures in place to contain the disaster and avert its most dire consequences. As I describe in chapter 4, at the beginning of the twentieth century averting medical and hygienic disaster was directly associated with international efforts to find a cure for sleeping sickness in Uganda, Angola, the French Congo, and the Congo Free State. This early form of humanitarian action was motivated largely by the colonial powers' economic interests in indigenous labor used to cultivate and gather wild rubber on colonial plantations for the export economy. Retroactive colonial humanitarianism justifies economic exploitation by finding the cure to the effects of colonial intervention. Finding the cure not only justifies the suspension of sovereignty rights under the colonial administration but perpetuates a system of inequality founded on the magical promise of technological modernity.

Admittedly, I attended the MSF lecture expecting a familiar apolitical vision of global humanitarianism given the recent history of MSF. The organization was initially composed of doctors interested in intervening politically on the basis of humanitarian rights, taking the side of the Biafrans in the 1967–70 Nigerian War in which Bernard

Kouchner publicly criticized the complicity of the Red Cross with the Nigerian government. Kouchner joined with Raymond Borel to create MSF in 1971, but the organization became more politically neutral with new leadership and through the expansion of its mandate by the end of the 1970s. MSF's secular humanitarian readiness has much in common with the legacy of the Pastorians, a cadre of French medical assistants and professionals who upheld Louis Pasteur's principles of social, hygienic, and medical reform in France and the colonies during the interwar period.

The evocation of an imperial global humanitarianism and the rhetorical tactics of rallying ecologically conscious potential donors in Santa Barbara in a European form of consciousness-raising mark another example of niche-marketed activism. The university-sponsored lecture was a means of evoking the normally invisible racialized "other" while laundering a vague sense of guilt for their inattention to and insularity from such questions. In the media flow of victimization, the throbbing head, bulging eyes, and shrunken body of the victim cries out for help to the consuming individuated Western subject, who can pay for a life by choosing to donate income that would otherwise be spent on the frivolity of attending the opera, installing a swimming pool in the backyard, or buying a bloated but possibly hybrid sports utility vehicle. Such arguments attempt to frame humanitarian action in opposition to the culture of consumptive gluttony.

An essential point of this book is not, however, to resolve the conundrum of a hierarchy of needs but rather to analyze the myths that underlie how the figure of the geographically remote "victim" figured in French colonial humanitarian consciousness during the interwar period. If the rhetoric of humanitarianism has shifted away from the development of a national consciousness, it remains with us, wrapped in layers of imperial hubris simultaneously unraveling and being reinvented across national boundaries. In the spirit of global capital flows, several of the better-known nongovernmental organizations (NGOs) circulate in the same social orbit of international corporate capital that exists in parasitic relationship to the increasingly indistinguishable international corporate and political class of actors. Or, as Agamben puts it, they "[maintain] a secret solidarity with the powers they ought to fight," thus depoliticizing disaster, obstructing an understanding of its local and global contexts, and producing victims as passive ciphers devoid of political agency.[3] Co-opting local suffering as international interventionism is categorically separated from the circumstances that create the disaster in the first place. The transformation of the humanitarian ethic into NGOs has its origins in nineteenth-century nation-state building projects grounded in ideas about geographic difference and successive constructions of "natural man."

This book addresses the parameters of French colonial documentary cinema as a history of a French colonial media apparatus. It does this in the spirit of understanding the rhetorical claims for humanitarian responsibility founded on security, human catastrophe, and civilization. The "apparatus," a term rooted in a psychoanalytic and Marxian analytic paradigm, is at once a machine that produces meaning and an overdetermined political and social context that forms the basis for ideology.[4] It is for this reason that chapter 1 begins with an analysis of the history of ideology in eighteenth-century Europe. In a survey of film-related inventions, scientific methods, and documents used to measure and visualize geographic difference, I explore a series of interrelated archives that illustrate how they served as the basis for the creation of a series of humanitarian myths that were primarily focused on remaking the French male body in relation to "natural man" from the Franco-Prussian War (1870–71) until the end of the interwar period (1918–40) of the Third Republic (1870–1940).

The transformation of "natural man" as a recurring figure beginning with Jean-Jacques Rousseau's *De l'inégalité parmi les hommes* (*Discourse on the Origin of Inequality,* 1755) was grounded in the history of physiology and gymnastic training and incorporated into the project of French colonial reform. The title of this book, *French Colonial Documentary,* refers to a corpus of documentary films that were made from the dawn of chronophotography in the late nineteenth century to the end of the interwar period, but also to an intersecting photographic and visual archive that simultaneously infiltrated and provided an authoritative context for colonial consciousness.

In chapter 2 I discuss the relationship between an archive of imagery and psychoanalytic categories defined through the projection and internalization of these images in relation to the history of the Tirailleurs sénégalais, or Senegalese Sharpshooters. Beginning with Roland Barthes's well-known analysis of the saluting soldier as the exemplary figure of French imperialism, I argue that Barthes's misrecognition of the figure in the photograph on the cover of *Paris-Match* is symptomatic of a broader history of misrecognitions depicting an evolutionary iconography of childhood—materialized as Bamboula, the "y'a bon" buddy, used to promote Banania, the French breakfast cereal. I examine representations of the Senegalese Sharpshooter through an archive of early postcards and documentary films that locate this figure as the sentinel of the French colonial empire. Initially renowned in France for their service in Morocco, the Tirailleurs sénégalais became famous for their service in Europe during World War I. I examine the manipulations of stereotyped imagery and its relationship to the history of shell shock, colonial psychiatry, psychoanalysis, and subsequent critiques.

Whereas the myth of the Senegalese Sharpshooter is focused on the body and gestures of the figure himself, it is the geographic mise-en-scène that serves as the focus of chapter 3. Through an examination of the interwar trans-Saharan crossing films sponsored by the automobile manufacturer André Citroën, I explore how the Saharan Desert figured in the French colonial imagination as the ultimate decompression chamber of the West. The crossing films were an extension of a longstanding national vision of creating a railroad itinerary to link Algeria to sub-Saharan Africa. In addition to outlining the expeditions and the never-completed Transsaharien Railroad project, I examine the role of the automobile as the foundational mode of transportation, which, in turn, became intricately associated with the film camera. The crossing vehicles themselves, like the mechanisms of a watch, were cued to the temporal structuring of the motion picture camera in their kinematic functionality. French colonial documentary is typically associated with the archive of Citroën films because of the way in which colonial geography became the ultimate vanishing point for a myth of humanitarian values in the machine aesthetics of modernity. The automobile and the camera became symbols of humanitarian action and the construction of tourist adventure. In the aftermath of the nine-month Croisière Noire (Black Cruise) expedition (1924–25), a well-attended exhibition of objects and films from the journey was held at the Musée des Arts Décoratifs, contributing to an evolving geographic mental picture of an African mise-en-scène in the metropolitan exhibitory imagination. Further, the crossing expeditions came to define French colonial documentary as an experience and genre of masculine adventure.

Making the colonies visible was focused not merely on a network of sites within the French colonial domain, but, as I illustrate in chapter 4, on diagnosing invisible agents that can be detected only by technologies of vision and know-how. Techniques of magnification and rendering the invisible visible as part of a medical discourse of hygienic reform drew on the scientific authority of photographic representation to make arguments about the social and moral imperative to transform the colonial landscape. In analyzing a 1924 short-subject film about sleeping sickness titled *Trypanosoma gambiense: Agent de la maladie du sommeil* (Gambian trypanosomiasis: The agent of sleeping sickness), I describe how techniques of editing and magnification support the construction of medical and hygienic authority. I also discuss the evolution of the educational medical hygiene films in France and the colonies initiated by the French parasitologist Raphaël Blanchard and address the impact of the Rockefeller-sponsored film hygiene campaigns mounted immediately following World War I.

In addition to promoting a medical infrastructure for colonial reform, colonial documentary was a government-sanctioned initiative subsequently redefined by the 1931 Parisian Colonial Exhibition, as I discuss in chapter 5. Instilling colonial consciousness among French citizens during the interwar period was directly integrated into a series of French colonial documentary initiatives. In addition to several films commissioned expressly for the 1931 exhibition, educational cinema was the basis for colonial documentary. Some of the earliest and best-developed efforts began in French Indochina under the tutelage of Albert Sarraut, the well-known architect of French colonial policy during the interwar period. Initiatives to produce colonial documentary films drew on advertising techniques and the discourse of crowd psychology in order to promote an ethic of colonial consciousness. The title of chapter 5, "Infiltrate the Crowd with an Idea!" refers to the perceived instability of the crowd and the need to manipulate its purportedly infantile undulations through the application of communication techniques in the service of geopolitical containment.

In chapter 6 I study a series of chronophotographs of a female Wolof potter as the starting point for ethnographic film and discuss the terms of its emergence in the history of anthropology. This history became associated with the role of educational film as a supplement to the study of human geography and with Albert Kahn's project known as Les Archives de la Planète (Archive of the Planet), which served as the basis for the early documentary film collection at the French National Film Archives.

This archive was conceived as a map of the world through Lumière color autochrome photography and documentary films financed by Kahn himself. Through a discussion of various expeditions that he sponsored, I analyze the context for obtaining these images and their role in the broader terms of internationalism and a Bergsonian vitalist approach to asserting the authority of the photographic image as the sign of meaningful difference and a basis for political action.

Some of the initiatives developed by Kahn carried over into the work of the League of Nations' Institute for Intellectual Cooperation (CIC). Henri Bergson's involvement with Kahn's initiatives and service as the first president of the CIC was significant, I argue, because of the way in which philosophical arguments about duration in particular became associated with institutional priorities of the period. In this context I discuss the debate between Bergson and Einstein on the nature of relativity and discuss how Bergson's reading of Einstein's work reinforced colonial imperatives by claiming that there is one master clock as opposed to separate clocks indicating times that can never be reconciled. Totalizing concepts of difference and projecting them informed the work of Kahn's Archives de la Planète, the CIC, and the League of Nations' Rome-based International Institute for Cinematographic Education.

The book concludes with a return to the theme of "natural man" and suggests potential sites for his reinvention. As another type of performance spectacle, related to the figure of "primitive man" illustrated in my discussion of Antoine and Lugeon's 1928 film *Chez les mangeurs d'hommes (Land of the Cannibals)* in chapter 1, African American boxers (Jack Johnson and Panama Al Brown) served as positive images of America for the Parisian avant-garde, signaling the materialization of natural man in dialectical opposition to the negative view of Americanization as Protestant uplift, standardization, Taylorization, and Fordism. As a counterweight to the positive image of the African American performer as natural man, the Senegalese boxer Battling Siki, who defeated Georges Carpentier in a reportedly fixed match, presented a negative vision of natural man because of his identification as a colonial subject dethroning the French champion who symbolized a French gymnastic ideal. The semiotic square that I just described repositioned the role of natural man through the popular sporting spectacle of boxing in an emerging international media apparatus during the interwar period that redistributed values of masculinity and colonial difference.

In the final chapter I also discuss the role of French masculinity in relation to Cocteau's stint as Brown's short-lived boxing manager and his analysis of feminine display in the case of the American trapeze artist Barbette. The masquerade of civilized femininity in relation to the racialization of "natural man" can finally be understood as contributing to the elaboration of a colonial media apparatus that drew on the history of bodily training at the intersection between black American boxing and French gymnastic techniques.

Research for this work has been conducted at archives in France and the United States and was initially connected to debates concerning the role and significance of colonial iconography in France during the 1990s. Most of the research related to the films examined in this project were initially screened with colleagues in France work-ing in an orbit of researchers connected to an associative structure known as Associa-tion des Connaisances Historiques de l'Afrique Contemporain (ACHAC),[5] but actual access to the films was crucially undertaken over an extended period at the French National Film Archives, while the collection of colonial films was being evaluated by Youssef el Ftouh with Manuel Pinto. In fact, without the support of Eric Le Roy and Michèlle Aubert at the Archives du Film at the Centre National du Cinématographie–Bois D'Arcy I would not have been able to screen these films or embark on research that has since led me further afield. Eric Le Roy writes that more than a thousand French colonial films were produced from 1896 to 1955, and only 820 have survived.[6] Interrogating the relationship between French documentary realism and the colonial enterprise is the central focus of this book. While Le Roy's useful filmographic cate-gorization of colonial cinema addresses, among others,[7] films that were filmed in the French colonies, I extend the parameters of colonial documentary as archive, myth, and visual index to the discourse of humanitarianism.

1. TUPI OR NOT TUPI

NATURAL MAN AND THE IDEOLOGY OF FRENCH COLONIAL DOCUMENTARY

"Tupi or not tupi, that is the question."

—OSWALD DE ANDRADE,
The Anthropophagic Manifesto (1928)

Jean-Jacques Rousseau's vision of a carefree, healthy, and happy "natural man" in opposition to a degenerate "civilized man" is deeply etched into the Western imagination. While Rousseau's well-known *De l'inégalité parmi les hommes* (*Discourse on the Origin of Inequality,* 1755) argues that civilization creates more ills than it can remedy, successive generations of nineteenth-century French hygienic reformers claimed that "civilization" improves health conditions and the general quality of life.

In this chapter I trace successive representations of "natural man" as they pertain to the legacy of ideology and the origins of French colonial documentary cinema. As an emergent mode of perception, the cinema drew on the legacy of the human sciences and later became a primary means of representing "natural man" in conjunction with a primitivist revival. Visual technologies used to measure and classify difference are inscribed into the very foundation of the French colonial encounter. An important starting point for arguments against Rousseau's positive vision of natural man can be found in the work of François Auguste Péron, the "pupil zoologist" who accompanied Nicholas Baudin on his voyage to Australia in 1800. While traveling with Baudin, Péron conducted some of the earliest anthropometric measurements on foreign soil by using a device known as the dynamometer to answer questions about the natural state of human existence. The superior physical strength of "savages" was thought to parallel their sexual instincts and desires. Péron, however, challenged the accepted wisdom that civilization led to the increased sublimation of the sexual instinct and hence to a diminished capacity for physical strength. He marshaled his measurements to prove the very opposite, that is, that civilization lends itself to increased physical capacity and sexual prowess. Through two kinds of measurements conducted with the

Dessine par C. A. Lesueur
15 sous avant la mort de son ami

Gravé par Lambert.

F^ois PÉRON,

Naturaliste et Rédacteur du Voyage Aux Terres Australes Correspondant de l'Institut Impérial
Membre de la Société Philomatique de la Société de l'École de Médecine, de celle médicale d'émulation &c

Né le 22 Aout 1775 & mort à Cérilly Départem.t de l'Allier le 14 Décembre 1810.

FIGURE 1. François Péron (1775–1810), naturalist and author of *Voyages aux terres australes,* sitting at his desk fifteen days before his death. Drawn by C. A. Lesueur, 1810. In *Voyage de découvertes aux terres australes, exécuté sur les corvettes le Géographe, le Naturaliste, et la goëlette le Casuarina, pendant les années 1800, 1801, 1802, 1803, et 1804,* ed. Louis Freceynet (Paris: Impr. impériale, 1807–16). Copyright Bibliothèque Nationale.

dynamometer, Péron ranked the capacity for civilization manifested by three groups of Australian aborigines in relation to French and British test subjects.

The British test subjects were consistently stronger than the French, a difference Péron attributed to the relative health of the test subjects after their long and treacherous journey. The results of Péron's study, reported in "On the Physical Strength of Savages," were considered credible upon his return to Paris.[1] Their scientific value was refuted only, as Jean Jamin suggests, more than fifty years later in the context of mid- to late nineteenth-century evolutionary debates initiated by anthropologist Armand de Quatrefages.[2] Crucially, the dynamometer also represents an ideological *physiology* associated with the development of chronophotography, that is, serial motion photography, by Etienne-Jules Marey. The transformation of philosophical ideas about the nature of sensation into a series of scientific experiments led to the development of a cinematographic instrument used to measure and visually reproduce movement in time. It is this Sensationalist legacy of cinema that became a source of colonial knowledge about the world in the register of cinematic realism. In the archive of Sensationalist thought, narrative fragments foregrounding a differential hierarchy of sensation formed the basis for French colonial documentary cinema. An accomplished expression of the French colonial documentary form is best examined in André-Paul Antoine

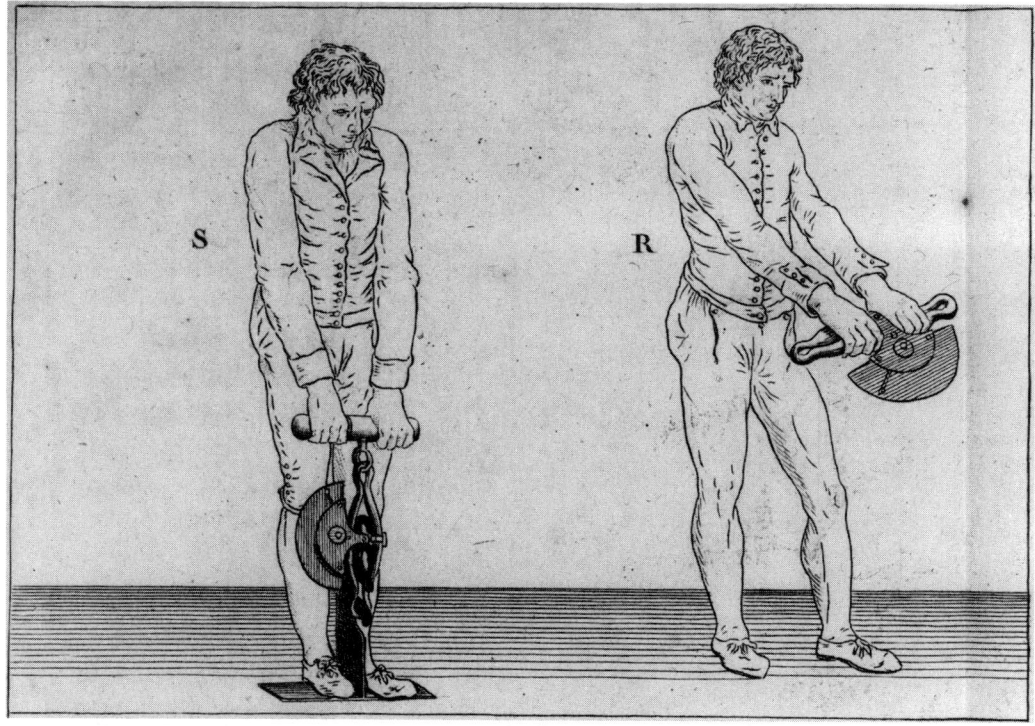

FIGURE 2. Edme Régnier's dynamometer illustrated in two positions: measurement of abdominal strength (S); measurement of strength in hands and arms (R). Jean-Baptiste Rondelet, "Expériences avec le dynamometre de Régnier," in *Traité théorique et pratique de l'art de bâtir,* vol. 2 (Paris, 1804), 21. Copyright Bibliothèque Nationale.

and Robert Lugeon's *Chez les mangeurs d'hommes* (*Land of the Cannibals*, 1928), which uses the trope of cannibalism in the South Pacific as its narrative hook.

IDEOLOGY, CINEMA, AND SENSATIONALISM

The legacy of "natural man" begins with conceptions of ideology. It is at the intersection between natural man and ideology that the cinematographic apparatus can be understood in relation to French colonial documentary. The natural, wild, and savage properties of humankind are presented along an evolutionary axis of civilization that was subsequently transformed into mimetic techniques of audiovisual representation. The history of ideology as it relates to the cinematographic apparatus is not merely a question of how cinema mediates representations of the real as addressed in the writings of Jean-Patrick Lebel and Jean-Louis Comolli during the 1970s,[3] but the specifically Kantian question of how we know the world. In *Anthropologie in pragmatischer Hinsicht* (*Anthropology from a Pragmatic Point of View*, 1797), assembled from a series of lectures delivered near the end of his life, Immanuel Kant set out to interrogate "how we know the world" by undertaking a systematic treatment of mankind. While

FIGURE 3. Title card for *Chez les mangeurs d'hommes (Land of the cannibals)*, 1928. Copyright Collection des Archives du Film et du Dépôt Légal du Centre National de la Cinématographie.

Kant acknowledged the prescience of a physiological knowledge of "man" that seeks to understand "what Nature makes of man," he asked what "man" makes of these sensory attributes as a freely acting being.[4] Kant formulated his anthropological perspective as "knowledge of the world" beginning with an interior investigation of the human faculties in search of universal forms. His emphasis on the willed nature and selective deployment of the human faculties remains paramount to the development of a pragmatic perspective.

Simultaneously in France, a materialist-based Sensationalism served as the foundation for acquiring objective knowledge under the influence of the *idéologues,* who were preoccupied with questions of how to distinguish the internal workings of the mind, the production of thought, and the observation of the natural world.[5] The human being as a unity was posited as a machinelike organism with an internal physical and psychic ordering that exists in relation to its sensory capacity to perceive the world. This conception of the human organism does not simply reinscribe John Locke's insistence on reflection as well as sensation, but serves as the physiological and grammatical foundation for ideology.

While much of the discussion to follow charts the history of ideology within the terms of the philosophical tradition of French Sensationalism (or Sensualism), I suggest that cinema might be understood as an ideological apparatus that is integral to defining and expanding human perceptual fields of inquiry.[6] By invoking chronophotography and machines that are part of an archive of inventions that sought to replicate and magnify the human capacity for perception, I draw out cinematic invention in the realm of physiological perception. As an educational device, cinema serves as an instrument used to train the human mind; it functions as a scientific technique for the observation of the natural world through the expansion and magnification of the human senses.

At the beginning of *Élémen[t]s d'idéologie* (Elements of ideology, 1801), the eighteenth-century French idéologue Destutt de Tracy proclaims that "ideology is part of zoology." This statement inaugurates a longstanding lineage between ideology and the scientific observation of the natural world, which lends itself to the unfolding of a "naturalist pedagogy." This conception of ideology defines two poles within the developing Western ideology of the natural world: an *ideological physiology* that addresses the physical and biological parameters of human sensibility and an *ideological rationality* that refers to the psychological and logical aspects of the human mind.[7] In an interrogation of the shared history of scientific modes of observation and the heritage of the moving image, ideology represents the initiation of an emerging scientific pedagogy in search of representational objects.

A physiological ideology serves as a generative reference point from which to analyze the development of scientific instruments used to measure the "physical and biochemical dimensions of human sensibility." In the French Enlightenment tradition, the evolution of a physiological ideology is positioned in terms of Abbé de Condillac's *Traité des sensations* (Treatise on the sensations, 1754) and his discussion of endowing a sculpture with human qualities. Condillac's treatise outlines the application of a rational aesthetics to human qualities. He underscores the sense of touch as the elemental sensation because it is precisely with the sense of touch that animal life begins.[8] Condillac's metaphor of endowing a sculpture with human qualities was subsequently adapted to a civilizing model in which the rational geometry of pure sculptural form is transformed into a realm of human sensation.

A Condillac-inspired notion of ideology also ties the cinematographic apparatus to the history of cinema as a device for measuring and magnifying bodily sensation. This Sensationalist rendering of cinema also suggests that graphic methods of inscription used to measure internal bodily signs with a pulse writer—the predecessor to the electrocardiogram—served as the foundation for an experimental device used to record, reproduce, and diagnose bodily movements. As an inventor of chronophotography, Jules-Etienne Marey pioneered the development of graphic writing as a viable diagnostic form within the French physiological tradition.

The "invention of cinema" as rather a nonteleological event with multiple origins can be meaningfully traced to the French ideological tradition of materialist thought. More than simply an inventor, Marey was a pivotal figure within French physiology. His work and the research conducted at the experimental station known as the Institut Marey point to a vision of the cinematic apparatus as an experimental means to picture motion in space and time.[9] Conceived as a scientific instrument, this rendering of "ideology and cinema" is an early dominant that positions the role of spectacle and reception as an effect of the popularization of scientific approaches.

As a historically grounded representational system of knowledge, the developing terms of ideology serve as an indexical site for the observation and critique of human affairs. Integral to the systematic examination of the natural world, the study of man as a zoological creature lends itself to a series of classificatory schemata intended to map out the nature of mankind, its morphology, and its sensory realm. While biology, economics, and philology have come to define the nodal points of an ideological science in the work of the idéologues, the trajectory of the concept of *ideology* owes much to contextualizing and systematizing an object of study. If ideology is part of zoology, man is part of a zoological system grounded in physiology and rationality. This evolutionary conception of man as descendant from the animal kingdom initiates a search for the biological origin of thought and its representation.

The Société des Observateurs de l'Homme (Society for the Observation of Man, hereafter Société, 1799–1805)—founded by Louis-François Jauffret and composed primarily of intellectual figures from the circle of the idéologues, including Destutt de Tracy—initiated a series of investigations into the natural sciences. The moral and conceptual framework of these investigations was established through a series of case studies. The search for universality throughout humankind led to numerous demonstrations of pathologies, including a comparison of skeletal morphologies and a profound interest in the study of physiognomy and movement. In the founding statement of the Société, Jauffret claimed that "the observation of physical man is intimately linked to man's morality; furthermore, it is practically impossible to study the body or the spirit in isolation."[10]

Pierre-Jean-Georges Cabinas, a member of the Société and an intellectual figure associated with the idéologues, was especially concerned with how Sensationalism could be translated into the thought process. To express the character of this action, Cabinas established a well-known analogy that equated the way the brain produces thought to the way the viscera—the brain, stomach, and sexual organs—act on nutrients.[11] Processes internal to bodily functioning were thus positioned as equally important and worthy of study as the apprehension of the sensory. In effect, Cabinas ushered in the study of illness and health as key to understanding human psychology, anticipating the nineteenth-century school of psychophysiology, which linked the physical and the moral.

More generally, this very indissociability of the moral spirit and the physical body in the work of the Société was also a claim for the use of scientific methods to study humankind. Human morality and the spirit could be included as part of the scientific study of mankind in terms of the *sensorium commune,* literally, "the seat of the soul." In effect, the *sensorium commune* was a way to demystify the spiritual implications bound up in human sensibility while asserting scientific authority in the face of theological and philosophical debates. The Cartesian mind–body dualism, along with Albrecht von Haller's earlier distinction between sensibility and irritability, became a means of directing questions of the soul to the realm of sensation, thus developing a scientifically codified language with which to observe and describe bodily movement.[12] As developed by the Société, this method was articulated through the study of human pathologies in a number of well-known case studies leading to a series of questions about human nature. While these methods anticipated Destutt de Tracy's notion of ideology, ideology was defined not as a purely objectivist form of observation, but rather as a philosophical system of ideas. As Michel Foucault explains,

> Ideology does not question the foundation, the limits, or roots of representation; it scans the domain of representations in general; it determines the necessary sequences that appear there; it provides the links that provide the connections; it expresses the laws of composition and decomposition that may rule it. It situates all knowledge in the space of representations, and by scanning that space it formulates the knowledge of the laws that provide its organization. It is in a sense a knowledge of all knowledge.[13]

Although the notion of ideology among the idéologues was somewhat less unitary than Foucault implies, its conceptual formulation was intricately connected to operational techniques for observation. As Jean Copans and Jean Jamin suggest, the concerns of the idéologues were articulated in two basic questions: What is the human faculty of thinking or perceiving? What is it to think about mankind, nature, society, and history?[14] As a master science and purveyor of representations, ideology was the formulation of observational methods. A number of significant case studies were undertaken by the Société that would initiate broader questions about human nature. A celebrated case study that led to an exploration of innate and acquired human characteristics involved a twelve-year-old "savage" child found in the Caune Woods of Aveyron, in the Midi region of France.

Victor, known as the "Wild Boy of Aveyron," was captured by a group of hunters and brought to Paris under the authority of the minister of the interior to the Institution Nationale des Sourds-Muets (National Institute for the Deaf and Mute), where he was put into the care of Dr. Jean-Marc Gaspard Itard at the institute.[15] Victor was studied by a commission of well-known figures from the Société, such as Georges Cuvier, Joseph-Marie Degérando, Louis-François Jauffret, Philippe Pinel, and Roche-Ambrose Sicard, who also served as director of the institute itself.[16] The case study conducted underscored a debate about the influence of "civilization" and "society" on the development of human nature. Victor represented the possibility of examining and distinguishing innate from acquired qualities. An educational training program was used to study, chart, and analyze Victor's responses. Historian of science Georges Gusdorf has noted that "Victor's education was conceived as a means of tracking an evolving human intelligence, step by step, from an initial state of nature, upon his discovery in the woods, to the fullness of human consciousness."[17] Education, as a form of observation, permitted a step-by-step developmental progression that imposed a structure of normative response.

In spite of the efforts of the institute, Victor's education was of limited success, and he remained incapable of expressing himself through spoken language. Itard describes Victor's difficulties with language and cultural adaptation in the context of Jean-Baptiste Lamarck's evolutionary theory of Transformism. The first of the two laws essential to Lamarck's treatise *Philosophie zoologique* (Zoological philosophy, 1809) served as a significant marker for diagnosing Victor's potential for reform. The first law specifies that in every animal that has not yet outgrown the goal of its development, the frequent and continued use of an organ gradually strengthens, develops, and enlarges it while bestowing a strength on it that is related to the duration of its use; however, the continued disuse of an organ gradually renders it weaker and finally causes it to disappear.[18]

Victor's development was stifled because "vital organs of learning" were permanently dysfunctional from never having been used. According to Itard, the complete lack of exercise of these organs limited his ability to be educated. That is, isolation during the early years of his development was diagnosed as a permanent impediment to the normal maturation of the nervous system, which is normally activated and energetic during the early years of life. As a corollary to the normal functioning of the nervous system within Itard's developmental schema, the imitative function serves as a crucial means of early socialization, allowing for the disciplining of the body and the learning of speech.[19] Following Itard's observations, Degérando noted that, unlike younger children whose developmental capacity for language is usually slow, Victor was simply disinterested. "[He] takes little interest in imitating our own pronunciation and his attention is scattered among numerous other objects."[20] Finally, Degérando cultivated the hope that more time and further mental exercise would elevate Victor's condition.

François Truffaut's film adaptation of this story in *L'Enfant sauvage* (*The Wild Child*, 1970) underscores the role of language as the focus of Itard's efforts. Truffaut frequently demonstrates the inability of Victor (Jean-Pierre Cargol) to pronounce vowels in the French alphabet to the utter frustration of Itard (Truffaut), which is, in turn, encoded as Itard's inability to express affection toward Victor as more than an adopted test subject. Through the figure of Victor, Truffaut points to the Sensationalist philosophical legacy of cinema as a meaning-producing machine.

Successive constructions of natural man throughout the nineteenth century served as parables for the larger philosophical questions concerning the nature of human knowledge. In this light, Victor represents an ongoing scientific fascination with the "wild" subject as representative of the possibility of training the human faculties. The story of his education foregrounds the "natural state" of his subjectivity. The question of the deaf-mute, for which Victor served as the nominal subject, was not merely a question of hearing and speech impairment, but rather implied that language was a civilizing force.

As Abbé de Sicard, director of the institute, wrote: "The uninstructed deaf-mute who lacks the facility for language is a living automaton, whose unstructured mind is less capable of action than that of an animal. If we call him savage, we are simply emphasizing his unfortunate condition."[21] Degérando, who also served on the commission, noted that the untutored subject who is deaf and mute from birth can be likened to Abbé de Condillac's inert statue, incapable of exercising the intellectual faculties. In his two-volume *De l'éducation des sourds-muets de naissance* (On the education of deaf-mutes from birth, 1827), Degérando continued to note that the very inability to communicate gradually weakens the other senses unless a helping hand pulls the deaf-mute out of this nightmarish state of existence. Finally, he asserted that, without any form of instruction, the deaf-mute is not merely less than human, but a directionless ambulatory machine.[22]

Degérando's invocation of the ambulatory machine not only referred to Victor's condition and the generalized state of the deaf-mute from birth, but emerged from an earlier mechanical determinist philosophy. Diderot's "Lettre sur les sourds et muets" (Letter on the deaf and mute, 1751) sought to explain "natural" communication as part of a logically reasoned grammatical structure that links gesture to language. Here the deaf-mute subject stood in for natural man, who was to undergo the process of becoming a socialized human being. Gestural hieroglyphs provided the foundation for the ordering of language that led Diderot to conclude somewhat arbitrarily that the French language is the most natural ordering of these gestures. A vision of natural man emerged in his discussion, founded upon a mechanistic conception of the human body, which functions like the moving parts of a clock, in which the heart serves as the pulsating timepiece and the other internal organs function as moving parts.[23]

The tension between a mechanical determinism as represented by Diderot's discussion of the deaf-mute and a vitalist anthropology of investigation in contradistinction to Degérando's emphasis on instruction remains important to understanding the functionality of the human faculties. The example of the deaf-mute was not merely an example of the savage but was the staging of a pedagogical debate on how to diagnose and educate the pupil through language. The subject who was deaf and mute from birth served as a figure of contemplation for Diderot and Degérando precisely because this subject lacked language. While Diderot's mechanistic philosophy and Degérando's nascent vitalism could prescribe a similar form of instruction and an interrelated search for a universal gestural language, repairing or building the clock, in the terms of Diderot's analogy, is not the same as understanding its nature. The natural as a rational form of mechanical functionality complements a vitalist rendering of natural language as universal but does not account for an object of investigation endowed with its own subjectivity.

Pantomime, lipreading, and sign language serve as the primary performative resources for the deaf-mute subject. The standardization and eventual technological enhancement of these "natural" languages are long-standing tropes that were reinvested with a technological form by the end of the nineteenth century. Georges Demenÿ, Etienne-Jules Marey's close collaborator from 1881 to 1893, recorded a series of chronophotographs as a form of visual education for the deaf and mute through the moving image with Hector Marichelle, the director of the Institution Nationale des Sourd-Muets. As Demenÿ wrote, "The use of chronophotography as an analytic method, so well adapted to the study of locomotion in general, can also be applied to more delicate gestures, such as the movement of facial muscles."[24] As a new analytic method capable of recording "micromotions," chronophotography established a trajectory for picturing a potential field of visual observation and demonstration.

The invention of mechanical auditory and visual devices used for amplification and projection led to the development of an array of prosthetic apparatuses to accommodate sensory attributes of the deaf-mute subject. Demenÿ's Phonoscope emerged from Marichelle's interest in using close-up images of silent filmed speech as a guide to lipreading and helping children understand how to form vowels with the movement of their lips.[25] He wanted to recreate the visible dynamism of speech for the deaf-mute pupil in such a way that it could be replayed over and over again. To meet these requirements, Demenÿ created a derivation of the zoetrope, which consisted of twenty-four positive photographic images positioned in equidistant holes cut to fit around the circumference of a circular glass disk. Unlike in several phenakistoscope projectors based on the magic lantern, Demenÿ used a hand crank to move the disk in relation to an alternating shutter. As Laurent Mannoni explains, Demenÿ's Phonoscope was one of the first motion picture projectors, in spite of the fact that it was poorly illuminated and had no viable future as a disk-based projector.[26]

Demenÿ described the experience of testing his new invention on three young deaf-mute subjects from the institute by visually recording, in close-up, his recitation of the sentences *Je vous aime* (I love you, 1891) and *Vive la France* (Long live France, 1892).[27] One of the pupils recognized the two sentences almost immediately, but the others had difficulty figuring out where the phrase began and ended, leading to some confusion. Furthermore, the varying speeds at which Demenÿ turned the hand crank of the Phonoscope determined how quickly the pupils would recite the phrases. The blind repetition of these phrases by the test subjects following the jerky sped-up and slowed-down motion of the Phonoscope led to Demenÿ's half-joking claim that it could be likened to a hurdy-gurdy.[28]

As a visual complement to the re-creation of auditory sound, Demenÿ's Phonoscope was part of a longstanding tradition of graphic inscription associated with the German school of psychophysiology. The development of optical-acoustic movement pioneered by Hermann von Helmholtz followed earlier inventions, such as Johannes Müller's artificial larynx, which could imitate animal sounds, and Rudolf Koenig's vocal gas light, which illustrated the movements of the larynx.[29] More specifically, Koenig's dancing flame would mimic vocal vibrations, creating a visual spectacle. While these inventions seem more like fairground attractions than laboratory instruments, promoters who were willing to pay large sums for the rental of Demenÿ's Phonoscope dulled its scientific and pedagogical pedigree. Heralded for a brief time as the visual equivalent of Edison's sensational phonograph, Demenÿ's invention was the progenitor of a series of cameras and projectors, later sold and licensed to Léon Gaumont.

Magnification of the visible as a prosthesis for the deaf-mute subject demonstrated the potential for magnifying and enhancing the senses. The adjustability of the senses was closely associated with the possibilities for mechanical reproduction. In this regard, it is not coincidental that Walter Benjamin cites the example of larynx surgery (known as the otorhinolaryngeal procedure), asserting that the boldness of the cameraman is analogous to that of a surgeon. Benjamin specifies that the "acrobatic tricks of larynx surgery have to be performed following the reversed picture in the laryngoscope."[30] Citing the French essayist Luc Durtain, Benjamin makes reference to a series of complicated surgical techniques related to the ear and the eye undertaken by the surgeon qua cameraman, equipped with an expanding set of visual implements. In Benjamin's essay the restoration of speech through larynx surgery also parallels the emergence of the sound film that added voice to the silent picture and mechanically reproduced audible sound in a theater.

Benjamin's surgical cameraman harks back to Victor's mentor, Jean-Marc Gaspard Itard, who developed the otorhinolaryngeal procedure with the understanding that most deaf-mute patients retained some form of rudimentary hearing, and thus invented new therapeutic techniques for ear surgery. Because Itard disagreed with the accepted wisdom that deafness was absolute and could be attributed simply to the paralysis of the auditory nerve, he invented an audiometer to test the hearing of deaf subjects and also developed a technique of lipreading with his collaborator, Jacob-Rodrigues Pereire.[31]

With a strange sense of historic monumentalism, the great-grandson of Pereire,

FIGURE 4. Georges Demenÿ recites "Vive la France" (Long live France), recorded on the Demenÿ Phonoscope for Hector Marichelle's Deaf-and-Mute Institute. Georges Demenÿ, "Les photographies parlantes," *La Nature* 20 (April 16, 1892).

Eugène Pereire, held a scientific conference at his home to present the Microphono-graphe, a new invention developed from Itard and Pereire's work on lipreading. Created by the Geneva-based physicist F. Dussard, the Microphonographe attempted to activate the cerebral cortex by stimulating the acoustic nerve and nerve endings near the ear canal. Dussard used an amplified telephone receiver designed in the shape of head-phones to project the sound waves.[32] Dussard's device was based on a stylus-driven rotating cylinder that could record the softest sounds on a wax surface and amplify them. Dussard's invention sought to circumvent sensory dysfunction by tapping into the ancillary structure of the nervous system. A significant element in Dussard's invention was the sensitivity of the microphone used to record sound, developed by his assistant, George F. Jaubert. This microphone was so sensitive that it could record the fluttering of an insect's wings and the sound of ants marching in formation—at the same time that Marey was beginning to analyze and film the flight of insects with a high-speed chronophotographic camera.

Dussard's invention was conceived as a fairly simple recording and playback device. It was later adjusted to work as a telephone answering machine, but it might also be considered an early predecessor of the hearing aid. A final genesis of Dussard's Microphonographe was the creation of a Cinémicrophonographe, which could synchronize speech and gesture. The Cinémicrophonographe, an idea developed by Pereire and Jaubert, was prepared for the 1900 Universal Exhibition in Paris as the centerpiece of the pavilion sponsored by the Compagnie Générale Transatlantique, the shipping and cruise ship concern led by Pereire. Pereire's idea was to feature short sequences with dialogue illustrating a departure on a luxury ocean liner, life on board, the chatter of sailors, and the sound of dropping anchor. In addition to showing the principal French ports of call, Pereire wanted to demonstrate the arrival of French troops in Madagascar and other French colonies that served as economic and cultural gateways to raw materials and indigenous cultural traditions.

The coupling of implements for sensory enhancement with an experience of the hitherto unknown began with the ambulatory state of the deaf-mute and developed into a popular attraction. The magnification of sound and sight not only compensated for the sensory limitations of the deaf-mute subject but also simultaneously opened onto a previously invisible spectrum. The expansion and magnification of human faculties was bound up in arguments related to the status of natural man. While the deaf-mute subject demonstrated the potential of the civilizing force of language, the core of the human faculty for perception, following Condillac, was considered to reside not in the sense of sight, hearing, taste, or smell, but rather in the sense of touch.

Condillac's theory of the sensations served as a cornerstone for the work of the idéologues, which was foundationally grounded in the sense of touch. Condillac introduced the metaphor of the statue in *Traité des sensations* with the gift of the rose and the corollary sense of smell. He demonstrated the interlocking nature of the senses by beginning with what it means to smell a rose. He theorized that time-based memories are created as well as the capacity for comparison, judgment, and the formation of the passions. The development of one sense founds all faculties of perception, with the maturation of the olfactory sense as a model. For Condillac, human consciousness as associated with thought *is* the ability to feel, which is not merely the sense of touch. Further, the sense of touch becomes transformed into the measurement and quantification of sensorial capacities beginning with the study of fatigue.

MEASURING FATIGUE

The ergograph, developed by the Italian physiologist Angelo Mosso in 1884, was the first of the dynamometric devices that could measure fatigue with any accuracy. As Mosso writes in his entertaining study *La Fatiga* (1891), the dynamometer was developed by Edmé Régnier in response to the interest of Georges Louis Leclerc, Comte de Buffon, in establishing comparative measurements of human force across age-related, racial, and environmental categories.[33] Though these differential criteria became overdetermined categories by the late nineteenth century, Mosso's ergograph mediated them as part of an emerging late nineteenth-century physiological dominant—the study of fatigue through the dilation of muscular fibers.

Marey's early experiments were grounded in techniques of graphic inscription initially deployed to measure internal bodily movement, such as use of the sphygmograph (to measure the pulse) and the myograph (to measure muscular contractions). As Mosso dutifully acknowledged, Marey's work served as an immediate predecessor to the development of the ergograph.[34] Specifically, this device measured muscle fatigue in the

FIGURE 5. The ergograph in Angelo Mosso, *Fatigue (La Fatiga),* trans. Margaret and W. B. Drummond (New York: G. P. Putnam and Sons, 1904 [1891]), 90.

forearm through the rhythmic exercise and eventual exhaustion of the middle finger. A stylus was attached to a cord that connected the finger to a suspended weight, which graphically recorded the process of fatigue through the lifting and dropping of a weight.[35] As Anson Rabinhach has observed, this rudimentary instrument was based on the notion that muscle fatigue is represented by the lessening of muscular force through exercise.

The isolation of an articulated movement as associated with measurable muscular fatigue initiated a broadly applicable technique for studying fatigue. As Georges Ribeill explained in his indispensable overview of the early history of ergonomics in France, three schools of ergonomics developed in France between the Franco-Prussian War and World War I. These three schools focused on aspects of ergonomics that, though interconnected and overlapping, are broadly identified as the isolation and measurement of muscular articulations, such as the movement of the finger described in Mosso's work; a conception of functional energy as tied to muscular tissue that was associated with thermodynamics and developed by the French physiologist Auguste Chauveau; and the analytic tracing of physiological movement, pioneered by Marey's graphic method of inscription.[36]

The study of fatigue can be localized more generally within a German physiological tradition of scientific materialism that grew out of the defeat of liberal ideas in the public sphere following the revolution of 1848.[37] A number of Marey's inventions were simply improvements on devices developed within this tradition. One of Marey's earliest inventions, presented as part of his medical thesis, was a portable sphygmograph. It was adapted from Carl Ludwig's kymograph (1847), which harnessed the blood pressure of a dog's artery as a form of graphic writing by adapting a mercury manometer to a floating writing stylus.[38]

Tracing the movement of mechanical force was a significant nodal point of Marey's work, and it addressed an evolving nineteenth-century physiological field of research that sought to measure and identify the mechanisms at work in the transmutation of forces. The kilogram-meter (also known as the foot-pound) quantifies work in terms of physical force. It refers to the amount of energy exerted in raising a mass of one kilogram one meter.[39] The study of fatigue as the direct consequence of work and the exertion of physical force was a significant subject of physiological research that also responded to broader social questions. Representative of a search for the broader terms of regeneration, fatigue-related studies sought to provide an antidote to social degeneration within the realm of physical mechanics.

It was within these broader terms of regeneration that an early collaborator of Marey, Auguste Chauveau, claimed that physiological work can be described as a "metamorphosis between the initial chemical reactions implied by movement and the final production of sensitive heat and mechanical work."[40] Just as Marx localized the economic cell-form within the value-form of the commodity, Chauveau identified physiological work with the contraction of the muscle, leading to its subsequent elasticity and the creation of heat. Further, the economy of the human motor in relation

FIGURE 6. Testing fatigue through the exercised finger in Mosso, *Fatigue,* 92.

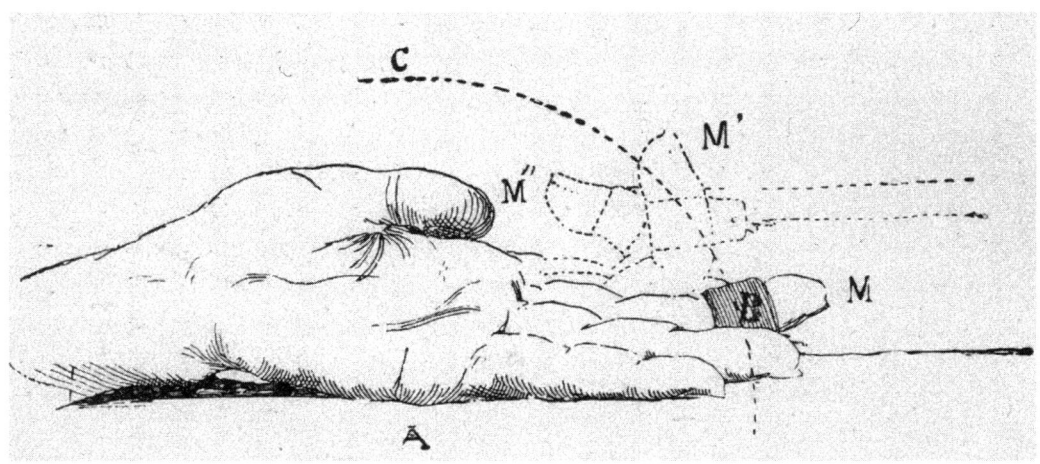

FIGURE 7. Positions of the fatigued finger in Mosso, *Fatigue,* 101.

to the steam engine was an analogy frequently invoked by physiologists. In light of the steam engine, Gustave-Adolphe Hirn's early experiments sought to measure the exertion of human work by enclosing a human test subject in a hermetically sealed room as a means of measuring the heat produced by the subject's body temperature after exercising on a treadmill.[41]

Just as Hirn's experiment (conducted on prisoners) became an early point of reference for studying the creation of heat in relation to movement, the production of heat by the "animal mechanism" was correlated with the efficiency of the steam engine. The mid-nineteenth-century French medical researcher and scientist Jules Gavarret wrote that "man's muscular system is infinitely superior to the best built devices in the service of science and industry."[42] He went on to note that the superiority of certain muscles is even more astounding; a muscular apparatus such as the heart is at least eight times more powerful than the most forceful locomotives used to traverse the steepest Tyrolean mountaintops in Austria. Gavarret finally cited Helmholtz's invocation of the superior objective capacities of the animal mechanism when he wrote: "The animal body differs from the steam engine not only through its means of creating heat and work, but through its means of directing these forces to its special goals."[43]

Helmholtz's experiments measuring human blood pressure as a model for the efficiency of machines became closely associated with the emerging science of thermodynamics. Marey described thermodynamics as the science that measures the relationship between heat and mechanical work.[44] In a similar way, the mechanical mediation of work represented a promise of regeneration. Although there was significant collaboration and continuity between French and German physiologists both before and after the Franco-Prussian War, France's defeat underscored the urgency of the development of techniques to revive a fatigued national body. The physiological study of the contractions and properties of muscular tissue became a privileged site from which to analyze and direct human movement.

PINPOINTING BONES, MUSCLES, AND MIND

A number of comparative studies determined the relationship between mechanical work and muscular morphology at Marey's Physiological Station. In order to understand the relationship between human locomotion and muscular morphology, Marey compared the thick and corpulent calf muscles of white Europeans to the long, thin calf muscles of black African subjects. The differences between them, he claimed, lent themselves to different forms of locomotion. The black African, for example, would be prone to engage in more extended movements and could be associated with distinctly marked articulations of the muscles to the bone structure; more precisely, Marey specified that the heel bone of the African tended to be longer on average than that of the European by a ratio of seven to five.[45] Marey's explanation of a Lamarckian anatomical adaptation, in effect, accounts for what he called the "incontestable aptitude for walking" among black Africans.[46]

More precisely, Marey deployed the term *nègre* for black Africans. That was a rather generalized appellation for those descendants of the so-called Ethiopian race in polygenist terms where the most salient characteristic was "lustrous black skin." In Bouillet's *Dictionnaire universelle d'histoire et de géographie* (1867), already in its twentieth edition, the definition of *nègre* was inextricably tied to midcentury evolutionary concepts that became firmly linked to the ascendancy of phrenology. As Bouillet notes, "Black Africans *('nègres')* possess a less pronounced facial angle than white Europeans *('blancs')*, a compressed cranium, a low forehead, a flattened nose, prominent cheek bones, thick and sagging lips, wool-like hair, and vigorous limbs."[47] Marey's comparative discussion of the relationship between human musculature and skeletal anatomy was derived from a concurrent reservoir of racial typologies, but his study of limbs also underscored an emphasis on functionality in opposition to a previous emphasis on muscular corpulence.

Just as the relational dimensionality of muscular tissue became a characteristic by which to evaluate muscular force, the anthropometric cephalic index within phrenology sought to establish a classificatory relational index. This index charted the relationship between the width of the skull and its length in order to derive generalizations concerning human mental aptitudes. The development of craniometry as a credible measurement technique, positioned as indispensable in the decoding of moral and intellectual capacities, was part of an anatomical framework in the French Enlightenment tradition. A branch of anatomy and physiology, phrenology is synonymous with the work of the eighteenth-century anatomist Franz Josef Gall, whose work established the brain as the locus of mental activity.[48]

Over the course of the nineteenth century, phrenology, with its topography of the brain as a series of measurable surfaces by which to evaluate and identify potential centers of activity, came to be associated with a popular fascination with the wonders of science.[49] Popular versions of phrenology, an immediately visible form of "observational" decoding, became analogous to a form of palm reading with the imprimatur of science, similar to later quasi-scientific demonstrations heralding the advent of X-ray photography. Gall was a contemporary of the idéologues, and his work more accurately approximated the physiological ideal espoused by Destutt de Tracy, in which ideology is part of zoology. A practicing physiologist who actively examined zoological specimens, Gall produced an oeuvre that was much closer to an experimentally tested physiological ideology than the more intellectually fertile abstractions developed by the idéologues.

A highly regarded anatomist, Gall criticized the Sensationalist approach inspired by Condillac in favor of the empirical localization of mental faculties identifying twenty primary qualities. Gall's associate Spurzheim coined the term *phrenology* (from the Greek *phren,* meaning mind) and served as the dominant popularizer of Gall's work, claiming there were thirty-five primary qualities.[50] A fascination with enumerating the faculties of the mind was parallel to an urge to classify the races, which was subject to various numerical estimates, ranging from two in Julien-Joseph Virey's late eighteenth-century classification to as many as thirty-four in Ernst Haeckel's late nineteenth-century schema.[51] This is the sense in which the study of bodily movement undertaken by Marey is indebted to a tradition of comparative anatomical functionality present in Gall's phrenology and is situated on a continuum with racial classification schemata.

CIVILIZING GYMNASTICS

The discussion thus far of muscular force in relation to functionality parallels the development of a subsequently extended geographic body. An abiding preoccupation under the newly founded Third Republic (1870–1940) was the regeneration of the national body. Metaphors of geographic expansion associated with anatomical functionality replaced an emphasis on muscular force. Péron's former insistence that the superiority of "civilization" directly translated into virile and physical strength gave way, following the Franco-Prussian War (1870–71), to an emphasis on the degeneration of the civilized. The rise of functionality, initially allied with anatomy, was particularly relevant to a search for strategies of regeneration.

As a result, the science of physiology associated with mechanistic conceptions of bodily movement was rearticulated as an experimental regenerative ethos. The clearest articulation of an emergent anatomical functionality can be tied to the application of physiological studies to military training that related to the soldier's gait in particular. In his extended introduction to the French translation of Angelo Mosso's *L'Éducation physique de la jeunesse* (On the physical education of youth, 1895), Commandant Legros explained that "a new school of thought, under the flag of physiology, has sought to develop a program of bodily training on a national scale that will reconstitute and reactivate atrophied organs so essential to military fitness."[52]

As Alain Ehrenberg notes in his account describing the training of the French soldier, the introduction of military training in the late 1880s was something of a novelty.[53] Until then, horsemanship had been the best-known and best-developed form of military training. Furthermore, because military strategists valued technology over technique, the development of faster and longer-range guns was considered more essential than the soldier who might use them. Studies that focused on the soldier's physical and psychological condition in conjunction with weaponry emerged only with the outbreak of World War I. Jean-Marie Lahy, whose subsequent work can be associated with Mosso's emphasis on measuring muscular articulations within French ergonomics, conducted a series of studies on soldiers equipped with machine guns in the trenches during the War to establish the parameters and effects of fatigue.[54]

Ehrenberg attributes the general disinterest in a developed form of physical military training before the 1880s to the dominant belief within the military that muscular force was not subject to significant alteration through any form of physical education. That is, the opposition between the civilized and the savage served as a marker differentiating the vital subject from one who was passive, weak, and fatigued. An earlier emphasis on geographic milieu as the overriding factor in determining the physical and mental capacity of the recruit came to be overshadowed by excessive discipline modeled on dominant modes of educating children. In effect, this form of military training was less concerned with developing bodily force or functional capacities than with forging the infinitely obedient soldier.[55]

Absolute obedience to military authority was a quality for which the Tirailleur sénégalais (Senegalese Sharpshooter) was highly regarded by military leaders. As I mention in chapter 2, the efficient expeditionary columns composed of Tirailleurs sénégalais and led by Lieutenant Colonel Louis Archinard on the African continent during the late 1880s were an inspiration for General Charles-Marie-Emmanuel Mangin's argument for an expanded conception of West African infantry divisions.[56] In an oft-quoted training manual concerning the emotions and aptitudes of the West African infantryman, Captain Hippolyte-Victor Marceau elaborated on why black Africans should be considered "overgrown children." In a discussion paralleling Mangin's description of West Africans as eminently suitable soldiers, Marceau claimed that a form of military discipline founded on obedience was both a moral imperative associated with colonization and the pedagogical duty of every French officer in the colonies.[57]

The reform of military training as directly applicable to the soldier's body was largely associated with the efforts of Marey and Demenÿ. In fact, the granting of land for the creation of Marey's Physiological Station was tied to Demenÿ's government contacts and to an argument that emphasized the utility of chronophotography to military instruction. One of the best-known chronophotographic studies produced by Marey and Demenÿ was an extended series that demonstrated different forms of human locomotion. Although a significant number of pathological subjects were surveyed, cadets from the École Normale (for gymnastics and fencing) at Joinville-le-Pont served as the primary test subjects. These studies provided durable visual evidence that justified the reform and refinement of military training. Although they signified a marked shift from Péron's static conception of muscular force in terms of savage versus civilized, Demenÿ was still preoccupied with the formation of "elite subjects," which he conceived as a means of imposing a form of positivist gymnastics. As Jacques Ulmann suggests in his epistemological account of French physical education, "Demenÿ sought to impose an ideal of physiological vitality as the norm in the tradition of John Stuart Mill's 'competent man.'"[58]

Demenÿ conceived of physical education as a pedagogical form of movement, to be illustrated and refined through chronophotography. While the resulting images served as guides to optimal physical movements, the question of how best to train military recruits was the subject of divisive debates simultaneous with the introduction of physical education exercises. Demenÿ was critical of the emerging tendencies in applied gymnastics that sought to impose a "gymnastic empiricism," creating a mechanized theatrics in the gymnasium as well as an exaggerated sense of athletic training, following what he called the "dogmatism" of the Swedish Gymnastic approach.[59] Demenÿ was a significant figure in the development of physical education in France with an impressive record of publications and experimental practice; but his lack of military and medical credentials was used to justify his eventual marginalization as an advocate for specific methods of military training.

To recapitulate, under the early influence of Marey and Demenÿ's chronophotographic and dynamometric studies of walking, running, and jumping (1883–85) at the newly christened Physiological Station, the modulation and exercise of the soldiers' movements provided a wealth of visual and statistical data for the subsequent redesign of French military training. Furthermore, Marey's comparative study of the calf muscles and skeletal morphology of European and African soldiers was used to demonstrate how muscular force follows the laws of physical mechanics. That is, the adaptability of the muscles to weight, mass, and environmental conditions explains how muscular corpulence is merely reflective of variations in measurable conditions. This vision of the body closely paralleled that of the steam engine and also heralded physical education as a mechanistic bodily science. Following the work of Marey and Demenÿ, fine-tuning the human organism could be reduced to an equation-based science of physical mechanics in relation to conceptions of natural man.

The calculation of bodily force and physical education was almost immediately applied to the study of human locomotion. Various studies sought to establish preliminary parameters concerning the articulation of walking and running to develop training exercises for the French navy.[60] Marey and Demenÿ's earlier findings concerning the utility of the flexioned gait was of great interest to military planners and strategists. Positioning the body closer to the ground by keeping the knees bent was shown to be less fatiguing than prevailing postural theories. The anthropologist Félix-Louis Regnault and artillery squadron leader Albert de Raoul undertook a study of the flexioned gait at Marey's Physiological Station in order to test earlier hypotheses developed by Marey and Demenÿ.[61]

The 1898 publication of de Raoul and Regnault's study, *Comment on marche* (How to march), established the efficiency of the flexioned gait with a variety of comparative data. The comparative anthropological perspective established the flexioned gait within a temporal evolutionary schema. Marey's introduction to the work, in fact, cites Léonce Manouvrier, the nondeterminist anthropologist allied with Paul Broca, who claimed that prehistoric man performed the flexioned march "naturally."[62]

Regnault cited numerous examples—from Tunisian *rékas,* who were long-distance dispatch couriers, to rural Belgium postmen—to underscore the prevalence of the flexioned posture. Regnault specified European and non-European examples alike, but non-European examples were transhistorically inscribed, while the European examples were associated with the rural reserves of European civilization, only marginally within the orbit of an emerging modernity. The crucial evolutionary transition of man from quadrupedal primate to bipedal *Homo erectus* endowed with consciousness served as an index for the civilizing process. Keeping the body closer to the ground through the "artificial" bending of the knees in the flexioned gait was a means of distinguishing the "natural" posture of the savage from the "artificially" bent, conscious posture of civilized man.

Regnault viewed civilized man as less inclined to remain close to the ground than his less civilized brethren and pinpointed a series of walks in order to explain why the upright European gait might be impeded or artificially induced. His extended classification of walks was a serious attempt to diagnose the human subject still inscribed within the domain of comparative anatomy. The kinds of walks that Regnault enumerated not only are racially determined but describe human forms of motion as diagnostic categories. Though this particular classification of walking postures was published several years after his collaboration with de Raoul, Regnault proposed a classification schema to distinguish superficially conditioned movement from "natural" movements revealing a deeper anatomical structure. Briefly, he showed that walks induced by specific professions, styles of dress, emotional propensities, disciplinary authority, and overwork are of a different nature than the "naturally" flexioned gait.[63]

Regnault concluded that "the savages do practice their own ethnic walks, specific to their overgrown or marsh-like habitat, dependent upon whether they walk along narrow paths, or use their feet as instruments of grasping."[64] The morphology of the foot as analogous to a prehensile extension found in apes was a subject of sustained commentary throughout Regnault's work. Following the renowned Italian criminologist, Cesare Lombroso, Regnault likened those flat-footed human subjects with markedly spread metatarsal and phalangeal bone structures to apes in a discussion of colonized peoples who use their feet to climb trees and swing on branches.[65] Lombroso even claimed that the presence of the prehensile foot among prostitutes was a more significant atavistic anomaly than the same anomaly found among criminals.[66]

Regnault's series of chronophotographs taken on the Champs de Mars in Paris juxtaposed West African climbing techniques against those of the white European.[67] Describing the climbing techniques used by a cross section of colonial subjects from Senegal, Mali, New Caledonia, and New Guinea, he drew a final physiologically grounded opposition between the European and an amalgam of colonized peoples with direct implications for a racially based evolutionary hierarchy. The comparative study of tree climbing cannot be read simply as a neutral test measuring physiological difference. The climber's ascension was punctuated by the presence of the tree itself and the tree's signification within concurrent evolutionary debates. That is, the tree was a morphological arboreal model of ascent in the descent of man and a physical object used to demonstrate respective climbing styles that revealed evolutionary racial typologies.

The chronophotographic series on tree climbing evoked a powerful metaphor applicable to the dominant French evolutionary polygenist paradigm, "a forest of trees."[68] The notion of separately planted trees neatly specified the French adaptation of Darwinian natural selection to a polygenist Transformism. In opposition to the single branching evolutionary tree, "a forest of trees" implied a cartographic spatial organization demarcating current levels of progress among the races and offered the potential for growth specific to the respective milieu. This very potential for growth and progress was in step with a time-based classificatory system used to describe the level of civilization attained within the French colonies.

champs, embrassent le tronc de leurs bras. Mais les pieds sont posés à plat, l'un contre l'autre, dans la ligne du corps et appuyant contre l'arbre, du côté des pouces, dans la position que prennent les pattes d'une grenouille à la nage. »

De même les Annamites, qui grimpent aux arbres avec les mains et les orteils, surtout avec ceux-ci, et ne se servent jamais des genoux. Les Bahnars, indigènes de l'intérieur de l'Indo-Chine, ont même pratique.

La plante du pied est donc appliquée sur l'arbre, bord interne

en haut, et c'est en serrant l'arbre entre les deux faces plantaires opposées que le grimpeur prend point d'appui. Le muscle qui a cette action est le tibial postérieur et, dans une moindre mesure, le fléchisseur commun.

On peut donc en conclure que, chez le sauvage, ces muscles sont plus développés que les adducteurs des cuisses qui, chez le grimpeur européen, comme chez le cavalier, permettent de serrer les genoux.

De plus, il y a un écartement plus considérable du gros

Grimpeur soudanais. — Chronophotographie de M. Comte.

orteil et une mobilité plus grande des orteils, ce qui permet au pied de mieux s'adapter à la surface de l'arbre.

Les sauvages ont employé divers appareils pour faciliter la montée sur l'arbre. Les Schanars, du sud de l'Inde, apprennent tout enfants à grimper aux palmiers; leur vie se passe à récolter le vin de palme, et toute la journée est employée à grimper. Pour éviter la fatigue, ils joignent par un lacs leurs deux pieds, tout en laissant un intervalle suffisant pour embrasser l'arbre. Mais, si celui-ci est trop gros et que les mains ne puissent l'entourer, ils allongent leurs bras au moyen d'une corde qui embrasse l'arbre et dont ils maintiennent les deux extrémités. Tir et Ilavar, aux Indes, font de même.

Au lieu de maintenir la corde avec les mains, il est plus commode de la faire passer par les reins, qui sont plus forts. Nous arrivons ainsi à une pratique extrêmement répandue. Le grim-

peur se sert d'une corde qui entoure à la fois le corps et le tronc d'arbre et forme ainsi un anneau mobile. Une exposition de nègres soudanais au Champ-de-Mars nous a permis, grâce à l'aide de M. Comte, de prendre, avec l'appareil de M. Marey, de nombreuses chronophotographies de ce mode de grimper. Il nous est, par suite, facile d'en révéler le mécanisme.

Là encore le grimpeur prend point d'appui tantôt inférieur, tantôt supérieur. Le point d'appui inférieur est, comme chez les sauvages, exclusivement plantaire. Le genou n'y est pour rien. Le point d'appui supérieur, au lieu d'être aux bras, réside aux lombes, grâce au lacs qui les enceint.

Le point d'appui étant aux membres inférieurs, le sujet élève son corps. Mais, au lieu de pratiquer une élévation des membres supérieurs et l'extension des inférieurs, comme le grimpeur européen, il lui suffit d'élever son lacs. Pour ce faire, par la

Grimpeur européen. — Chronophotographie.

flexion énergique d'un coude, il attire en haut la partie correspondante de la corde. La même contraction dégage les lombes qui ne touchent plus la corde. Celle-ci s'élève sur l'arbre, et de perpendiculaire à ce dernier devient oblique. Par suite, le buste du grimpeur se rapproche de l'arbre et la tête s'élève.

Les muscles qui paraissent agir le plus sont, d'une part, les fléchisseurs du coude et surtout les biceps qui élèvent la corde et qu'on voit énergiquement se contracter sur les chronophotographies; de l'autre, les adducteurs du pied, tibial postérieur et fléchisseur des orteils, qui maintiennent le point d'appui.

Prenant point d'appui sur les lombes, par le moyen de sa corde, le grimpeur fait alors un pas en élevant un des membres inférieurs. Le bras correspondant à ce membre élève alors la corde et l'autre pied repart, et ainsi de suite.

Parfois le pas n'est point accompli d'un coup, soit pour cause de faiblesse, soit qu'il s'agisse d'un arbre défavorable : un premier effort mène la jambe inférieure, la gauche par exemple, à la hauteur de la droite, puis il élève le lacs avec le bras correspondant et il repart encore du pied gauche, qu'il élève au-dessus de l'autre. Il tirera alors avec le bras correspondant au pied le plus bas.

Nous avons vu le même nègre (pays des Rivières, en Guinée) pratiquer successivement ces deux variantes.

Cette méthode du lacs paraît économiser davantage les forces et être plus rapide que l'ascension directe. Mais il est nécessaire d'avoir les muscles adducteurs du pied puissants, car ici le genou ne peut servir de point d'appui.

Cette pratique est usitée à Ceylan, chez les Indiens de l'Amérique du Sud. Elle est extrêmement répandue en Afrique. On la trouve en Égypte, à Loango, en Guinée, dans les Rivières du Sud. Une image en bois de l'Exposition des colonies nous représente cette attitude au Gabon.

Sans aller aussi loin, les habitants d'Elche, dans la province d'Alicante, pour faire la récolte des branches montent ainsi, avec un lacs qui leur ceint le corps, en haut des palmiers.

Dr Félix REGNAULT.

FIGURE 8. Comparative climbing techniques of a European (below) and a West African (above). Félix-Louis Regnault, "Le Grimpeur," *Revue encyclopédique* (1897), 905.

In his 1910 reflections on the French colonies, the former deputy, senator, and minister of war Albert Messimy superimposed an evolutionary grid of humanity on the development of Western civilization. While he claimed that some of the inhabitants of Central Africa were simply forgotten by humanity in its ascension, other inhabitants of the colonies can be understood as part of a social awakening. He defined three classes of humanity, those who resembled "our ancestors" of the Bronze age, such as the Senegalese; others, such as the Annamites of Southeast Asia, who had attained the level of civilization of the Iron Age; and finally, at the highest level of civilization, among the colonized, the Kabyles in North Africa, with the most advanced customs and institutions, reminiscent of "our Middle Ages."[69]

The development of human capacities among "the savages" was thus seen to depend on a vision of milieu, which had to account for a wide range of environmental conditions. It was within the terms of what Claude Bernard calls *milieu intérieur* that an evolutionary paradigm was justified through the study of physiologically grounded anatomical difference. In a brief study of climbing, Regnault concluded that "while the flexor muscles and the muscles behind the shinbone are more highly developed among 'savage peoples,' the strong adductor muscles of the thigh among the European climbers account for their respective differences in climbing techniques."[70] This comparison of the calf and thigh muscles, analogous to Marey's comparative discussion of the heel bones of Senegalese and Europeans, kept us firmly within an oppositional realm of nature and civilization, in which savage movements were opposed to movements of the civilized. This opposition of savage and civilized founded on a skeletal and muscular morphology was also applied to the mechanical nature of labor power. While the rationality of physical mechanics was implicated in the physiological study of movement, the human form was still inscribed within an evolving civilizing gradient. The analysis of functional anatomy established a chronology of human development associated with racial and geographic difference.

CANNIBAL LANDSCAPES

André-Paul Antoine and Robert Lugeon's 1928 film *Chez les mangeurs d'hommes* presents the search for the primitive state of humankind in Melanesia as the encounter of the objective camera with the natural state of human existence. Shot on the New Hebrides Islands in the South Pacific (now the Republic of Vanuatu), this film was commissioned as part of a corpus of fictionalized documentaries about the French colonial empire. An early example of the popularized fictional documentary film genre, it presented a popular primitivist rendering of the search for natural man with imagery from a far-flung region of empire. As a silent film, later edited with a musical sound track for the extensive film program at the 1931 Colonial Exhibition in Paris, it became part of an emerging catalogue of moving images featuring French colonial possessions around the globe.

The production context for *Chez les mangeurs d'hommes* was directly related to French colonial propaganda efforts at a time when technological improvements in the film medium, such as the introduction of sound, made it a predominant form of popular entertainment. As part of a series of feature documentaries launched by the Colonial Film Propaganda Committee, *Chez les mangeurs d'hommes* was re-edited and premiered at the 1931 Colonial Exhibition. In principle, this initiative sought to edit and supplement existing representative documentary footage held by the Economic Affairs Agency for each of the colonies that I discuss in chapter 5.

In the terms of an emergent interwar French colonial humanism, cinema became an effective means to promote humanitarian values of "civilization." The role of cinema as a means of condensing and assembling the works of empire on the screen paralleled the very goal of the Colonial Exhibition itself, which attempted to condense the geographic extensions and differences of empire into a manageable "theme park" of attractions. At the numerous colonial fairs and exhibitions during the interwar period, cinema as well as the display of industrial innovations contributed to an ascendant "radical realism," designating empire as a phenomenal realm of action that came to be associated with "great works" and "great men."[71] The presentation of these "works of empire" was associated with an aesthetic of "rayonnement," or radiance, bringing light to that which lies beyond.

The monumental spirit of the colonial exhibitions presented a series of "great works" that demonstrated the very existence and expanse of empire. Medical campaigns and literacy efforts, among other "works," served as examples of successful and incontestable civilizing endeavors. The 1931 Colonial Exhibition presented itself as consonant with a series of rhetorical and material symbols related to colonial humanism that had been successively articulated throughout the 1920s. The oft-repeated slogan "the work of human solidarity" facilitated both its adoption as a rhetorical platform and its adaptation within a series of social practices.

Chez les mangeurs d'hommes offers insight into the historical relationship between cinema and the French colonial encounter; it was one of the few films of this period that actually featured the movie camera as an animate technological object of curiosity. In most documentary-style films of this period, the invisibility of the camera asserted an omnipotent narrative perspective. It is for this reason that critics of the day, such as Georges-Michel Coissac, claimed that it was more inventive than a colonial film because it presented the values of educational cinema as a civilizing force for humanity.[72]

As a fictionalized feature-length documentary, *Chez les mangeurs d'hommes* was filmed with the participation of a Christianized village, Small Namba, in the New Hebrides Islands, named after the Scottish Islands by Captain James Cook. Upon the film's release, its realist-documentary style led popular audiences to accept its cannibalistic premise. Only later was it declared a hoax by the host of the filmmaking expedition, the Bishop of Port Vila.[73] However, labeling this film a hoax misses the crucial point that most French colonial documentary films of this period were fictional representations of otherness. The staging of so-called realist documentary representations in the colonies was ideologically bounded by a post–World War I vision of economic and social revival. The opposition between natural man and the movie camera displayed the technological superiority and moral authority of civilized man, capable of manipulating geographical and temporal boundaries. It must also be conceded that the island cast was, at least in part, aware of being in on the hoax, presenting a Western image of the state of nature.

The magical arrival of filmmakers Antoine and Lugeon on Malekula Island during a typhoon is prefaced by the warning that "the British Colonial officer Bridgis and his three children were eaten by cannibals in February of 1924 (four years earlier), and two subsequent retaliatory Franco-British expeditions were prudently abandoned." Accompanied by a group of hired men from the nearby islands, Antoine and Lugeon retrieve their film equipment and make contact. Their shipwreck serves as a narrative hook to motivate an encounter with cannibalism.

Their exploration of the island begins with their cameras and rifles intact. After eight days without seeing an indigenous tribesman, they find traces of fresh footsteps in the sand, cut branches, and a knife sheath—familiar structural elements derived from the American western film genre. The explorers decide to set a trap for an unsuspecting tribesman, who has been watching them. Placing faith in the stereotype of the "savage" who is easily seduced by alcohol, Antoine and Lugeon dig a trench in which they booby-trap a bottle of spirits by hooking it up to a camera and a light source, which enables them to catch the perpetrator in the act of drinking. They capture the tribesman on film, but he easily jumps out of the trench, leaving only the emptied bottle behind.

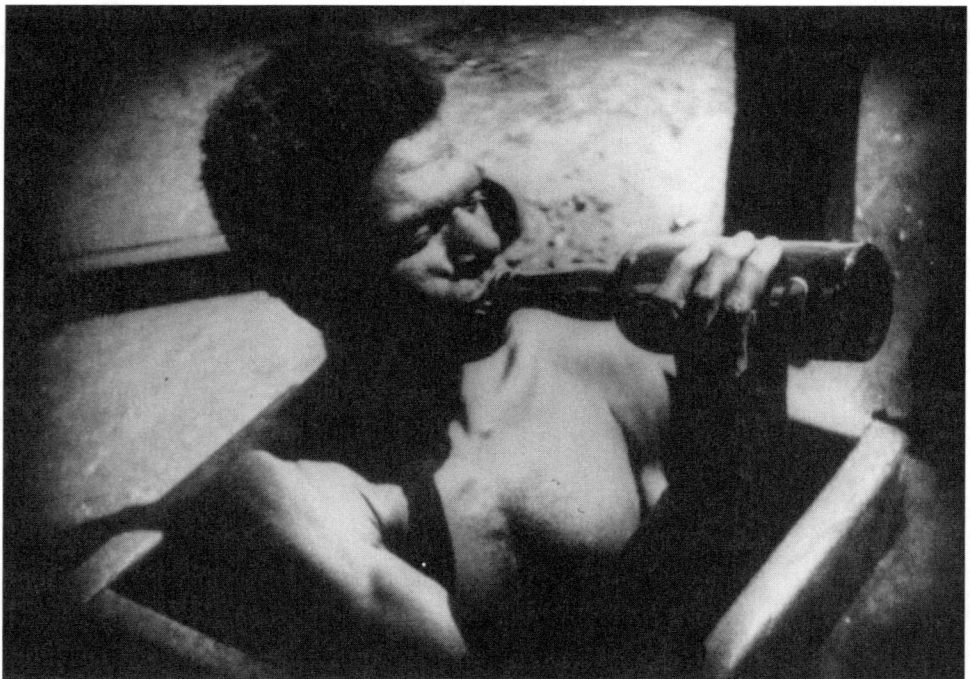

FIGURE 9. The tribesman drinking as stereotype in *Chez les mangeurs d'hommes*. Copyright Collection des Archives du Film et du Dépôt Légal du Centre National de la Cinématographie.

This particular segment demonstrates how the camera is a more effective means of studying the inhabitants than the trap the explorers set. The trench setup is both an allusion to the trench warfare of World War I, with the camera standing in for a machine gun, and a preindustrial means of capturing animals. Recording the tribesman in the act of drinking, unaware of being filmed, is a statement about the power of the camera as a symbol of industrial civilization as opposed to simply catching him in the flesh. The distance between physical capture and the effectiveness of the camera as a form of surveillance points to a new humanism, a humanism that posits the ubiquitous gaze of the camera in opposition to physical capture.

The following day, fifteen tribesmen armed with bows and arrows confront Antoine and Lugeon. Though somewhat surprised, the explorers remain calm. They set up their two cameras to run automatically, stand ready with their rifles in hand, and initiate a truce. In spite of being woefully outnumbered, the explorers direct the scene with their frightened assistants and a two-camera setup. The movie camera serves as the focus of this potentially hostile encounter. After the explorers meet with the village headman, Meltetali, the camera fascinates rather than frightens their hosts, serving as a ritual object of modernity. Meltetali then invites the explorers to be his guests, and Antoine and Lugeon show the tribesmen how the camera works. This scene serves as a temporary narrative reversal; instead of eating the filmmakers, as they did the British officer Bridgis and his three children, the tribe succumbs to an all-consuming fascination

FIGURE 10. The camera as witness in *Chez les mangeurs d'hommes*. Copyright Collection des Archives du Film et du Dépôt Légal du Centre National de la Cinématographie.

with the camera. Another initiation rite is being performed, an introduction to the technological totemic practices of modernity. The infinitely versatile camera as the locus of cross-cultural communication is not simply an objective witness but a peacemaker and civilizing machine.

This transformation of potential armed conflict into curiosity before the camera points to a history of machines used to record and study human difference. As a knowledge-gathering instrument, the camera partakes in an unfolding ideological science of discovery. This notion of ideology tied to a scientific mode of investigation was by the end of the eighteenth century relevant to the status of the camera as a viable instrument of discovery and a method of mediating representations of the unknown. As the arbiter of geographic, cultural, and physical difference, the camera represents the legacy of technological implements used to graphically represent the other. The rational technological modernity of the camera is the all-powerful metaphor in *Chez les mangeurs d'hommes* in confrontation with the irrational primitivism of cannibalism.

Antoine and Lugeon are taken to Meltetali's village, as the intertitles explain (italics in the original), "across an unknown river *not identified* on their maps." The rationality of the camera and the erratic eating habits of the filmmakers' hosts are constantly counterpointed throughout the film. This sequence leads the filmmakers further into

FIGURE 11. Meltatali gets behind the camera in *Chez les mangeurs d'hommes*. Copyright Collection des Archives du Film et du Dépôt Légal du Centre National de la Cinématographie.

the unknown, relying on the good faith of their hosts. Antoine and Lugeon's seeming immunity to fear of the unknown demonstrates their almost sovereign right as witnesses to the state of nature. The film narration does not clarify whether Antoine and Lugeon are honored guests or simply the catch of the day, duped into returning with the tribesmen.

After settling into the village, Antoine and Lugeon come to see, as the intertitles declare (italics in the original), "the soft, hospitable, and *almost entirely* vegetarian side to the tribe." They stay on as Meltetali's guests for six months and introduce members of the tribe to the camera, each with a specific trait: Elten the hunter, Malektsell the musician, Nalé the canoe builder, Malcekem the sleepy one, and Lawak the sorcerer. These descriptions of individual personalities are followed by a demonstration of their roles in the life of the village. This segment of the film is a storybooklike demonstration of the natural state of human existence in all its abundance and draws on Rousseau's *De l'inégalité parmi les hommes,* where the natural state of human existence was featured as "carefree, healthy, and happy."[74]

In essence, *Chez les mangeurs d'hommes* recounts the long-standing historical debate about the relative value of the natural state of human existence. The distinction between "savagery" as uncivilized and the "natural state" as akin to human purity before the fall was used to mediate both the encroachment of civilization and the desire for preindustrial authenticity. The ambiguity of *Chez les mangeurs d'hommes* as a fictionalized representation of cannibalism plays on a somewhat fetishistic revival of a Rousseau-inspired primitivist adaptation in the late 1920s and early 1930s. Although the discourse of French colonial humanism during the interwar period promoted the values of "civilization" as education, it also contained a dialectical response in the form of a return to the state of nature.

The anthropophagic trope, conceived as an essential opposition to "civilization," was also representative of resistant and reversible excess taken up by French Dadaist and Surrealist currents associated with the Brazilian avant-garde.[75] Following the publication of Francis Picabia's 1920 *Manifeste cannibale* and the subsequent Dadaist journal *Cannibale,* "Tupi or not tupi, that is the question" was a natural response to the civilized rationality of colonial humanism.[76] Reappropriating anthropophagi as a discursive strategy also implied a reversal of terms in such a way that anthropophagi as a primitive stage in the course of human history served as a point of reflection and a strategy by which to critique its contemporary other, mechanized destruction and the profoundly destablizing effects of World War I. In other words, the opposition between cannibalism and civilization masked their effective complementarity, whereby industrial mechanization devoured human labor power.

Oswaldo de Andrade's notion "Tupi or not tupi," proclaimed in his 1928 *Anthropophagic Manifesto,* re-emerged under the sway of the Brazilian Tropicalist movement of the 1960s and 1970s. In Nelson Peirera dos Santos's film *Como era gostoso o meu Francês* (*How Tasty Was My Little Frenchman,* 1971), the unnamed Frenchman (Arduino Colasanti) says, "The savages walk totally naked, and we walk unrecognized" upon being captured by the Tupinamba in the seemingly untended Brazilian landscape. In this film, set in the mid–sixteenth century and loosely based on the diary of the German explorer Hans Staden, who was captured by Brazilian tribesmen and managed to escape, the Frenchman is actually a military deserter. The apocryphal sentence "The savages walk totally naked, and we walk unrecognized" refers to the fact that he cannot be recognized as French through language or his possessions. The Frenchman is misidentified as Portuguese, and his captors are allied with the French against the Portuguese. In fact, no matter what the Frenchman does to demonstrate his Frenchness or his loyalty to the Tupinamba, including fighting with the chief Cunhambebe (Eduardo Imbassahy Filho) against the Portuguese and the enemy Tupiniquim, it does not change his status as a condemned man. The Frenchman is also given a wife, Sebiopepe (Ana Maria Magalhães), while he lives with the tribe and attempts to create the impression that he has magical powers to create gunpowder. The transformation of the condemned native savage into the French captive witness is a storytelling strategy that harks back to the mythology of the Tupinamba, popularized as the last vestiges of "natural man" in Claude Lévi-Strauss's subtle structuralist anthropological rendering of this world in his self-conscious travelogue *Tristes tropiques*. It is within the captive witness genre, however, that Pereira dos Santos stages the eventual sacrifice of the Frenchman in order to upend the project of colonial domination through the lens of the indigenous Tupinamba, whose language is also the primary language spoken throughout the film.

By contrast, a discourse of authenticity foregrounds the static, "primitive" state of nature in *Chez les mangeurs d'hommes*. Furthermore, "primitive authenticity" serves as an important rhetorical foundation by which to chart the "progress" and "dynamism" of industrial civilization. The "discovery" of civilizations, lost in time, is also a claim for a positivist vision of human history. As in the film, the inaccessibility of lost civilizations is almost always presented as a secret to be revealed by the explorer who magically arrives in an uncharted temporal and geographic zone.

Geographic, temporal, and political consolidation as presented at the 1931 Colonial Exhibition was a claim for the civilizing powers of modernity. The promotion of the colonial idea at the exhibition included a response to Rousseau's vision of the natural state of human existence.[77] Natural man could be maintained, protected, and appropriately civilized only through the expansion of the French colonial empire. At the exhibition, a differential grid of humanity was imposed to assert the authority and values of "civilization."

The revival of Rousseau's vision of natural man in conjunction with the conflicting tendencies of bourgeois society under the Third Republic was an inversion of natural man as a prerevolutionary challenge to the divine right of the monarchy and the degenerative effects of private property. The reappearance of natural man allied with colonial consolidation was used to justify political and territorial domination. The impossibility of Rousseau's natural state, in which inequality was practically nonexistent, served as a political prescription that the French Republic could claim as its revolutionary divine right. This readjustment of the natural state to the protective agency of the

French state substituted a state-driven consciousness as natural. This way of rehabilitating Rousseau's natural state illustrates how symbols of social justice are appropriated in pursuit of the functional exercise of power.

The ongoing search for natural man remained a significant paradigm in exploration narratives and the defining terrain for French anthropology as an ideological science of man. Savage man, following the French translation of *sauvage* as natural, raw, and untended, became a mythological point of comparison by which to evaluate successive civilizing moments. The implied cannibalism was decidedly forbidden and irrational, lurking in the realm of human passions. The measurement of strength both quantified potential labor power and lent itself to a new calibration of human force through the evolving terms of "race" and "civilization."

Although Péron's findings were based on a series of misunderstandings about human difference and actual mismeasurements, his work points to a collective unconscious rendering of otherness that isolated the physical, moral, and sexual characteristics of natural man. Péron's unpublished diaries, rediscovered by Ernest-Théodore Hamy in 1890, pointed to yet another wrinkle related to the sexual life of the savages, complicating Péron's own published conclusions about their virility. He noted, in passing, that the propensity for sexual stimulation among aboriginal men seemed far more frequent than among healthy civilized men.[78] While Péron did not use this observation as proof of their actual virility, his observations served as a lively subject of debate.

Primitive sexuality was used in counterpoint to the virility of civilized man, who in France was under the spell of low birth rates and a pervasive movement toward *dégénérescence* by the end of the nineteenth century. The discourse of "civilization" under the Third Republic was associated with a campaign of virilization and nationalist revival. A program for the physical and moral regeneration of civilized man even led to some of the earliest uses of serial motion photography as a technique for bodily training. To restore the virility of civilized man, dwarfed by the power of industrial modernization, a series of educational techniques and exercises was developed to restore the physical attributes of natural man. The reintroduction of natural man as a desirable model for the physical regeneration of the French race was exemplified by the work of physical education reformers, such as Georges Demenÿ and his disciple Georges Hébert. Hébert claimed that an overriding "physical morality" could guide the regeneration of the French race, and he developed a series of eight indispensably utilitarian exercises as part of the "natural method" he used to train the mind and body of the recruit.[79]

The central role of virility in the rehabilitated vision of natural man under the Third Republic extended a fascination with cannibalism and its sexual charge. Devouring the human body dangles the specter of sexuality before the spectator. In *Chez les mangeurs d'hommes,* the idyllic natural state of the islanders is interrupted by an arrow of provocation, shot by a "wife-stealing" bandit from a neighboring clan. Clearly the transition from the idyllic agrarian lifestyle to warfare is marked by the arrow, challenging the honor of the village headman, Meltetali.

Meltetali's tribe responds in kind after a meeting of the Conseil des Suprèmes, which approximates a religious war council. The decision to attack the neighboring village is taken not only out of revenge but to acquire prisoners for the forthcoming "Festin du clan," the seasonal human sacrifice. The visual reference to the beating of the drums combined with the blowing of a seashell horn signals the battle cry that precipitates the invasion of the neighboring village. The attack itself leads to the almost immediate capitulation of the neighboring village. In fact, these villagers begin burning down their own village and flee into the forest. Upon their arrival, Meltetali's warriors continue the pillage by burning down the village totems, stealing a pig, and capturing numerous prisoners.

In the final section of the film, visual allusions to hypnotic "talking drums" become a device of transgression under whose spell, we are informed, the celebration ends with a human sacrifice. However, before we see the actual sacrifice, the idea of the sacrifice enters the realm of the symbolic: members of the village are transformed into performers, wearing costumes and headdresses resembling sailboats, shark heads, long-necked birds, and, to reinforce the theme (though irrelevant to the actual costumes), the identification of a performer as the Man-Who-Wants-to-Eat. The seemingly authentic-artistic quality of a final series of dance and theatrical spectacles, though completely misconstrued and maligned to serve the myth of anthropophagi, serves as the central "educational" demonstration of the film.

In effect, the dance sequence becomes the moment at which the popular myth of the man-eating tribe is transformed into an ornamental art form and is documented as an ethnographic ritual that evokes the specter of human sacrifice. The ritual provides a substitute for the public execution that so excites the European imagination; it does not enact the orgiastic moment of death but rather provides a continuous flow of convulsive movement, performed in a trancelike state. Because Antoine and Lugeon are "prevented" from filming the final ritual of human sacrifice, it is represented as even more forbidden, potentially unrepresentable.

As a form of titillation, cannibalism stands in for a spiritual realm that remains obscured. During the final dance ritual, two rifles appear as part of a ceremony and are depicted as instruments of divination rather than war. The spatial and temporal distance of the sacred realm also implies an array of spiritually coded objects that mediate a relationship with the invisible nonmaterial world. These objects are endowed with meaning associated with spiritual practice and are dissociated from the circuit of exchange value or practical utility.

In effect, the final series of ceremonies provides a primitivist point of reference for the ultimate transgression of Western rationality. The trance-dance of movement—which Jean Rouch later applied to the act of filmmaking itself, calling it *ciné-trance*—is at once the unleashing of libidinal bodily impulses and an indivisible act of creation. The representation of trance serves as a referential core for the study of ritual and transgression that has been a touchstone of the French sociological method since Durkheim. Moreover, the trance scene is an illustration of the "primitive" who is part of a preindustrial religious history to be categorized and retained as part of a vanishing past.

As a means of measuring and detecting movement, the camera in *Chez les mangeurs d'hommes* finally documents the ritual. The initial search for real-life cannibals by the hungry treasure-hunting explorers enters a diagnostic register that establishes a primitivist symbolic aesthetic, attributing value and humanity to the cannibal. The extended trance sequence in *Chez les mangeurs d'hommes* underscores the potential for objective visual documentation. The nonrepresentation of a human sacrifice contributes even more powerfully to the mythology of the cannibal, whose ritual of sacrifice can only be imagined.

Finally, the story of cannibalism as it relates to appropriations of natural man is a historically recurrent tale. Natural man serves as a prescription for a new political order that is intended to remake the social fabric. The cannibalism attributed to the preindustrial savage masks the ever more devastating destructive power implied by postindustrial processes of production. The question remains: tupi or not tupi?

2. MYTHOLOGIES OF THE
TIRAILLEURS SÉNÉGALAIS

CINEMA, SHELL SHOCK, AND FRENCH COLONIAL PSYCHIATRY

The figure of the Tirailleur sénégalais, or the Senegalese Sharpshooter,[1] is perhaps the ultimate cipher of France's colonial legacy. Portrayed as the infinitely obedient soldier who served France on European battlefields during World War I, the Senegalese Sharpshooter was etched into the collective French imagination as the "sentinel" of France's colonial empire. In Morocco, Algeria, Indochina, Madagascar, and beyond, he served as a symbolic agent of French political and territorial ambitions, functioning as a powerful threat in the international racial and sexual unconscious.

I examine the Senegalese Sharpshooter as one of a series of fragmented images embodying a projected colonial gaze that crystallized an expanding humanitarian enterprise. The visual articulation of the Tirailleurs sénégalais as formerly "ransomed" West Africans who were transformed into a loyal French fighting force is a mainstay of colonial mythology. In fact, Roland Barthes's well-known essay "Myth Today," first published in 1957, refers to the *Paris-Match* cover photo of a saluting African soldier as "the exemplary figure of French imperiality."[2] Although Barthes analyzed this image to illustrate the role of myth, explaining that the photograph naturalized the dilemma of being a subjugated African subject and an obedient French solider, this instance of "split subjectivity" was described in the subsequent development and critique of French colonial psychiatry. I examine how the legacy of the Tirailleur sénégalais has been represented and projected from the perspective of a shifting imago founded on the imperatives of the French colonial legacy.[3]

Barthes described the colonial myth of the African soldier as an example of a social and ideological construction of embedded meaning. Reexamining this image fifty years later, we see that the saluting African figure was not a solider but an African

35

LE NAUFRAGE DE RIVA-BELLA

•

Les enquêteurs recherchent les responsabilités et revivent par la photo les dix minutes d'horreur de

LA TRAGÉDIE DU MANS

LES NUITS DE L'ARMÉE

Le petit Diouf est venu de Ouagadougou avec ses camarades, enfants de troupes d'A.O.F., pour ouvrir le fantastique spectacle que l'Armée française présente au Palais des Sports cette semaine.

FIGURE 12. Cover of *Paris-Match* 326 (June 25–July 2, 1955).

teenager wearing a Boy Scout uniform.[4] The fact that the African figure was neither solider nor icon of the Tirailleur sénégalais is yet another essential displacement of the photograph's significance. The image of the Senegalese Sharpshooter was so abundantly present in French interwar and postwar consciousness that it remained the point of reference for Barthes's analysis of the African figure even though that was unspoken in the essay itself. The fact that the "soldier" was a teenager as opposed to an adult is foundational for articulating the African soldier's identity in French colonial consciousness. That is, the African soldier is almost always a child in the framework of French imperialism. Saluting the unseen fold in the *tricoleur* flag, as Barthes posited, served as an indexical starting point for the more contemporary evolutionary discourse of "development."

Terence Ranger explains that African volunteers were attracted to serve in the newly formed Tirailleur sénégalais battalions by snappy uniforms, modern arms, Koranic oaths of allegiance, and crash courses to evoke the glory of the French military tradition. Crucially, it was even suggested from Paris that the children of the Tirailleurs should be provided uniforms and miniature equipment similar to those of their fathers as a means of instilling a sense of military sartorial codes.[5] Projecting a vision of military genealogy onto the Senegalese Sharpshooters at the very outset was part of an ongoing strategy of assimilation and incorporation specific to managing and extending France's colonial dominion.

FIGURE 13. Postcard of a Senegalese man with children outside tents as part of the Moroccan Campaign, 1907–8. Grébert Photo, Casablanca, ca. 1910. Copyright Research Library, the Getty Research Institute, Los Angeles, California (970031).

In the extensive archive of picture postcards that depict the Tirailleurs sénégalais in Morocco as of 1907, serving as a French proxy expeditionary force to quell the first of many uprisings, an important subject was the image of the Senegalese soldier with his family, particularly his children, standing at his side outside of huts in the wind-swept Moroccan landscape. The fact that the soldier was depicted with his children transformed the Senegalese family into vassal settlers in relationship to the French settlers who moved to Algeria following the Franco-Prussian War. As opposed to the French settlers, however, the Senegalese Sharpshooters and their families were depicted as living in a presettler nomadic state of existence, thus "naturally well adjusted" to the rigors and dangers of defending French military occupation and expansion. In fact, the evolutionary ideology of "a struggle for survival" marked this vision of the civilizing process.

French colonial rule established a series of African soldiering and labor contingents in West Africa from 1758 to 1817, eventually culminating in the creation of the Tirailleurs sénégalais by decree in 1857 through the efforts of Louis-Léon-César Faidherbe, the French governor general of Senegal from 1854 to 1861 and from 1863 to 1865. The formation of the Senegalese Sharpshooters as a French fighting force had its origins in French official policy for the eradication of slavery and the rhetoric of an extended French fraternity. An early scheme for the organization of troop and labor contingents took the form of "ransomed" service in which French commanders sanctioned the purchase of men from African slave traders. These slaves were "freed" from

FIGURE 14. Postcard of Senegalese men and their families in Morocco. R. Schmitt, Rabat, 1912. Copyright Research Library, the Getty Research Institute, Los Angeles, California (970031).

FIGURE 15. Image of Louis-Léon-César Faidherbe inset in a map of Senegal in *La France est un empire*, 1939. Copyright Collection des Archives du Film et du Dépôt Légal du Centre National de la Cinématographie.

their African masters only to be transformed into "volunteers" under the condition that they serve the French government for a minimum of fourteen years in order to repay their debt. The "ransoming out of slavery" system actually encouraged the slave trade, because African slave traders served as suppliers for this lucrative French market.[6]

In addition to the soldiers inducted through this "ransoming" system, the French navy also recruited a more stable group of less indentured Soninke and Fuulabé Muslim "volunteers" known as *laptots,* who initially served as sailors, guides, armed boatmen, and defenders of commercial vessels before being recruited to serve the French navy during the 1830s and 1840s as part of the expanding troop contingents. Their expanding role as guarantors of French shipping led to the formation of the first company of Wolof soldiers who had the same rights as the Algerian Zouaves,[7] with their own distinct vestmental identity printed on a ribbon attached to their patent leather hats that read "Compagnies noires du Sénégal" and "Chasseurs du Sénégal."[8]

With the economic conversion from the slave economy and gum arabic to the groundnut economy by the mid-nineteenth century,[9] French colonial interests in West Africa expanded beyond the previously settled Four Communes area,[10] and a reliable military and work force became essential to expanding the groundnut economy. In the spirit of economic expansion cast in the language of political and civil rights, demands concerning pay, dietary needs, and tentative liberties to establish their own households without interference from French authorities influenced the formation of the Tirailleurs sénégalais. In fact, as Mamadou Diouf, Abdoulaye Bathily, and other historians of Senegal have shown, indigenous leaders such as El Hadj Umar rivaled French administrative authority outside of the Four Communes and remained an ongoing semiautonomous force within Senegal itself.[11] Faidherbe signed more than one peace treaty with El Hadj Umar, who was sent into exile, then repatriated, and the indigenous Kajoor power structure managed to maintain an important element of political autonomy through the complicity of these men in organizing the groundnut economy that served as an elemental vanishing point for French interests.

The creation of a thoroughly "voluntary" African military force reflecting French republican values was not resolved by the creation of the Senegalese Sharpshooters. In spite of an increase in pay, substantial enlistment bonuses, a reduction in the service requirement from fourteen to four years, new uniforms, and a right to the spoils of military campaigns, the "ransoming" system remained in place until European colonial expansion in Africa reached its zenith in the 1880s. Expanded regiments of Senegalese Sharpshooters were created in 1884 under Lieutenant Colonel Louis Archinard, and the reputation of the Senegalese Sharpshooters began to shift from that of "ransomed slaves," known to be unreliable and potentially mutinous, to that of disciplined soldiers who began marrying into African royal families.

The spoils of the extensive military campaigns in Equatorial Africa during the 1880s and 1890s, such as the Mission Crampel (1891)[12] and the Mission Voulet-Chanoine (1898–99),[13] led Senegalese Sharpshooters, once "ransomed slaves" themselves, to "ransom" women (and their children) into their service as wives, cooks, and servants. By this time, the Senegalese Sharpshooters were among the few African men who could reliably provide protection against the ravages of the all-consuming Franco–British–German–Belgian scramble for African territory. The transformation of the identity of Senegalese Sharpshooters into that of brave and powerful soldiers beyond reproach who were universally praised by their French superiors was finally complete with their deployment in Morocco. The historian Marc Michel explains that the first two battalions of Senegalese Sharpshooters were sent to Morocco in 1908 and that close to ten thousand Senegalese troops were stationed there by the outbreak of World War I.[14] The French press widely publicized their exploits in Fez, Meknès, Marrakech, and Sefrou, which became their testing ground for eventual combat on the battlefields of Europe.

Morocco served as an initial incubator for the accumulation of imagery depicting the Tirailleurs sénégalais as obedient soldiers on the one hand and as living memorials of the Bronze Age on the other. The emerging iconography of the Tirailleur depicted him as both physically violent on the battlefield and sexually predatory. In an image that dates from World War I, a Tirailleur holding a severed ear taken from his Moroccan adversary says, "Ça y'a bon zareilles Marocaines. Y'a gris-gris." In the guise of a half-serious cartoon, the Tirailleur demonstrates an arrested state of linguistic, psychological, and spiritual development. The contraction "y'a bon" refers to the well-known advertisements for the chocolate- and banana-flavored French breakfast cereal known as Banania, which became an emblem of the half-civilized Tirailleur sénégalais. In the context of the image, "zareilles" refers to *oreilles,* or ears, to be used as a good luck charm, and is, once again, suggested half jestingly.

The language of the Sharpshooter was used to place him along a civilizing index. In place of the correct form *c'est bon,* meaning "that's good," "y'a bon" was from a French African pidgin dialect called *petit nègre. Petit nègre* was spoken among African recruits after a short-lived French attempt to impose Bambara as the major vehicular language of the region failed; this ensured a rudimentary level of French language competency—just enough for the soldiers to understand orders but not enough to challenge them verbally.[15] "Y'a bon" echoed the stereotyped response of the Senegalese troops to their superior officers using the phrase *Y'a bon, capitaine* ("Yes Sir, Captain"). "Y'a bon" also drew on stereotypes of drunken African soldiers who discovered the joys of cheap French table wine, known as *pinard.* "Y'a bon pinard," which appeared in subsequent advertisements of the interwar period, meant "That's good wine," but

FIGURE 16. "The French Army in Morocco: Tastes good, Moroccan ears. Like a lucky charm." R. Tugot, artist; published by M. Kerambrun et P. Cousin, Rabat, 1912. Copyright Research Library, the Getty Research Institute, Los Angeles, California (970031).

also suggested in a half-mocking tone that the African was "naturally" a drunkard who could not speak French correctly or hold his liquor.

The multiple meanings of *y'a bon* are directly related to the ambivalent laughing grin of the Senegalese Sharpshooter appearing in the ubiquitous Banania posters promoted during the war and throughout the interwar period. The Tirailleur personage, branded as "l'ami y'a bon" (the "*y'a bon* buddy") and in a later iteration "Bamboula," was designed by the graphic artist De Andreis in 1915, after the product was initially launched in 1914 with the image of an Antillean woman. The Banania recipe was patented by the French journalist Pierre-François Lardet after sampling a similar recipe while traveling in Nicaragua, but became associated with sweetness and was submerged in the prospect of *créolité*.[16] The mixed-race figure of the *assimilé* had already been established in France beginning with the infusion of Rouen-based merchants that first established the transatlantic slave trade linking West African labor to sugar and spices in the Antilles. The strategically orchestrated image of Banania, however, drew on the playfulness and the seeming uncalculated spontaneity of the Senegalese Sharpshooter. Denoting the good taste of Banania, the "y'a bon" slogan connotes the good life in France and, by association, the good taste of battle.

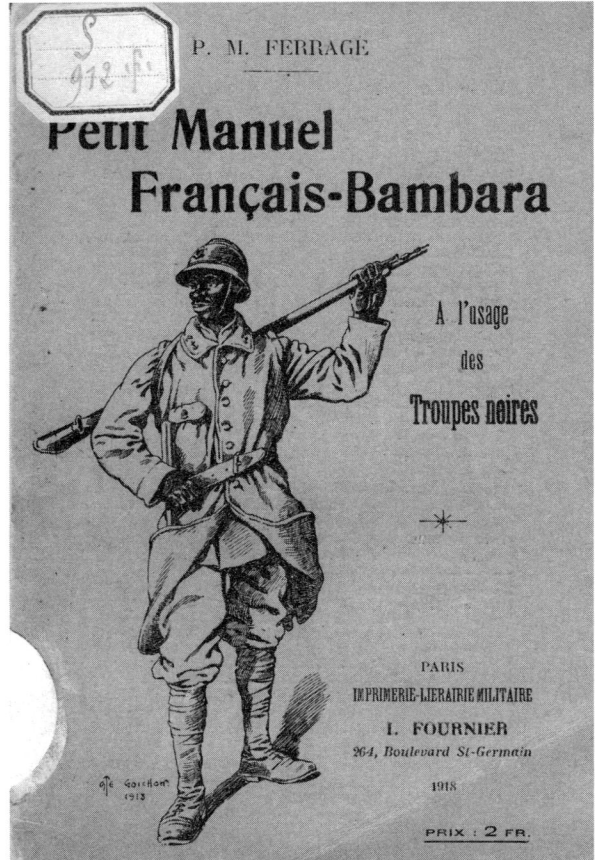

FIGURE 17. Cover of French–Bambara language manual for use with African troops. Published in Paris by L. Fournier, 1913. Copyright MHC–BDIC.

FIGURE 18. Early Banania poster of an Antillean woman. Charles Tichon, artist; Maus, Delhalle and Urban, publisher; poster, 1914. Copyright Musée Roybet-Fould.

The Banania advertisements in France became the ascendant stereotype of the Senegalese Sharpshooter, which associated the state of an inarticulate primitive blackness with the category of taste, or the "flavor" of African difference. The juxtaposition of the grinning Senegalese Sharpshooter as part of the French fraternity, uttering "y'a bon" while sitting on a box of breakfast cereal, half-mockingly conveyed that the best way to cajole and civilize the "primitive" and "childish" Senegalese Sharpshooter was though his stomach, that is, with "delicious sweet food for delicate stomachs" as indicated on the Banania box.

The unprecedented proliferation of colonial imagery continuing through World War I into the interwar period is often referred to as the "Banania years" because "declinations of the stereotype," as Mireille Rosello puts it, branded the European and African imagination.[17] The Banania advertisements were so ubiquitous in France that Léopold Sédar Senghor registered his disgust with the image of the grinning Bamboula in the final line of his well-known *Poème liminaire* by writing, "I will tear all the Banania laughs off every wall in France."[18]

The "*y'a bon* buddy" paired with "Banania" in the name of French fraternity on the European battlefield evokes the banana as phallus, condensed in the grinning expression of Bamboula. The sexualization of the Tirailleur was part of an extended battlefield

FIGURE 19. Banania poster showing the most frequently reproduced Banania image. The box reads: "Exquisite Sugared Breakfast. Delicious Food for Delicate Stomachs, Sold Everywhere, factory in Courbevoie, y'a bon." De Andreis, artist; Camis Paris, publisher; 1915. 163 × 123 cm. Copyright Bibliothèque Forney, City of Paris.

of imagery. An archetypal image that appeared as comic imagery in popular journals, postcards, and posters during World War I was that of the mixed-race couple, featuring the wounded Senegalese soldier with a French nurse in his arms. Most often the Senegalese soldier was presented as very black, frequently grimacing and taking on a simian, or flexioned, posture. In many of these images of mixed coupling, the more black the African man, the more transparent the French woman.

Many of the more provocative images also depicted the wounded Senegalese soldier chasing after the French nurse in the hospital or, alternatively, the French nurse seducing the Senegalese patient, figured as the "grand enfant," wearing the signature red *chéchia* head cover and rendered with bright red, oversize, suckling lips while lying in bed. On the one hand, a semiotic correspondence was forged between the white virginal French nurse and the sexually potent black African male, translating the African "warrior" figure on the battlefield into a sexual predator in the hospital. The alternate scenario imagines the white nurse, who doubles as a Catholic nun, as sexually activated by the dumbfounded but sexually naive African soldier.

The stereotype of African male sexual prowess was projected onto the image of the white French woman, who was depicted as sexually knowing. Given the massive death tolls on the battlefield and the entrenched fin-de-siècle discourse of *dégénérescence,* the declining visibility of the French male in French civil society was transformed into the twinning of female promiscuity with the myth of African sexual bravura. The sexualization of African soldiers was almost always related to the promotion of their

FIGURE 20. Senegalese Sharpshooter (referred to as "Zoave" in the description of the image), with sexually knowing French nurse. Ea. Iolvo, artist; 1915. Copyright MHC–BDIC.

FIGURE 21. Senegalese Sharpshooter in arm and leg casts seduced by a sexually knowing French nurse. Ea. Iolvo, artist; 1915. Copyright MHC–BDIC.

exemplary performance on the European battlefield following their rapid deployment between 1914 and 1918 along with an expanded contingent of colonial troops.[19]

More than 134,000 West Africans were sent to Europe as soldiers and workers during the war. In spite of popular imagery suggesting that the infinitely brave and proud Senegalese Sharpshooter could not be stopped, Marc Michel estimates that more than 30,000 West African troops fell on European battlefields, and a significant number were wounded.[20] There have been conflicting claims about whether the mortality rate among the Tirailleurs sénégalais was higher than that of French troops, begging the question of whether they were deployed more carelessly. The death toll fluctuated at different moments during the conflict, but Michel estimates that the percentages of French and African troops killed were roughly equivalent.[21] When first deployed, Senegalese troops were especially ill prepared for the harsh European climate and lacked modern tactical training. After scores of Senegalese troops were massacred by Prussian soldiers during the first few months of battle, all arriving Senegalese recruits were sent to a training camp in Southern France to acclimatize them to the rigors of warfare in Europe.[22] The rising death toll among African shock troops led Blaise Diagne, the Senegalese-born French deputy and leader of African troop recruitment during the war,

_ Oh! non, pas la baïonnette!..

FIGURE 22. "Oh! no, not the bayonet!" n.d. Copyright Research Library, the Getty Research Institute, Los Angeles, California (970031).

to charge that they were being used as cannon fodder after half the soldiers of twenty-six Senegalese battalions perished in the battle of Chemin-des-Dames in 1917. The alarming death rates raised the specter of whether the blood tax of battle was too high in exchange for the granting of French legal and civil rights to the limited contingent of Senegalese *originaires*.[23]

In addition to photographs, postcards, and posters, there were hundreds of newspaperlike trench journals printed during World War I that were written and edited for and by soldiers, featuring an ongoing series of columns that were supposedly penned by Senegalese troops.[24] As Annabelle Melzer describes them, these articles referred to the Africans' interactions with French women while serving in Europe during the war. In fact, these stories, written by white French officers, were used to evoke the frisson of an encounter with sexually available French women; they incorporated letters supposedly sent by Senegalese troops to French *marraines de guerre* (pen pals), who would often send gifts such as hand-knitted socks to support them.[25]

Melzer examines an array of trench journals and trench scripts performed by and for the troops as an "utterance-marked" space of masculine display that, in turn, triangulates the draft-dodging white French soldier, the brave African Tirailleur, and the French woman as an expression of male hysteria. In other words, the imagined interaction between the oversexualized African male and the sexually available French woman was cemented through the absence of virile and patriotic French men. This scenario was then transformed into a fear of miscegenation that found expression in popular images and, subsequently, in official policy.

The symbolism of the Senegalese Sharpshooter carousing with the French nurse was so powerful that the military recommended segregated hospital settings and the use of male nurses and orderlies.[26] It has also been argued, less than conclusively perhaps, that the subsequent deployment of Senegalese troops as a French occupying force in the Rhineland at the conclusion of the war was motivated by an effort to quickly reduce their number on French soil in order to deflect a symbolic challenge to the fragmented state of French masculinity.[27] However, the limited presence of Senegalese troops in the Rhineland provoked a powerful reaction in the political centers of Hamburg, Berlin, and Munich, but not in the Rhineland itself. The government-led German propaganda machine, with an international array of unwitting allies, staged an international media campaign that was fueled by fears of miscegenation.[28]

While it is unclear exactly how many Senegalese Sharpshooters were stationed in the Rhineland at the conclusion of the war, it was certainly fewer than the forty thousand troops that German sources claimed. Sally Marks reports in her detailed discussion of this episode that American military statistics claimed that there were closer to fifty-two hundred West African troops along with twenty thousand Algerian, Moroccan, Tunisian, and Malagasy troops.[29] In fact, the Tirailleurs sénégalais were organized as battalions, each consisting of 800 to 1,200 men with variable patterns of deployment.[30] Additionally, the sparse Sudanese troops were shifted to Syria in June 1920 in order to deal with revolts there, and later the Malagasy troop contingent was sent to

Morocco to deal with more uprisings. An advance guard of French-led Moroccan troops in Frankfurt a year earlier had already been used to raise German fears of nonwhite domination, and the arrival of Senegalese troops motivated a political media event known as the "[Black] Horror on the Rhine." The prospect of African troops' violating the honor of German women first became popularized after a series of inflammatory editorials was published by left-leaning British journalist Edmund D. Morel in the New York–based *Daily Herald*.[31]

Posters bearing such slogans as "Protest der deutschen Frauen" ("German women protest [the Colored occupation of the Rhineland]") underscored the indignity of having African soldiers as occupiers in the Rhineland. Distortions and fabrications of incidents involving Africans engaged in rape, assault, and the spread of disease in the Rhineland were voluminously propagated through pamphlets, postcards, posters, press releases, demonstrations, radio programs, and newsreels subsidized by the German government in Berlin. Heinrich Distler's novel *Die Schwarze Schmach* (The black shame) claimed that the widespread rape of German women was perpetrated by Senegalese Sharpshooters; a popular film of the same title directed by Carl Boese was released in 1921, the year after Boese and Paul Wegner directed *Der Golem*.[32] The film played for a short time to large popular audiences in Stuttgart and was then made into a stage play that drew a full house of theatergoers in Munich. In fact, the popular press barely disputed the fallacious accounts of rape and other forms of sexual intimidation claimed in the film.[33] In addition, planted news stories and other ephemera were also systematically translated into English, French, Dutch, Italian, Portuguese, Spanish, and even Esperanto, underscoring the maligned underpinnings of interwar international humanitarianism.

THE TIRAILLEUR SÉNÉGALAIS IN FRENCH MILITARY DOCUMENTARY FILMS

The accumulation of postcards, posters, cartoons, and advertisements of the Senegalese Sharpshooter reveals contradictions at the core of the European male's sense of self under threat. In contrast, the sparse French documentary film footage depicting the Tirailleur sénégalais in France during World War I reveals a series of structured absences. At first, French newsreel footage of the war was forbidden, and then it was strictly censored until the Section Cinématographique des Armées (SCA) was established in 1915.[34] The SCA was charged with producing, distributing, and censoring films in support of the war effort. Initiated as a consortium of the best-known cinematographers and filmmakers of the period from Pathé, Gaumont, Éclair, and Eclipse, the SCA finally expanded its work to such an extent that more than 750 newsreel shorts were produced from 1915 until the end of the war.[35]

The short documentary films depicting the Tirailleurs sénégalais drew on newsreel compilations that presented them working, playing, training, marching, eating, resting, and praying following guidelines set by the SCA. A widely distributed documentary titled *Tirailleurs sénégalais en Alsace* (Senegalese Sharpshooters in Alsace, 1917)[36] demonstrates the complicit behavior of the Senegalese troops as screen actors, living up to their reputation as ferocious warriors, yet also buffoonish. In a short segment that begins with the French and English bilingual intertitle "Some types of Senegalese," one of the troops plays the role of the savage warrior, brandishing a sword before the camera, only to be restrained by two fellow compatriots. In another scene, two Senegalese infantrymen act the part of the buffoon: one soldier gently swings a strand of hair of another, whose head begins to bob back and forth, making his neck seem as flexible as rubber, not like other human necks.

While it might seem that the seemingly good-natured Senegalese troops were simply being tricked into playing the fool, this short film also reveals a self-consciousness of the stereotype in the name of comradeship and as a demonstration of good humor in deflating the perniciousness of the setup. The film also emphasizes the fact that the African troops are being well fed, with sequences detailing the preparation and serving of copious portions of rice, eating, and their being given adequate time to rest after the meal. As stipulated by SCA guidelines, the film demonstrates the troops' good morale while avoiding any specific depiction of actual fighting or death.[37] In fact, occupying Alsace with the aid of Senegalese Sharpshooters more than forty years after it was annexed by Germany was a symbolic act of reintegration. The loss of Alsace-Lorraine as a result of the Franco-Prussian War redirected French national consciousness toward colonial conquest. Thus, in the context of the film, the presence of the Tirailleurs sénégalais in this nearly sacred territory of French national consciousness underscored the point that the project of colonial education and military training enabled the territorial reintegration of France itself.

Another film from 1918, known as *L'Aide des colonies à la France* (Aid to France from the colonies) consolidated the myth of the Senegalese Sharpshooter by reference to Sergeant Mamadou Diarra, known as Tirailleur 4053.[38] The intertitles in the film explain that Diarra captured 130 German prisoners, 30 officers, and 7 machine gunners, all supposedly single-handedly. Quotations from speeches given by Generals Galliéni, Bonnier, Dodds, and Gouraud, interspersed with footage of the Tirailleurs on active duty, pay homage to their dedicated service. Variations on the quotation "They are a first-class fighting force: loyal, brave, and equally adept on the battlefields of Africa and Europe" were not only reiterated throughout the film, but became part of a broader propaganda initiative that justified the continued deployment of these troops in France and throughout the empire in the interwar period.

This short-subject film begins with a "history lesson" on the glory of French colonialism; it opens with a semicircular rotating bust depicting Jules Ferry, with an intertitle that reads, "A great Frenchman, Jules Ferry, had the marvelous vision that a great nation must have colonies." A series of animated geographic images demonstrates the relationship between France and its extended colonies, now integrated into *la plus grande* France. The film first justifies the conquest of the colonies by asserting, "In Morocco, the latest addition to the French colonies, the Sultan provides wheat and provisions to revitalize General Lyautey's admirable soldiers and robust workers." As yet another example of reinventing tradition and co-opting local leaders, this quotation legitimizes the French military occupation as a form of rescue in the name of a civilizing enterprise.

L'Aide des colonies à la France depicts the project of a greater French empire as embraced by French colonial subjects from around the world, certified by their willingness to sign up and volunteer to defend France against "German aggression." The film reinforces the message that these subjects have finally internalized French humanitarian ideals and are now ready to stand up for them as emerging citizens. The second part of the film is devoted to the history of the Tirailleurs sénégalais, who are portrayed as the most loyal of all the colonial troops with the most elite fighting units. They are shown to be well adjusted and agile. Footage of them throwing grenades from the trenches and setting up barbed-wire fences testify to their competence. A segment depicting them donning gas masks and undergoing rigorous physical training demonstrates that they are valued soldiers: fearless, capable, and willing to go "over the top" of the trenches at the front on command.

The film ends with the accomplishments of Mamadou Diarra as the archetypal Senegalese warrior. Diarra was a decorated war hero who managed to stay on duty all night in a trench in a German-controlled sector during the Battle of the Somme in 1916 after his lung was punctured by a bullet fired into his stomach. In one description, it is claimed that in addition to fighting all night and killing several German soldiers who were attacking French positions, Diarra helped evacuate his comrades to the nearest barracks by marching all night and was seen by a doctor only the next morning, thirty-six hours after he was wounded.[39] Although Diarra's story is not summarized in the film, it was widely known at the time and contributed to the legend of the indomitable Senegalese Sharpshooter. The final quotation from the film exclaims, "France expresses its appreciation to the colonial army," subsuming Diarra's accomplishments into an expression of homage to all colonial troops.

Sequences depicting the Senegalese Sharpshooter were continually recycled and replayed in a number of feature documentary colonial films until the 1950s, providing a broader historical context for Barthes's analysis of the *Paris-Match* image. Films such as *La France est un empire* (France is an empire, dir. Gaston Chelle, Hervé Missir, Georges Barrois, Raymond Méjat, and André Persin, 1939) and *Les Sentinelles de l'Empire Française* (Sentinels of the French Empire, dir. Jean D'Esme, 1938) used the image of the Tirailleur as the dutiful sentinel who guaranteed the seamless coordination of the component parts of the colonial puzzle. The lone patrol that always maintains at least two Senegalese soldiers was always present in fiction and documentary films alike during the interwar period, remaining consistently loyal to the task at hand.

A wide array of footage recorded on the front lines during World War I was censored by a committee of representatives from the SCA, the Ministry of War, the Ministry of Foreign Affairs, and Police Headquarters.[40] According to Marcel Pierre's early analysis, some of the most spectacular footage was shot, once again, during the Battle of the Somme. However, it was not the heroics of Mamadou Diarra, but footage filmed by the cameraman Emile Pierre depicting a group of open communal gravesites and a psychologically disturbed soldier walking between the lines of battle bearing signs of shell shock that was "amputated" on the cutting room floor at the request of the censors.[41]

DEFINING SHELL SHOCK AND FRAGMENTARY IMAGES

It was the agitated psychological state of the soldier, in opposition to tales of bravery on the battlefield, that inexorably led to the role of shell shock as yet another crucial opposition in the narrative memory about the Senegalese Sharpshooter. The appellation *shell shock* was first coined to describe a condition with its own etiology by the British psychologist Charles S. Myers while working as a consulting psychologist in neurological centers located in Paris and at Châlons-sur-Marne in 1915.[42] As a result of the widespread use of the term among soldiers themselves, *shell shock* was subsequently excised from the diagnostic medical vocabulary by the Allied Army Medical Service in 1917.[43] Myers claimed that the unprecedented conditions of warfare, such as the strain of immobile trench fighting and the preponderance of inexperienced non-professional soldiers, led to widespread neurological breakdown among the troops. The

FIGURE 23. Senegalese Sharpshooter at attention in *La France est un empire*. Copyright Collection des Archives du Film et du Dépôt Légal du Centre National de la Cinématographie.

condition was also described as "pithiatism" by the French psychiatrist Joseph Babinski, and there was no widely agreed-upon diagnosis and treatment for the array of symptoms associated with shell shock during the war itself.[44]

French medical discourse did not initially cast the figure of the brave Senegalese Sharpshooter as experiencing shell shock symptoms due to his presumed neurological and civilizational lack of development. Professor Emmanuel Régis, one of the most respected figures in early French colonial psychiatric literature, claimed that nervous disorders such as paralysis were "a thermometer serving to measure the relative mental acuity of a race."[45] That is, more "advanced" European races experienced these disorders, whereas "less developed" people in the colonies did not. This perspective was challenged only during the interwar period by such figures as François Cazanove, who argued that a historical and cultural perspective must be incorporated into a study of mental disorders in the colonies.[46]

General Mangin, the mobilizing figure in the French military establishment for African troop recruitment, proclaimed that military bodily training was the best way to civilize African subjects. As Mangin wrote, "The recruit is to be instructed through a regime of imitation and by suggestion. He has barely learned to think before enlisting and we expect an unconscious spontaneity from him that barely registers in his consciousness."[47] Mangin's assertion that military training *civilizes* the African soldier was also aimed at *virilizing* the French recruit. African soldiers served as comparative test subjects in an ongoing campaign aimed at retraining the French male body in the name of national revitalization. Mangin was so preoccupied with fears of depopulation and with what he considered the tendency toward degeneration that he proposed physical and moral training as the antidote. Mangin even advocated that the state instill "the duty of paternity" into young French recruits and encouraged the creation of the Ligue pour la Race, with a central committee composed of eminent fathers.[48]

The relative absence of Senegalese Sharpshooters in the public discourse on shell shock coded them in opposition to the complex of male hysteria found among French soldiers. In fact, intermittent early reports on the poor performance of African troops on the battlefield were often construed as a criticism of Mangin and others who had argued so vigorously in favor of their deployment on European soil. A nineteenth-century male code of honor was projected onto the Senegalese Sharpshooter, who was positioned in a hierarchy of colonial difference. In fact, the colonial boundary between self and other that existed for French soldiers serving in the colonies shifted when colonial troops arrived in Europe for the first time en masse. Africans, among other colonial soldiers, were outsiders to the fault lines of European nationalist difference on entering the war. However, they became keenly aware of cultural differences within France itself and started to see how the hierarchical logic of centralizing culture, values, and language conspired to establish the edifice of colonial difference.

Although the humiliation at the hands of Germany during the Franco-Prussian War remained a vanishing point in French collective consciousness, newly developed mechanized techniques of warfare marked a perceptual shift toward an emerging aesthetics of the fragment. Longer-range explosives, tank warfare, mustard gas, mechanized artillery, and airplane bombings shifted perceptions of the soldier from a physical entity engaged in hand-to-hand combat to a technician in a projected space of battle. Technical mastery over machines as opposed to physical mastery over an individuated adversary transformed the soldier into a nearly immobile assembly-line worker instructed to obey orders. In the commotion of the mechanized battlefield, shell shock emerged as an array of symptoms that was closely associated with hysteria. Babinski's notion of "pithiatism" drew on his own earlier discovery that a magnet could be used to transfer hysterical disorders not just between different parts of the body but between different patients.[49] This meant that the solidarity among soldiers, considered a crucial element in recruiting and maintaining morale, could have a negative effect given the contagious nature of shell shock.

The vocabulary of contagion and hysteria associated with shell shock was closely

FIGURE 24. "The Bravery of the African Soldier: Me not afraid! Bullets cannot pierce African skin." The missing lower section reads: "The African is a soldier of exemplary bravery / Can you see how little this 'turco' fears death? / Also, France loves him, and he wants to please her / Carries himself like a hero, consistently, without effort." André Rosa, artist; 1915. Copyright MHC–BDIC.

linked to the negative attributes associated with late nineteenth-century visions of the crowd. Gabriel Tarde's narrower and evocative conception of "unconscious imitation," in which members of a collective imitate each other's gestures, reinforced Gustave Le Bon's broader assertion that the crowd is a lower evolutionary form of human consciousness.[50] Babinski's work, however, was directly associated with that of his mentor, Jean-Martin Charcot, the preeminent nineteenth-century French neurologist who opened the door to the study of hypnosis and hysteria and drew on a form of interventionist medical practice that was so prevalent at the turn of the century.[51]

Charcot's collaboration with Duchenne du Boulogne, who pioneered the use of electrical faradizations in illustrating muscular contractions, exemplified the interventionist method that was documented in a series of well-known photographs of Adrien Tournachon published in Charles Darwin's *Expression of the Emotions in Man and Animals* (1872).[52] Disbelief and ignorance characterized the attitude of most practicing physicians concerning the seriousness and causes of shell shock during the war. Duchenne du Boulogne's experiments with electrical faradizations became a frequently appropriated technique in medicine, and painful electrical shocks using high voltage and low amperage were applied to the affected regions of the patient's body. Electrodes were applied to the larynx of a deaf-mute shell-shocked patient until the subject would presumably scream. In spite of the fact that these patients would frequently lapse into their prior condition, this form of treatment, also known as *torpillage,* was favored by most British, French, German, and Austrian doctors.[53]

The treatment for shell shock was at once a form of punishment and an effort to reanimate the patient based on earlier tendencies associated with mesmerism and the demonstrated effectiveness of applying electrical shocks. The figure of the automaton in E. T. A. Hoffmann's story *The Sandman* (1816) returned as the shell-shocked patient with a disarticulated nervous system whom doctors attempted to put back together again. The abuse of this technique and the harm it did to the shell-shocked patient were later investigated when a less invasive mode of talking therapy became the preferred technique for treatment by the end of the war. This actively interventionist physiological approach was reinforced by Claude Bernard's notion of the "experimental method" in which the experimenter prods the test subject in order to provoke a reaction. In Bernard's well-known opposition of the observer and the experimenter, he explained that whereas the observer seeks to record what nature reveals, the experimenter applies simple or complex techniques to vary or modify natural phenomena with a precise goal in mind.[54] Provoking the shell-shocked subject to vocalize some form of response was not based on careful observation of the symptom. Instead, it denied the psychological purchase of the condition.

The tradition of British social psychology initially developed a nuanced approach based on observation to examine the symptoms of shell shock, particularly in the work of Charles S. Myers. Myers and his colleague, William McDougall, were both trained as experimental psychologists under the tutelage of William Halse Rivers Rivers. While at Cambridge University, Rivers was asked by his colleague Alfred Cort Haddon to assemble a team to accompany him on his second voyage to the Torres Straits in 1898. Rivers invited Myers, McDougall, William Seligman, and others to accompany him and Haddon on the voyage, which became a founding moment for the development of fieldwork methods that established the Cambridge School of Anthropology.[55] Significantly, the voyage resulted in several anthropological films and wax cylinder audio recordings that referred to dance and initiation ceremonies among the Mer (Murray) Islanders in the Eastern Torres Straits, located in the Northern Australian province of Queensland.[56] Though they were primarily reenactments, the five surviving films remain significant because they emphasize the role of gesture in a symbolic system of religious and social ritual, much in the same way that linguistic phrasing might be analyzed or a medical symptom diagnosed. Further, the recording and examination of the ritual as a performative act in situ grounded a newly emerging form of ethnographic analysis.

The stereotype of the Senegalese Sharpshooter was projected to frighten German soldiers and serve French military objectives in the name of shared values of republicanism. However, it was the unfamiliar aboriginal subject in the Torres Straits who heuristically oriented Myers's ethnographic approach to understanding shell shock as a profoundly social symptom among French and British soldiers. Following Myers's early work, a debate about the definition, causes, and effective treatment of shell shock was initiated by the British psychiatrist William Brown in 1919, with Myers and McDougall serving as respondents. Crucially, this debate framed shell shock in relation to hysteria and the utility of hypnosis in its treatment.

Whereas Brown argued for evoking the emotions associated with the traumatic event through a form of hypnotic abreaction, Myers and McDougall claimed that accurately recalling the repressed memory should be the focus of hypnotic suggestion. While this exchange was primarily about emphasis and therapeutic technique, Myers and McDougall pointed to the importance of the traumatized soldier's gaining knowledge of (or relation to) himself by recovering memory of the traumatic event.[57] In spite of the fact that Freud's work on the unconscious, repression, conversion neurosis, and mental conflict were mentioned in their discussions, the primary role that Freud ascribed to sexuality was considered beside the point.[58] For Brown, Myers, and McDougall, the primary conflict for European soldiers afflicted with this condition was not the question of male sexuality but the way in which "fear" and "duty" lead to a "flight into illness."[59]

An underlying element of this debate addressed how shell shock might function as a form of trauma and memory formation that could be effectively treated by hypnosis. To this end, Brown used the metaphor of the filmstrip to demonstrate the indelible reservoir of memory.[60] More specifically, he wrote that "there is at least a continuous thread of actual experience being deposited in memory from moment to moment, like the successive photographic views on a cinematograph ribbon, and these early memories can be revived in the exact form in which they were originally laid down as the mind passed beyond them to new experiences."[61] Paralleling human memory to the filmstrip recalls Henri Bergson's influential discussion in *L'Évolution créatrice* (*Creative*

Evolution, 1907), in which he likened memory to the filmstrip as formatively acquired internal memory images.[62] Brown asserted that formative or traumatic experiences become submerged in the unconscious and can be recalled through the act of hypnosis. If we extend Brown's metaphor of the filmstrip, segments that have been edited out, or are seemingly forgotten in conscious waking life, remain a defining mark of personal identity. For Brown, reactivating these memories through hypnosis and the psychodynamic process of reliving them in the present leads to an adaptation of Freud's notion of "working-through," allowing the intensity of the symptom to subside.[63]

Brown's indelible images of memory lodged in the archive of the unconscious are approximated in the notion of the "complex," which refers to a locus of strongly invested emotional thoughts and interests. Freud remained deeply skeptical about this term, which is rarely used in psychoanalysis, because of how it had been turned into a form of dreaded psychologism. Nonetheless, the term is frequently modified to describe and isolate conditions such as the Oedipus complex, Prospero complex, Nero complex, and other relational structures.[64] In an attempt to define the role of the complex more clearly, Carl Jung coined the concept of the "imago" to emphasize the role of a psychic hierarchy within the emotional complex.[65]

The imago is a useful means by which to reestablish the relationship between shell shock and the evolutionary hierarchy promulgated through the colonial imagination, which positions the colonial subject in a developmental educational model based on the French language, physical and moral training, and sacrifice for national ideals. Following Laplanche and Pontalis, the imago is "an acquired imaginary set, as opposed to an image per se," which takes on the form of a stereotype that models the way we see the other.[66] This developmental approach is based on the emotionally invested nature of perception and its relationship to the reproduced image itself, which can never be neutral, but instead takes on a series of "inaccurate self-replications."[67] The formation of the imago through perception creates a collective imaginary. However, the role of the image as a point of reference that exists in the public and private space serves to guide the way in which the imago may be simultaneously formed and projected.

MEMORY MITRIALLÉ AND THE 1916 LEBEL MODEL RIFLE

The image of the Tirailleur sénégalais exists at the nexus of an archival imaginary, positioned within the coded imagery during World War I but first mapped in turn-of-the-century picture postcards. By 1900, the rapidly expanding photographic postcard editors began mapping the geography of Senegal for metropolitan France and the *assimilé* elite in Senegal itself. The colonial urban spaces within the Four Communes of Senegal were *mitriallés,* with the camera standing in for the rapid fire of a machine gun, as Philippe David asserts, "street by street, building by building, tree by tree, well by well."[68]

Until modern methods of postcard production took hold in the 1960s, David claims that the period between 1902 and 1914 was the most prolific period of postcard

ÇA Y PAS BON MANGER...
ÇA VACHE ENRAGÉE!

L. Géligné. Imp. Édit. DÉPOSÉ.

FIGURE 25. A Senegalese Sharpshooter says, "Not good to eat / those mad cows!" L. Gelingne, publisher, 1914. Copyright Research Library, the Getty Research Institute, Los Angeles, California (970031).

production in Senegal, when there were as many as fifty-four editors located in Dakar and other cities.[69] Postcards were abundantly sold, seen, and sent throughout France prior to World War I. The Dakar-based picture postcard production output by Edmond Fortier, the largest and best known of the Dakar-based postcard editors, depicted racial stereotypes of West African ethnic groups, such as the Lébou in Saint-Louis, that were well known to the French expatriate photographers.[70]

Such photographic collections were part of an expanding anthropometric faith rooted in evolutionary paradigms with an extensive scientific pedigree. Racial characteristics came to be associated with their utility in battle, and ethnic groups known for their qualities on the battlefield were called "warrior races." On a French West African ethnic map of the period, the "warrior races" were articulated as a geographic tapestry of racial stereotypes that could be deployed throughout the region. As Joe Lunn explains, units comprised of Wolofs, Serers, Tukulors, and Bambaras—all deemed "warrior races"—were thought to be the very "best" combat formations.[71] These groups were also considered part of the *non-* or *semi-évolués* Senegalese populations whose origins, aptitudes, and personalities were minutely mapped in a series of guides published for officers, such as Captain Hippolyte Victor Marceau's *Le Tirailleur soudanais.*[72]

Although I have focused almost exclusively on the question of how the Senegalese Sharpshooter was represented in the French colonial imagination as a symbolic intermediary, the role of the imago as an internal image that might respond to visual imagery among other stimuli can be partially explored through an analysis of French colonial psychiatric case histories, as articulated by the patients themselves. In the history of French colonial psychiatry, one of the earliest studies of Senegalese psychiatric patients was described in Paul Borreil's 1908 medical thesis on the internment of Senegalese patients in Marseilles.

One of Borreil's case studies describes a female patient known as LR who repeats for hours on end the phrase "Le propriétaire du grand pont Faidherbe,"or "[I am] the owner of the great Faidherbe bridge." Her "folly of grandeur," as Borreil put it, was accompanied by other psychiatric symptoms, most notably that of eating her own feces.[73] Le grand pont Faidherbe was completed in 1897 and was a technological marvel of the era, after which time it served as a visual emblem of colonial Senegal. The bridge linked the two halves of Saint-Louis, the detached political capital and the industrial city on the mainland. The industrial city, known as Sor, became an important railroad station in the groundnut export economy, linking it to Dakar, the future capital. Before the steel bridge was built, a floating bridge was constructed in 1860 under

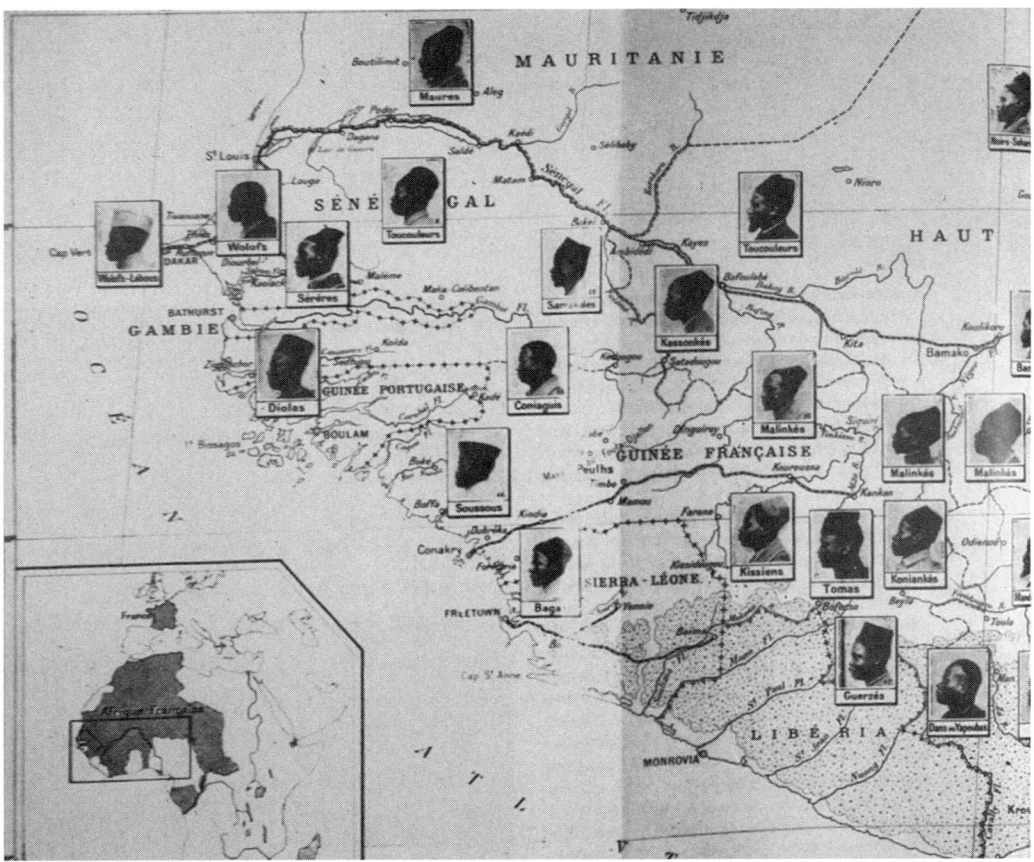

FIGURE 26. The geographic origins of West African races of Senegalese Sharpshooters in *La Dépêche coloniale illustrée* (January 1916).

Faidherbe, who played an important role in securing political and civil rights for the assimilated Franco-Senegalese elite of the period.

While the case history is sparse, the fact that the patient LR repeats "[I am] the owner of le grand pont Faidherbe" indicates that her history and identity were intertwined with the completion of the bridge. Borreil remarked that the patient was Muslim, twenty-five years old, and born in Nioro, a village located in present-day Mali. She arrived at the asylum in Marseilles in 1906. We can deduce that the patient was not part of the mixed-race assimilated Franco-Senegalese Catholic elite, nor was she among the *originaires,* and thus she would not normally have had French citizenship rights, and yet she was sent to an asylum in France, indicating that she did have the rights of a citizen. To speculate further, LR might have been taken to Saint-Louis as a former wife of a Tirailleur sénégalais or a French soldier, officer, or engineer while he worked on some aspect of the construction project. But once separated from the mediating presence of the bridge, she claimed her ownership of it. In her repetition of this phrase, she spoke of owning a public symbol of colonial assimilation as proprietor, not merely as a pedestrian who depended on its utility.

Numerous scenarios can be constructed around why the bridge figured in LR's verbal discourse, but this case, among others described in Borreil's medical thesis, demonstrates that West African subjects with some form of mental illness were programmatically treated in France as of 1897, when the first Senegalese patients were evacuated to Marseilles. According to Borreil, "From 1897 to 1907, seventy-two Senegalese patients were evacuated to Marseilles."[74] Borreil further explained that the African patients sent to Marseilles survived on average for only twenty-seven months. The question that arises from his discussion is whether they were treated humanely; significantly, Borreil reaffirmed the conventional argument of the period, that only a minute percentage of the population of Senegal suffered from mental illness in comparison to the percentage of the French population.

This type of argument corroborated the accepted wisdom of the early to mid-nineteenth century, which followed Alexander von Humbolt's assertion that "insanity was absent in the life of the savages." However, Borreil questioned whether these Senegalese patients should be sent to Marseilles when so many of the patients died during their treatment. René Collingnon, who has written extensively on the history of psychiatry in Senegal and on West African psychiatry in general, explains that whereas 1897 marked the transfer of the first "alienated" West African patients to France, 1938 marked the beginning of the use of psychiatric medical units in French West Africa. During the period in between, he writes, adaptive measures were employed that did not fully address the issue.[75]

At the conclusion of World War I there was a need for an asylum in Senegal to house wounded and shell-shocked West African troops returning from the European front. An infirmary set up in 1917 at Thiaroye, just outside of Dakar, was unable to address the demands placed upon it, so all of the psychiatric patients were sent back to France for treatment.[76] Thiaroye was to serve as the functional equivalent of the Hôtel des Invalides in order to care for and reintegrate war veterans. Since that time, the town of Thiaroye has functioned as a multiple signifier related to the treatment, training, and manipulation of Senegalese troops.

Thierno Faty Sow and Ousmane Sembene's 1987 film *Camp de Thiaroye* portrays the Senegalese Sharpshooter as a victim of false French promises and the nearby camp as the site of a massacre on December 1, 1944.[77] After being short-changed on the conversion of their wages from French francs to African francs and denied the right to a pension following their service in the European War, the African troops mutinied, taking over the camp and temporarily taking a French officer hostage. Retribution by the French was brutal; tanks and mortar fire leveled the camp along with the remaining African troops. Sembene's semifictional rendering addresses the event in the genre of a tragic farce. Although the film focuses on circumstances surrounding this event, artifacts of World War I are ever present in his depiction of the Tirailleurs sénégalais themselves. Characters such as Captain Aloyse Diatta, the epitome of assimilation, who listens to classical music as he writes to his French wife, and Corporal Diarra, based on the example of the brave Senegalese warrior Mamadou Diarra, contribute to the stereotype of the Senegalese Sharpshooter. Each of the African troops in the film refers to others by their country of origin, such as Gabon, Congo, Niger, and Ubangi, and they communicate with each other in *petit nègre*. An African survivor of Buchenwald, known as Pays (Country), was so traumatized by the war that he can no longer speak. Wearing a German military helmet and on the lookout when French tanks arrive, Pays awakens the camp to warn them of an impeding attack. Pays claims that German tanks are surrounding the camp. Considering Pays delusional, they pay no heed to his warning. The tanks lie in wait, and at 5:00 a.m. Camp Thiaroye is awakened by tank fire and burned to the ground.

Sembene's vision of the Senegalese Sharpshooters evokes the differential history of colonial integration and occupation that characterized the French role in West Africa. This trauma and its legacy are also a primary focus of Franz Fanon's critique of colonial psychiatry in *Peau noire, masques blancs* (*Black Skin, White Masks*, 1952), a work whose starting point was Octave Mannoni's analysis of Malagasy subjects' dreams and his discussion of the recurrent presence of the Tirailleur sénégalais.

Mannoni's *Prospéro et Caliban: Psychologie de la colonisation* (*Prospero and Caliban: The Psychology of Colonization*, 1950) reveals a particularly disturbing artifact of the Senegalese Sharpshooter's presence in Madagascar immediately following World War II. Described alternately as an "angry black bull," the "black ox," or simply the "Senegalese soldier," the Senegalese Sharpshooter was portrayed as a victimizing agent in a group of dreams. Mannoni interpreted these allusions to the Senegalese soldier as a father image in Malagasy Merino cosmology. On the basis of this research he developed a far-reaching theory of dependency and inferiority that he defined as the Prospero complex.[78] Mannoni specified how colonial racism manifests itself as a form of sexual guilt. In other words, Prospero's mistreatment of the slave Caliban was motivated by the ambivalence of selfsame difference that came to be expressed as racism. In this way, Prospero projected his own intentions as those of the slave, cleansing his own conscience.[79] The sense of sexual guilt was expressed through a triangulation with French women and by the oversexualized representation of the Tirailleur sénégalais, as an example of how the guilt of imposing a hierarchical racial division reveals a confrontation with selfsame otherness.

Fanon did not disagree with Mannoni's theorization of the Prospero complex, but argued that Mannoni failed to understand "the real coordinates of the colonial situation." The dreams that Mannoni used to sketch his notion of dependency were taken up by Fanon to show that

> the enraged black bull is not the phallus. The two black men [who appear in another dream] are not the two father figures—the one standing for the real father, and the other standing for the primal ancestor. . . . The rifle of the Senegalese soldier (that appears in one of the dreams) is not a penis, but a genuine rifle, the 1916 Lebel model. The black bull and the robber [in another dream] are not *lolos*—"reincarnated souls"—but actually the irruption of real fantasies into sleep.[80]

In fact, Senegalese Sharpshooters were used, at least in one documented incident, as torturers in Madagascar at a time when eighty thousand Malagasies were killed, one in every fifty people, during the struggle for independence.

Mannoni worked in Madagascar from 1925 until 1947 as head of the Government Information Service and as a self-described amateur ethnologist. As Jock McCulloch explains, he maintained an interest in psychoanalysis and entered a training analysis in Paris with Jacques Lacan in 1947 before completing the original French version of *Prospéro et Caliban* two years later.[81] The abiding interest of his work focuses on themes of dependency and inferiority derived from Alfred Adler's writings. The dream work that evokes the figure of the Senegalese Sharpshooter as torturer, or a representative figure in Malagasy cosmology, demonstrates how these troops were used as colonial agents, burying themselves in the split subjectivity of French military service.

The Tirailleur sénégalais emerged as a memory image, and consequently as an artifact of the imago in the postcolonial imagination. While Fanon's position in this debate with Mannoni drew on the trope of shell shock as a form of traumatic memory, it suggests an abreactive reading of French colonial psychiatry itself as a form of trauma to be excised. Writing nearly twenty years after *Prospéro et Caliban,* Mannoni explained that an underlying element of his previous analysis of racism inevitably led toward a universalist theory of how difference is articulated against the grain of a personalizing liberalism.[82] He concluded that racism is fundamental to an analysis of colonial myths because it infiltrates the identity of all those who act on the basis of maintaining a position within this institutionalized framework.

It was in the name of universalism that Thiaroye, the site of a former convalescent hospital for returning West African troops, was transformed once again into a psychiatric hospital that became an important site for the development of ethnopsychiatric approaches to mental health under the leadership of Henri Collomb. Collomb worked with a team of French and Senegalese collaborators from 1959 to 1978, focusing on psychodynamic approaches that incorporated local epistemologies of trance in the treatment of mental disorders.[83] The collaborative approach to psychiatry that he embodied was part of a larger movement within French anthropology itself that had implications for broader transformations in the field itself.

Traces of an ethnopsychiatric approach to understanding the colonial symptom through spirit possession also appear in Jean Rouch's 1954 film *Les Maîtres fous* (The crazy masters). While most descriptions of this film have focused on the shocking nature of sacrificing a dog that the adepts eat while in a trance state, a less commented-upon segment in the film is the final sequence, in which Rouch says, "When looking at these happy faces and being told that they are among the best workers of the Water Works Department, and comparing these smiles with the contortions of yesterday, one wonders whether these men of Africa have found a panacea against mental disorders. One wonders whether they may have found a way to absorb our inimical society."

This concluding section of the film expresses some of Rouch's ambivalence about the content of the possession ceremony as a critique of the colonial administration. Instead he frames the trance state as a potentially therapeutic technique by which to reenact the contradictions of colonial Ghana and Niger, where most young men had served in French and British colonial troop detachments. Although Rouch subsequently acknowledged that this final narration diluted the implied critique of colonial power implicit in the possession ceremony, it was very much in keeping with ethnopsychiatric approaches developed during this period as part of a gradualist approach to decolonization.[84]

Like Manonni's *Prospéro et Caliban*, *Les Maîtres fous* was criticized from a number of different quarters, including that of Sembene himself, who considered it yet another instance of colonial anthropology that objectified the African subject in the genre of colonial stereotypes that supported languishing colonial myths.[85] However, there is much more to Rouch's depiction of how trance relates to the history of the Zabrama migrant phenomenon, which takes into account the transformative nature of ritual. In the same way that Myers had come to understand shell shock among French and British troops through his work among the Torres Straits islanders a half century earlier, Mannoni and Rouch forged a path toward the decolonization of a French colonial psyche they came to see as a universalizing project to be detached from the colonial episteme.

A common thread linking depictions of the Senegalese Sharpshooter and African troops in general was the act of shoveling, the universal symbol of work. In the history of ergonomics and work measurement, the lifting motion of shoveling can be calculated as a unit of work. In *Les Tirailleurs sénégalais en Alsace,* a primary form of work that is portrayed is none other than the digging of trenches in order to maintain the French strategic position in Alsace. In *Les Maîtres fous,* Rouch claims that several of the Zabrama adepts digging ditches are known to be among the best workers of Accra Waterworks. In Sembene's *Le Camp de Thiaroye,* the surviving Senegalese troops shovel graves for those who perished during the massacre. Finally, the image of the Tirailleur sénégalais shoveling serves as a symbol of his obedience to colonial authority and his victimhood as corpse and gravedigger. Perhaps it is the work of shoveling, as a catalogue of body techniques in its semiotic articulations, that is the most appropriate site for the positioning of the psychohistorical narratives bundled in the name of the Tirailleurs sénégalais.[86]

In 2005, Banania was disinterred, if only momentarily. The Banania trademark had been retired in the early 1980s, but Banania returned with the same ingredients

FIGURE 27. Remaking the Banania image: Nutrimaine, 2005.

after being bought by the company Nutrimaine from Unilever in 2003.[87] The relaunch of Banania as a breakfast cereal for children followed a resurgence of Banania memorabilia, which had been found in many boutiques and museum gift shops around the world since the mid-1990s. In response, a petition was launched by the forty thousand–member Antillean, Guyanese, and Réunionais Collective against the image of the "le bon nègre," as Hervé Mbouguen writes at the French Web site Grioo.com, because it ignored the fact that Africans are still given little consideration in contemporary French society. Mbouguen is referring to the difficult conditions that Africans face given current immigration restrictions. The image on the cereal box has been redrawn so the figure is no longer that of Bamboula, but that of a child wearing a red *chéchia* hat, with large red lips, bug eyes, and brows appearing on the headgear. The cereal box reads, "Le bon petit déjeuner équilibré," or "The tasty well-balanced breakfast."[88]

To whom does the Banania image belong? Is the shift of the image to the innocent child yet another replay of the image that Barthes misidentified as an African soldier in "Myth Today"? Is it a replay of the same pernicious colonial stereotypes? In Barthes's 1972 follow-up essay "Change the Object Itself: Mythology Today," he writes that the myths he has described relative to French society have not changed, but his own thinking about myths as *sociolects* has. Instead, he proposes the idea of *ideolectology*, a more formal and therefore more penetrating notion, whose operational concepts would no longer be sign, signifier, and connotation but rather citation, reference, and stereotype.[89] Finally, Barthes proposes the idea of changing the object itself to create a new object, a new science. It is in this search for a new point of departure that the return of Banania poses some important questions. While vestiges of colonial consciousness cannot be erased from the social imaginary, they can be transformed through a combined approach of recalling the repressed memory. This "working-through" hinges on repositioning the image in relation to a refracted colonial gaze in such a way that the revenge of the repressed is not transmuted to the image of the Senegalese Sharpshooter as the child of an immigrant African worker who no longer has meaningful economic or social rights.

3. The Trans-Saharan Crossing Films
Colonial Cinematic Projections of the French Automobile

From traversing space to mapping it, the French colonial crossing films of the inter-war period embody a classificatory gaze, projecting geographic itineraries across Africa, Asia, and the Middle East. The automobile served as a mobile platform of geographic mastery, traveling along a network of carefully plotted coordinates that territorialized human difference. From this point of origin ethnic and cultural stereotypes were represented in the omniscient realism of cinema.

The major French automobile manufacturers (Peugeot, Renault, and Citroën) began sponsoring film expeditions across the Sahara during the interwar period in the context of an emerging tourist economy. These expeditions served as potent symbols of the French automobile industry and the state's geopolitical ambitions. The best known of the films were the feature-length documentaries sponsored by André Citroën, founder of the Citroën automobile firm. They featured the movement of caterpillar-tread half-track vehicles known as *autochenilles*[1] across the French colonies and into adjacent territories. The movement of these half-track vehicles was featured in *La Traversée du Sahara* (Traversing the Sahara, 1923),[2] *La Croisière noire* (*The Black Cruise*, 1925), and *La Croisière jaune* (*The Yellow Cruise*, 1932).[3]

These crossing films, or *raids* as they were often called, given their aggressive and quasi-military nature, featured exotic landscapes from the perspective of an automotive expedition, indexing an archaeological, ethnographic, and geographic repertoire within the context of French colonial ideologies of hygienic, educational, and political reform. These films were presented as a moving visual catalogue of the French colonies, saddling a discourse of interwar humanitarianism with the expanding forces of leisure travel and tourism. The Citroën films featured the automobile as an emerging means of tourist discovery dependent on an extensive network of shipping and railroad lines. By 1923 it took only twenty-four hours to get from Marseilles to most of the North African port cities thanks to the expansion of the Compagnie Générale Transatlantique passenger ships, which were, in turn, linked to an extensive network of railway itineraries and hotel accommodations.[4] Given the history of the French conquest, occupation, and integration of Algeria as three *départements* of France by 1848 (these included Alger, Constantine, and Oran, as well as Les Territories du Sud [the Southern Territories] by 1902), it was a destination with a well-developed infrastructure for tourism.

North Africa became an appealing tourist destination because of its familiarity and its proximity to the Saharan desert, which was popularly perceived as the great decompression chamber of Western civilization. It was in this space, which had been minutely charted on numerous geographic and military expeditions, that a desert fantasy of sexual and temporal dislocation could be imagined. After World War I, the French fascination with the Sahara was evocatively illustrated in Jacques Feyder's 1921 feature film *L'Atlantide,* adapted from Pierre Benoît's popular 1919 novel. In the film, Queen Antinéa (Stacia Napierkowska) uses her ancient Egyptian charms to seduce a

FIGURE 28. André Citroën contemplates the itinerary from Algiers to Timbuktu for the Raid Citroën and the film *La Traversée du sahara,* 1923. Copyright Citroën Communication.

long history of eminent European men whose bodies are preserved as taxidermic tro-phies in her castle hidden away in the gorges of the Saharan desert.[5]

Significantly, the world of Antinéa was outside of time and history and a site of no return for those men who were seduced, trapped, and finally exhibited in her lair. Furthermore, as Abdelkader Benali relates, Feyder's adaptation of the novel empha-sized the lost civilization of Atlantis as the mysterious source of Antinéa's origins.[6] The mistress-slave complex implied by Antinéa's relationship to her servants and henchmen reinforced her despotic powers of leadership and seduction. By analogy, Antinéa's ser-vants reinforced existing colonial stereotypes, claiming that the Tuareg lived in a back-ward state of human history where master-slave relationships were still the norm. This stereotype associated Tuareg culture with a pre-Hellenistic Bronze Age (thirteenth and twelfth centuries BC). The relationships of domination and submission portrayed in the film stood in opposition to the democratic enlightenment impulse of French civ-ilization. Moreover, Antinéa and Atlantis were Egyptian referents, hidden away as if in a cryptlike forbidden zone of the Saharan desert. In this depiction of the Sahara, African civilization was constructed as barbarous and absent from history, serving as a crucial point of opposition in the elaboration of the Enlightenment project itself.

The sexual appeal of Queen Antinéa and the Atlantis referent were so powerful that in the published travel account of the Citroën journey across the Sahara, known as *Le Raid Citroën,* the subtitle for the work was *De Touggourt à Tomboutou par l'Atlan-tide* (From Touggourt to Timbuktu through Atlantis). It also appeared as a heading on each page of the text. "Par L'Atlantide" appeared on all of the right-hand pages of the volume, associating it directly with Benoît's novel and Feyder's film. "De Touggourt à Tombouctou," which appeared on the left-hand pages, referenced the politically con-tentious Transsaharien railroad project.

THE TRANSSAHARIEN RAILROAD PROJECT

The Transsaharien was the French trans-Saharan railroad project that sought to cre-ate a railroad link between Algeria and sub-Saharan Africa. The Touggourt–Timbuktu railroad itinerary was a subject of ongoing debate in the French political sphere. The Transsaharien was initially proposed by Henri Duveyrier, a French explorer who first traveled to the Sahara in 1859 and made contact with various Tuareg leaders in the region.[7] Duveyrier suggested a trans-Saharan route from Algiers to Timbuktu in order to establish a gateway to an intersecting sub-Saharan east–west junction between Sene-gal to the west, in French West Africa, and Djibouti to the east, in the French Soudan. Duveyrier's suggestion was followed by a report about the viability of the project by the engineer Adolphe Duponchel, funded by the Commission for the Transsasharien.[8]

Four major expeditions into the Sahara were funded by this commission. The last of them, under the command of Lieutenant Colonel Paul-François Flatters, turned into a brutal massacre, acquiring the status of myth. It consisted of ninety-two men, including ten French army officers and engineers, forty-seven Arab soldiers, two French noncommissioned officers, two orderlies, and thirty-one Chaamba guides and camel-eers. The expedition left Laghouat, Algeria, in November 1880 and returned with only thirteen half-dead Chaamba survivors, who arrived in Ouargla on April 4, 1881. Mem-bers of the expedition were massacred and poisoned, and incidents of cannibalism among men on the expedition were reported in the final month of the expedition.

The outcome of the Flatters Expedition led to the temporary abandonment of plans for the Transsaharien until it was revived with the Foreau–Lamy expeditions.[9] A pattern of administrative embrace and rejection of the Transsaharien continued for nearly a century. The traumatic effect of the Flatters Expedition was so significant that all films of expeditions passing through the Ahaggar Saharan outpost of Ouargla make at least passing reference to the Flatters monument located in the town center, with its sprawling arcades, with Ouargla serving as an "orientalized" example of the Amer-ican Western frontier town. References to the American western frontier were made in Duponchel's initial Transsaharien report,[10] and the American novels of James Fen-imore Cooper and Mayne Reid made their way into the published travelogue account of Le Raid Citroën[11] in evoking a brush fire on the dune-swept plains near Tabankor, Niger, which the expedition encountered just before reaching Timbuktu.[12]

A network of railroad lines was built throughout Northern Algeria, Tunisia, and West Africa during the second half of the nineteenth century. Extensive railway ser-vice was established in Northern Algeria as early as 1862 with the Algiers–Blida line, and as of 1890, eighteen hundred miles of railway track linked port cities along the Alger-ian and Tunisian coast to inland regional centers.[13] By 1918, the Biskra–Touggourt line had been built, and the end of this railroad itinerary in Touggourt was the launching point for the first of the Citroën expeditions, led by Georges-Marie Haardt and Louis Audouin-Dubreuil.

The automobile journey across the Sahara became part of prevailing public debates about the Transsaharien. The Citroën half-track vehicles were a powerful substitute for the railroad, as if their caterpillar tread, with its tractorlike capacity, had cleared the way for a phantom railway system. The caterpillar tread's continuous imprint attempted to unify the colonies as part of "greater France," in the rhetoric of the day, through the extension of the railroad.

A compelling feature of the half-track vehicle was the looping of the metallic-rubber caterpillar tread that imprinted the geographic landscape, almost like the move-ment of a mechanical clock, echoing the constancy of modulated propulsion. In other words, the half-track vehicle defined distance and territory in terms of the temporal movement forward. The movement of the clock, which has been so instrumental to the development of the film transport system for the motion picture camera, relies on the interaction of gears and the counteraction of propulsion and stoppage. To para-phrase the media archaeologist Siegfried Zielinski, "The clock acquires its hold on time by continually and forcibly disciplining it and not allowing it to run freely."[14]

The kinematics of the motion picture camera and the automobile are based on the modulation of interlocking mechanisms embodied by the clock. Therefore, *kinematics*

FIGURE 29. Traveling in the *autochenilles,* or half-track caterpillar-tread vehicles, during the Raid Citroën in 1923. Copyright Citroën Communication.

refers to the principles underlying the motions that occur in mechanisms, and, by extension, *kinetic synthesis* is the design of linkages to produce a given series of motions for a particular purpose.[15] The imposition of time implied a regime of regulation that standardized the movement of film through the registration gate of the motion picture camera and the controlled movement of the cylinders of an engine that, in turn, activated the axles and put the tires of an automobile in motion. The modulation of the clock underlay the chronological indexing of civilization in the crossing film genre. It also inferred the dominant model for the diffusion of human civilization of the period, based on an Indo-European cultural inheritance.

Whereas the people and landscape on the African continent were depicted as being lost in time and history, the automobile was the symbol of European modernity. This view of modernity positioned Africa as a static entity that could be reawakened only by the agency of Western modernity. These images can be understood as part of an Aryan diffusionist perspective that denied the significance of African civilization.[16] Furthermore, it was a perspective that could not conceive of an existing African modernity born through the struggles implied by the slave trade and the historical significance of African and Asian contributions to the development of civil society in the West.

The crossing films illustrated the Aryan diffusionist perspective, claiming that the origin of human civilization was derived from the Indo-European origins of ancient

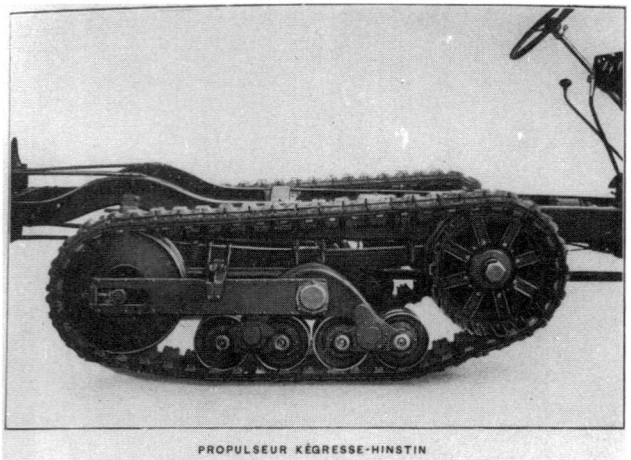

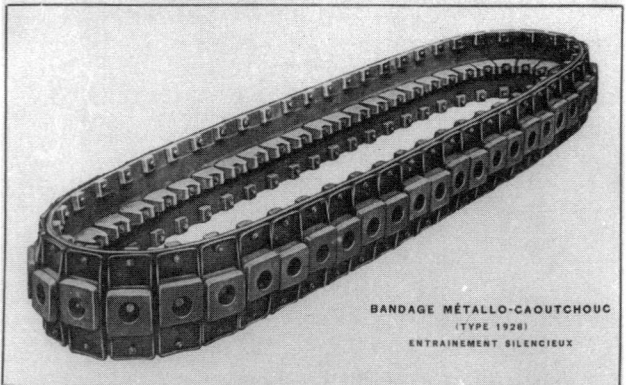

FIGURE 30. *Top:* The Kégresse-Hinsten propulsion unit. *Bottom:* The metallic-rubber caterpillar tread. Copyright Citroën Communication.

Greece, which, in turn, led to the invention of Europe. The search for purity in a lost historical era of human civilization served to support and specify a racially specific depiction of African geography. The disciplining of time implied that metropolitan France was the most advanced state of industrial and cultural agency and the automobile industry was a leading force. With the introduction of American-inspired scientific industrial management practices on the Citroën assembly line under the stewardship of Ernest Mattern by 1922, the Saharan landscape represented the ultimate challenge to the chronometric rhythms of industrialized production.[17] The alliance of Taylorist industrial efficiency and colonial propaganda coalesced around the half-track vehicle, on a mission to discipline the landscape in the service of an itinerary. Over the course of the expeditions, they charted relative human difference through the hypnotic regularity of the caterpillar tread in motion, overcoming geographic and cultural obstacles.

La Traversée du Sahara featured the automobile as a survey vehicle, illustrating geographic contours of the desert landscape as a metonym for a civilization lost in time and history. The expedition embodied the values of industrial rationality, with seemingly neutral manned half-track vehicles traveling through nomadic Tuareg communities in the Saharan desert. The vastness of the luminous desert landscape was a site of psychohistorical projection for European fantasies of otherness, a "lost" sociocultural historical past, and an empty space to be mapped, contained, and ultimately used to undertake the first French nuclear testing at In Eker (Algeria) in 1961.[18]

As the starting point of the Raid Citroën expedition, Touggourt represented the beginning of the proposed central railroad itinerary through the Sahara initially proposed by Duveyrier. An early guidebook for North African automobile tourism describes the area surrounding Touggourt as an evocative mise-en-scène for Saharan tourism:

> Alas, the sand makes normal automobile excursions nearly impossible. Fortunately, half-track vehicles have passed through and opened up innumerable paths for Saharan tourism; let us gaze at the sunlight languishing on the dunes, intersecting with towering palms that weave a magical background for the sandscapes of "Antinéa," the site where principal scenes from *L'Atlantide* were filmed.[19]

This passage links the recently completed Citroën expedition with the evocative landscapes that served as an exterior shooting location in Feyder's *L'Atlantide*. The

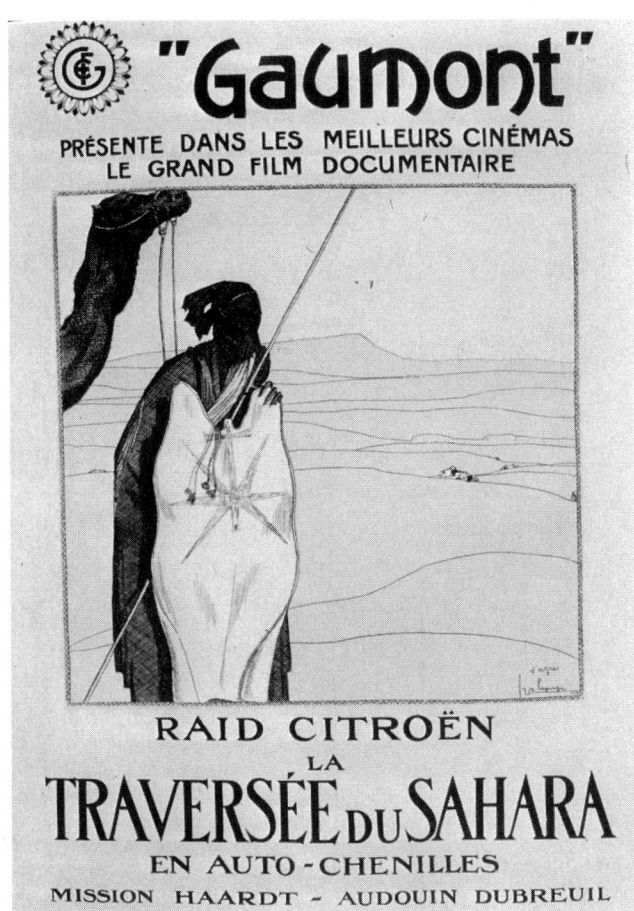

FIGURE 31. Gaumont poster for *La Traversée du Sahara* (1923), featuring a black-veiled Tuareg tribesman and camel. Copyright Citroën Communication.

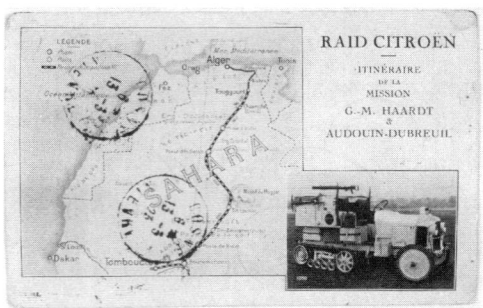 

FIGURE 32. (Left) Le Raid Citroën itinerary. (Right) Stamped travel itinerary from Timbuktu to Touggourt, signed by the expedition copilot, Louis Audouin-Dubreuil, 1923. Copyright Citroën Communication.

rhetorical interplay between sunlight, sand, and the feminine charms of Antinéa evoked a visual spectacle that appealed to an emerging tourist economy. On the basis of French Touring Club statistics, Patrick Young has claimed that 35,000 tourists visited Algiers in 1910, and by 1923 more than 350,000 tourists traveled from France to Algeria and Tunisia on a yearly basis.[20] Tourists were attracted to the extended desert geography, where the automobile became an increasingly viable form of adventure. It was in this way that a form of ethnographic tourism emerged. Automobile tourism promised a mediated encounter with authenticity, symbolized by the collection of "folk" artifacts and the act of writing and photographing their own travelogues.

André Citroën explained that Le Raid Citroën was envisioned partially as a topographic survey for the projected expansion of the railway line through the Sahara and that the half-track vehicles were best suited to this task because they functioned as "moving rails" along this difficult terrain.[21] After more than fifty years of wrangling over specific itineraries for the construction of a trans-Saharan railway, the Touggourt–Timbuktu central route appeared to be a likely itinerary for the construction of the trans-Saharan railway. In fact, subsequent public debates about railroad itineraries shifted south of the Sahara.

By the time *La Traversée du Sahara* was released in 1923, public debates about the Transsaharien were overshadowed by the trans-African railroad project, known as the Transafricain. It was to be a "continental" railroad route serving as the "vertebral column" of the French colonial empire on the African continent, linking raw materials to ports while allowing the swift deployment of large-scale military and labor contingents.[22] At the same time, it challenged British ambitions of creating a Cairo–Capetown railway axis. *La Croisière noire* (1925), the best known of the Citroën crossing films, served as the geographic visual compendium for potential continental African itineraries.

It was argued that the Touggourt–Timbuktu Saharan itinerary remained critical to unifying the various trans-African railway lines, but, ironically, it was never built; the dream of the Transsaharien never materialized. Instead it became the ultimate testing ground for the French automobile after World War I.

THE AUTOMOBILE AND THE SAHARA

Automobile excursions in Northern Algeria, Morocco, and Tunisia were first introduced by private companies in response to trade and tourism from 1898 to 1908, but were later used by the French army in the Sahara immediately following World War I.

The French military pacification of the Sahara was seriously destabilized during World War I. As Jeremy Keenan has explained, within weeks of the outbreak of the war, the Sennusi tribe, instigated by the Turks, revolted against the French and Italian presence in the Sahara. After the Italians were driven out by the Sennusi and abandoned their positions at Ghat in 1914, the Sennusi began to attack French Saharan territory. In February 1916, an organized contingent of a thousand armed Sennusi combatants attacked the French garrison of Djanet. They laid siege to the town for

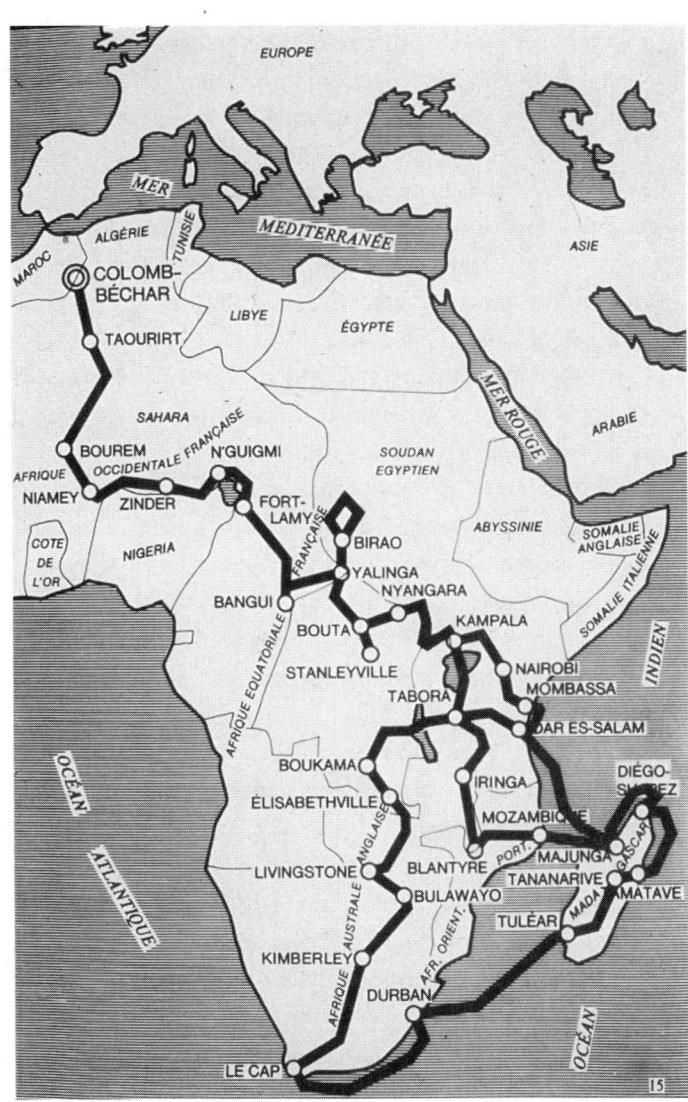

FIGURE 33. The Croisière Noire itinerary, 1925. Copyright Citroën Communication.

eighteen days, and the men at the garrison surrendered. French forces retook the garrison two months later, but just as they began reoccupying the villages that had been overtaken by the Sennusi, further military action ceased and the French forces abandoned their positions by order from Paris.[23]

Following the perceived retreat of the French forces, revolt spread throughout the Sahara, culminating in the assassination of Charles de Foucauld, the aristocratic French missionary who had written the first systematic linguistic guide to the Tuareg language. The introduction of the automobile to the Sahara by 1916 coincided with this renewed spirit of Tuareg defiance, which might explain why the first Renault and Citroën automobiles were, in fact, militarized reconnaissance vehicles. The importance of a road linking Touggourt to the Ahaggar region via Ouargla and In Salah was recognized by French military leaders as early as 1915,[24] and one of the first Saharan automobile itineraries was a twenty-day, 289-mile journey from Ouargla to In Salah with two vehicles.[25] As Commander Bettembourg, one of the participants, remembers, only one of the two vehicles arrived at In Salah. The second was abandoned along the way, and the vehicle that arrived benefited from "the combined effort of wooden planks, the shovel, camels, and elbow grease."[26] This itinerary later culminated in subsequent automobile and airplane excursions used to establish road itineraries and refueling points, transforming the landscape into nodes of transit. It was during one of the early Saharan airplane itineraries in 1920 that General Laperrine, memorialized in the colonial archive as the architect of French military strategy in the Sahara, died from injuries resulting from a plane crash.

The cult of men piloting dangerously fast machines who sought to master the desert landscape was established from this early moment and continues into the present with the Paris–Dakar auto rally. The desert was the ultimate test not merely of machines but of the endurance and virility of men manifested as machines of speed in a race against time. After World War I, fears of depopulation and the death of more than a quarter of the active French male population on the battlefield revived the discourse of *dégénéréscence*. The will toward the values of speed and endurance embodied by the automobile, capable of overcoming the hardship of the Saharan desert, galvanized aspirations of revitalizing the French national body, still traumatized by the effects of the war.

The initial Saharan expeditions sponsored by Citroën prior to Le Raid Citroën began in 1921 and were used to test the half-track vehicles in the desert sand. Certain members of the initial Citroën expedition had significant military experience with automobile and airplane reconnaissance in the Saharan desert. Lieutenant Louis Audouin-Dubreuil, the copilot of the three Citroën expeditions, and Commander Bettembourg, a participating military adviser on the first two expeditions, had extensive French military experience in Algeria. In fact, they were chosen to participate in the Citroën expeditions because they had led military detachments with the use of automobiles in contested regions of Algeria starting in 1919 as part of the larger French strategic initiatives in the region.[27]

La Traversée du Sahara begins with the following set of intertitles: "From the dawn of antiquity, communication across the desert could only be assured by camel-driven caravans . . . Which slowly crossed the immense desert landscape. . . . The vast French colonial domain in Africa requires more rapid communication. . . . This is being made possible by courageous men, with the help of the *auto-chenilles*."[28] These opening intertitles are complemented by a series of long shots starting with a group of camels being led by nomads, followed by a vacant desert landscape and an image of the half-track vehicles. The nomadic lifestyle associated with camels, caravans, the desert landscape, and the fully veiled nomads is opposed to the modernity of the half-track vehicle in this opening segment of the film. The opening intertitles stress the importance of rapid communication, which serves as an oppositional framing device throughout the film. Rapid communication facilitated the efficient deployment of French troops, the promotion of French hygienic and medical techniques, mail service, and French educational efforts based on the "universality" of the French language. Short segments throughout the film illustrate these efforts.

The opposition between camel-driven salt caravans and the *autochenilles* is yet a more complicated story. The salt caravans depicted in this opening scene were a response to an entrenched network of French zones of occupation that altered grazing patterns for livestock and crucial access to water. The French territorial expansion in the region not only shifted how Tuareg groups secured their livelihood, but transformed power relationships between tribal leaders in the region. In the archive of French colonial documentary cinema, Jean d'Esme's films, particularly *Peaux noires* (Black skins, 1932) and *Sables du feu* (Sand of fire, 1935), attempted to evoke the lyricism of the salt caravans and ancient trade routes while ignoring the disruptive colonial presence that had dramatically transformed the economy of the region in the first place.

Amenoukal Akhamouk, who appears in a brief segment of the film exchanging gifts with leaders of the expedition, is introduced as the sovereign leader of the Ahaggar region, which was the largest section of the desert itinerary. Amenoukal was a leadership role that the French had greatly expanded under Akhamouk's predecessor, Moussa ag Amastane. In the film, the image of Amenoukal Akhamouk, whose face and body were fully covered by the black-veiled garment known as the *litham*, reinforced the mystery of the people and landscape of the Sahara.

The even more elaborate greeting and tea ceremony used to introduce Amenoukal Akhamouk in one of the short films,[29] derived from the same footage used to make *La Traversée du Sahara*, illustrates Terence Ranger's observation that "indigenous traditions" were formalized and ritualized in the colonial context as a means of accentuating "traditions of subordination."[30] Public displays of traditional authority figures supported the contention that French colonization efforts were part of a civilizing process, echoing an Aryan, but seemingly respectful, geographical diffusionism. However, there is something disturbing about the ceremonial function portrayed by these African figures. Their relationship with the French adventurers, military officials, and administrators authenticates the representation of "African tradition," stereotyped as an object of curiosity.

La Traversée du Sahara is structured as a travelogue organized through a set of intertitles interspersed with a brief series of shots. Significantly, the camera was almost exclusively positioned on or in the vehicles themselves in a number of mobile point-of-view shots. The film introduces the significance of the caterpillar-tread vehicle as a swift and reliable means of communication across the Sahara desert, and this is followed by an illustration of the genesis of caterpillar-tread technology and the organization of the voyage under André Citroën's sponsorship. The film then presents the actual itinerary of the voyage in three segments, culminating in their arrival at Timbuktu, where they embark on a brief hunting expedition in Niger. Before returning to Touggourt, André Citroën, his wife, and Aldolfe Kégresse greet members of the expedition at the halfway point of the abbreviated return itinerary.[31]

Aldophe Kégresse was the inventor of the half-track vehicle. Born and educated in France, Kégresse started as a mechanic and was then manager at the Jeanperrin de Glay automobile factory. He was employed for a time as an inventor at the Russian Imperial Garage under the tutelage of Prince Orloff in St. Petersburg. At the Imperial Garage he developed a half-track vehicle that could reliably function in soft snow conditions as well as on icy roads without interruption or a reduction in speed.[32] In France he helped engineer the first Renault tanks that were introduced by General Estienne during World War I and worked in collaboration with Jacques Hinstin, André Citroën's original partner. With Citroën's backing, Kégresse and Hinstin developed the patented Kégresse–Hinstin propulsion unit, which was applied to a variety of vehicle prototypes. The vehicles built for Le Raid Citroën represented the first adaptation of the half-track vehicle for Saharan tourism.

O 6 2 11

FIGURE 34. A half-track vehicle carriage fitted with front-wheel skis, n.d. Copyright Citroën Communication.

FIGURE 35. Diagram of the half-track vehicle's component parts, 1926. Copyright Citroën Communication.

With ten members of the expedition, five vehicles, and their mascot Flossie the dog, Kégresse and Hinstin set out, and in *La Traversée du Sahara* there are frequent references to maps of the region, the tracing of their itinerary, and the ritual departure of the vehicles.[33] As early prototypes of the all-terrain military amphibious vehicle, these half-track vehicles were equipped with machine guns, built-in expandable tents, and flip-down sinks with running water. They transformed a military expedition into a slightly dangerous camping adventure in which the threat of indigenous people was considered of the same order as the fear of wild animals. The film is a virtual tour of French military pacification efforts in the Sahara, reflecting familiar motifs associated with colonial adventure—the desert sand, the automobile, the all-male military unit, and stereotyped imagery of geographically specific ethnic populations. The recurrent motif in this film is the half-track vehicle mechanism itself, which is at once a capable tractor, an armored vehicle, and a phantom railroad touring car, able to surmount almost any obstacle while leaving a continuous mechanical footprint in its wake. *La Traversée du Sahara* was finally edited into a fifty-minute documentary film for the general public.

Georges-Marie Haardt, the copilot of the expedition, told Léon Poirier, the filmmaker hired to accompany the Croisière Noire expedition less than a year later, that *La Traversée du Sahara* was made by a film operator who specialized in the travelogue format, so the film does not convey the full intensity of the desert.[34] Haardt wanted Poirier to portray the visual sensation of the desert landscape in *La Croisière noire*, transforming the documentary conceit of the film into an evocation of the desert in the first part of the film. Paul Castelnau, the filmmaker who directed *La Traversée du Sahara*, was a geographer by training whose involvement with cinematography began through his association with the geographers Jean Brunhes and Vidal de la Blache, who established a school of geographic thought known as *la géographie humaine.*[35] This school of thought linked geography to ethnography in a Bergsonian-inspired colonial encounter. To paraphrase Achille Mbembe, Bergsonian colonialism reduced the colonized to animals in their native habitat, where familiarity and domestication subsequently served as the dominant tropes of servitude.[36] This mode of colonial engagement is even more apparent in Poirier's *La Croisière noire,* which has been re-edited numerous times, in part because of its self-assured approach to depicting African subjects as native fauna specific to particular regions of the continent. Castelnau worked as a traveling film operator whose most important benefactor was Albert Kahn. As I mention in chapter 5, Kahn commissioned Castelnau to make numerous films in Asia, Africa, and the Middle East.

As was true of many pedagogical films of the period, there was more than one version of *La Traversée du Sahara* in circulation. In the two versions of the film that I have screened, the title was completed with *en automobiles* for one and *en autochenilles* for the other. Other variations in its length and the use of intertitles were also present,

FIGURE 36. Portrait of Léon Poirier, director of *La Croisière noire,* n.d. Copyright Citroën Communication.

marking the different exhibition histories of the two versions. Whereas *La Traversée du Sahara en autochenilles* was distributed by Gaumont on a national and international public circuit, *La Traversée du Sahara en automobiles* was distributed in schools and public education lending libraries. In addition to multiple versions of the same film, a twelve-part series of short films known as *Le Continent mystérieux* (The mysterious continent, dir. Paul Castelnau, 1924) was released the year after *La Traversée du Sahara*. According to Pierre Leprohon, this film was released in a serial format at the request of distributors anxious to provide a steady flow of exotic imagery.[37] It featured extended thematic reflections using excess footage from particular aspects of the itinerary, such as the Saharan oasis, indigenous scenes, extended views of the desert landscape, and views at In Salah, Ouargla, Timbuktu, and along the banks of the Niger River. Each short film of *Le Continent mystérieux* started with the trademark opening title card indicating that the films were the equivalent of ethnographic field notes taken over the course of Le Raid Citroën. The presentation of these short films served to further saturate the public with images of the Citroën expedition in anticipation of the completion and release of *La Croisière noire*.

A recurrent theme in the Citroën films was the depiction of African women in various states of undress. In contrast to the image of Antinéa as vamp in *L'Atlantide*, African women were depicted as alternatively titillating, submissive, or burdened with

FIGURE 37. Postcard of a Nailiyat (Oued-Naïls) woman wearing traditional jewelry and dress in the Scènes et Types postcard genre, ca. 1912. Copyright Research Library, the Getty Research Institute, Los Angeles, California (970031).

arduous forms of domestic labor. Women of the Ouled-Naïl tribe (known as Nailiyat) are shown performing *la danse du ventre* (belly dance) in the fourth episode of *Le Continent mystérieux,* known as "Scènes indigènes à Ouargla." The Nailiyat are introduced, in opposition to their "warrior" male counterparts, as "sirens of love." Marnia Lazreg has described the precolonial situation of the Nailiyat as a group of women from the Ouled Naïl tribe who enjoyed a degree of sexual freedom that was not uncommon among women in nearby communities. These women would leave their rural milieu and entertain men in nearby towns with song and dance. Nailiyat women did not solicit or ask for money, but depended on the generosity of their clients to help their families pay taxes on land used for farming.

The town of Bou Saada, located on the plateau of the Ouled Naïl Mountains, became known as the capital of Nailiyat dance performance. While these dancers typically performed fully clothed, the French Syndicat d'initiative, or tourist bureau, in the region influenced the character of their performances and insisted that they perform nude before their European visitors, transforming them into tourist spectacles by the 1880s. This shift toward tourism initiated a process in which the dancers' freedom of

FIGURE 38. Attributed as *une almée,* or Egyptian dancer, in the Orientalist imagination, Algiers, ca. 1914. Copyright Research Library, the Getty Research Institute, Los Angeles, California (970031).

movement was restricted, and women associated with Nailiyat dance performance were issued identity cards classifying them as prostitutes subject to periodic medical check-ups.[38] By the interwar period, the Nailiyat became synonymous with prostitution in France thanks to the expansion of French tourism in Algeria and the vigorous development of the picture postcard market. Malek Alloula and Leïla Sebbar have described the way North African women were visually depicted to titillate and promote their availability as part of an emerging colonial tourist fantasy.[39]

The population of Algerian prostitutes, though stereotyped as Nailiyat, were in fact part of the same population of orphaned girl children, as Leïla Sebbar suggests, who were taken in by the French Catholic missionaries and trained in silk weaving and Arab lace making.[40] Some of the women became practitioners of the highly sought-after lacework made by this technique, which is abundantly visible on serialized postcards depicting Arab women in various poses. Images of their work are presented in *Le Continent mystérieux* and associated with homage to Cardinal Lavigerie, founder of the Catholic African Missions. In fact, a glimpse of the Catholic mission in *La Traversée du Sahara* conceivably depicts orphaned young women creating the Arab lacework that appears on the postcards.

The Nailiyat were recurrent subjects in a number of expedition-related films of the period. A series of shots show three young bare-breasted women dancing in the same installment of *Le Continent mystérieux*. An older woman, dressed in white, then gestures toward the camera, inviting us to watch the other dancers. This segment is followed by an image of the Chaamba *fantasia* celebration, with warriors on horseback shooting into the air as they gallop by a group of spectators. These images were later recycled in *La Croisière noire,* as well as in at least two of the more than fifty short films made over the course of the Croisière Noire expedition.

In one of these short films, *Lève Africaine* (Raising the African woman, dir. Léon Poirier, 1925), recycled images of the Nailiayat dancers reappear. This time, however, one of the dancers is identified as Zina, who is presented as a woman who responds to her clients' desires, but, as the intertitles explain, she chooses them carefully and leaves it to her servants to please the crowd. This is followed by an extended dance sequence with images of musicians and Nailiyat dancers. In the film, however, prostitution, the profession with which the Nailiyat became nearly synonymous, is identified with Congolese women, who are even further removed from an Indo-European diffusionist point of origin. The Nailiyat practice of prostitution is merely referenced in the intertitle, "Arab penetration did not include the introduction of Nailiyat dancing or their practices of prostitution." In one way, this intertitle refers to Nailiyat prostitution as an art as opposed to its less refined form as practiced by Congolese women. The expansion of prostitution under the French occupation of Algeria was formalized by the "Arab bureau" and was restricted at first to certain quarters of the French colonial cities catering to the appetites of the French military and subsequently to the desires of European travelers.[41]

Further, "Arab penetration," the term used by the intertitles in *Lève Africaine,* casts

FIGURE 39. *Type de femme de l'Algérie du nord,* or rather, nude North African girl in a pose suggestive of bondage, chromolithograph, ca. 1912. Copyright Research Library, the Getty Research Institute, Los Angeles, California (970031).

Arab men as the ravishers of Congolese women, imagining Arab men as sexual predators. This also implies that although Arab women could serve as potential sexual partners for French men, Arab men were denigrated as the victimizers of defenseless Congolese women. The *fantasia* segment that follows the Nailiyat dancers in *Le Continent mystérieux* features Arab soldiers firing their guns in the air on horseback, reminiscent of warriors from the Bronze Age, trapped in the historical past. The depiction of Africans in *La Traversée du Sahara* and *La Croisière noire* uses geography as a means of charting their historical and "civilized state" relative to the norms of metropolitan France. The fairgroundlike depictions of live African, American Indian, and Asian ethnic groups, who appeared throughout Europe from the mid-nineteenth century until the Second World War, suggested a colonial geographic theme park of cultural and historical attractions. These attractions were codified once they began to appear as popular ethnographic exhibitions in France, and were later inscribed into a cinematic travel itinerary. In Paris, affluent families could present themselves in their automobiles as they motored through the Bois du Boulogne and glimpsed the reconstructed ethnographic villages populated with live "natives" on display.

CINEMATIC ILLUSIONISM AND THE COLONIAL LANDSCAPE

Images of the African continent constituted an archive of visual stereotypes that were integrated into a series of public exhibitions. The trope of the mysterious Sahara was firmly rooted in the French imagination by the mid-nineteenth century, following the legacy of the Napoleonic Egyptian campaigns and the invasion of Sidi-Ferruch (Algeria) in 1830. Visual references to the Sahara abounded from the Algerian School of Realist painting, images of early Romantic photography, and French Romantic literary novels by Eugène Fromentin.[42] The Algerian landscape was incorporated into a literary and aesthetic vocabulary of conquest, settlement, and sexuality. It was from the perspective of the Egyptian conquest that Edward Said's critique of Orientalism and colonial ideology began.

Possibilities for travel were incorporated into early panoramas and film exhibitions at the Universal and Colonial Exhibitions. One of the first attempts to bring back images from the African continent was sponsored by a Belgian railroad company in the Congo for presentation at the International Colonial Exhibition at Tervueren in 1897. The film operator attempted to film the work that was underway by Congolese laborers for the construction of a railroad line between Boma, Matadi, and Kinshasa in the Congo, but due to technical difficulties the film was not properly exposed and

FIGURE 40. Animal tusks displayed in front of the half-track vehicles and their occupants in Faradje, Congo Free State (now D. R. Congo), during the Croisière Noire expedition, April 4, 1925. Copyright Citroën Communication.

could not be shown.[43] These short films were to appear as part of the Zoographe exhibition of short films, featuring Demenÿ's Phonoscope.[44] This early attempt to make a film illustrating the construction of an African railroad project was part of a pattern of colonial imagery that promoted the technology of travel.

The 1900 International Universal Exhibition in Paris included numerous variations of the panoramic voyage on exhibition. The Trans-Siberian railway panorama had visitors sit in a stationary train carriage while they watched the unrolling of various landscapes along the Moscow–Beijing itinerary. These landscapes were painted on canvas and rolled across the windows over the course of a forty-five-minute "ride." As Emmanuelle Toulet has described, one of the most spectacular displays was the "Maréorama," an animated panorama installed in the center of a large edifice reproducing the bridge of a steamer. It attempted to convey the experience of a Compagnie Générale Transatlantique passage from Marseilles to Constantinople by way of the Algerian coast.[45]

Large-scale panoramas at the 1900 Universal Exhibition represented aspirations for the development of a French colonial geographic axis from the Atlantic Ocean to the Red Sea. Panoramas of Fachoda, the strategic village located at the base of the Nile River that served as a short-lived French strategic foothold in East Africa, momentarily resuscitated the imagined imperial grandeur of the Napoleonic Egyptian conquest.[46] By 1900, numerous films were presented, including an exhibit featuring imagery from Egypt and Algeria, as part of the Algerian Cinématographe pavilion. Lest we forget, imagery of Egypt remained the Orientalist root of the nineteenth-century European imagination.[47]

The ubiquity of representative artifacts from the colonies, as well as fully reconstructed villages and architectural designs, created a foundation for the transformation of the colonial environment itself. From the *rue du Caire* to the *rue d'Alger*, the colonial city was reconstructed at a series of international European exhibitions throughout the late nineteenth century, inhabited by traveling indigenous African, Asian, and American Indian performers. The continual reappearance of the colonial city and its familiarity among urban Europeans has led Timothy Mitchell to assert that the attempt to create a representation of the "other" was a blueprint for the development of the metropolitan colonial city. It was a city divided in two—one that was part of the exhibition and the other serving as a natural history museum. The exhibitionary side of the colonial city was perhaps best embodied by Lyautey's Rabat, as Paul Rabinow has described it, with its Cartesian design of public buildings, the centrality of the railroad station, and the minute ordering of public spaces.[48] The natural history museum was all the rest, a live ethnographic exhibition, a survey of the past. While the ethnographic exhibitions presented a live tableau of an idyllic African scene, the colonial urban spaces on exhibit were an attempt to establish the majesty and certainty of the colonial administrative order.

The theatricality of the exhibitions asserted colonial authority in the ordering of collected objects. Whereas these exhibitions were focused on establishing parameters for the colonial city, the crossing films mapped regional and continental geographies. The itineraries for Citroën, Peugeot, and Renault crossing films were structured to sequence and display the unfolding of geographic space as a spatiotemporal extension of the colonial exhibition. Unlike an exhibition, the crossing films could present a grand narrative of civilization that could be photographically mapped through the act of editing.

The shift from establishing a differential colonial index of civilization to manufacturing that experience as part of a tourist adventure is at the heart of the crossing film genre. The European exhibitions served as referents for the transformation of colonial geography. Colonial cinema served to authenticate the exhibitions at a moment when the colonial cities were being completed. It was the simulated encounter with "natives" and ethnographic objects at the Colonial Exhibitions that encouraged a particular kind of travel itinerary and experience of the metropolitan "exotic" simulation in situ. The exhibitions further prepared the spectator for the experience of travel, isolating the sensations and making them feel "realer than real" with such international attractions as Hale's Tours, where the spectator boarded a "train," paid a dime to the "conductor," and sat in a theater that resembled a passenger carriage.[49] In some of the more elaborate shows, the theater itself rocked and creaked in order to simulate the experience of being in a railway car.[50] This would often result in a doubling effect in which the experience of the voyage and the depiction of the spaces would simulate the tourist adventure.

The Citroën films were symptomatic of the shift from images celebrating colonial conquest to a civilizing project represented as moving images. In the aftermath of World War I, the terms of colonial occupation had shifted from colonial conquest toward maintaining a colonial administrative presence while espousing the values of a postwar humanitarianism. The argument for a continued colonial presence on the African continent became part of a larger effort aligned with postwar reconstruction. Rebuilding the African continent along the lines of hygienic reform existed in an uneasy alliance with the drive toward metropolitan tourism.

CONSTRUCTING THE SAHARAN AUTOMOBILE AS A VEHICLE FOR TOURIST ADVENTURE

Automobile travel became explicitly associated with privileged access to exotic landscapes. As André Citroën and Louis Renault vied for a leadership position in the French automobile industry after World War I, the Sahara became the new theater for automobile performance allied with the trappings of the expedition. The success of Le Raid Citroën was followed by a series of Renault expeditions that culminated in the development of a vehicle outfitted with six large twinned tires for the Mission Gradis.[51] The Mission Gradis also introduced a new itinerary that departed from Colomb-Béchar, Algeria. A newly completed railway station in Colomb-Béchar represented a new beginning for the Transsaharien, tracing a western itinerary that was the shortest distance across the desert into French West Africa and a powerful node of the French colonial officers' corps.

The competition between Renault and Citroën began with the expansion of their factories to serve the military during World War I, with Citroën applying Taylorist techniques of assembly line production to produce artillery shells in record time. The intersecting itineraries of Citroën and Renault expeditions continued on the African continent throughout the interwar period. While the Renault-sponsored expeditions did not overtly seek to advertise the vehicles themselves, the Citroën expeditions were an expression of André Citroën's flair for publicity and willingness to devote substantial resources toward their organization and presentation to the public. Between 1924 and 1926, two travelogue films used Renault vehicles on the African continent as part of an extended itinerary across the Sahara and beyond. The first of these films, about which only scant written information still exists, was made over the course of the first Mission Gradis.[52] The second film, known as *Les Mystères du continent noir* (Mysteries of the dark continent, 1926), presented select material from the eight-month Mission Gradis–Delingette and followed a trans-African itinerary from Oran to Capetown.

Les Mystères du continent noir treats the African continent as a series of faunalike pathologies. The version of the film that I have seen is tinted red.[53] Red tinting was a technique that distributors would often use to indicate danger or fire or to foreground emotional, sexual, and primitive impulses. The film is significant to the extent that it goes beyond the usual denigration of African rituals to focus on various techniques of self-mutilation, particularly of women. Various scarification techniques as well as bodily incisions are demonstrated with close-ups. The incisions used to insert lip disks in the Saras-Djinas ethnic group near Lake Chad are presented in explicit detail. The upper and lower lips are cut to form an elastic joint that holds upper and lower wooden plates in place. The shock value of this demonstration is posited on its decontextualization and the mutilation of a significant erogenous zone, the lips.

The numerous views of the Saras-Djinas women inserting and removing the plates from their distended lips are presented as a barbarous parody rather than as part of what was intended to be a betrothal ritual. Other examples of tattooing, skin discoloration, and the purportedly violent popular game called "massa" all function as part of a dehumanizing fascist spectacle of Africans living in a dystopic state of nature, calling out for a civilizing locus of authority. The mere organization of these cultural rituals as part of a film about the "dark continent" demonstrates the omnipotent perspective of Western modernity, asserted through the automobile, the airplane, and the camera. These technologies function as an unseen presence in this film. The film production itself supports a myth of objectivity, allowing the camera to present phenomena typically inaccessible to the larger public.

Georges-Michel Coissac, one of the most prolific French film critics of the interwar period, wrote that a film featuring Renault automobiles was released in 1924 titled *La Première traversée rapide du désert (329 heures)* (The first rapid crossing of the Sahara [329 hours]), following an itinerary from Colomb-Béchar to Niger led by Gaston

Gradis.[54] The title of the film was a direct challenge to Citroën's *La Traversée du Sahara* given the increased speed and agility of the Renault vehicles.

The "rapid crossing of the Sahara" as opposed to "the crossing of the Sahara in half-track vehicles" evokes a theme central to the earliest public displays of the automobile—the overland auto races. The automobile itineraries across the Sahara by Citroën, Renault, and Peugeot capitalized on the enthusiasm in France for open-road auto races that established a testing ground for the first automobiles. A Peugeot film, shot over the course of the Prost–Peugeot expedition, was released as *Images d'Afrique* (dir. Jean Vallée, 1926). It traced part of what came to be known as the Paris–Dakar auto rally with a round-trip Algiers–Dakar itinerary that departed from Paris. This film appeared in numerous versions, re-edited and supplemented until 1942.

As with the beginning of cinema, France led the development of automobile construction. In 1895, the same year that the Lumière cinematograph was patented, the first nonstop 730-mile auto rally was staged from Versailles to Bordeaux and back. The open-road automobile itineraries in France drew spectators from villages and cities alike, successfully transferring the enthusiasm for professional cycling competitions to

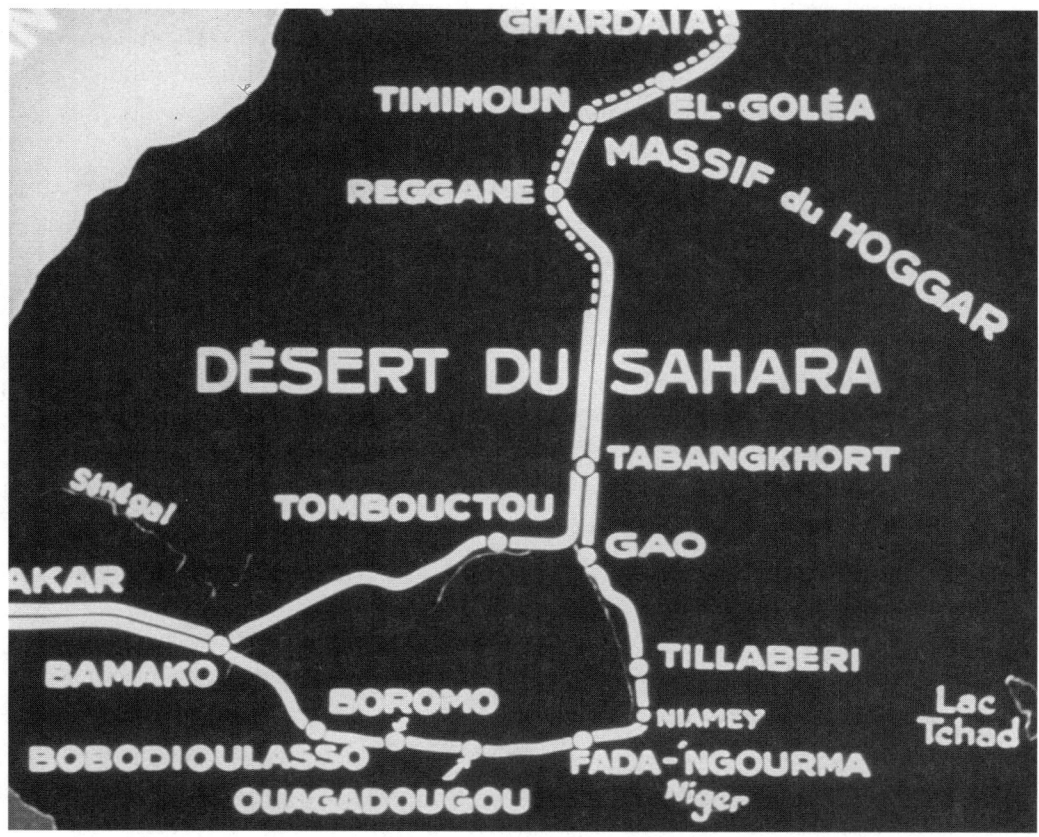

FIGURE 41. Trans-Saharan itinerary for the Prost–Peugeot expedition, in *Images d'Afrique*, 1926. Copyright Collection des Archives du Film et du Dépôt Légal du Centre National de la Cinématographie.

the speed and agility of the automobile. A community of spectators that validated the cinematograph as a founding apparatus of cinema was also present to witness the automobile as a physical means of travel. The automobile was a vehicle of exploration that could penetrate the most remote corners of the country, reaching beyond the circumscribed railroad itinerary.

The most popular early open-road automobile races in Europe included the Paris–Marseilles–Paris race in 1896, the Paris–Bordeaux race in 1897, and the Paris–Amsterdam–Paris race in 1898, along with many shorter contests.[55] The Citroën half-track vehicles were a bridge to a new type of travel experience that promised protected panoramic views of colonial landscapes. Distant landscapes were becoming accessible to an affluent metropolitan clientele thanks to the automobile. The confluence of the automobile and a new kind of travel experience in the Sahara was recognized by both André Citroën and Louis Renault. The success of *La Traversée du Sahara* convinced Citroën that he should develop an overland travel package itinerary for affluent European tourists, and Renault followed with his own Saharan overland tourist itinerary.

Citroën's travel package was an exclusive twelve-day adventure that incorporated a variety of motorized vehicles, including the caterpillar-tread vehicles, automobiles outfitted with rubber tires, and a recently patented hydroplane as part of various segments of the 3,355-mile itinerary from Oran to Timbuktu. Citroën created a transportation company called La Compagnie Transafricaine Citroën (CITRACIT) to undertake preparations for this tourist itinerary, which was promoted to a wealthy and influential clientele of travelers. CITRACIT began by acquiring territory in order to build elaborate camping sites along the way. These travel packages consisted of a twelve-person travel expedition, projected to accommodate 324 passengers per year, with numerous automobiles and technicians at their service.[56] King Albert II of Belgium, a popular figure in France at the time, and Marshall Pétain, who was still revered for his victory at Verdun, were to be among the first passengers. Citroën's trans-African travel company implied that a future travel itinerary would traverse the length of the continent, complementing the highly publicized Crosière Noire expedition.

Along the itinerary, Citroën commissioned carefully built *boudj*-hotels, which were luxurious tentlike structures, each adjoined to an elegant dining room. As one of the advance publicity brochures explained, these were intended to create an ambience for men in smoking jackets, women in gowns, and dancing to live music under the stars.[57] In spite of the monumental planning and great expense, all plans for the Citroën tourist adventure were canceled when a telegraph sent by General Dinaux, based in Aïn-Sefra (Algeria), indicated that the security of the expedition could not be guaranteed because there were reports of "tribal unrest" on the Southern Moroccan border near Colomb-Béchar. When King Albert withdrew his participation from the first voyage, Citroën abandoned the project.[58]

The circumstances regarding Citroën's decision to cancel the whole project and the significance of the so-called tribal unrest have remained ambiguous. Alain Frèrejean explains that it was reported sometime after the Citroën expedition was canceled

FIGURE 42. CITRACIT poster for the twelve-day Paris–Timbuktu tourist adventure that was finally cancelled, 1925. Copyright Citroën Communication.

that there was no threat of imminent danger to the tourist excursion. He further paraphrases an item that appeared in the popular magazine *Fantasio* claiming that "tribal unrest" might have been invented by Renault partisans in order to sabotage the Citroën expedition.[59] Undoubtedly military officers such as General Dinaux, who made their careers in North Africa, were less than comfortable with the prospect of the Sahara being transformed into a European tourist destination. In a subsequent Renault-sponsored guidebook, there are references to the "Citroënausaurs," a derogatory term used to denote the army of indigenous workers employed by the CITRACIT project to build hotels and shore up roads in anticipation of a new tourist economy. These abandoned workers now approached European tourist-adventurers in their Renault vehicles in search of employment.

Nonetheless, Renault had participated in an alternative tourist adventure package that did not intend to equal the level of luxury and expense proposed by Citroën. In addition to following General Estienne's advice about developing a vehicle that used six twinned tires for earlier Saharan itineraries, Louis Renault created an alliance with Dal Piaz, director of the powerful Compagnie Générale Transatlantique. They managed to establish an agreement in which Renault vehicles would ferry passengers along a desert itinerary for which Piaz would build a series of hotels along the way.[60] Gaston Gradis, the scion of a Bordeaux shipping family and leader of two expeditions that used the modified Renault vehicles, served as the organizer, establishing the Compagnie Générale Transsaharien, which undertook the initial surveys for the project, and later served as the principal in the booking agency that managed the Colomb–Béchar–Niamey itinerary. The reappearance of *Transsaharien* as the name of the company symbolized a return to establishing a railroad corridor across the Sahara. By 1927, Gradis's Compagnie Générale Transsaharien had started regular Renault automobile service between Algeria and Niger, with newly opened Compagnie Générale Transatlantique hotels in Reggane, Gao, and Niamey.[61]

LA CROISIÈRE NOIRE

The Croisière Noire expedition began in Colomb-Béchar (Algeria) on October 24, 1924, with eight caterpillar-tread vehicles and reached its final destination of Tananarive, Madagascar, eight months later, on July 26, 1925. Once the expedition was completed, it became the best-known French crossing expedition and was recorded in the most famous documentary film of the era. The will to create an exhaustive itinerary on the African continent was so powerful that once the expedition reached Kampala, it split up into four different units in order to traverse to several different destinations, Cape Town (South Africa), Mombasa (Kenya), Dar es Salaam (Tanzania), and Beira (Mozambique). Approximately 88,582 feet of film was shot over the course of the journey, then edited into short-subject documentary films that simultaneously specified and visually stereotyped the continent.[62] These documentary shorts were presented as supplemental travelogues and educational films that were finally used to demonstrate the context of the various objects that were collected over the course of the expedition.

Those objects were the subject of a popular exhibition held at the Musée des Arts Decoratifs in 1926, which served as one of the models for the large-scale 1931 French Colonial Exhibition. Significantly, Léon Poirier's feature-length documentary of the expedition was featured at a number of prestigious venues in France and Belgium.[63] The film premiered with a live orchestra at the Opéra Garnier on March 2, 1926, with Gaston Doumergue, the French president of the republic, in attendance. The film was dedicated to the youth of France and became a symbol of French colonial humanism on the African continent. It illustrated a trans-African itinerary along the length of the continent, and by special arrangement with the minister of the colonies, the various subitineraries were consolidated in such a way that they converged at the port of Majunga, Madagascar, in order to ceremoniously complete the expedition in Tananarive, the capital of Madagascar. This final leg of the itinerary demonstrated the geography of the French colonial African empire as a unified body that could be revitalized and infused with the spirit of metropolitan France.

Metaphorically speaking, the brain, as represented by metropolitan France and deprived of its full national extensions after World War I, sought to manage, inspect, and transform these extended bodily parts of the French colonies. As the French historian Gilbert Meynier has written, the French colonial empire represented a body to be activated, strong but incapable of action, in need of centralized mental conditioning emanating from the French mind.[64] In France, the crossing films demonstrated these geographic bodily extensions as a conflation of untended geographic landscapes and ethnic populations. Therapeutic reconditioning was promoted in an extended archive of colonial films that prescribed an interrelated set of industrial, medical, military, and physical activities in the spirit of an interwar discourse of colonial humanism.

The relentless movement of the half-track vehicles physically stamped a surface as it ground forward, and the film emulsion recorded surfaces through its modulated exposure to light. In the Citroën crossing films, the half-track vehicle and the motion picture camera were both used to create the illusion of a totalizing geographic picture, analogous to a Heideggerian "World Picture" imagined as a global geographic itinerary and structured as moving pictures. Creating a totalizing geographic picture of the African continent was precisely the goal of *La Croisière noire*. This film illustrates the extensions and accessibility of the French colonies across the African continent to France. The logistics for the expedition required numerous military supply lines, as well as airplane and hydroplane support. *La Croisière noire* was the equivalent of a large-scale military survey operation, in spite of the fact that there were only eighteen men who were identified as the actual members of the expedition.

FIGURE 43. Alexandre Iacovleff at the easel during the Croisière Noire expedition, 1925. Copyright Citroën Communication.

The culmination of the numerous events planned throughout 1926 was the well-attended Crosière Noire exhibition, which was held in six large halls at the Musée des Arts Décoratifs, located in a wing of the Palais du Louvre, for several months. Georges-Marie Haardt's caterpillar-tread half-track vehicle known as La Scarabée d'Or stood at the center of the largest room surrounded by a menagerie of taxidermically preserved animals. The other rooms, as reported in the *Bulletin Citroën,* held a "treasure trove" of objects, including jewelry, religious articles, pottery, and musical instruments that had been collected over the course of the expedition. Three dioramas were also constructed that attempted to depict three different scenes from the continent. In addition, one of the rooms was dedicated to an array of drawings produced by Alexandre Iacovleff, the artist sent to accompany the expedition.[65] Finally, adjoining the exhibition halls, a theater projected a steady stream of fifty-two short documentary films that were filmed over the course of the expedition.[66]

The films created a self-assured colonial context for objects on display at the exhibit and served as a point of reference for French colonial cinema that merged educational cinema with travel and leisure. For the numerous galas that were associated with La

FIGURE 44. Belgian poster for *La Croisière noire* depicting a Mangbetu woman and her shadow as the true geography of the African continent, 1925. Copyright Citroën Communication.

Croisière Noire, Josephine Baker was a reigning presence. André Citroën was such an avid fan of her dance and music that he gave her a Citroën B14 Sports Cabriolet automobile. John Reynolds writes in his biography of André Citroën that Baker returned Citroën's adoration by singing that she had only two loves in her life, her country and Citroën.[67] In one celebrated episode, Baker donned a hat and hairstyle that referenced the Mangbetu coiffure, which remains a key image appearing on a well-known poster advertising *La Croisière noire*. In the Belgian poster used to promote the film, a female African figure is depicted with the distinctive Mangbetu hairstyle, casting an expanded shadow that functions as a partial outline of the African continent, and her nose, lips, and breasts are an invitation to the feminized ornamentation of the continent. The Mangbetu hairstyle was featured in *Vogue Magazine* in 1926, and Madame Agnès, a Parisian hair designer who worked with the fashion houses in the La Madeleine area, developed this fashionable hairstyle for an affluent clientele.[68]

The Mangbetu were a people in Northeastern Congo who were represented in numerous texts by German explorers throughout the nineteenth century. The nineteenth-century "Mangbetu myth" depicted them as noble savages who engaged in cannibalism but lived in the splendor of a royal court culture. Christraud Geary asserts that in popular and scholarly thought of the period, the Mangbetu variations in physiognomy and skin color were attributed to a mixture of Bantu with Semitic and Hamidic races, which occupied a higher position in the European racial hierarchy.[69] The image of the Mangbetu that appears on the poster was modeled from a photograph taken during the expedition. The elongated head shape served to sexualize the image of the African woman, with the open end of the headdress a point of entry into the African geographic body. The image of the Mangbetu woman, like that of Queen Antinéa in *L'Atlantide,* pegs female sexuality to the mystery of the African landscape. However, it is part of an open text in which the lineage of the Mangbetu has been traced to Egypt, particularly to the ancient Egyptian iconography of Nefertiti.

This discussion of the French colonial crossing films has traveled full circle, from specifying the contours of French colonial stereotypes to describing the geographic diffusion of European civilization and explaining how the colonial crossing films were an extension of the colonial exhibitions. The Croisière Noire exhibition portrayed myths about the African continent that finally served to promote Citroën vehicles at home and create the terms for a tourist adventure on the African continent. A significant displacement resulted from this transformation of the exhibition into tourism. The African tourist itinerary became a space of projection for idyllic landscapes, colonial cities, and racial stereotypes that were embodied by the colonial exhibitions. Through the procession of the live ethnographic displays to motion pictures of the African continent, tourist itineraries were an attempt to create a safe simulation of the real, mitigated by the insularity of the automobile.

4. DIAGNOSING INVISIBLE AGENTS

BETWEEN THE MICROBIOLOGICAL AND THE GEOGRAPHIC

There was a time when Mohamed ben Chegir was as strong
as a lion, as fast as a greyhound, as agile as a panther.
He possessed more stamina than the best camels and was
as handsome as a summer's day. But something happened.
A cold sore appeared on his lip.

These sentences open *Conte de la mille et une nuits* (Tale of a thousand and one nights, 1929), a ten-minute animated film illustrated by Albert Mourlan. This film, produced by Jean Benoît-Lévy (one of the best known and most prolific French educational filmmakers of the interwar period), was part of a vast archive of short-subject educational films incorporated into a vision of hygienic reform based on the reterritorialization of microbiological and geographic space in France and its colonies.

Conte de la mille et une nuits opposes Mohamed's natural, healthful state (emphasized with animated drawings of a lion, a greyhound, and a panther) to his present state of physical decline. Some years later, an automobile arrives bearing French doctors, nurses, and a free movie. In the local cinema hall, the curtain unveils the film's opening title: "Les Maladies Vénériennes" (Venereal disease). The first shot of this film-within-a-film reveals a photographic image of a distorted Arab face with the intertitle "Syphilis can lead to insanity," then another of a blind Arab man gesturing for alms with the intertitle "Syphilis can lead to blindness." A quick succession of photographs appear: a medium shot of a child born with syphilis, a close-up of syphilitic lesions on a man's back, and an extreme close-up of a cold sore. The last words of the film-within-a-film (emphasis in original) are an appeal to those in Mohamed's predicament: "If you presently have, or ever have had these seemingly inconsequential lesions, even if they did not hurt, see the doctor right away. *The doctor—and the doctor alone—is the only one who can cure you.*"

FIGURE 45. The film within the film *Conte de la mille et une nuits* in a "native" North African theater, 1929. Copyright Comité Français d'Éducation pour la Santé.

The doctor who diagnoses and treats the patient is the irreproachable symbol of French colonial humanism. *Conte de la mille et une nuits* was widely circulated in France and North Africa during the interwar period and was eventually set to French and Arabic narration tracks some years later. The Orientalist parable of "A thousand and one nights" drew on the powerfully charged *contes arabes*—tales of romance, exoticism, and mystery that presented a vision of spectacle for the pleasure-seeking voyager. Traces of these stories are revealed in nineteenth-century French colonial novels, photographic ephemera, and French feature-length films that invoked tales of sexuality, capture, and exotic landscapes.[1] In fact, *Conte de la mille et une nuits* demonstrates the hygienic revenge of this well-known Arab fable, where French medical agency becomes not merely the sole cure for syphilis, but the only way that the fantasy of "A thousand and one nights" may live on as an imagined "natural" state of French masculinity.

When Mohamed understands that the cold sore is no mere "bobo" and walks over to the village dispensary, the film conveys a hope that we may all return to a Rousseauesque state of nature, uninhibited by the paralyzing effects of contagious disease produced by "civilized life." The arrival of French public health campaigns thus implied a modernist regenerative mythology. The appearance of the automobile, the screening of an educational film, and the incontrovertible authority of French medical expertise all contributed to the spectacle of modernity, which promised a form of spiritual and social renewal as the "restoration" of a simpler life.

FIGURE 46. The arrival of the hygiene caravan from the Office Nationale de l'Hygiène Sociale (National Social Hygiene Bureau) in *Conte de la mille et une nuits*. Copyright Comité Français d'Éducation pour la Santé.

More generally, French interwar documentary cinema established a vital link between microbiological agents and geographic landscapes. Popular demonstrations of the all-powerful microbe became associated with the Pasteur Institute before World War I and contributed to an emerging visual culture of magnification and spectacle. These demonstrations became emblems of a scientific diagnosis beyond question, justifying a widening geographic theater of curative action in both France and the colonies.

A substantial group of prewar and interwar documentary films represents this ideal of social reform. The technique of matching sequences from different archival sources was a frequently used editing convention in most French educational documentaries of the period. In fact, because key sequences depicting the work of the Pasteur Institutes in Africa and Southeast Asia were often recycled and then later restaged and supplemented as part of a developing corpus of medical assistance films, educational films can be understood as archival composites whose origins can be heuristically traced while their meaning shifted through subsequent editing and exhibition.

EXAMINING AN EDUCATIONAL FILM COMPOSITE:
TRYPANOSOMA GAMBIENSE

In the short-subject film *Trypanosoma gambiense: Agent de la maladie du sommeil* (Gambian trypanosomiasis: The agent of sleeping sickness, 1924), an optics of scale demonstrates the effects and causes of sleeping sickness. This four-minute film was composed using three basic camera positions in three different spaces. It begins with a medium-long shot of an African "patient," followed by a close-up of the tsetse fly, and concludes with a series of microcinematic illustrations of the trypanosome protozoa parasite that transforms the morphology of normal blood cells into sleeping sickness (or the final stage of human trypanosomiasis).

These three sequences define sleeping sickness as a set of typological associations. The opening shot establishes an African context for sleeping sickness. While at first glance nothing seems obviously wrong with an African man breathing heavily outside of a hut, the intertitle informs us that he is afflicted with sleeping sickness. His medical condition seems invisible, yet he is transformed into a pathological subject. A still image of the *Glossina palpalis* species of the tsetse fly dangles on the end of a needle. It is an entomological specimen that transmits the Gambian (West African) variety of sleeping sickness in the form of a parasite adapted almost exclusively to humans.[2] The film then cuts to an entomological photo of the fly, affixed by a pin to a white backdrop with its antennae, sensor, proboscis, and stinger labeled as part of an anatomical demonstration with the aid of a pointer.

The Gambian variety of sleeping sickness, typically transmitted by the *glossina* genus of the tsetse fly, was identified in 1901 by British scientists when a forty-two-year-old officer aboard a steamer on the Gambian River came down with a fever that was initially thought to be malaria.[3] He had been working on the ship for six years and had experienced several previous bouts with malaria. However, upon closer examination at the British Colonial Hospital in Bathurst, Gambia, the attendant doctor noticed that the officer's blood was infected with a different type of protozoa. Subsequently, Robert Michael Forde and Joseph Everett Dutton identified it as a trypanosome parasite, which causes a disease they specified as Gambian trypanosomiasis.[4]

In the final and longest segment of the film, the camera moves into the cellular universe of the microscopic sample. At first normal circular blood cells with lymphocytes appear, but a further magnified view detects the telltale wormlike strands of the microorganism that causes Gambian sleeping sickness. The invading organism is identified, like the fly itself, as a series of component parts with a nucleus, flagellum, and undulating membrane. On contact with the parasites, normal circular-shaped blood cells mutate into octagon-shaped cells at the microscopic level, recombining in a quilted pattern. This brief demonstration shows how the trypanosome protozoa, which causes sleeping sickness in humans and livestock, infects the blood sample by reconfiguring and transforming "normal" blood cells.

The microcinematographic typanosomiasis footage was put in the service of a circulating archive of educational films that were often edited together to create new compilation films for use in different contexts. *Trypanosoma gambiense* is itself a composite of film strips from other documentary films of the same period. Despite the frequent reappearance of the same sequences in different educational films, they remained convincing pedagogical demonstrations. Their patchwork quality created the effect of authenticity in spite of subtle incongruities.

The composite nature of *Trypanosoma gambiense* is revealed by certain internal inconsistencies. One wonders, for example, why the intertitles indicate that Gambian trypanosomiasis is shown infecting a sample of rat's blood as opposed to the blood of the African man who appears in the first sequence. While the African man simply sits outside of a hut breathing heavily, the intertitles describe his behavior as a form of lassitude or laziness and thus a symptom of sleeping sickness. These discrepancies form part of a deeper web that points to conditions of production and circulation. Each segment of the film was drawn from a longer cycle of explicitly "educational" film subjects, with specific components such as microbe-specific demonstrations, schematic diagrams with pointers, and generic images of the African landscape that were combined and presented to the French public.

This film primarily originated from a group of early Pathé–Consortium–Cinéma educational films and was widely circulated in French rural communities as part of

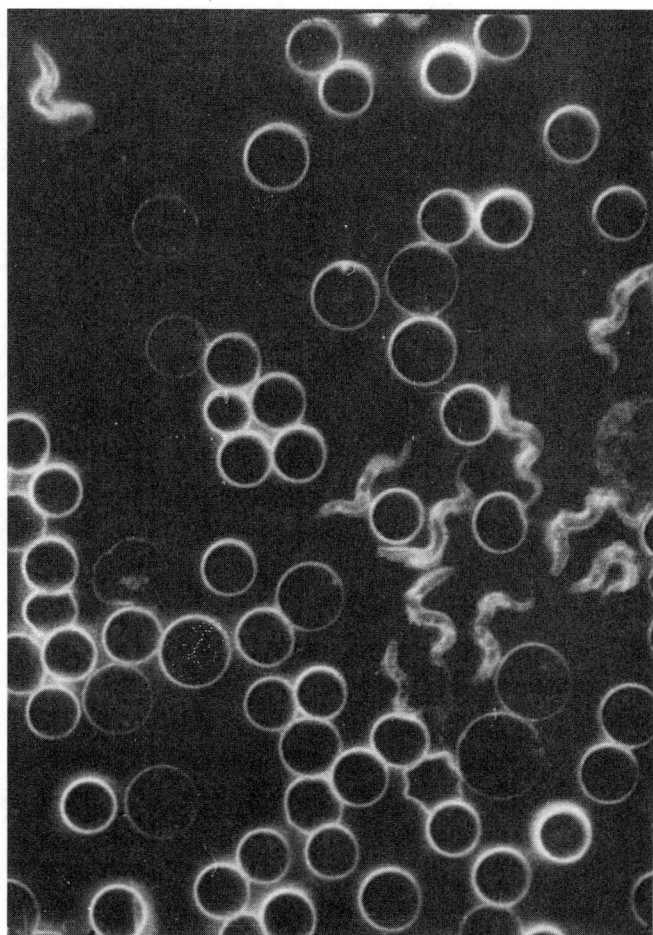

FIGURE 47. Microscopic view of the subject organism in *Trypanosoma gambiense: Agent de la maladie du sommeil,* 1924. Copyright Les Documents Cinématographiques.

an educational demonstration. Still images that demonstrate the anatomy of the fly separate the African context from the microscopic images. The final microcinematic sequence can be identified as part of Jean Comandon's oeuvre. Comandon pioneered the use of a variable-speed motion picture camera adapted for use with an ultramicroscope in order to document his bacteriological research on spirochetes of syphilis as early as 1908.[5] A series of Comadon's first films was presented to the French Academy of Sciences the following year, and sleeping sickness figured as one of his earliest demonstrations.[6] To develop the microcinematographic apparatus, Comandon collaborated with technicians at Pathé Frérès, where he also worked in varying capacities from 1908 until 1926.[7] *Trypanosoma gambiense* has become known as a Jean Comandon film primarily because of the extended microcinematographic sequence, consisting of fourteen shots that comprise more than half the length of the film. These images were filmed while Comandon worked at Pathé and, as nearly as I have been able to surmise, it was exhibited within the context of the circulating agricultural and medical educational films in France by the early 1920s.

MICROCINEMATOGRAPHIC RELOCATIONS: REPRESENTING THE VAMPIRE

The startling microcinematographic demonstration of sleeping sickness in *Trypanosoma gambiense* is part of a catalogue of Jean Comandon's earlier scientific experimental films, which Jean Painlevé, the documentary filmmaker and scientific film archivist, later compiled and distributed as founder of the Institute for Scientific Cinema.[8] Painlevé used portions of the same microcinematic footage in a more generalized way to dramatize the effects of a vampire bat's bite in his short film *Le Vampire* (The vampire, 1939–45). Given Painlevé's reputation as a documentary filmmaker who had made a number of nature and scientific films, the Pasteur Institute loaned him the Brazilian vampire bat (known as *Desmodus rotundus*), a recent acquisition of their private zoo.

Painlevé vocally described the vampire bat as a diseased opportunist analogous to the human vampire in F. W. Murnau's *Nosferatu: Eine Symphonie des Grauens* (*Nosferatu: A Symphony of Terror*, 1922). He used a series of outtakes of the haunting Professor Orlock (Max Schreck) perambulating in a nondead state to illustrate the bat's monstrous character. Before the 1897 publication of *Dracula* by the Irish writer Bram Stoker and its 1920 translation into French, a number of other French works had featured the theme of the vampire throughout the nineteenth century.[9] In the popular and scientific imagination at the fin de siècle, the story was that men became afflicted with syphilis on contact with "women of ill repute," underscoring an anxiety about shifting gender roles. The abundance of female vampires in the literary and cinematic imagination after the turn of the century thus was an expression of emasculation, provoked by fears of losing "control" over female sexuality.[10] This schema also echoed a medical discourse of vector and victim in which uncontrolled female sexuality was seen as the vector that transformed the unsuspecting male victim by disarticulating a French male code of honor.[11]

In the lexicon of early cinema, the invention of the "vamp," or the female vampire, was first associated with the figure of the Danish actress Asta Nielsen in her early Danish and German films directed by Urban Gad. However, the figure of the vamp had a specifically French connotation in the publicity surrounding the emergence of the Cincinnati-born American actress Theodosia Burr Goodman. Her stage name, Theda Bara, was fabricated by Fox Studio publicists as an anagram for "Arab Death." She was promoted internationally as a mysterious figure who possessed supernatural powers as a result of having been born in the Saharan desert to a male French artist and his Egyptian concubine.[12] "Arab death" was a reference to syphilis, and it was in this offhanded popular American reference that the connection between syphilis and the danger that women pose to men was spelled out. In France, Irma Vep, an anagram for "Vampire," was the vamp played by Musidora, who appeared in Louis Feuillade's well-known serial *Les Vampires* (1915–16).

Painlevé's *Le Vampire,* however, does not specifically focus on the feminine; instead it portrays the vampire bat as a physically unappealing infantile creature. Comandon's microcinematic depiction of sleeping sickness reveals that the bat is an agent of trypanosomiasis. In contrast to the medical needle used to draw blood and supplement it with a vaccine, the bat's blood-sucking quivering lower harelip is an organ that spreads contagion. For the purposes of demonstration, Painlevé uses multiple close-ups of the harelip and demonstrates the extractive acumen with which it is used on a soon-to-expire somnambulant guinea pig. Moreover, a distinctive gesture of the vampire bat in which it stretches out its wing in a "Heil Hitler"–like salute was, as Painlevé acknowledged, an attempt to allegorize the deathly vampiric nature of Nazism.[13]

In the spirit of the Parisian avant-garde's preoccupation with American jazz, *Le Vampire* is set to two musical numbers by Duke Ellington, "Black and Tan Fantasy" and "Echoes of the Jungle." The "scientific" story of the little-known bat species depicted is set to these representative echoes of the jazz age, connoting not only the slumming character of the bat but also its underground cavelike habitat, analogous to the archetypal catacomblike jazz nightclub. The specter of vampirism is also present in Dudley Murphy's RKO short *Black and Tan Fantasy* (1929), a vehicle for the emergence of Duke Ellington along with the light-skinned African American actress Fredi Washington.

Painlevé's *Le Vampire* was completed only in 1945, even though it was initially commissioned in 1939. Once the film was shot, Painlevé explained, the zookeepers at the Pasteur Institute gassed the bat to death when the war broke out because they feared it would escape during the German bombing raids and spread infectious disease.[14] The pairing of the vampire bat with Comandon's footage motivates the final shot of a horse afflicted by Carderas disease, yet another type of trypanosomiasis that destroyed livestock, in which the back of a horse is transformed into a decayed living carcass à la Francis Bacon.

Le Vampire and *Trypanosoma gambiense* refer to the same microscopic cellular blood sample as the origin of bodily transformation. In both cases, the effects are negative and underscore the role of the vampire bat and the fly as agents of contagion. The theme of vampirism has been associated with syphilis in the popular vernacular, in which men become weakened as a result of their contact with dangerous women. In the extensive critical commentary about the theme of the vampire in Victorian literature, imperial male racial decline has been associated with the allure of the feminine exotic, where the vampire as a feminine vamp became an important figure. The physical features of Dracula in Stoker's *Dracula* have been described as analogous to Cesare Lombroso's "criminal type," with a Semitic curve to his vampirelike nose.[15] This understanding of Dracula as a potentially Eastern European Jewish émigré of criminal difference transforms him into another type of feminized male other who turns women into his agents in order to attack other men by poisoning their blood.

Luise White imaginatively used the extraction of blood from an unsuspecting victim as both an element of the vampire discourse and a category of critical historical analysis. In one instance she described the story of sleeping sickness through a reading of Northern Rhodesian vampire accusations in 1931 and described how the medical discourse of tsetse control was transformed into African rumors of vampires that pointed to blind spots within the colonial mindset.[16] The use of the vampire in the African popular vernacular has emerged as an area of inquiry in African studies. In T. K. Biaya's works on the female urban migrant in the Congo during the 1950s and 1960s, the woman, known as a the *ndumba* (free woman), was often referred to as a vampire who lived off the meager earnings of single male wage earners. The use of the term *vampire,* Biaya asserts, was symbolic of a Congolese version of a Christian castration complex.[17] The various interpretations of the vampiric as involved with the "extraction of blood" were likewise grounded in a colonial epistemology referring to the microscopic examination of blood in the medical sciences, but also to a coercive structure of colonial labor whereby African men were deployed in the service of extracting primary resources for export.

SLEEPING SICKNESS AS AFRICAN PATHOLOGY

Trypanosoma gambiense begins with an eight-second shot of an African man sitting outside a hut. This opening shot is representative of an emerging cycle of documentary films about the African continent that attempted to identify and classify African physical and racial characteristics in relation to specific ceremonial and ritual events. Many of the earliest filmed expeditions on the African continent, such as the extended two-month expedition led by the emerging twenty-five-year-old filmmaker Alfred Machin in 1904, were film survey expeditions sponsored in the spirit of Charles Pathé's attempt to "conquer the world" through cinema.[18] Most of the significant filmed "documentary" expeditions on the African continent before World War I were of two basic types: geographic survey expeditions illustrating European public works projects in the context of colonial pacification or scientific pursuits and explorer-driven narratives of conquest, often featuring a British-style hunting expedition as the purported goal, as did those made famous by the American filmmakers Martin and Osa Johnson.

The sequence depicting the African man sitting outside a hut as an illustration of sleeping sickness could have originally been filmed to illustrate any number of elements. It might have been part of a series of outtakes associated with the earliest Citroën-sponsored film expeditions, with this particular footage used to illustrate the racial characteristics of a particular ethnic group, such as the Songhay, and not specifically an example of the ravages of sleeping sickness.[19] Nonetheless, several documentary expeditions by the mid-1920s along the Ubangi-Chari River Basin corridor (which extends beyond the Central African Republic into Chad and the Republic of Congo, i.e., Congo-Brazzaville) could not help but chart the devastation of sleeping sickness, if not explicitly, then through exclusion, simply because of the extensive scale of the epidemic. In Marc Allégret and André Gide's 1926 documentary *Voyage au Congo* (Travels in the Congo, 1925), the section of the film dealing with the Saras-Djinas people of Chad focuses almost exclusively on women at a time when men were disproportionately struck by sleeping sickness through their exposure to the tsetse fly near the riverbanks while clearing brush as colonial laborers and fishing to feed their families.[20]

However, the opening segment of *Trypanosoma gambiense* is significant because it is here that visual stereotypes of African pathological illness are positioned. The film opens with an art nouveau–style silhouette framing the title of the film, followed by the first intertitle, which reads, "Negro *[nègre]* suffers from sleeping sickness." This is followed by a shot of an African man sitting outside, leaning against a small hut for livestock in an isolated area of a village compound. With one leg outstretched and the other clenched at the kneecap in such a way that his thigh and calf are barely distinguishable, the man's state of malnourishment is revealed by his outstretched leg. His diminished calf muscles and the lack of musculature on his thigh accentuate his gaunt appearance. In the background a short, thick, Y-shaped wood branch has been driven into the barren earth. Behind this, a covered structure with larger wood supports appears, and a small amount of straw on the ground can also be discerned. It seems as if this man, who wears a leather-encased gris-gris around his neck, is in some kind of indeterminate distress, because an inscrutable grimace appears on his face; he barely glances at the camera.

In most medical assistance films of the period, the patient afflicted by illness is presented in a hospital environment with a doctor or nurse present. Instead, the African man's condition can be discovered only by reference to the intertitles and not by visual cues in the shot. In fact, the man's visible condition is a pretext for the indexicality of the microbiological realm. That is, his physical appearance is less revealing than what can be seen under the microscope, which is the organism leading to the ultimate diagnosis of the African "condition."

The African's lethargic condition, attributed to sleeping sickness, justified the rhetoric of French colonial humanitarianism as a potential cure. It posed the question "Is the man's lethargic state a medical condition, an acquired characteristic, or an innate racial disposition?" This film takes the position that his condition is primarily a medical condition, with the tsetse fly as the vector that can be controlled and the condition "cured" thanks to modern medical techniques. However, by presenting the black man as merely an unidentified patient in an African setting, the film equates the African subject with sleeping sickness. The rhetorical position evident in the film was adapted only after sleeping sickness was identified as a form of trypanosomiasis and Europeans became affected by the condition. Although Pasteur had established a germ theory of disease by the 1860s, displacing earlier theories of spontaneous generation and miasmata, this theory had a limited impact on dispelling ideas of innate racial difference.[21] In fact, theories of racial difference became more pronounced with the development of the French colonial empire after the Franco-Prussian War under the Third Republic.

A 1904 article that appeared in *Le Caducée,* a French colonial medical journal for practicing military doctors, begins with the statement "It has now been acknowledged that Europeans can be infected by sleeping sickness. It does not only afflict the natives."[22] The article then explains that this has been established only recently in three documented cases: one involving a British missionary in the Congo, another afflicting a Trappist monk who had lived in Equatorial Africa for five years and later died in Antwerp, and a third that the author, H. Dupont, had been observing.[23] Dupont's twenty-four-year-old patient, referred to as "V," was from Antwerp. He had been trained as a salesman and served as a soldier in the Belgian Congo. V had been sent back to Antwerp after disciplinary action was leveled against him by his superiors. In a report on his activities, it was claimed that he was drunk on duty, refused to obey orders, and threatened the indigenous population with provocative gestures. Furthermore, the report explained that V's conduct was frequently irrational. He would often speak incomprehensibly while also making deceitful or mean-spirited remarks. In a follow-up to the first report on his condition, the editors of *Le Caducée* informed readers that this patient had died some weeks after the first article was published, and although his behavior had reverted to a "gentle and intelligent demeanor driven by the best of motives to serve in the Congo," he was, by that time, already on his deathbed.[24]

The article about V's case is significant not only because it documents yet another verified instance of sleeping sickness among Europeans, but because psychiatric symptoms were also described and connected to sleeping sickness. French colonial psychiatry, as distinct from French psychiatry, began to develop through a series of documented cases involving sleeping sickness only after the turn of the century. In one case that the French psychiatrists Gustave Martin and Georges Ringenbach describe, an African soldier named Paté-Kamara, originally from the French Soudan (now mostly Mali), had been deployed in the French Congo and later hospitalized in Brazzaville.[25] Paté-Kamera, a name that evokes the Pathé crackerjack-box motion picture camera and projector in use by 1903, was a soldier known to be obedient, healthy, and strong and was well regarded by his superiors. However, his wife noticed, his character began to change.

The change became obvious on the job, too. One day Paté-Kamera did not return to his barracks and was forcibly brought back from the forest. When asked why he had not returned, he replied incoherently. When the troops were called to assemble later that evening, Paté-Kamera tried to attack the sergeant in charge. He was restrained and subsequently barricaded himself in a room. Emerging sometime later, dressed in full military attire, he was put under observation. Later that evening he experienced a bout of shivering, crying, and wild gesticulations lasting three hours. At 1 a.m. he attempted to leave the military camp. He pushed past the guards on duty and grabbed a bayonet that he wanted to use against them, but was finally disarmed and later taken to a wing of a hospital for mentally ill patients in Brazzaville.

Martin and Ringenbach explain that Paté-Kamera's condition seemed to stabilize, but six weeks later he escaped from the asylum, stole another bayonet from a policeman, and went to a nearby cemetery, where he dug up a grave, uncovered a casket, and stabbed the body through the casket with the bayonet. It took five men to restrain him. Three days later he returned to the graveyard, but before uncovering another body he started to swallow dirt at the gravesite before being restrained. In Martin and Ringenbach's account of this incident, the particular gravesites were not identified, nor did the authors explain how Paté-Kamera's personal history might have explained his actions. Instead they described his act as a form of vampirism and said he was yet another patient afflicted with sleeping sickness who exhibited symptoms of "catatonic and suggestible" behavior. In Richard von Krafft-Ebing's classic work *Psychopathia Sexualis* he discussed the mutilation of corpses in the following manner: "When no other act of cruelty . . . [other than cutting a corpse into pieces] . . . is practiced on the cadaver, it is probable that the lifeless condition itself forms the stimulus for the perverse individual. It is possible that the corpse—a human form absolutely without will—satisfies an abnormal desire, in that the object of desire is seen as perfectly subjugated and without resistance."[26]

Paté-Kamera's condition mimicked the nature of his own subjugation to French military authority, which became dislodged by a neurological response to sleeping sickness. His desire to subjugate the dead body, a body without will, could be interpreted as a means of digging up his own identity, submerged in the discipline of French military authority. It was in the realm of powerful psychiatric responses that the unseen discipline of colonial ultimatums was enacted in an encounter with the phantom of the nondead corpse, an encounter between a subjected self and the will toward resisting the subjugation.

DIAGNOSING THE VECTOR: THE FLY

The fly that appears in the middle section of *Trypanosoma gambiense* is a recurrent figure in early hygiene films. Flies were part of a group of vectors, which included rats and the less bountiful bats, which were identified as sources of contagion. The tsetse fly anatomy lesson is the most didactic portion of the film because it includes a needle dissection pointer that identifies the component parts of the fly using a somewhat static photographic, as opposed to a dynamic cinematographic, mode of presentation that is reminiscent of a genre of educational stop-action films in their film strip–like presentation. The tsetse fly was identified as the primary mode of transmission of

Gambian trypanosomiasis, whereas another, faster-acting and more virulent, variety of sleeping sickness, known as Rhodesian typanosomiasis (caused by *Trypanosome rhodesiense*), found in the savannahlike topography of British Rhodesia (present-day Zimbabwe), was most often transmitted from animals to people.

The physiology of the fly figured prominently in the work of Raphaël Anatole Émile Blanchard (1857–1919). A founding figure in the development of tropical medicine and parasitology in France, Blanchard was also one of the first to champion the use of educational films about medicine and social hygiene before and immediately after World War I. As early as 1910, Blanchard showed a series of Comandon's microcinematographic films on sleeping sickness at the French Psychiatry Convention in Brussels, contributing a form of microscopic evidence to explain the root of a lethargic behavioral pathology that had been considered endemic to the colonized, particularly in the Congo.[27] It was also thanks to Blanchard's initiative that the first French medical sleeping sickness survey expedition to the French Congo was launched in 1903, at a moment when sleeping sickness had become the most significant medical threat to the colonial powers on the African continent.[28]

In France, the preoccupation with the spread of microbes became part of a national campaign, and Blanchard established an associative movement in 1914 known as La Ligue Sanitaire Française contre la Mouche et le Rat (The French Hygiene League against Flies and Rats, or LSF), which drew on this momentum but featured the role of parasitic agents transmitted by flies and rats.[29] As the film historian Thierry Lefebvre has described, Blanchard developed a structure for early public health campaigns that included films and posters before the larger-scale Rockefeller public health initiative introduced a well-equipped structure for health promotion and assistance throughout France. The fly dangling on the end of a needle in *Trypanosoma gambiense* is reminiscent of these early film campaigns promoting hygienic reform throughout France, in which the fly was featured as the symbolic agent of disease.

La Mouche domestique (The housefly, Pathé, 1917) and *La Mouche bleue de la viande* (The parasitic bluebottom fly, Gaumont, 1917)[30] were among the first educational hygiene films slated for national distribution by the LSF, and, as Lefebvre suggests, these films were variations on earlier prewar films but treated the same subject in a more promotionally adroit way. Blanchard had envisioned traveling hygiene lecture-demonstrations using the lure of a film screening to attract audiences. The hatching of fly larvae on rotted meat or flies picking up worms from an infected food source and releasing them on an infant's pacifier were the kinds of graphic examples used in these short-subject hygiene films.[31] Such compelling graphic illustrations established a clearly defined public hygiene effort in which visual magnification revealed that the fly was analogous to enemy fighter planes, dropping worms rather than bombs and establishing a new visually coded battlefield of hygienic reform. An expanding educational documentary film culture that had first been developed by Pathé, Gaumont, and Éclair before World War I became a popular medium used to promote hygienic reform during the interwar period.[32]

Just as the colonial effort against sleeping sickness facilitated the internationalization of colonial medicine at the turn of the century, the targeting of rats and flies as vectors of contagious disease became an important element in the development of national public health movements in England, Denmark, the United States, Holland, and France. An excerpt from the first bulletin published by the LSF explained that the spread of infectious diseases by flies, attracted by waste that was not properly disposed of, endangers the lives of children. Edouard Herriot, the mayor of Lyons and a radical Socialist who later served as a cabinet minister and premier, went on to explain that the development of a new science of insect and rat extermination, which he described as *désinséction* and *dératisation,* was one of the most useful contributions to public hygiene.[33]

Blanchard defined a new structure for the mobile presentation of educational hygiene films in 1915 using a portable hand-cranked film projection unit outfitted with an electric light bulb.[34] He explained that after researching film projection equipment, the League was able to order a film projection unit weighing approximately thirty-six pounds that folded into a box equivalent to a regular piece of hand luggage. He envisioned ordering a dozen of these film projectors and called for the training of twenty projectionists. The first films proposed would address not only how flies spread contagious disease but also the role of mosquitoes, the need to boil water to create potable drinking water, the importance of washing one's hands, and the dangers of alcoholism, among other subjects.[35]

Blanchard also proposed the use of posters as a means of illustrating the work of hygienic reform, and he wrote enthusiastically about an emerging array of public health posters. The Board of Public Heath in Minnesota sent him instructional posters depicting flies and typhoid fever. Dr. A.-J. Salm, his former student and a Dutch medical officer stationed in the Dutch East Indies, sent him multilingual color instructional hygiene posters addressing cholera and the spread of malaria by mosquitoes, among other subjects.[36] Significantly, a print of *Trypanosoma gambiense* with Dutch intertitles was sent to the Batavian Hygiene Service in Malaysia, underscoring the international collaborative spirit of public health media instruction.[37] As Blanchard conceived it, promoting public hygiene through film and posters was an international effort that was not bounded by territorial colonial rivalries.

Blanchard's efforts in creating hygiene films were preceded by Comandon's work with Pathé–Consortium–Cinéma, where he created a collection of twenty-five short films that were among the first films to define the educational hygiene film genre.[38] Another important contemporaneous group of social hygiene films was produced by La Société des Établissements Gaumont for educational settings that focused on questions of oral and bodily hygiene.

These early educational film initiatives, which later culminated in the hundreds of short-subject social hygiene films that Jean Benoît-Lévy produced through his firm Édition Française Cinématographique, established a structure for the social hygiene educational film movement during the interwar period. An underlying tenet of this movement was that educational reform through the medium of cinema was the solution to reimagining public health after World War I. The magic of educational cinema was the way in which it conjured invisible agents in relation to the gleaming project of modernity. It was within this context that humanism played a crucial role in transforming colonial occupation into a form of medical humanitarianism. Diagnosing the colonies reinforced a knowledge structure of master and pupil that framed the "natives" as pupils left back in time and history. The invention of norms for social hygiene and disease control was illustrated by reference to the colonies in order to serve as an example for metropolitan France. Significantly, the symbolic fly was represented as at its most virulent in the form of the African tsetse, capable of decimating human populations and positioning the African continent in a state of nature not yet capable of establishing the rule of law.

Raphaël Blanchard remains a crucial figure at the intersection of hygiene films and colonial medicine because of his instrumental role in both arenas. In addition to initiating the use of film for public health campaigns before World War I, Blanchard was an instrumental figure in promoting colonial medicine in France under the rubric of parasitology. As founding editor of the influential medical journal *Archives de parasitologie* (1898–1911), Blanchard published numerous articles during the run of this journal that were directly related to his pivotal role in establishing the Institute of Colonial Medicine in 1901, including the founding statutes and a record of the institute's activities.[39]

The fly as symbol and vector of parasitic contagion that could be magnified, animated, and diagnosed was identified in Western medical discourse only at the turn of the century. Prior to the late nineteenth century, trypanosomiasis was referred to as a "species of lethargy" of unknown origin by Thomas Masterman Winterbottom in his *Account of Native Africans in the Neighborhood of Sierra Leone,* published in 1803.[40] Winterbottom explained that this condition had been widely recognized for centuries in West Africa, particularly among resident ethnic groups, all of whom had a well-developed vocabulary to describe it.[41] He also explained that slave traders were well aware of this condition and often associated it with the presence of small tumors or swollen glands in the neck (later known as "Winterbottom neck"), and he said they would try to avoid acquiring those afflicted, or "get quit" of those who demonstrated symptoms.[42]

A flurry of Western medical research on the vector (or agent) of trypanosomiasis transmission began in response to a series of epidemics that alarmed colonial authorities and led European governments to organize medical expeditions to the African continent. In 1901, Portuguese physicians were sent to Angola, a London-based British team was sent to Uganda in 1902, and a French medical expedition to the French Congo was organized in 1903.[43] In 1903, another group of British physicians based in Liverpool was sent by King Leopold of Belgium to the Congo Free State. Leopold feared the demographic and economic collapse of his recently established colony, already under scrutiny for incidents of forced labor and atrocities that were reported in the European press. As a result, medical teams were sent out to determine whether preventative action needed to be taken in response to the spread of the disease, which ended in the deaths of more than twice the 250,000 afflicted in the Ugandan outbreak.[44] The high productivity required of colonial workers who gathered wild rubber vines and worked on the colonial plantations is evidence that controlling the spread of sleeping sickness was an imperative for the maintenance of colonial economic interests.[45]

André Gide later referred to the nature of the colonial rubber trade in his travel narrative *Voyage au Congo,* in which an undercurrent of sleeplessness—or insomnia—characterized his narrative voice and state of consciousness throughout the expedition. Russell West has even argued that in this film Gide's insomnia and the prospect of sleeping sickness exist in a dialectical relationship, contributing to "Gide's nascent critique of Western expansion in Africa."[46] In Allégret's filmed version of his expedition (1926), Congolese workers were depicted collecting wild rubber and bringing it to be weighed at the local colonial depot. Rubber collection had become an important form of wage labor by this time, but with the increased demand for rubber from the developing automobile industry in France the cultivation of rubber became an increasingly organized form of arboriculture in Indochina.

New adaptations of the automobile led to the next major shift in the history of the educational hygiene film. Although Blanchard promoted the idea of mobile film screenings, a project initiated by the Rockefeller Foundation allowed mobile medical teams to use films as part of a tuberculosis (TB) prevention campaign using specially equipped automobiles.

LES ROULOTTES D'HYGIÈNE:
FROM THE ROCKEFELLER ANTI-TB CAMPAIGN TO INDOCHINA

Lucien Viborel, a leading French public health educational campaigner in the 1930s, traced the beginning of the French educational film movement to the Rockefeller-financed anti-TB campaign in 1918, which supported traveling caravans that toured France from 1918 to 1922 featuring films that depicted the disease-carrying fly.[47] The internationalization of public health initiatives was crucial to the promotion and establishment of a national French public health service. Following the American Red Cross's involvement with child welfare reform in France before the war, the Rockefeller anti-TB mission assisted with the creation of local committees and clinics throughout France. Before a medical infrastructure could be put in place, the battle against TB was staged by five circulating hygiene caravans, or *roulottes d'hygiène,* as they were known. Each caravan consisted of a five-person team, along with projection equipment, short-subject films, and forty-two exhibition panels, as well as a stock of brochures, tracts, postcards, and posters for distribution throughout France.[48] In the numerous lectures on hygiene that accompanied the films on TB, invisible microbiological agents were identified as threats to public safety.

The American statisticians who accompanied the caravans reported that the anti-TB campaign reached 1,338 cities, presenting 2,327 lectures to adults on TB and 4,403 lectures on general and household hygiene, each followed by a film presentation. These lectures were voluntarily attended by 1.25 million French adults, and 1.5 million children attended the 5,000 school lectures.[49] Many of the films shown were accompanied by live narration and were considered a novelty. Among the physician-impresarios traveling throughout France with the Rockefeller mission was Louis-Ferdinand Destouches, later known as Céline, subsequently the author of *Voyage au bout de la nuit* (Journey to the end of the night, 1932). Near the end of his life, Céline spoke with Claude Bonnefoy about his experience with the Rockefeller mission:

> We held meetings in schoolhouses about tuberculosis. We held as many as five or six a day. The farmers whom we addressed spoke [only] local [French] dialects and did not seem to follow our scientific explanations most of the time. . . . They listened patiently [however], without saying a word. . . . [Nonetheless], they paid close attention to the films. . . . They would see flies walking in milk. . . . The film would break every five minutes, or skip. That wouldn't matter . . . we would fix it.[50]

Céline's brief account of his experience explains that the films were perceived as potentially enthralling in spite of the fact that many people in the linguistically distinct rural communities in France could barely understand the doctors who spoke about them. The public health meetings drew on the resources and ideology of the secularized public education system as part of a national effort against TB. Hygienic reform was both an educational mission to "protect" French citizens and a civilizing endeavor.

With the effectiveness of the Rockefeller anti-TB film campaign demonstrated on a national scale, an activist secular educational cinema began to flourish throughout France. National and regional film-lending institutions sought to integrate cinema into the public education system as well as public health and agricultural assistance campaigns. The expansion of the educational cinema movement in France created a series of interdependent educational film-lending libraries that used variations of the same short-subject films.

A variation of the structure used by mobile vaccination drives, with film projections accompanied by lectures from medical doctors, functioned as an almost immediate substitute for the heavily used recruitment footage in Indochina.[51] The shifting parameters of battle, from protecting metropolitan France against German aggression to protecting "greater France" against invisible microbiological agents that weakened and wiped out communities, became an important justification for the continued establishment and fortification of colonial authority. As Bruno Latour suggests, the microbe, detectable only under the microscope, was identified as the invisible agent that coded human mortality.[52] The power of the microbe was demonstrated through highly publicized medical campaigns led by the Pasteur Institutes that were subsequently established throughout the colonies.[53]

The microbe constituted an infinitely divisible subject capable of justifying all kinds of large-scale invasive sanitary efforts. Witnesses of "the geometric and mechanical splendor of mechanical destruction" during World War I now became spectators to an emerging hygienic spectacle staged in a microscopic and geographic theater of action.[54] Just as the specter of vast mechanical destruction lies beyond the scope of individual casualties, the microbiological realm defines a world beyond the mental and physical state of the patient. From a patient's body to a microscopic sample or a geographic landscape, curative agency is precisely the capacity to penetrate the body, to see beyond the limitations of human sight, to interpret and define parameters for action.

The war itself was marked by the success of preventative medical measures following the biomedical innovations of Jenner, Pasteur, Laveran, and Koch. The sanitary efforts undertaken during the four years of battle in the trenches were orchestrated with no major epidemics, neither typhus, typhoid, nor cholera, demonstrating the superiority of European medical techniques.[55] This moment of superiority of European medicine left the soldiers in a sound state of health, only to be successfully dismembered in new ways by an increasingly effective war machine.

The Pasteurian approach always consisted of the same method. As Anne Marcovich describes it:

> The first step consisted in carrying out field observations of a disease, observing its progress, differentiating it from other diseases that might be similar, isolating the agent, and determining the type of transmission and the sequence. At this point work began on a serum, and then on the vaccine. Such research showed a continuous pendulum movement between laboratory and field observation that narrowed the gap between the exterior (natural) environment and the interior (artificial) environment.[56]

The keen adaptability and malleability of Pasteurian methods, as delineated by Anne-Marie Moulin, to different kinds of cultural and geographic environments inspired the late nineteenth-century French anthropologist Arthur Bordier to claim that Lamarkian Transformism in medicine was Pastorism; the adaptability of Pasteurian methods to new cultures was its political credo, just as the adaptability of virulent biological cultures was its scientific one.[57] *Pastorians*, as opposed to *Pasteurians*, refers to those doctors, nurses, and technicians who instituted a structure of insertion and application of Pasteurian conceptions of epidemiology in which notions of physical well-being were tied to systematic hygienic practices.

Finally, the Pasteurian method developed a new conception of a given bacillus or virus by considering these agents as living organisms requiring specific conditions in order to live and reproduce. Once they were understood, the next step was to reproduce the agents under controlled laboratory conditions, and from them to produce a vaccine. A cadre of Pastorians executing Pasteurian methods functioned as auxiliaries to the establishment of colonial authority. They posed as objective agents to identify the affliction and prescribe social as well as medical agency for the recovery of a given individual or community.

It was in the context of a Pastorian ethic that Eugène Jamot, the French Pasteurian most often associated with the "battle" against sleeping sickness, emerged as one of the most frequently appearing subjects of numerous kaleidoscopic documentary films about the great works of French colonial humanitarianism during the interwar period. Jamot had directed the Pasteur Institute in Brazzaville after it was initially set up in 1906 as an experimental laboratory to support and extend the work of the first large-scale sleeping sickness expedition. The 1906 expedition was significant as an illustration of how the ideology of colonial occupation became increasingly dependent on the discourse of medical humanitarianism. It was sponsored by the French Société de Géographie (Geography Society) and the Société Antiesclavagiste (Anti-Slavery Society), asserting its fundamental humanitarian character associated with secular republican values of equality, education, and the transformative spirit of colonial volunteerism.

TIRAILLEURS MÉDICAUX

A documentary film widely distributed both in France and throughout Europe under the auspices of the League of Nations, *Le Réveil d'une race au Cameroun* (The awakening of a race in Cameroon, 1930), by Alfred Chaumel, exemplifies how the microscopic

FIGURE 48. Title card reading "Sleeping sickness in Cameroon," in *Le Réveil d'une race au Cameroun* (The birth of a race in Cameroon), 1930. Copyright Collection des Archives du Film et du Dépôt Légal du Centre National de la Cinématographie.

and the geographic came to be reconciled. The film addresses the success of Dr. Eugène Jamot's pioneering work (1926–30) in reducing mortality rates due to sleeping sickness in Cameroon.

Jamot had organized a network of mobile prophylactic medical units throughout Cameroon armed with microscopes, charts, and vaccines to outpace the spread of the epidemic. The film demonstrates the transmission of sleeping sickness by optically magnifying the sting of the tsetse fly and by demonstrating its paralyzing effects on indigenous subjects. It also demonstrates the cure, established through Jamot, whose work is shown being carried out by a small army of trained Cameroonian assistants. These assistants, depicted as a unit of loyal and adept infantrymen seemingly lifted from the ranks of the Tirailleurs sénégalais, are portrayed as coextensive with Jamot's medical equipment: the rifle is replaced by the microscope and the syringe, which represent the diagnostic and preventative aspects of the cure. Jamot's patients, on the other hand, are presented as walking zombies, bewitched by a magical spell: apathetic, sleepy, and weakened by the effects of the parasitic protozoa. In the film, the cure for sleeping sickness becomes a means of awakening and reviving the evolutionary progress of Cameroon, stupefied before the march of history.

FIGURE 49. Title card reading "Infected patients are given a medical form indicating the prescribed treatment by the European doctor," in *Le Réveil d'une race au Cameroun*. Copyright Collection des Archives du Film et du Dépôt Légal du Centre National de la Cinématographie.

As Dr. Jamot closely surveys his medical team working in tents equipped with folding tables, microscopes, and a large indigenous medical corps dressed in white lab coats, the foregrounded Cameroonian landscape underscores the locale as an isolated experimental laboratory. A medically inscribed whiteness is used to diagnose, annotate, and reveal the state of the patient's illness: dark bodies constituted test subjects that were marked with indelible white paint to indicate the current state of their treatment. Like the blackboard slate upon which French grammar exercises could be continuously generated in white chalk, the patient's body was used to inscribe a medical condition: the letter *S*, for *sommeil* (as in *la maladie du sommeil*, or sleeping sickness), signified a diagnosis of contamination.

White markings on the Cameroonian patient's body functioned to extend and reroute the geographic and evolutionary itineraries so often evoked in fiction and documentary films about the colonies, where images of geographic circulation and the flow of men and machines throughout the empire became an important motif. The interwar Citroën crossing films (discussed in chapter 3) transformed manifest images of men, automobiles, and a geographic itinerary into latent signs of European mechanization and nature through an "adventure narrative" involving a wild, untrammeled setting uninhibited by the conventions of European civilization. Likewise, Jamot's pioneering medical campaign against sleeping sickness (which gave rise by 1930 to the first mobile prophylactic medical teams on the African continent, organized on the model of small military assault units) took place during the war in the Ubangi-Chari region. These medical teams were divided into twenty-eight sectors, with the participation of thirty doctors, several European auxiliaries, and 150 indigenous medical assistants, as well as numerous porters and boy servants.

Ironically, Jamot's extensive experience brought to light a significant parallelism between European expansion and the movement of sleeping sickness. In 1929, after tracking the spread of trypanosomiasis (beginning as a military doctor in Ouadaï, Chad, and then assuming several directorship positions starting with the Pasteur Institute–Brazzaville in 1916),[58] Jamot wrote:

> In bringing peace to these countries, age-old barriers separating diverse ethnic groups have been violated. Formerly epidemiologically closed communities were now subject to new communication networks and commercial links that connected the coast to the interior. The movement of military personnel, porters, and boy servants recruited from all over the continent and beyond resulted in population dislocations. Healthy indigenous workers were mixed with others from contaminated zones. It is in this sense that the European was the true agent of its spread.[59]

Jamot's modest successes in Cameroon were sufficient for the creation of an expanded theater of operations for his work. He was also keenly aware that the intense contact of indigenous populations in the service of large-scale colonial works projects during the war had had a decisive impact in Franco-German embattled Cameroon on the spread of trypanosomiasis among Cameroonians. The effects of colonial rivalry, the formation of colonial armies and labor crews, and the exploitation of natural resources in these regions had led to a series of demographic and geographic displacements. Several documentary films from the 1920s and 1930s illustrate the movement of men and machines through Cameroon and the Ubangi-Chari region, which contributed to widespread social disequilibrium.

This particular region figured as a familiar geographic site in early educational films, such as *Mission en AEF* (1920), and constituted a significant corridor for numerous adventure-oriented geographic documentaries, such as the popular film and printed catalogue *Peaux noires* (Black skins, Jean D'Esme, 1932).[60] In this film, which also features the work of Jamot, Ubangi-Chari is introduced by the arrival of an automobile, which establishes the village as a mere backdrop for the work of colonization. This scene is followed by a pronunciation lesson for young schoolchildren from the region. The blackboard reads:

> Banda has a big tent.
> Samba is in good health.
> Mbi killed thirty elephants.
> A panther devoured a child.

These sentences are shown with the proper liaisons on a blackboard for the students to repeat after the teacher in an open-air classroom. In the exercise, a big tent and good health are juxtaposed with the act of killing thirty elephants and the image of a panther devouring a child. Thus seemingly innocent parables for children feature the laws of nature that depict Africans as passive subjects. This viewpoint is reinforced cinematically by showing acts of leisure (a slow-motion image of youths jumping into a lake) and an extended sequence of funerary rituals, after which the automobile as civilizing agent returns to the dock, ready for its next mission.

Another film that portrays Jamot's work at the Pasteur Institute in Brazzaville is *Promenade en AEF* (A stroll through French Equatorial Africa) by J. K. Raymond-Millet, produced for the 1931 Colonial Exhibition. This film frames the process of social disequilibrium as offset by the benefits accrued when French know-how is installed in the colonies. Successive images of professional trade schools, woodworking shops, and blacksmithing techniques build up to a low-angle shot of the towering Pasteur Institute in Brazzaville, in all its pristine medical whiteness. Jamot appears, a bearded man with microscope in hand, wearing a white lab coat and using a colony of apes as experimental test subjects. These are suddenly replaced by "possessed" human subjects, that is, those afflicted with sleeping sickness.

This abrupt evolutionary substitution of humans for experimental test animals was to have tragic predictive overtones when the doubling and sometimes tripling of the sanctioned dosage of the prescribed medicine caused the deaths of numerous patients and permanent blindness in more than seven hundred victims.[61] Jamot was later prevented from returning to Cameroon by Governor General Marchand when an unauthorized increase in the vaccine dosage carried out by one of his trusted medical auxiliaries in Bafia was discovered.[62]

Nevertheless, the creation of controlled geographic zones emerged as a crucial element in Jamot's work, which continued in what is now Burkina Faso and Ivory Coast. The cure that controlled the epidemic, but also caused side effects such as blindness, was positioned in terms of a geographic conception of contagion. The idea of an epidemic as a geographic phenomenon created by demographic shifts and social disequilibrium made it seem possible to control its spread through the creation of new micro-organizational structures. Jamot and his fellow Pastorians functioned as social actors who could reveal and control these invisible microbiological agents through their own geographic mobility. For Jamot's medical team, the mastery of geographic movement was essential for the containment of microbiological contagion.

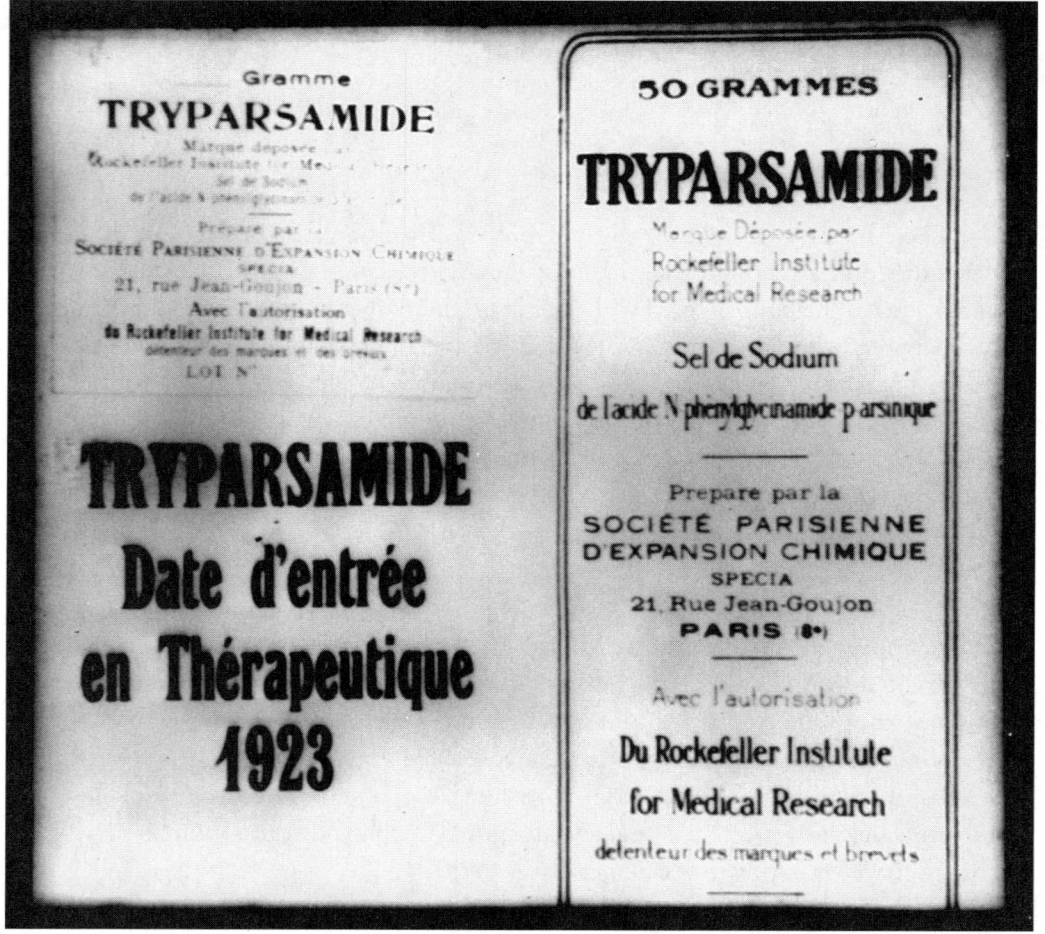

FIGURE 50. Tryparsamide is an arsenic-based treatment for sleeping sickness that was used as of 1923. From *Le Réveil d'une race au Cameroun.* Copyright Collection des Archives du Film et du Dépôt Légal du Centre National de la Cinématographie.

Jamot was head of the medical unit charged with eradicating sleeping sickness in French West Africa during the early 1930s, but he failed to contain the unprecedented spread of trypanosomiasis.[63] Controlling the circulation of the parasite meant suspending economic development in the region, as well as strictly regulating population movements. Colonial authorities were more interested in exacting inexpensive labor power than in limiting the spread of sleeping sickness. Metropolitan administrators were already bewitched by another form of sleeping sickness—financial crisis. The need to strictly control infected populations and the economic imperative of rapid manpower deployment were not immediately reconcilable objectives in the French colonies. Though Jamot's recommendations were adopted elsewhere, it was not until the dawning of World War II, after Jamot's death, that his mobile prophylactic methods were deployed.[64]

True to his Pastorian conception of duty, Jamot had written, "The relentless fight against the spread of trypanosomiasis everywhere by the Great Powers fulfills not only a great humanitarian responsibility but also an obligation to a higher standard of justice."[65] At this juncture we can understand how the Pastorian, a social technician zealously engaged in prophylactic and educational efforts, outstripped the conflicted political will of the colonial administration itself. The Pastorians, as health assistants, educators, and doctors, were hygienists committed to Pasteurian conceptions of diagnostics and treatment. For them the extension of a social scientific technical agency became an overriding element that went beyond the political and economic contingencies of the colonial mandate and served as a basis for humanitarian action.

PASTEURIZING FRENCH COLONIAL DOCUMENTARY CINEMA

Jean Benoît-Lévy and Marie Epstein produced roughly three hundred short-subject films serving the cause of public health during the interwar period.[66] Epstein's collaboration with Benoît-Lévy began when he commissioned her brother, Jean Epstein, to direct his first film, *Pasteur* (1922), commemorating the centenary of Louis Pasteur's birth.[67] As a Pastorian, Benoît-Lévy was part of a cadre of medical activists committed to instituting and promoting a broad political and social agenda that tied notions of physical well-being to systematic hygienic practices.

Benoît-Lévy, who upheld the great works of Louis Pasteur as a model for educational cinema, considered educational cinema a technological remedy for social pathologies—an interwar palliative to the devastation of World War I. Paraphrasing Pasteur's writings to emphasize the opposition between nihilistic destruction and humanitarian values, Benoît-Lévy wrote:

> Two opposite laws today seem to be in conflict: a law of blood and death, which, by inventing a new method of combat every day, forces people to remain in a perpetual state of readiness for the battlefield, and a law of peace, work, and health, which has as its sole aim the deliverance of man from the evils that assail him. The first seeks only

violent conquest, the other only the solace of mankind. The latter places the life of
a human being above all victories, the former would sacrifice hundreds of thousands
of lives for the ambition of one.[68]

The shifting parameters of battle, from protecting metropolitan France against
German aggression to eradicating microbiological invisible agents that weakened and
wiped out human communities, became an important justification for large-scale
invasive sanitary efforts throughout France and in the colonies. Mobile vaccination
drives carried out by workers armed with film projection equipment functioned as an
immediate substitute for the heavy use of newsreel footage presented in more than
twelve hundred cinema projection stations in military barracks and depots during
World War I.[69] Microbiological discoveries fostered successive waves of large-scale
hygienic public works projects that included the draining of lakes and rivers, the building of sewers, and the destruction of unsanitary indigenous housing as a result of geographical and economic occupation.[70]

The extensive corpus of educational films produced and directed by Benoît-Lévy
and Epstein were part of a discrete matrix of national social hygiene campaigns. With
the subsequent establishment of the French national hygiene organization (La Commission Générale de Propagande de l'Office National d'Hygiène Sociale), several specialized national public health leagues commissioned films on venereal disease, TB,
alcoholism, child protection, cancer, and diphtheria and more general films on medical assistance.[71] The short film within *Conte de la mille et une nuits* is, in fact, an excerpt
from another Benoît-Lévy film, *Les Maladies vénériennes* (Venereal disease, 1925), which
he produced for the National League against Venereal Disease.

Benoît-Lévy characterized the goal of his numerous sex education films from the
interwar period as "a call to life," which was rather different from the morbid approach
typical of the genre. He elaborated this "call to life" as "that powerful compulsion coming from nature herself, who desires that every living creature, between birth and death,
should propagate itself."[72] In *Conte de la mille et une nuits* this "call to life" is set in an
exotic North African setting that draws on an imaginary vision of near-otherness—
outside the geographic boundaries of metropolitan France and yet under reconstruction through the "great works" of French colonial reform.

In their 1934 feature-length film *Itto*, Benoît-Lévy and Epstein addressed the introduction of French medical assistance to Morocco. This film was made on location in
the Atlas Mountains, where the exotic landscape served as the mise-en-scène for a
story of forbidden love and tribal rivalry that served as a counterpoint to the "great
works" of French colonial humanism. The film features Pierre Darrieu (Hubert Pre-
lier), an exemplary agent of French medical expertise who has been assigned to lead
medical campaigns throughout the Atlas Mountains. Having been introduced to a
Berber village by French soldiers who were being held hostage, Darrieu proves his powers of healing to the local population by saving their sheep herd from the ravages of
an epidemic. As a true scientific healer, in opposition to the local sorcerers who appear

intermittently throughout the film, Darrieu consistently demonstrates his magical abilities to heal the sick.

Itto (Simone Berriau) is named for the daughter of the Moroccan resistance fighter Hamou El Amrar (Moulay Ibrahim). The story of the film is based on this legendary figure, who fought against French pacification efforts between 1914 and 1920.[73] Itto's lover, Miloud (Ben Brick), is the son of the leader of a neighboring clan, and their relationship is forbidden by Itto's father, though tolerated at first. Itto and Miloud consummate their love and attempt to elope, but are stopped by Hamou's men, who wound Miloud and return Itto to her father, pregnant. Miloud is then picked up by a French patrol squadron and is nursed back to health by Darrieu. During this time, Itto's pregnancy comes to term and she gives birth to a baby girl in difficult circumstances.

Another newborn appears when Françoise (Simone Bourday), Darrieu's wife, has a child who, in narrative terms, makes up for the loss of her brother Jean (Roland Caillaux) in a desert skirmish. Jean had introduced Darrieu to Françoise in the opening segment of the film, and the symbolic exchange of her brother for the newborn represents Françoise's initiation into the perils of French humanitarian colonial frontiersmanship. Shortly thereafter, Itto's daughter falls ill and the servant girl, Aïcha, suggests that the "white sorcerer" examine the child. After walking all night with Itto's child, Aïcha arrives at the souk where Darrieu makes his weekly rounds. Darrieu determines

FIGURE 51. The resistance fighter Hamou El Amrar (Moulay Ibrahim) in *Itto*, 1934. Copyright Collection des Archives du Film et du Dépôt Légal du Centre National de la Cinématographie.

that Itto's daughter has diphtheria and inoculates her with the vaccine. When a diphtheria epidemic ensues, Darrieu is sought out by other mothers from the region.

Meanwhile, the stockpile of diphtheria vaccine, mistaken for crates of ammunition by Hamou's men, is stolen in a raid on a nearby French supply depot. With no serum left, Darrieu's own newborn child becomes infected with diphtheria and Darrieu is resigned to waiting for the arrival of more serum. It begins to snow. When the stolen serum is pawned for more ammunition at the souk, a group of women from the nearby village recognize the vials of vaccine. They confiscate them and undertake a treacherous journey through sleet and snow to dispatch the medicine to Darrieu, who is then able to save his own child.

The arrival of the vaccine represents a new kind of cooperation between the concerned Berber mothers and Darrieu. The Berber women's retrieval of the vaccine serves the greater community, but their trek is presented as an expression of concern for the well-being of Françoise and Pierre Darrieu's infant. Better acclimated to the rigors of the environment than the French medical supply truck, which is stuck in a snowdrift, the heroic Berber women contribute to the effectiveness of French medical agency. This scene demonstrates that the Berber mothers' actions indirectly support the process of conversion from traditional beliefs and customs to French colonial medical and social renewal. The close association between vaccination and colonization recalls some of the earliest French inoculation campaigns in Algeria in the mid–nineteenth century, in which the invasiveness of medical and hygienic efforts were directly in line with military pacification efforts.[74]

Once the epidemic is vanquished, Itto's daughter is taken back to the Darrieu household for protection as Hamou prepares for his final stand against the French. Hamou encourages everyone under his command to surrender, but remains a valiant warrior until the bitter end. Itto returns to ask for her father's forgiveness and stands in solidarity with him against the French forces. Tragically, Hamou and Itto are shot down by two stray bullets, fired against the orders of the French colonel, who respects Hamou's courage. In the final scene of the film, Françoise adopts Itto's daughter and offers her breast to her, symbolizing mother France (Françoise) nurturing the growth of a newborn Morocco.

The theme of protecting the newborn child in *Itto* and *Conte de la mille et une nuits* serves as a metaphor for France's efforts to rebuild and regenerate after World War I. Following the success of Benoît-Lévy and Epstein's film *La Maternelle* (*The Children of Montmartre*, 1933), which dealt with the nurturing of slum children in a nursery school located in the working-class neighborhood of Montmartre, Pierre Boulanger reports that Eden Productions gave the filmmakers a free hand to make *Itto*.[75] Although Benoît-Lévy and Epstein established themselves as the leading French educational filmmakers of the interwar period, the success of *La Maternelle* demonstrated that they could make compelling narrative films from subject matter with seemingly little popular appeal.

CURING MOHAMED BEN CHEGIR

Although geographic mastery and military pacification are preconditions for meaningful social and medical reform in these films, the healthy future of children serves as the final and most important cause. Children represent universal salvation and are shown to be nurtured best by French medical treatment and education. For example, Benoît-Lévy and Epstein's *Conte de la mille et une nuits* demonstrates not merely that Mohamed ben Chegir can be cured of syphilis but that he can still become the proud father of many healthy children. In *Itto,* Darrieu's newborn child represents an evolving cooperation between Berber mothers and a French father and mother, who also represent French medical assistance; Françoise's final offering of her breast to Itto's daughter symbolizes triumphant French colonial humanitarianism. Françoise's own conversion from a skeptical French citizen to a committed colonial humanitarian turns on the power of motherhood, a vocation that blurs national boundaries.

Vaccination was an all-purpose antidote protecting children, and it became an important theme in the oeuvre of Benoît-Lévy and Epstein. In *Itto* the diphtheria vaccine is almost a magic potion, recalling the prominence the Pasteur Institutes had gained throughout the French colonies.[76] Although Emile Roux had invented the diphtheria vaccine in 1894, a major stumbling block to its initial acceptance was the long distance that had to be traversed to relay the laboratory tests and vaccines from the Pasteur Institute laboratories to qualified local care providers. The colonies served as experimental test sites and proving grounds for a new generation of military doctors and medical reformers trained in Pasteurian methods and techniques. Films and short excerpts that demonstrated the work of the Pasteur Institutes in the colonies emphasized the superior nature of French technical know-how as the foundation for humanitarian values and political reform. Pasteur Institutes were established even before World War I for primary research and the production of vaccines throughout the French colonies, launching the illustrious careers of Alexandre Yersin, Adrien Loir, Eugène Jamot, and others.

From the animated drawings of *Conte de la mille et une nuits* to the more realistic portrayal of the Moroccan landscape in *Itto,* the French colonial experimental laboratory justified the agency of modernity as the only cure for medical and social pathologies. *Itto* combines an educational, hygienic demonstration with a compelling narrative focused on the destiny of Morocco. Itto's daughter represents hope for a new Moroccan future, no longer hindered by the guerrilla resistance movement of Hamou El Amrar but part of the normative healing agency of the Darrieu household.

Frantz Fanon has written that the concept of the normative rests on the notion of a closed society in which the family comes to represent the nation. Thus, "A normal child who has grown up in a normal family will become a normal [person]."[77] The introduction of a cure mediates an opposition between the normal and the pathological. Just as the pathological subject becomes the pretext for action, the cure overdetermines the symptom.

Colonial reform was not simply about civilizing the French colonies, but was aimed at reforming hygienic and social behavior in France itself. In *Conte de la mille et une nuits,* Mohamed's return to his former "state of nature" through French medical expertise poses the underlying question "Who does Mohamed represent?" I would suggest that for more assimilated North African and French metropolitan audiences he represents the conveniently "uncivilized" North African Arab stereotype. Yet although he may function as this "uncivilized" Arab stereotype, he also represents "natural man," who does not merely live in a state of nature but is part of nature, indistinguishable from the illustrated North African landscape. This figure represents a desire to return to preindustrial primitivism and demonstrates that this desire can be reconciled with hygienic forms of disease prevention and treatment.

Mohamed is cured; he is once again as strong as a lion, as agile as a panther, as fast as a greyhound, as tireless as a camel, and the happy parent of many healthy children. Storybook images of the lion, the panther, the greyhound, and the camel (which illustrate Mohamed's return to health) are followed by a series of powerful photographs depicting syphilitic children that are then juxtaposed against shots of Mohamed's

FIGURE 52. Mohamed ben Chegir with a syphilitic cold sore in *Conte de la mille et une nuits.* Copyright Comité Français d'Éducation pour la Santé.

healthy children. A final warning proclaims, "Do not trust false remedies or false healers that result in a loss of time, a loss of money, and diminish the possibility for a cure." The diagnosis and treatment of syphilis in the film thus serves as a call to political reform under the banner of French medical agency.

The work of French colonial humanitarianism is represented in these films as parallel to the magic of educational cinema. The layering of educational films in the service of hygienic reform was part of a larger political and social agenda in which an extended French colonial political body could be articulated and animated from an indivisible scientific and spiritual metropolitan center. The power to diagnose invisible agents was used to project political and territorial objectives across microbiological, cultural, and geographic boundaries, advanced through the colonial administration of the all-powerful "scientific" cure.

5. Infiltrate the Crowd with an Idea!

Colonial Educational Cinema and the Threat of Imitative Contagion

The opening sequence of a 1931 French colonial educational film begins with a young man pacing in his asphyxiating cell-like room, opening and closing the window and unable to focus his energy.[1] As he sits down and begins to look through a picture book about the French colonies, the pictures are progressively enlarged into moving images of street scenes from Indochina and the Saharan desert punctuated by the turning of a page. These moving images represent the young man's imagination, which is making the still images move and inspiring him to sign up at the recruiting office for service in the colonies.

After four months of military training, intercut with the flash-forwarding of calendar days, the new recruit wears an officer's uniform and boards a steamer in Marseilles. In the next scene he has a new life in an unidentified colonial outpost, training African troops for battle. Military training and exercise give him purpose and authority upon landing on colonial soil. The colonial picture book becomes a source of cinematic possibilities, so that the act of joining up to participate in the colonial enterprise is a way of effecting change in an emergent world picture of humanity.

The notion of a book coming to life as a series of animated images was a frequently used convention in French educational cinema. Photographic imagery of the colonies was a window into the exotic world often associated with the colonial exhibitions in metropolitan France. The French colonial exhibitions initially began as parts of international universal exhibitions, starting in 1878, and developed as their own genre of smaller-scale exhibitions in Rouen, Bordeaux, Marseilles, and Roubaix from the late nineteenth century until World War II. The idea of mounting a large-scale international colonial exhibition emerged from the popularity of the colonial pavilion at the

1900 Universal Exhibition.[2] After a resolution was reached to hold this large-scale exhibition at the Porte Dorée in Paris following the supplemental 1906 and 1922 Colonial Exhibitions in Marseilles, major architectural construction was undertaken that included the building of a sectional near-replica of the Cambodian Angkor Wat temple in its distinctive Khmer architectural style. The 1931 Parisian Colonial Exhibition was the largest exhibition in Paris since the Universal Exhibition of 1900, selling more than thirty-three million tickets and drawing as many as three hundred thousand visitors per day for the six months that it remained open.[3] The exhibition functioned as a geographic simulacrum of empire, as Herman Lebovics suggests, meshing modernity with the exotic distancing of colonial life.[4] Furthermore, it was a veritable theme park of colonial attractions in which educational cinema played an important role as a form of instruction and entertainment.

The moving picture book motif also served as the organizing principle for the creation of a series of films that were commissioned for the Parisian Colonial Exhibition. The organizers were intent on creating a *livre d'or* of moving images consisting

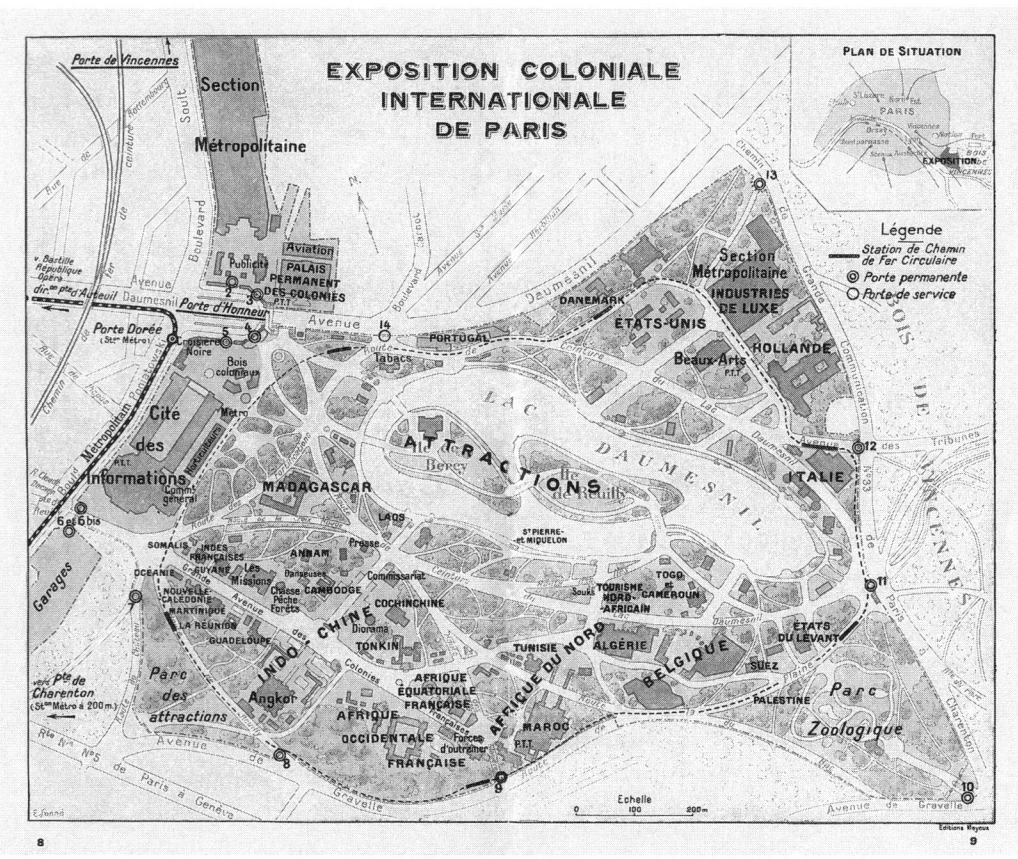

FIGURE 53. Map of the 1931 Parisian Colonial Exhibition in *Guide offert par les grand magasins au Bon Marché* (Paris: Maison A. Bouciacau, 1931), 6–7.

of feature documentaries celebrating the economic vitality and history of French involvement in each of the colonies.[5] Documentary cinema that featured a diffusionist geographic perspective was used to monumentalize the work of colonization in action. A primary theme that emerged from the films was the transformation of the colonial project from a doctrine of conquest and commercial domination to interwar humanitarianism that encouraged popular participation in the "great works" of empire at a time when a majority of French people were turning against the rhetoric and realities of colonial occupation.

"Making France known to the colonies, and the colonies to France" was the guiding policy for colonial film education established by the well-known French politician Albert Sarraut, who served as governor general of Indochina twice and as minister of the colonies, among other ministerial positions during the interwar period, making him the most significant political figure in establishing French colonial interwar policy.[6] My analysis of this formula of "making known" initially focuses on the establishment of the Colonial Film Committee in association with the 1931 Colonial Exhibition and is followed by a discussion of the first film that it commissioned, *La Marche vers le soleil* (Marching toward the sun, 1928). Using newspaper accounts to illustrate the narrative, publicity, and context for this film, I examine how this film, directed by René Le Somptier, was an instrumental part of the broader architecture of colonial documentary educational filmmaking first established in French Indochina through the Agences Économiques (Economic Affairs Office) and then used to promote Indochina in France and France in Indochina through photography and documentary film.

Indochina is an important site for the beginnings of French colonial educational cinema because of the pivotal role that education played in the establishment of French adminstrative authority under Sarraut's mandate. As I will argue, educational politics in Indochina was directly linked to the creation of educational cinema in France itself, where the education of children became a focal point of this effort. I maintain that educational cinema, as a cinema of reform for the education of children in metropolitan France, was exported to the colonies as a means of rhetorically transforming colonial subjects into citizens. With the appeal and ubiquity of American films in the colonies, however, and a limited infrastructure for colonial education efforts, the promotion of educational cinema in most of the colonies was barely sustainable. The establishment of censorship regulations in the French colonies became a means of restricting American and some French narrative features, which it was feared would imperil the integrity of the colonial ideal. Finally, the advertising slogan "Infiltrate the crowd with an idea" was transformed to protect the colonial and perhaps protoproletarian subject from the contagion of the crowd both in the colonies and and at home; instead, the colonies were to serve as a model for an emerging modernity of travel, secular values, and the remaking of the French national body. L'Abbé de Condillac's metaphor of the statue successively endowed with each of the senses thus came to be pinned to the modeling of French colonial subjects in the transitory state of becoming in order to stabilize and consolidate French national identity.

THE COLONIAL FILM COMMITTEE

As a step toward popularizing the colonial idea, the Comité de Propagande Colonial par le Film (Colonial Film Committee) was established in 1928 to produce films and re-edit others for the 1931 Parisian Colonial Exhibition. The Film Colonial production unit was launched to expand, edit, and supplement representative imagery that was first developed as part of a system of lending archives for educational, industrial, and fairground exhibitors, known as the Agences Économiques. The Agences were set up by Albert Sarraut in 1918, then governor general of Indochina before becoming minister of the colonies in 1920, to promote the colonies and encourage economic exchange in the name of education.[7] The promotion of colonial educational cinema was auxiliary to a vision of colonial humanism, articulated in the Sarraut Plan, that linked economic development to moral, political, intellectual, educational, and social values.[8]

Using an "American-style" treatment to be evaluated by government officials, newsreel-quality footage was assembled alongside newly scripted material to be shot on location in each of the colonies. This series of popular feature documentaries was to highlight the history of colonization, public works undertaken, natural resources available, geographical markers, living standards, anthropological referents, and a vision for future development in each of the respective colonies. Films treating Indochina, the Antilles, Guyana, Madagascar, the Pacific Islands, West Africa, Equatorial Africa, and the Somali Coast were envisioned for widespread distribution by la Société Aubert, primarily in France and Belgium. It remains unclear how many films were actually completed under this specific mandate. Seven million French francs were requested for their production as well as free passage for several filmmaking teams consisting of five- or six-member crews.[9]

The "popular" documentary compilation film initiative sought to engage French filmmakers such as Abel Gance, who was to make a film on the history of Guyana;[10] Roger Lion, who was to make a film based on an Élissa Rhaïs novel;[11] and René Le Somptier, who was commissioned to make *La Marche vers le soleil*. Press clippings from a variety of colonial affairs journals and film magazines attest to the production of several compilation films, but only fragments of these films have survived.[12] One of the restored films from this group, J.-K. Raymond-Millet's *Promenade en AEF* (A stroll through French Equatorial Africa, 1931), begins with the assertion, "Many of the documentary segments from this film belong to the Economic Affairs Office [Agences Économiques] for French Equatorial Africa," and the address of the office appears at the end of this three-reel, fifty-minute film. The film is organized as a geography lesson showing colonial works throughout the Congo, Gabon, and Cameroon. Shipping, automobile travel, and the building of the railroad along the Congo River are shown to facilitate health initiatives to cure sleeping sickness, promote educational initiatives, encourage large-scale building projects, and provide a transportation network for the exportation and cultivation of cacao.

Although *Promenade en AEF* is a silent film, the 1931 Colonial Exhibition featured documentary talkies such as *L'Histoire de la Plus Grande France* (The history of Greater France, 1931). According to George-Michel Coissac, one of the best-known film journalists of the era, this film traced the history of French colonization, beginning with Henri IV along with Richelieu and Colbert, followed by Galliéni in the nineteenth century, and culminating in the twentieth century with Maréchal Louis Hubert Gonzalve Lyautey, the model colonial officer-administrator and official commissioner of the exhibition itself.[13] A contemporary of Albert Sarraut, Lyautey was also involved with an early government-sanctioned colonial educational film project that commissioned Léon Gaumont to make a series of educational and documentary films in 1917 to publicize the economic resources of Morocco in France. Albert Sarraut used the very same argument about making the economic resources of the colonies known to France in a policy statement referred to as the Sarraut Plan in 1920 while serving as minister of the colonies.[14]

Most of the films presented at the Parisian Colonial Exhibition were short educational films, but they were supplemented by compilation films such as Millet's *Promenade en AEF,* feature documentaries such as *La Croisière noire* (discussed in chapter 3), and fictionalized documentary renderings such as Jean Renoir's *Le Bled* (The outback), initially commissioned for the 1930 Algerian Cententary. According to the multivolume

FIGURE 54. Maréchal Louis Hubert Gonzalve Lyautey in *Lyautey, batisseur d'empire,* 1947. Copyright Collection des Archives du Film et du Dépôt Légal du Centre National de la Cinématographie.

Rapport général documenting the exhibition, at least three hundred films, or "a million meters of film," were shown in the fifteen-hundred-seat theater at the Cité des Informations.[15] A million meters of film divided among three hundred films suggests that there was a plethora of educational films of shorter and longer lengths, averaging thirty-five minutes. In addition, there were numerous films presented at each of the individual region-specific and theme-specific pavilions, such as the smaller Croisière Noire pavilion.

Furthermore, numerous films beyond those included under the Film Colonial mandate were commissioned or re-edited for the exhibition and related events through myriad public and private initiatives. Among them were Baron Napoléon Gourgaud's *Le Vrai visage de l'Afrique: Chez les buveurs du sang* (The true face of Africa: Among the blood drinkers)[16] and André Antoine and Robert Lugeon's *Chez les mangeurs d'hommes* (In the land of the cannibals, discussed in chapter 1). Léon Poirier, the director of *La Croisière noire,* which remained the key colonial documentary of the interwar period, was appointed artistic director of the film program for the Cité des Informations theater, an effort that he acknowledged was extremely frustrating and haphazard given the numerous other events that often took precedence in the same venue.[17]

In spite of the spotty organization of the colonial film program, from the Colonial Exhibition itself emerged a vision of centralized authority that included interconnected

FIGURE 55. The Cité des Informations at the 1931 Parisian Colonial Exhibition in *Vues de l'Exposition coloniale de 1931,* 1931. Copyright Collection des Archives du Film et du Dépôt Légal du Centre National de la Cinématographie.

French colonial contact zones that bordered on the fantastic, projecting a totalizing world of simultaneous communication. Or, as Dudley Andrew and Steven Ungar suggest, displays of difference were transformed into contained encounters with otherness.[18] The Cité des Informations edifice was constructed as the central point of orientation for the exhibition, capable of providing a storehouse of information concerning all existing empires in every European language, including a wide array of current visual information. Four planispheres were mounted inside, as Catherine Hodeir and Michel Pierre have described, "displaying up-to-the-minute information concerning existing air routes to the colonies, radio and telegraph links, as well the principal sites of production for colonial products. Another large illuminated scoreboard provided continuous news flashes from around the world by the Havas [travel] agency."[19] A studio for radio transmissions was also located in the Cité des Informations and initiated shortwave radio transmissions to the colonies. Radio-Coloniale began broadcasting with the opening of the Colonial Exhibition, transmitting the sounds and speeches of the exhibition and establishing an immediate and durable means of broadcasting to the colonies.[20]

As a prototype for a new modernist future of instantaneous communication, the Cité des Informations was equipped with a mountain of data related to the colonies, capable of serving financial investors, public health specialists, university researchers, journalists, and the less specialized schoolteachers or tourists. It served as a model control center for an emerging communications network and provided a key to maintaining imperial hegemony across the geographic divide. It was in the context of this emergent media semiosphere that educational colonial cinema was showcased as an integral element of the colonial media spectacle at the Colonial Exhibition.

RENÉ LE SOMPTIER AND DOCUMENTARY FILMMAKING AS A COLONIAL VOCATION

René Le Somptier's *La Marche vers le soleil* was the centerpiece of the Film Colonial production initiative. The intent of the fictional documentarylike form of the film, officially termed "un documentaire-romancé," was to adapt a fictionalized story to colonial instruction, which Le Somptier had claimed was the inspiration for his 1924 colonial feature film *Le Fils du soleil* (The child of the sun).[21] Georges Sprecht, the cameraman for *La Croisière noire,* guaranteed a sense of visual continuity as director of photography for *La Marche vers le soleil.*

La Marche vers le soleil was conceived as an orienting kaleidoscope, synthesizing the history and achievements of empire in French Equatorial Africa. Scenes portraying the building of railroads, road construction in the Ubangi-Chari region, the copper mines in Mindouli (in the Republic of Congo-Brazzaville [R. Congo]), and timber felling in Gabon were featured. Views from other colonial cities such as Bangui (Central African Republic [CAR]), Brazzaville (R. Congo), and Pointe-Noire (R. Congo) were interspersed with sequences depicting Eugène Jamot's efforts against sleeping sickness in Cameroon and a historical reconstruction of the conquest of Chad by the Mission Crampel.[22] Advance publicity circulated before the film's premiere drew attention to the state-financed colonial film initiative. As part of the on-site coverage of the production, a still photographer was sent along with the production team.[23] According to the press reports and reviews, the "gift" of European civilization was the primary narrative thread. The inevitable corollary to this so-called gift was the Equatorial African Esperanto word *matabiche,* or tip for services rendered. A discussion of this term is integrated into an advance publicity chronicle penned by the actress Marquisette de Bosky, who played a reporter in the film itself.

In one of the five diarylike installments that appeared in the popular French film magazine *Ciné-miroir,* de Bosky incorporated the translation of a song that four of the porters started to sing while carrying the film production equipment. According to de Bosky's translator, the last two lines of the song meant, "Yes, we are able and strong, and the white man will give us a well deserved *matabiche.*"[24] *Matabiche,* de Bosky explains, was the first word that she heard upon arriving in Equatorial Africa and the last she heard upon leaving. Hundreds of local workers were used to facilitate the production, particularly paddlers for the sequences filmed on the Congo River, so the film itself became yet another large-scale colonial works project parallel to the Citroën *boudj*-hotel venture described in chapter 3.

La Marche vers le soleil reinforced the official discourse of colonial humanism and featured the Central African landscape as a theater for civilizing action, evoking the prospect of African subjects transformed through the pedagogy of modernity and associated with railroad construction, medical curative action, military service, and French language instruction. French Equatorial Africa (Afrique Equatoriale Française, or AEF) was familiar territory for Le Somptier, where he was the state-sanctioned filmmaker-in-residence in the region during the mid-1920s.[25] Raphaël Antonetti, governor general of AEF, was the driving force behind putting *La Marche vers le soleil* into production once the director of the AEF economic affairs office in Paris, Léon Mirabel, wrote the script at his urging.

The production of *La Marche vers le soleil* as a state-sanctioned film was the result of the efforts of a tightly knit circuit of civil servants allied with Aristide Briand, one of the most adept French political figures of the post–World War I era, who was also an advocate for the notion of a collective European identity, or "the European idea," associated with the "Film Europe" platform from 1924 to 1929.[26] The film historian Marcel Oms explains that Le Somptier's friendship with Briand facilitated his subsequent political career.[27] It also tied him to another close associate of Briand, Henry Paté, president of the Colonial Film Initiative for the 1931 exhibition, who ultimately commissioned Le Somptier to make *La Marche vers le soleil.* Colonial educational cinema drew on an extended fraternity of civil servants who were committed to the social regeneration of the French political and physical body articulated as a form of colonial service. Briand's engagement with anticlerical educational policy was complemented by the work of the newly established interwar Ministry of Physical Education, which was first directed by Paté, where Le Somptier served as the general secretary some years later. Taking hold of an extended geographic territory implied reanimating the inhabitants in order to enact an evolutionary logic in which physical education and educational cinema, among other endeavors, such as hygienic reform, were conceived as transformative acts in the civilizing process.

The Union Coloniale, which was the best known and largest of the industrial colonial lobbying organizations of the period, sponsored the premiere of *La Marche vers le soleil,* at which its president, Frédéric François-Marsal, began his public address with the following remarks: "At first the book and now the cinema put forward another demonstration, more grandiose, more striking, of the beauty of our colonial domain. . . . Today the cinema is our means of propaganda, and thanks to the collaborative work of artists showing themselves to be both gracious and intrepid, filmmakers have found a way to join pleasure with utility."[28]

The marriage between entertainment and social utility was thus conceived as a means of infiltrating the masses with the colonial idea, with cinema representing an essential social instrument to guide the flows and agitations of a nascent Debordian society of the spectacle. Though *La Marche vers le soleil* was praised for its evocation of "the colonial genius" in the predictable bombast on the occasion of its premiere, the film met with mixed reviews for its heavy-handedness and repetitiveness. As one critic noted, it lacked the poetic and popular properties so evident in Walther Ruttman's 1929 documentary *Melodie der Welt* (Melody of the world), a film commissioned by the German navigation firm Hapag-Lloyd that sampled newsreel footage from around the world set to music.[29] Furthermore, unlike so many of its American counterparts, *La Marche vers le soleil* was a silent film that did not draw on the experimental sound techniques already being used by the French avant-garde. Le Somptier had pursued his filmmaking career during the silent era and was primarily known as an "academic craftsman" by critics and filmmakers of the period.[30]

Le Somptier's filmmaking career began after World War I, when he directed *La Sultane de l'amour* (The sultan of love), which was co-directed by Charles Burguet and produced by a well-known producer of film serials, Louis Nalpas. The film is an American-style serial based on the "tale of a thousand and one nights," which recounts a love story of capture and rescue through the medium of a magical glass. The use and circulation of the magical glass serves as a powerful knowledge-gathering device revealing crucial scenes of parallel action and consequently demonstrates that ownership of the technology of vision determines the course and orientation of events. In fact, finding the magical glass and retrieving it from the entourage of the evil Sultan Malik (Paul Vermoyal) becomes an all-important prerequisite for the eventual rescue of the beautiful Sultane Daoulah (France Dhélia) by Prince Mourad (Sylvio de Pedrelli). A final rescue sequence is revealed through the magical glass, in the hands of Daoulah's father, Sultan Mahmoud El Hassam (Albert Bras).

Like the cinema itself, the magical glass becomes a source of magical power. "Seeing as knowing" is thus conceived as a means of identifying and establishing an object of study that later inspired a vision of geographic and intellectual mastery that was prevalent in French educational cinema. The use of the magical glass as a narrative device underscores the ubiquitous and mobile perspective of the camera, which promises a form of simultaneous transmission and remote reception. Its authoritative visual perspective represents the power to transform an exotic landscape through a form of "photogenic plasticity," a turn of phrase that Louis Delluc used to describe the vitalist aesthetic associated with the use of light in French cinema, the depiction of flesh in Italian cinema, and the early American cinema of D. W. Griffith and Thomas Ince.[31] Further, Delluc's *photogénie* became the basis for André Bazin's ontology of the film image and functioned as an aesthetic point of reference for French colonial cinema.

Le Somptier's magical glass had much in common with photography, phonography, and radiophony in that it could reveal, record, and transmit the previously undetected as part of an emergent optics of scale. In *La Sultane de l'amour* the retrieved magical glass illustrated the rescue of Daoulah by Prince Mourad, and yet it was used as an instrument of surveillance to capture her in the first place. Figuratively speaking, the magical glass functioned as a console viewer with the sort of documentary authority that one might find in the bourgeois sitting room within the spectrum of photographic viewers and optical toys by the turn of the century. While the use of the magical glass was presented as an illusionistic technique by which to illustrate parallel action in *La Sultane de l'amour,* Le Somptier's 1924 eight-part serial *Le Fils du soleil* transformed it into the lens of novelistic colonial documentary realism.

Le Fils du soleil, in fact, served an explicitly colonial propagandistic agenda, analogous to that of *La Marche vers le soleil,* such that the opening intertitles explain that the film seeks to "show the great works accomplished in Morocco, where order and prosperity flourish" and is dedicated to "the patience and tenacity of the civilizers who have made Morocco into a new country."[32] As *Cinémagazine* reported in 1924, "Here is an example of how the Société des Ciné-Romans, with the release of *Le Fils du soleil,* has shown us to simultaneously instruct and entertain with the cinema, combining fiction with education while performing an act of patriotism and public instruction."[33]

Le Fils du soleil turns on a broken engagement between a young officer at the prestigious St. Cyr military academy, Hubert de Beauvoisin (Georges Charlia), and the daughter of a marquis, Aurore de Saint-Bertrand (Marquisette de Bosky, who was also the featured actress in *La Marche vers le soleil*). They are reunited through their search for economic and social renewal in Morocco. While Hubert joins the Foreign Legion to regain his reputation as an upstanding military officer after being falsely accused of stealing, Aurore accompanies her father, who seeks to rebuild his lost fortune by starting over as an engineer in Morocco.

As in *La Sultane de l'amour,* an oedipal triangle (with the absent mother) is established, alternatively triangulating the vulnerable father and the good daughter in relation to the good and bad suitor. In *Le Fils du soleil,* Aurore is figuratively held hostage by the profiteering and unscrupulous Baron Horn (Joë Hamman), who frames his rival, Hubert, and poses as a potential suitor capable of bailing out Aurore's father. The redeeming potential of the colonies, where military reputations and fortunes can be regained, is also a backdrop for the good couple on the frontier. The theme of redemption on the frontier, so common to American westerns and evoked by Joë Hammon's screen presence as an early Pathé western icon, was adapted to current events in Morocco. The film was released just when the Moroccan resistance leader Abd el-Krim had successfully driven the Spanish out of the Rif Mountain region of Morocco, and, as David Slavin notes, "threatened French imperial interests in the [Moroccan] Sultanate and neighboring Algeria," eventually leading to the Rif War (1925–26).[34] In fact, the war-profiteering Baron Horn supplies weapons to the nefarious Abel el-Kassem (Mario Nasthasio) in a direct reference to Abd el-Krim.

The production of popular fictional adventure films, derived in part from the colonial novel, formed a photogenic referent for an expanding reservoir of exotic imagery whose latent effect was reinforced with colonial propaganda efforts. Le Somptier's film served as a model for the Film Colonial effort because it featured colonial priorities as part of an affective strategy of personal engagement in which the audience was expected to identify with the colonial father and daughter, vulnerable to the vagaries of nature and natives on the colonial frontier. Further, Le Somptier, like J.-K. Raymond-Millet, Jean d'Esme, and Alfred Chaumel, was among the best-known French colonial documentary filmmakers by vocation. These men frequently appeared in their own films, functioning as patriarchs and linked to a previous generation of military men who had "settled" the colonial frontier. Alfred Chaumel incorporated his wife, Geneviève Chaumel-Gentil—the daughter of the explorer Émile Gentil, who had accompanied Savorgnan de Brazza on his conquest of Chad—into most of his films, appealing to the next generation of young men by creating aspirations to colonial service as a vocation and to a family lifestyle on the frontier of the French geographic imagination. These familiar adventurer-explorers served as a linchpin in the discourse of colonial education as a spatial enterprise orchestrated by men, humanized by women, and cleansed through the crucible of humanitarian values of hygienic reform and education that could then serve as a model by which to remake the French national body.

INDOCHINA AS THE FOUNDATION OF COLONIAL EDUCATIONAL CINEMA

Marcel Olivier, the de facto organizer of the 1931 Colonial Exhibition, sent out a questionnaire to gather information about all of the relevant films made in each of the colonies for the exhibition. Significantly, Indochina maintained the most comprehensive film holdings that were specifically focused on education.[35] The films produced by the Mission Cinématographique de l'Indochine served as the bulwark of government-sanctioned documentary film production, foregrounding the "colonial idea" as a means of humanizing industrial expansion in the name of high-minded republican educational objectives.

Films about Indochina were extensively presented at La Cité des Informations and the Indochinese pavilion itself at the Colonial Exhibition. These films were part of an evolving photographic inventory of architectural, geographic, and cultural sites that mapped Indochina as part of a territorial amalgam that became known as Indochine Française, or French Indochina. Shot by Constant Girel and Gabriel Veyre as early as 1898, they were among the first colonial short-subject films. Veyre met the governor general of Indochina, Paul Doumer, who facilitated his travels in Indochina, leading him to exhibit existing catalogue reels to the emperor in Hué. He was also contracted to shoot footage for the 1900 Universal Exhibition in Paris and for another exhibition in Lyon.[36]

Panivong Norindr locates the hyphenate "Indo-Chine" between India and China as a new physiognomic political geography of the region.[37] Following Norindr's geographic and political interpretation, Nicola Cooper points out that when Indo-Chine was referred to as the French "Pearl of the Far East," it was also set in opposition to India as the British "Jewel in the Crown."[38] This rhetorical framing points to a form

FIGURE 56. René Têtard, head of the Mission Cinématographique de l'Indochine, with unidentified Indochinese auxiliaries standing beneath a projection booth in an outdoor theater, n.d. Copyright Serge Dubuisson, CAOM.

of feminine and royal adornment that can be admired for its brillance only by being set into place as part of a geographic configuration of empire.

Consisting of present-day Vietnam, Cambodia, and Lao PDR, Indo-Chine did not specifically refer to India per se; the prefix *Indo* may be best understood in relation to proto-Indo-Europeans from the Calcolithic or Copper Age, who were supposedly seminomadic people defined by polytheistic forms of worship, animal husbandry, and a sacral kingship structure of governance. The Copper Age construct was part of a nineteenth-century founding myth of European nationalist superiority that established Africa, Asia, and Oceania as being on a sliding evolutionary scale on which Asia was considered among the most "civilized" areas in the French colonial order. The contiguous Chinese landmass was perhaps a more essential geographic referent for Indo-Chine given that British influence continuously threatened French economic hegemony in the region, as in Siam to the West. In the French imagination China transformed the evolutionary notion of proto-Indo-Europeaness into a French Orientalist fascination and commensurate mistrust of the "Orient."[39]

Indochina was the capstone of both the French colonial educational system and educational cinema. In fact, the extensive resources expended on developing educational institutions in Indochina (totaling close to 15 percent of total French expenditures in Indochina) led Sarraut to consider establishing Saigon as a second metropolitan axis of empire—an idea that was swiftly rebuffed, because it was claimed that it would rob metropolitan France of its spiritual centrality.[40] A two-tiered French and Franco-indigenous educational system was established in which French students were channeled into the French schools through selective entrance exams, while Franco-indigenous schools were geared toward practical and professional training. Educational initiatives and the development of structured educational pathways became important mechanisms of colonial policy used to reorganize Indochina as a unified French dominion. Gail Paradise Kelly's detailed work on French educational policy in interwar Vietnam demonstrates that the substantial resources devoted to education in Indochina were part of a strategy to eliminate indigenous forms of educational training that could contribute to the development of an autonomous political elite.[41] Kelly notes that Vietnamese schoolteachers were among the first to organize and lead the resistance struggle following the first French invasion in 1858. The historical prominence of the schoolteacher in Vietnam represented, as Kelly puts it, "the backbone of a political network that was capable of organizing armies."[42]

Vietnamese resistance leaders associated knowledge about modern scientific techniques with education as the key to regaining national autonomy. In some respects, there is a striking resemblance between the struggle for republican values in France among the ranks of schoolteachers, as opposed to the clerical values associated with the Catholic Church, and the struggle of schoolteachers associated with "modern" Vietnamese education. An early example of "modern" Vietnamese education was the short-lived Dong Kinh Free School in Saigon, which was based neither on Vietnamese educational traditions nor on colonial educational models, but rather integrated the study of French, Vietnamese, and Chinese with that of modern European scientific methods and even developed scholarships for students to study in Japan and China.[43]

Furthermore, there were instances of cooperation between local leaders with the French colonial authorities in the "reform" and co-optation of indigenous educational methods, as was the case in Annam and Tonkin. French educational politics throughout Indochina was chaotic before 1917, and it was only with the series of subsequent educational reforms developed under the tutelage of Sarraut that the Indochinese educational system came to be centralized and standardized under the French colonial administration. As Pierre Brocheux and Daniel Hémery have argued, the imposition of French reforms established education as an emergent site for geographic consolidation, which inadvertently spawned a corresponding Vietnamese nationalist resistance movement opposed to French occupation. Crucially, traditional Chinese characters were translated into the Latinate Quôc ngu initially developed by French missionaries in the seventeenth century. Quôc ngu later served as a vehicular language for Indochina and, in turn, became the first step toward familiarizing Indochinese people with the French language.[44] Quôc ngu became the language of political debate and modern Vietnamese literature during the interwar period. In effect, the Vietnamese independence movement directly countered Sarraut's fraternal policy of "making France known to the colonies, and the colonies to France" with the politics of rupture that refigured education and "making known" as a form of colonial resistance.

French educational films were incorporated into secondary school education throughout Annam (Central Vietnam centered around Hué, also known as Troung Ky) and Cochinchina (the Mekong Delta region around Ho Chi Minh City [Saigon] in the former South Vietnam, also known as Nam Ky). As an official memo from the period reports, the most extensive film archive was held by the Patronage Laïque Cochinchinois, a French lay educational initiative based in Saigon. With thirteen projectors, the organization developed an archive of no fewer than 840 films and presented approximately 5,000 recreational screenings—presumably American westerns and comedies along with some European films—and at least 1,000 filmed educational lessons and hygiene films from 1922 to 1927.[45]

American junk prints made their way into Indochina primarily through China, where close to 75 percent of the films shown during the 1920s were of American origin and were primarily shown in Chinese theaters. Hollywood, or "Film America" as it was frequently referred to during the era, with British participation also financed Chinese motion picture production using Chinese screenplays and actors. The largest production houses in China during the 1920s included the British American Tobacco Company, the Peacock Film Company, and the Commercial Press, which specialized in commercial and travel films.[46] These initiatives led to an early French effort to integrate Vietnamese performers into a film adaptation of the best-known Vietnamese epic, *The Tale of Kieu,* under the title *Kim Van Kieu* (New accents of a heart-rending song, 1924). Though it was originally written in the sixteenth or the early seventeenth century by an author using the pen name Thanh Tam Tai Nhan, Nguyen Du adapted it in its popular epic form in the early nineteenth century. Focusing on two lovers who cannot marry because of a family prohibition, the story became a nationalist allegory that is part of an ongoing troubadour tradition.

The release of this film in 1924 was a heavily publicized event related to French film production in Indochina. *Kim Van Kieu* was the first production effort financed by the independent French production company known as La Société Indochine Films et Cinémas, directed by E. A. Famechon.[47] The film was released with intertitles in Chinese, Quôc ngu, and French to attract audiences throughout Indochina, but also in Tonkin and in the ill-defined region of the border with the Chinese province of Yunnan. According to French Governor General Merlin, the release of *Kim Van Kieu* was part of a broader effort to develop French propaganda, particularly given the hegemony of American films in the region.[48] However, the film was a commercial failure and was most likely produced to drive out competition, using domestic elements in its production in spite of the fact that the film was also an attempt to exclude Vietnamese producers. As Dean Wilson has suggested, the head of Indochine Films, Charles de la Pommeraye, started working in Indochina as a distribution agent for Pathé Frères and served on some of the early censorship boards, thus orienting policy in the direction of his own interests while driving out the competition.[49]

French educational and hygiene films were conceived as a counterweight to the popular cinema in the name of education, drawing on the extensive development of educational film lending libraries at the Musée Pedagogique, the Cinémathèque Nationale du Ministère du Travail et de l'Hygiène (1923),[50] the Cinémathèque du Ministère de l'Agriculture (1923), and the Cinémathèque de la Ville de Paris (1925).[51] The Musée Pédagogique, one of the founding pillars of the Third Republic, was initially established as a lending library that produced and lent magic lantern slides that came to be supplemented by a burgeoning collection of educational films. By 1921, the Musée Pédagogique had already established a catalogue of more than six hundred films, and it became an important source for an emerging educational cinema movement throughout France, known as *le cinéma éducateur*.[52] As Raymond Borde and Charles Perrin have written, this early system of educational film production and distribution in the school system was a social movement that resisted the influence of the church and promoted secular educational values of community, pacifism, and workers' rights.[53]

Regions of Indochina and Algeria became pilot sites for the development and integration of educational cinema seeking to contest the influence of the church while promoting secular educational values. Indochina, in particular, became a testing ground for the educational film movement's broader agenda, which attempted to merge colonization with anticlerical republican values founded on the primacy of the child's mind as a blank slate to be instructed through the dynamism of cinema. The child did not merely represent the French primary or secondary school pupil, but was synonymous with the mind of the colonial subject in the developmental logic of colonial humanitarianism. The mind of the pupil as the fundamental formative entity brought together educational and colonial cinema.

EDUCATIONAL CINEMA AS COLONIAL CINEMA

The language of conquest as a form of instruction was part of a broader strategy attempting to position France at the apex of a hierarchy of mind, knowledge, and civilization. Cochinchina became one of the first testing grounds for educational policy in Indochina, and French educational films were incorporated into the curriculum as early as 1921. The 1917 *Educational Film Report* undertaken by Auguste Bessou documented one of the most significant government-mandated studies on the definition and uses of educational film in the classroom.[54] It established three categories of educational cinema, which included instructional *(instruction)*, educational *(éducatif)*, and scholastic *(scolaire)* films. Whereas instructional film was considered a form of documentary entertainment for the general public and educational film was defined as a more rigorous treatment of any given subject matter, scholastic film was considered analogous to a book illustration; a description presented by the teacher might be followed by footage demonstrating the matter at hand.[55] These categories elucidated potential criteria for their use and distribution and helped establish film production guidelines, but they finally blended into each other as the educational film movement expanded throughout the 1920s.

Just as the colonial enterprise was conceived and defined in part as an expanding system of national education, the founders of the new empire were also the originators of a developing public education system.[56] Jules Ferry, a significant catalyst in the Colonial Lobby (Parti Colonial) and prime minister from 1880 to 1881 and again from 1883 to 1885, was a key figure in the establishment of the Musée Pédagogique and the development of a national public educational system that was later transformed into an audiovisual lending library. The integration of cinema into a nationwide educational curriculum was founded on a belief in the photographic image as a knowledge-laden fragment exceeding the experience of the moment. This perspective led Emile Roux-Parassac, a member of the educational cinema commission, to proclaim that "seeing is almost knowing."[57] However, this position is bound up in a representational fallacy implying the ideological transparency of the image, so *know-how* refers to the visualization of imperatives established in the name of education.

Primary school students were identified as particularly responsive to the cinema, and short projected sequences were used in schools for vocabulary and composition exercises. In an appendix to the *Educational Film Report* on the uses of film in primary schools, Adrien Collette noted that "moving images allow students not only to apply their intellect but to exercise their faculty of observation and distinguish between a number of objects and actions: naming objects, finding their qualities and relationships as well as discovering the verb that represents an action."[58] The role of film was then positioned within the context of a *dictée* exercise of comprehension and repetition that is transformed into a creative act when the students are asked to write their own description in a free and personal manner as presented by the film.

As one of the authors of the report explained, the use of cinema in the classroom

FIGURE 57. "France is our country" is written on the blackboard in a scene from *La France est un empire,* 1939. Copyright Collection des Archives du Film et du Dépôt Légal du Centre National de la Cinématographie.

can be particularly effective in educating children because "the imagination and attention of the child are best guided by a form of teaching that uses visual aids rather than simply the voice of the instructor. In combination with the spoken word, course material illustrated by the cinema can bewitch and enlighten with its dazzling light."[59] The *Educational Film Report* promoted the use of cinema in educational settings as an auxiliary to the teacher—that is, as a means of crystallizing and projecting his or her word, not simply as a technological replacement for the teacher. For this reason, the capacities to enlarge the still image and to slow down, arrest, and speed up movement were essential qualities of this new instrument of vision and pedagogy.

The long-standing focus on the effects of the moving image was probed, especially in relation to child developmental psychology. Children between the ages of eleven and fourteen, still under the protection of the state, were to serve as the primary subjects in the formation of this educational initiative. Just as the beginning of a national public education system can be linked to the emergence of the Colonial Lobby and Jules Ferry, sustained efforts by colonial propagandists to incorporate natural history, political science, biology, geography, and industrial techniques into the educational curriculum defined the basis of what were known as the "colonial sciences."

A detailed program of action, established at a national meeting on colonial promotional techniques during the 1931 Colonial Exhibition, sought to influence public opinion in order to create *une mentalité coloniale.* Two overlapping forms of action were proposed, one targeted at adults and another at childen; the latter was designed to take effect over the longer term. Accordingly, this second form of colonial propaganda, *propagande scolaire,* "should inspire children to understand our unflagging efforts, in spite of the innumerable obstacles before us, and evoke a belief and admiration of the civilizing role that France has so brilliantly fulfilled."[60] Some of these efforts would include field trips, as well as pedagogically oriented public events and festivals in which cinema played an instrumental role.

Colonial documentary shorts were featured at small-scale colonial exhibitions and fairgrounds in France and Belgium prior to World War I. One of these popular film exhibits was sponsored by a well-known regional spirits firm, Amer Picon, and was featured at the French West African Pavilion as part of the 1906 Colonial Exhibition in Marseilles.[61] The exhibitions attempted to create an atmosphere of wonder, with the majority of the attractions geared specifically toward children. In addition to colonial-themed festivals and events, such as La Semaine Coloniale, the *Petit Journal* newspaper inaugurated a free film series in 1923 to promote the colonial idea to young adults.

Encouragement from educational officials of the period supported a loosely defined group of colonial educational films used in public school curricula.[62] The slogan "Educate our young people, win over the older ones, and lead them on the path to knowledge of our colonial domain" echoed Albert Sarraut's notion of "making the colonies known to France."[63] The use of documentary cinema to influence a young public by equating the moving image with the real was further reinforced through its adoption in the public schools, where many of the films were used in conjunction with courses focused on geography, industrial techniques, archeology, architecture, and social hygiene along with native techniques of preindustrial production and religious rituals.

It was within the context of educational priorities that Sarraut launched the Agences Économiques initiative parallel to the media production and library lending structure of the Musée Pedagogique. Specifically, the films held at the economic affairs office for Indochina were often lent to teachers for their regular classes and for Thursday and Sunday matinees. The collection provided numerous views of Indochina, mirroring and extending the still images appearing in colonial picture postcards and projected in magic lantern slides.[64] These views would then be inserted into various metropolitan contexts, such as secondary school geography lessons, anthropological conferences, architectural and archaeological study groups, and more generalized industrial and cultural exhibitions.

Sarraut was keenly aware of cinema's utility as an instrument for revitalizing and elaborating a national vision. His policy statements concerning the reorientation of promotional efforts after World War I articulated a program in which the image was to be used as an influential tool to educate metropolitan adults and children as to their responsibility toward the French colonial empire:

> It is absolutely indispensable that a methodical, continuous and earnest propaganda through the word and image, the press, public conferences, film screenings and exhibitions . . . be used to activate both children and adults alike. We should sharpen and expand the brief coverage on the history and diversity of our imperial domain in our primary and secondary schools. A more vital form of instruction should be deployed, both more vivid and practical: a form of instruction which projects still and moving imagery that amuses and informs our young citizens who might be unaware of their colonial dominion.[65]

Sarraut's understanding of film as a compelling form of public instruction complemented educational efforts seeking to integrate film into primary and secondary school education. The use of film thus became a means of validating a field of action through the development of a system of representation, which not only identified empire as a world to be remade, but fixed it as a program of action for educated metropolitan citizens. It was in this sense that economic development could be propelled under the adage "Colonialism, the work of human solidarity"—that is, a colonial humanism proclaiming the right of all human beings to a better life by using the world's abundant material resources in combination with a system of moral values serving the needs of all. In Sarraut's words, "The fruits of this double abundance (material and moral) can only be achieved through a forthright solidarity among races, where natural resources can be exchanged and maximized by the creative faculties of innovation."[66] This exchange of know-how for raw materials represented the responsibility of France to uphold the values of universalism.

From 1924 to 1927, an extensive archive of documentary film footage from Indochina was made available in France. During this period, the Agences Économiques lent out films on 1,500 separate occasions.[67] By 1925, 220 short films (fifteen to thirty minutes in length) and 500 slides were already in circulation.[68] According to correspondence from the period, the most popular subjects were the application of modern industrial techniques and tourist views, such as the ruins of Angkor Wat. By 1924, the Mission Cinématographique de l'Indochine had established an early model for official film production units and a distribution network between France and the colonies. Indochine Films took over the documentary film production effort from the Mission Cinématographique de l'Indochine in 1924, setting up offices in Hanoi and Saigon, establishing a five-year contract with the French administration to produce a minimum of 2,700 meters (8,860 feet) of film per year.[69] This effort resulted in a critical mass of circulating films about Indochina in France, with on the order of 152 different films in distribution through the Paris-based Indochinese economic affairs office by 1927.[70] In addition to producing photographic and documentary footage, Indochine

Films was also charged with showing French propaganda films in towns and villages throughout Indochina under orders from the French administration as agents of French colonial policy.

The Agences Économiques served as public relations offices for the French colonies in Paris, later contracting production houses such as Pathé and Gaumont to produce footage for their various popularization efforts. Pathé even produced a monthly magazine, *Pathé mensuel,* promoting its film production services in North Africa for both state and commercial interests. The first issue appeared in 1920 and promised "a convenient service addressing the needs of an industrial clientele established in North Africa."[71] The paradigmatic quality of the imagery realized through this system of contractual film production becomes clear through the continual reappearance of the same footage with reworked intertitles and sequencing arrangements. The amount of footage required, measured in meters, determined the cost for commissioning industrial and educational films, with the subject matter determined by an already established repertoire of visual imagery and pedagogical imperatives.

PROMOTIONAL TECHNIQUES AND VEHICLES

Like the increasingly codified nature of colonial views, the colonial exhibitions were tied to the notion of the sample, such as the photographic reproduction, the tactile exhibit, the live spectacle, and the mouth-sized taste. As an influential guide to modern advertising techniques put it, "The sample is a unit or fragment of merchandise permitting an identification of the object in question, allowing the consumer to make judgments for a future purchase."[72] As the guarantor of product quality, the metonymic sample identifies the whole and provides the foundation for a future relationship with the prospective client. Although distribution of the sample was a dominant technique for product identification at the commercial fair or exhibition (which also made ample use of the documentary short), one of the emerging foundations for advertising culture became the use of indirect methods of promotion, transforming the role of the salesmen.[73]

Indirect advertisements encapsulating wish fulfillments were also used to promote values of education and public health.[74] State-sanctioned initiatives and an indirect advertising culture for industry were often mutually reinforcing. Public health initiatives were crucial opportunities for advertisers, who could capitalize on fears of the microbe through hygienic and nutritional antidotes. In fact, more than one highly successful advertising campaign, such as those for Banania, focused on developing a line of nutritional food products that featured the language of *l'aliment pur,* accenting their nutritional or health value.[75]

The crossover between state-sponsored and private sector initiatives was often indistinguishable in the industrial development of the colonies. As Jules Ferry once claimed in a well-known speech concerning colonial initiatives, "Colonial policy is the daughter of industrial prescription."[76] Another prime example was the privately financed Croisière Noire expedition, for which the president of the republic, Gaston

Doumergue, requested that the itinerary be altered so that the expedition would finish in Madagascar, linking the French colonies by means of the automobile. Indeed, an abundance of films demonstrated the building of railroads in Indochina, the use of the airplane linking the colonies to France in record-breaking time, and the ease of the automobile as a vehicle of encounter. The cinema functioned crucially as the preferred publicity vehicle, suggesting possible wish fulfillments associated with the colonies.

Mobile commercial exhibitions were often held in vehicles of transit themselves and used to showcase the promise of spatial and temporal deliverance. One such exhibition, on a luxurious ocean-going vessel, *La Belle France,* was equipped with a screening room as well as numerous stands promoting French industry, publications, luxury items, wine, liqueur, music, and French cuisine while en route to major port cities around the world.[77] A genre of traveling train exhibitions, which came to be known as Trains-Expositions Coloniales, were used with the explicit purpose of promoting the colonies. These exhibits were usually held in railroad stations and consisted of a dozen or so train cars opening into one another. Each colony would be granted one or two of these railway cars in accordance with its budget and economic significance, following the example of an effective Canadian commercial venture that sought to publicize Canadian products throughout France in the aftermath of World War I.

According to a report presented at the 1931 Conference for Colonial Promotion and Action, these colonial train exhibitions met with limited success due to a host of logistical problems, but they led to a variation based on the train car as an attraction.[78] This form of promotion used railway cars that could be lifted off the tracks, adapted with tires, and tugged by tractor into any given town center. This followed the tradition of the Soviet agitprop trains used in early Bolshevik newsreel distribution, most often associated with Dziga Vertov's early filmmaking endeavors. However, still more effective were the pickup trucks armed with generators that projected amplified recorded spectacles, echoing the mobile cinema campaigns used to recruit troops and promote public hygiene. Music and sounds from the colonies, as well as speeches and a cinema of attractions, were found to be the most popular in the French countryside in the tradition of the traveling sideshow and festival culture.

"INFILTRATE THE CROWD WITH AN IDEA!"

Obtaining adequate government subsidies for colonial promotional campaigns became an increasingly contentious issue with the creation of numerous colonial committees throughout France. These interwar *comités coloniaux* were not usually centered around promoting one colony in particular, as had their prewar predecessors, but rather were focused on regional commercial and industrial needs. Just as the colonies were perceived as a means of national restoration following the economic crisis of 1929, these committees took on an increasingly active role.

The close association between French economic development and colonial expansion also marked an evolving consolidation of commercial and political promotional goals. Marius Ary-Leblond, a novelist and former colonial administrator who became the first director of the Musée Colonial, even called for the privatization of colonial promotional efforts on the model of a successful publicity campaign that was launched for an industrial firm in Rouen.[79] Ary-Leblond's approach was symptomatic of a perceived need to renew a conception of colonial promotional activities beyond public instruction and turn it into a more active form of conversion—that is, to mobilize the seemingly complacent and disinterested metropolitan masses. The lack of general interest in the colonies, addressed by public and private initiatives from 1928 to 1932, paralleled the declining influence of the Catholic Church. Lay republican ideology transformed religious imperatives into humanitarian values associating colonial service with a *solidariste* platform, submerging religious values and the rhetoric of faith into a nationalist credo, as in the Union Coloniale slogan "Buying colonial is buying French," thus interpellating a patriotic collective subject.

A 1932 edited volume incorporating articles by media specialists from the Catholic Church, titled *Comment propager nos idées* (How to propagate our ideas), opens with the following quotation: "For the sake of making the Truth clearly known, there is no alternative but to make it known [by any means necessary]."[80] As in the case of the rhetorical principle of "making known" that guided the organization of the Agences Économiques, in this case the truth was tied to seizing public opinion with techniques of modern advertising. Following a well-known adage of American advertising culture, "Infiltrate the crowd with an idea," the authors cited commercial advertising techniques as the new instruments for spreading the word of God.[81] Modern advertising techniques were adapted by Canon Joseph Reymond, who established a popular service known as the Cinema Mass that drew crowds to the massive Greek temple–like La Madeleine Church in Paris throughout the early 1920s.[82]

Renewed efforts to shape the image of the Catholic Church in relation to contemporary techniques of communication converged with the advertising techniques used to inspire colonial consciousness in metropolitan France. Turn-of-the-century notions of crowd psychology popularized by Gustave Le Bon and Gabriel Tarde as well as group psychology methods were promoted as effective means of seizing public opinion. Gérin and Espinadel's widely influential 1927 book *La Publicité suggestive* (The advertising of suggestion) was cited as an essential source on which to model publicity campaigns for the Catholic Church. Following Gérin and Espinadel's model for the circulation and propagation of a commodity, Canon Reymond articulated a notion of screen practice for the church that associated the effectiveness of a film with the passivity of the spectator, which, in turn, would enhance reception and the potential for internalization.[83]

The method of presentation was conceived within the terms of an operational effect. Gabriel Tarde's work on crowd psychology, *L'Opinion et la foule* (Opinion and the crowd), tied the question of social knowledge to a series of imitative acts that followed a geometric pattern of extension through a chain of intermediaries.[84] Tarde's theory of imitation was tied to the universalizing acts of repetition, opposition, and adaptation, in accordance with an evolutionary model in natural history in which each newly formed variation of animal or plant life is generated according to a geometric progression. A notion of imitative contagion was then grounded in the same principle as that of an army of ants at work, where individual initiative is followed by imitation.[85] Gérin and Espinadel's emphasis on processes of affirmation, intensity, and repetition for an advertising campaign followed Tarde's microsociological imitative principles of cognition inspired by contagious acts of repetition, opposition, and adaptation.

Tarde's conception of imitation also carried over into a theory of innovation in which an invention inaugurates a new series of imitations, such as the invention of gunpowder, the windmill, or the Morse telegraph. While the invention marks a vitalist act of creation for Tarde, the crowd is an undifferentiated mass existing at the intersection of rhythms, undulations, and vibrations of an abundant flow. It is in this sense that Tarde wrote, "The state of the social, like a hypnotic state, is only that of a dream, a dream of ultimatums, a dream of action. Hypnotic suggestion encouraging spontaneous belief—that is the illusion of the sleep-walker as well as socialized man."[86] Perhaps this is one of the clearest statements of how a social imaginary might be constituted and sustained through a series of hypnotic, imitative flows. The validity of a given public address is thus linked to the speed at which it is deployed in such a way that immediacy establishes a discernible register of public perception. The metaphor of hypnosis and the dream state for public opinion, as well as for socialized man, not only resonates with parallel developments in social psychology but is also tied to a hypnotic register of visual perception in which the eye is capable of being seduced and tricked.

The idea of public opinion as a flow of energy that tends to degrade the individual has also been developed in physiological terms. In his 1891 treatise on collective psychology, *La Folla delinquente* (The crowd as criminal), Scipio Sighele asked how emotions are communicated through a mass of individuals.[87] For Sighele, the nervous system, rather than the rationalizing limits of the mind, is keenly sensitized to the staging of an emotional agitation. That is, the representation of an emotional state provokes its repetition among those who witness it. Physical expression acts as a hypnotic form of suggestion, which led to Sighele's theory of imitative-suggestion, through which he sought to explain the criminality of the crowd as contagion and epidemic. Gustave Le Bon's 1895 *La Psychologie des foules (The Crowd: A Study of the Popular Mind)* rejected Sighele's conclusions while incorporating his insights into a critique of the popular mind. Like his predecessors, Le Bon reaffirmed the mental unity of the crowd and identified this social agglomeration with evolutionary regression. For Le Bon, "impulsiveness, irritability, the inability to think rationally, the incapacity to judge or think critically, as well as exaggerated expressions of sentimentality are specific to crowds who can be likened to inferior evolutionary forms, such as the child and the savage."[88]

PICTURE PALACES AND A CINEMA OF THE INSTINCTS

The crowd figured as a flow without content, an indiscernible amalgam, volatile yet malleable. The profoundly negative charge of the public sphere in a series of works about crowd psychology echoes the characterization of native subjects as undifferentiated and barely inserted into a logic of colonial becoming. Guided by the science of anthropometrics and by long experience in maintaining an indigenous soldiering force, the fear of the crowd in the colonies was not necessarily associated with indigenous resistance movements per se (as was the case in Madagascar and Morocco), but rather was tied to new forms of public assembly ushered in by colonization. In this sense, the motion picture theater, known as the picture palace, functioned as a site of public association for the French settler population and the local middle-class urban populations with a film program that was considered a potential threat to colonial authority.

By 1926 there were 252 movie theaters throughout the French colonies, the large majority in Algeria (118), Morocco (34), and Indochina (29).[89] The continued expansion of picture palaces as well as second-run and third-run theaters throughout the colonies by the early 1930s led to rising fears that a cinema portraying lawbreakers and the underworld might damage the prestige of Europeans in the colonies.[90] The presentation of American westerns and an abundance of "third-rate melodramas" depicting the seamier side of life among the colonizers, where criminality, prostitution, and vice were rampant, were thought to have the power to erode the moral force of European civilization. As Aimé-François Legendre, a Sinologist charged with conducting numerous geological surveys throughout Asia, wrote:

> The cinema has become the master of the masses through . . . the power of its images, its realism, its appeal to the emotions, to all internal vibrations. Its control over the indigenous masses, dominating their child-like spirit, has been accomplished with great immediacy and totality. The cinema is all-pervasive, and its reach extends from the largest to the smallest village, even drawing the peasant from the distant rice paddy fields.[91]

In Legendre's extended discussion of cinema and the prestige of the white race in Asia, he associated the cinema with a great humanizing potential for Asians and yet decried the unscrupulous work of businessmen, especially the Americans who have infiltrated the cinema with values that undermined the civilizing forces of empire. Interestingly, the so-called pernicious influence of this predominantly American cinema was tied to the representation in fiction films of vagabonds, bandits, and prostitutes—the very same social actors who were associated with criminality in the crowd. While adventure films and melodramas featuring brigandage, detective stories, serials, and Charlie Chaplin comedies were exceedingly popular forms of international entertainment, communicating across linguistic and cultural boundaries, Hollywood productions were accused of pandering to base instincts and encouraging seditious conduct.

By 1921, French film censorship boards had been established in Hanoi and Saigon as a response to the American and British films that dominated the region. The question that surfaced once censorship restrictions were put in place was whether the presence of unsavory French characters with a less than upstanding moral compass would destabilize French colonial authority. Film censorship restrictions were first established in Tunisia and Morroco in 1916, prior to the establishment of the first censorship boards in France in 1919, under the Ministry of Education.[92]

Legendre considered the American films not indecent but rather inappropriate for indigenous spectators, who he claimed were incapable of seeing beyond the veracity of the photographic reproduction into the narrative at hand. As he wrote, "They understand the brutal realism of the images that pass before them due to their well-developed visual memory, but usually miss the moral lesson. A theatrical piece treating the same narrative does not produce the same consequences but the image creates a permanent impression in his mind forever."[93] Legendre imagined a cinema of the instincts that would indelibly mark the memory of the colonial subject, the way a child's memory is marked at a formative stage of maturity. Legendre's cinema of the instincts would immediately penetrate the mind of the colonial subject, in opposition to the educational but libidinally vacant cinema of instruction.

Just as educational cinema was aimed at children, Legendre's depiction of the Asian masses as easily influenced by the vice and crime depicted in the cinema drew, in fact, on an abundant literature concerning child criminality and the cinema. The long-standing trope of cinema as the corrupter of youth, so dear to religious and political figures, became an international issue, spawning one of the first international film distribution surveys concerning censorship restrictions worldwide.[94] Undertaken in 1928, this survey was conducted through the newly founded, Italian-based International Institute for Cinematographic Education under the auspicies of the League of Nations, and it was related to an already established area of international cooperation: child welfare.[95] Previously, a detailed report presented to the League of Nations Child Welfare Committee by Dr. F. Humbert, titled "The Effect of the Cinematograph on the Moral and Mental Well-Being of Children," had correlated a mass of statistical data in order to determine the relationship between violent scenes in films and child criminality.[96] Paralleling Legendre's statements concerning the mind of the native subject, Dr. Humbert, citing the conclusions of the Berlin psychologist Felix Lampe, wrote, "The film attracts the child because animated reproduction corresponds to his mode of thought, which responds to all that is in movement and is ignorant of the process of abstract logic. Children think by associating ideas that are principally visual."[97]

Accordingly, Legendre described the photographic reproduction as an unmediated sense impression that resolutely sealed the colonial subject's opinion of the white race because he was unable to distinguish the rule from the exception, precisely like a child. Legendre's tract concerning the cinema in the Asian imagination invoked child criminality while also reflecting a self-referential immediacy. The fear of the European few for the many natives, by whom they were outnumbered by more than a thousand to one, was an unstable state of affairs easily upset by the perceived sensationalism and immediacy of the cinema, which was thought to exacerbate the unreasoned, "feminine" hysteria of the crowd.[98]

Legendre's opposition between the dangerously popular American cinema and the less than popular educational cinema was inspired by a variant of crowd psychology that associated the menacing masses with the spread in Asia of communism, whose growth within the turbulent political power vacuum left in China was imagined as an emanating contagion that would potentially engulf French Indochina. The bordering regions of French Indochina, especially the poor and overpopulated valley regions of Yunnan province, such as Kouang-tong and Kouang-si (which had once been reservoirs of manpower for the French military during World War I), were considered sites primed for potential Bolshevik infiltration.[99]

In effect, in the generalized discussions of American commercial cinema it became the symbol of emergent economic forces threatening to undermine empire through a Wilsonian credo of "self-determination" for all peoples.[100] In fact, Legendre claimed that the American model of economic liberalization would encourage the spread of permanent developmental inequality, to which the inevitable response would be Soviet-inspired Bolshevik ideology.[101] The threat of Americanization, as associated with the cinema, was perceived to dilute and, even more alarmingly, reverse the "progress" of colonization. Interestingly, the fear that communist propaganda was a legitimate threat to colonial authority was founded on a parallel interdependency between propaganda and education. In this view, the political utility of crowd psychology became a powerful means of distinguishing between, on the one hand, the excesses of the crowd as associated with regression into a "savage" and "childlike" "primitive communism" and, on the other, an affirmative transformation of the masses into an individuated realm of disciplined segmentation.

The intimacy of American cinema was thought to translate into a negative stereotyping of the whole "white" race in a mirror image of racial classification. Psychic underdevelopment, as associated with the hypnotic forces of the cinema, was conceived as an active agent in crowd psychology. From the Tardian flows of public opinion to infiltrating the crowd with an idea, the domination of American films in the picture palaces throughout the French colonies gave rise to fears of humiliation before the colonized. The "caricaturelike" American cinema, with its scenes of betrayal, criminality, and sexuality as well as the defilement of religious values and symbols, was thus identified as the perpetrator of political instability.[102]

IMITATIVE CONTAGION

The question of how to define French colonial cinema was addressed in a series of debates in the Marseilles-based film weekly *Cinéma et spectacles* from 1928 to 1929.[103] With the number of potential colonial spectators exceeding that of the American population at the time, more than 100 million, the journalist Raymond Huguenard called for the creation of a colonial cinema as a means of forming and reeducating the colonial masses.[104] This debate occurred within the broader context of the 1928 Herriot Decree, which attempted to establish a newly expanded censorship policy that tied foreign imports to French exports in order to establish a broader market for French films abroad.[105] A subsequent editorial called for the development of cinema throughout North Africa, claiming that this part of empire was sufficiently "civilized" that the production and distribution of French cinema merely needed to be "fertilized."[106] Numerous agricultural and irrigation development schemes as well as economic potential invited the comparison of North Africa to California. In terms of geographic and climactic variables, North Africa was imagined as a potential rival to Hollywood, endowed with superior natural resources.[107] The burgeoning success of the Foreign Legion film, derived in part from the American western, as well as the abundance of exotic exteriors, excellent available lighting conditions, and a low-cost international cadre of film professionals, created a glint of hope for the French film industry, which was undergoing a period of internationalist transformation.[108]

Finally, in the last of this series of articles in *Cinéma et spectacles,* G. Moulan asks the question: "What sort of cinema can we offer to spectators abroad? A group whom we have every interest in 'curing'—for whom we must establish standards of quality and pass on an enlightened vision of our civilization."[109] Whereas Huguenard argued for increasing the production of documentary and educational films for the colonies, Moulan called for government subsidies to finance the exportation of the less commercialized "artistic" French feature films in the colonies.

American adventure films such as *The Mark of Zorro* (dir. Fred Niblo, 1925), starring Douglas Fairbanks, were said to "accentuate malicious tendencies" by French colonial censorship boards in Indochina and were thus censored. The American adaptation of *Arsène Lupin* (dir. Jack Conway, 1932), starring John and Lionel Barrymore, was also banned in Indochina because it portrayed scenes of theft in a positive light and presented French policemen in an uncomplimentary light.[110] The debates about inappropriate content for films in Indochina, for example, followed the example of censorship boards in the United States, which also played a powerful role in establishing tariff restrictions for foreign products.[111] Father Louis Jalabert, an outspoken advocate for a return to clerically inspired social values, protested against a number of the American and French "adventure" films, many of which were adapted from colonial novels and filmed in the colonies, such as René Le Somptier's *La Sultane de l'amour* (1919) and Jacques Feyder's *L'Atlantide* (1921). These French films were thought to encourage criminal tendencies even in France itself.

The unrelenting criticism of a dominant American cinema that might unhinge the sluice gates of colonial hierarchies emerged from a fear of instinctual individualism. Although this public discourse might have been suggestive of public fears, economic policy was another matter. As François Chevaldonné suggests, it was precisely the Hollywood model of production to which a large number of French film companies with production facilities in North Africa aspired.[112] Numerous international coproductions as well as the circulation of Hollywood financial credit in Casablanca (derived in part from the distribution of American films) were available for on-location shooting as well as full-blown, on-site productions. Multilingual Foreign Legion films, such as Rex Ingram's *L'Arabe* (1924) and *Le Jardin de Allah* (1927), used Western genre-specific conventions with motifs adapted from colonial novels.[113] Exotic exteriors, sexual innuendo, and native male bandits, which were so pronounced in screenplays filmed in North Africa, led the film critic Paul Saffar, based in Algiers, to claim that "the unreality in so many of these films reveals an excess of zeal on behalf of the filmmakers. By seeking to accentuate the natural wonder of this region with artificiality, the films are most often laced with a superficiality that contradicts the intended effect."[114]

This examination of French educational film, its presentation, and its transformation as a result of competition with American films, underscores the role of cinema in the colonies and of colonial cinema in France. Sarraut's dictum of making the colonies known to France and France known to the colonies ultimately defines French colonial documentary as part of a humanitarian educational enterprise that reveals a logic of French national consolidation. The opposition between educational and popular cinema in Indochina fueled contrasting visions of cultural modernity ultimately culminating in a revolutionary response. French educational initiatives were part of an anti-Catholic, colonial ethic that positioned cinema as an orienting kaleidescope for remaking the French geographic body from within and without. Like the magical glass in Le Somptier's *La Sultane de l'amour*, educational cinema was thought to promise simultaneity and reproduction of the real, but was considered potentially seditious when popular films led toward the anarchy of imitative contagion and militated against the formation of a unified French national consciousness. Imitative contagion as fear of the crowd finally established cinematic education as a promotional strategy in the service of geopolitical colonial containment.

6. HUMANITARIAN VISIONS AND COLONIAL IMPERATIVES

FÉLIX-LOUIS REGNAULT, ALBERT KAHN, AND HENRI BERGSON AS SEMIOPHORE-MEN

In the cause of promoting an international humanitarian image of France, interrelated educational film and photographic archives provided a realist foundation for evolutionary theories of difference. The pairing of hygienic reform and geographic consciousness recast the colonial subject as an avatar of French national consciousness. The new technologies of audiovision produced images that functioned as "material ideograms," providing the basis for French colonial interventionism.[1] A series of chronophotographs depicting an unnamed Senegalese Wolof woman potter illustrates the relationship between the colonial evolutionary paradigm and a civilizational hierarchy of humankind.[2]

FROM THE ETHNOGRAPHIC VILLAGE
TO THE EVOLUTIONARY MOVING IMAGE ARCHIVE

Fatimah Tobing Rony describes Félix-Louis Regnault's chronophotographic series of the Wolof potter as the spectacle of "language through gestures," reducing the Wolof woman's consciousness to the micromotions of toolmaking in a Neolithic order of human history.[3] The Wolof potter's performance was initially part of an open-air Senegalese village staged during the 1895 ethnographic exhibition held in the same mall-like setting as the 1889 Universal Exhibition, which had featured the first reconstructed Senegalese village in Paris as part of an emerging "exhibitionary complex."[4] The use of live ethnographic exhibitions initially developed following the Franco-Prussian War, as William Schneider explains, in order to increase attendance at the Jardin d'Acclimatation after the zoo was nearly destroyed during the German occupation. Albert Geoffroy

Saint-Hilaire, the director of the Jardin d'Acclimatation and grandson of the natural-ist Etienne, was in search of a new kind of spectacle to attract larger crowds. In 1877, exotic animals from the Horn of Africa were accompanied by fourteen Africans, whose inclusion in the exhibition was not considered significant by the organizers until their presence attracted a startling number of visitors.[5]

After this first group of East Africans (known as Nubians) were recognized as a popular·attraction for which one could charge admission, an assortment of "pure racial types" soon followed. These included Inuits from Northern Canada, Gauchos (cowboys) and Fuegians (popularized as "naked sea hunters" in the 1871 publication of Charles Darwin's *Descent of Man*) from Argentina, Kalina and Araucan Indians from (French) Guyana, Kalmyks from Mongolia, Native Americans as part of Buffalo Bill's Wild West Show, Dahomeans from Benin, Ashantis from Ghana, and Sri Lankans. Staged performances such as the Ashanti War Dance were part of the beguiling exotic supplement to the legacy of the eighteenth-century theatrical sideshow.

A committee from the Parisian Anthropological Society (Société d'Anthropolo-gie de Paris) was established to visit most of the exhibitions. This committee took the customary head form and body measurements, later publishing them as part of a fetishistic collection of statistical indexes of racial types in their scholarly journal.[6] The public appeal of such exhibitions and the notion of traveling exhibits that included "natives" on tour booked by European promoters provoked disdain within the French scientific community because it blurred distinctions between scientific inquiry and the twinning of the primitive with the popular. The physical anthropologists who domi-nated the Parisian Anthropological Society, however, hardly considered the theatrical import of such exhibitions because they saw the natives on display as representative eth-nic subjects to be incorporated into an anthropometric atlas of the world's populations.

This volumetric census of human types zeroing in on head form was so influen-tial during the last third of the nineteenth century that twenty-five million Europeans were subjected to anthropometric measurements.[7] Members of the Parisian Anthro-pological Society were on hand to conduct measurements for all of the human ethno-graphic displays presented to the Parisian public, and Regnault used Etienne-Jules Marey's equipment and studiolike laboratory to make chronophotographic images as a new type of measurement of three culturally specific scenes of the natives' imagined everyday life. Joseph Deniker, a fellow member of the society whose major work *Les Races et peuples de la terre* (*The Races of Man*, 1900) became an important synthesis of the polygenist perspective, had earlier collected a series of cranial and facial measure-ments from 145 non-Europeans with Louis Laloy, focusing on physical differences among West African subjects who had appeared at the 1889 Universal Exhibition.[8]

In an article documenting the same 1889 exhibition, anthropologist Ernest-Théodore Hamy wrote that the reconstructed Senegalese village was, "without exag-geration, the most curious of attractions."[9] Hamy established a historical context for the reenactment by referring to the eighteenth-century writings of Jean-François de Bourgoing, a French ambassador to Spain, who had proposed an exhibition outside the Prado Museum in Madrid that would showcase the everyday activities of all the exotic peoples who lived under Iberian rule. De Bourgoing imagined an exhibition of living communities as a guided tour, or "cicerone of voyagers" as he wrote, in which "the objects of curiosity act for themselves."[10]

Regnault's series of the Wolof potter fashioning a ceramic bowl was one of three chronophotographic views that he recorded in Marey's laboratory. He and his assistant, Charles Comte, recorded a scene of Muslim men bowing in prayer and a Wolof woman carrying an infant on her back. The Wolof woman fashioning a bowl without a potter's wheel remains the best-known image because it bridges the polygenist anthropological discourse of evolutionary measurement as a form of racialized statistical mapping with an ethnographic descriptive approach to cultural difference. Regnault's description of the Wolof potter at the 1895 Parisian ethnographic exhibition linked her gestures to a mechanistic determinism rooted in an archaeological history of unfired pottery and the origin of the potter's wheel.[11] Notably, the absence of the wheel and the animation of the female Wolof potter's movements as authentic gestures were attempts to reconstruct the living presence of humanity from the postglacial Neolithic age.

Jean Rouch, the ethnographic filmmaker and founder of the Ethnographic Film Committee at the Musée de l'Homme, cited Regnault's chronophotographic series depicting the Wolof potter as the beginning of French ethnographic cinema.[12] Although Rouch was aware that the original ethnographic spectacle was staged—and then restaged at Marey's laboratory—he was referring to Regnault as an institutional figure in the history of French anthropology. The chronophotographs thus functioned as meaningful

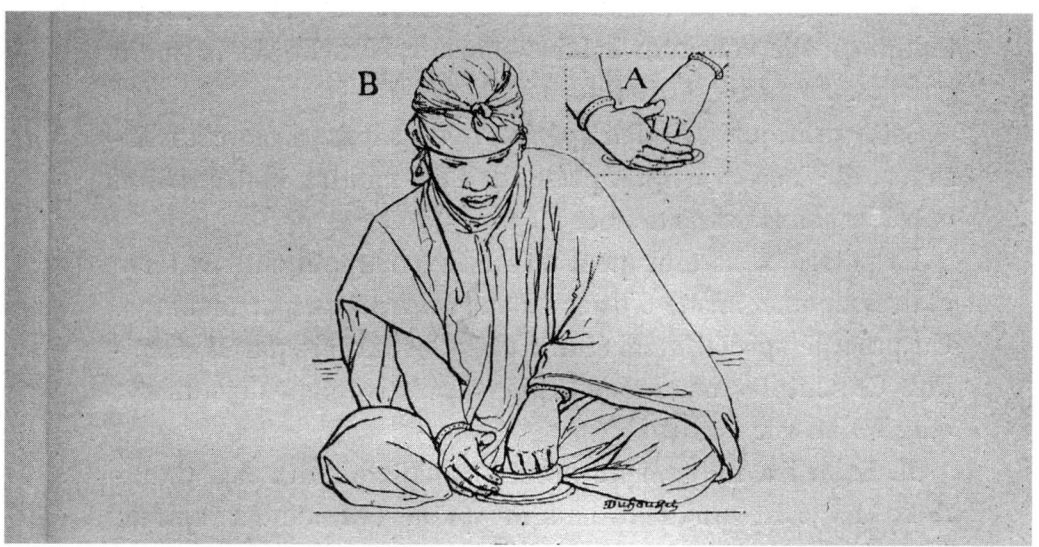

FIGURE 58. Female Wolof potter fashioning a bowl without a potter's wheel in Félix-Louis Regnault and Dominique Lajard, "Potterie crue et l'origine du tour," *Bulletins et mémoires de la Société de l'Anthropologie de Paris* (December 19, 1895).

archival statements in the revival of ethnographic approaches to the study of human-kind focused on the dynamism of human activity that deemphasized, but did not refute, the polygenist paradigm. The scene of the Wolof potter was based on the fallacy of authenticity, in which the ethnographic exhibition presented the colonial "other" in a space of temporal dislocation, which Johannes Fabian has described as being outside of time and history.[13] The disappearance of potterymaking unassisted by a potter's wheel was metonymically linked to its performance as a living cultural technique that could be preserved as a moving image.

As a point of origin of ethnographic cinema, Regnault's chronophotographic series leads to a broader analysis of the colonial documentary film archive as a time-based atlas of humanity. Throughout this work I have argued that a series of interlocking hygienic, educational, industrial, and travel film archives created a context for social myths of national belonging as the bulwark for the French colonial enterprise itself. In this chapter, however, I address how early documentary imagery was part of a reformist ethnographic orientation that was transformed into international colonial humanitarianism, as in the work of Albert Kahn's Archives de la Planète (Archive of the Planet, 1910–31) and the internationalist educational agenda of the League of Nations during the interwar period.

The interconnected nature of these archives and their shifting contextual relationships was finally grounded in an analysis that positioned the functionality of the fragmentary view as the basis for a realist cinematic montage of the colonies. The cinematograph, as a recording and projection apparatus, also served as a spiritually inflected platform for Henri Bergson's notion of mind as a function of time and memory. Following Bergson, duration was positioned as a vitalist category of human possibility that was set in opposition to a mechanistic approach to difference. To underscore this opposition, I compare the static nature of the Hottentot Venus as the sum of measurable body parts to the possibility for dynamic gestural movements enacted by Regnault's unnamed female Wolof potter.

THE EMERGENCE OF FILM IN THE ANTHROPOLOGICAL COLLECTION

The story of Sarah Baartman, otherwise known as the Hottentot Venus, is one of the most powerful examples of how the display of human difference was reduced to a collection of body fragments initially held by the Muséum National d'Histoire Naturelle (hereafter referred to simply as the Muséum), the foundational predecessor to the Musée de l'Homme.[14] Brought to Europe from the eastern cape of South Africa by Hendrick Cezar (the brother of Baartman's employer), she was featured as a widely popular sideshow attraction because of the shape of her protruding buttocks, produced by a condition known as steatopygia. Baartman's exhibition throughout Europe intersected with the prehistory of recorded media entertainment as a theatrical sideshow revealing the forbidden, through which she was presented as a zoomorphic spectacle. Crucially, however, upon her death from an inflammatory ailment in 1815, Baartman's body became the subject of an immensely popular autopsy report by the zoologist Henri de Blainville, and a later one by the French naturalist Georges Cuvier, which was reprinted at least twice during the 1820s.[15] Of greater interest to these natural scientists than the puzzle of Baartman's steatopygia were her genitalia, which had always been covered during her exhibition.

The autopsy report confirmed the nature of her steatopygia as the accumulation of fatty tissue, but Cuvier went on to uncover the presence of a genital flap, known as a *sinus pudoris* or *tablier,* which was taken as proof of a biological determinism, placing the Hottentot Venus on the lowest rung of the human evolutionary scale, more closely associated with the lower primates. The search for signs of anatomical difference was part of an evolving notion of racial hierarchy that sought to classify and "archivize" humans as geographically specific material artifacts. As Stephen Jay Gould explains, Cuvier dissected Sarah Baartman's genitalia so artfully that they remained intact, floating in a formaldehyde-filled bell jar above Paul Broca's leaking brain in the

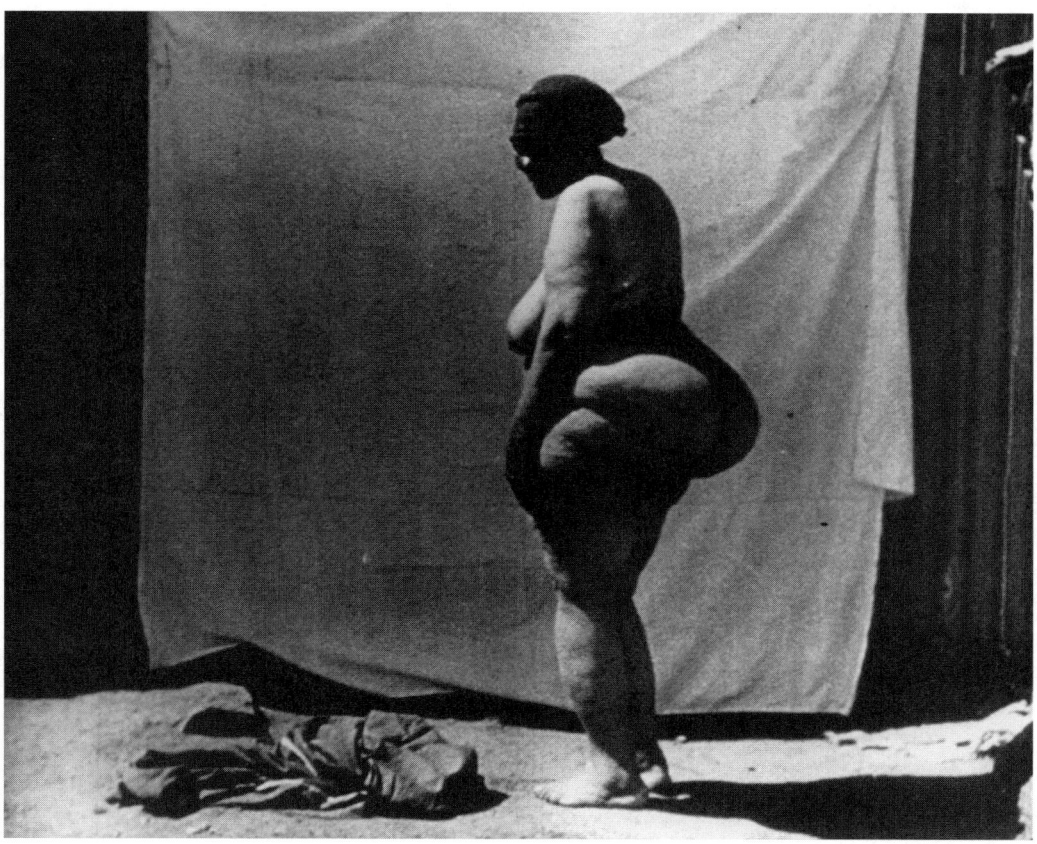

FIGURE 59. A Hottentot woman exhibiting steatopygia and the legacy of the Hottentot Venus in *Au pays des buveurs du sang* (In the country of the blood drinkers, 1943), a documentary remake of Napoléon Gourgaud's *Chez les buveurs du sang* (Among the blood drinkers, 1930/1931). Copyright Collection des Archives du Film et du Dépôt Légal du Centre National de la Cinématographie.

back reaches of the Musée de l'Homme.[16] There they remained until they were repatriated and ceremonially interred along with her other remains in her birthplace on the Eastern Cape, as Zola Maseko documents in her film *The Return of Sarah Baartman* (2005).[17] Though Cuvier's conclusions from the presence of a genital flap were both erroneous and preposterous, they were part of a shift toward a polygenist anthropological paradigm asserting the static nature of certain non-European races, who could not be "civilized" and thus entered a phase that Paul Broca called "phyletic exhaustion." As the historian of anthropology Claude Blankaert suggests, this schema subsequently gave moral license to acts of brutality undertaken in the name of colonial conquest.[18]

The body of the Hottentot Venus not only served a popular fascination with human pathologies, it stitched medical concepts of the normal and the pathological to geographic contingencies, supporting the long-standing Enlightenment argument for the predominance of milieu, in which geography determines race and culture in a diffusionist order of civilization. Baartman's live exhibition and subsequent dissection served as a significant case study used to assess the respective roles of morphology and functionality, a crucial debate in France during the 1830s that established the basis for neo-Lamarckian evolutionary models.[19]

Fragments such as Sarah Baartman's remains were held in the collection at the Muséum and later supplemented by a burgeoning institutional infrastructure emerging from the Parisian Society of Anthropology. The society was founded in 1859, the year of the publication of Darwin's *Origin of Species,* under the leadership of Paul Broca,

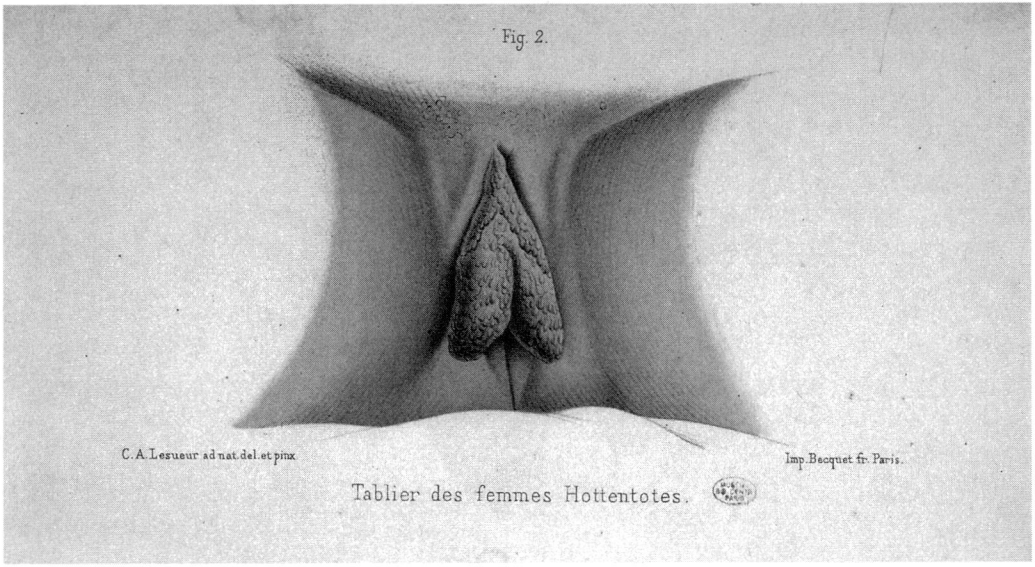

FIGURE 60. An illustration of the *sinus pudoris,* frontal view, by artist C. A. Lesueur. Raphaël Blanchard, "Une etude critique sur la stéatopygie et le tablier des femmes boschimaines," *Bulletin de la Société de Zoologie de France* 8 (1883). Copyright Bibliothèque centrale du Muséum national d'Histoire naturelle, 2004.

who became the generally acknowledged founder of physical anthropology, dominating the field until his death in 1880.[20] According to its first statute, the society was set up for the scientific study of human races, and "concerned itself with the origins, filiations, migrations, and mixing of numerous and diverse groups that compose the human genus."[21] As Thomas G. August explains, the approach of Broca and the society was primarily biological, and most of the society's members were medical doctors.[22] By 1872 it had begun publishing a review, and in 1876 it formed the École d'Anthropologie, consisting of a laboratory, library, and museum that became world renowned for establishing an anatomical classification system for visible racial differences.[23]

The polygenist perspective espoused by Broca emerged as the dominant view by the second half of the nineteenth century; it ascribed racial difference to particular forms of hybridization resulting from the multiple sources of evolutionary humankind. These multiple sources of origin were then classified as "types" and "races," thus challenging the originary couple of the Adamic myth in the name of science but masking the inherent hierarchical absolutism of this supposition. Armand de Quatrefages (de Bréau), the first chair of anthropology at the Muséum and Broca's contemporary, countered the polygenist argument with what was considered the orthodox monogenist position at the time by claiming the unity of the origins of human beings. Nonetheless, both contingents agreed on an evolutionary approach to human difference and collaborated in defining the expanding field of anthropology. While the polygenist approach was instrumental in defining physical anthropology, monogenism defined ethnography as the descriptive study of race, culture, and society.

The culturally descriptive perspective associated with de Quatrefages, his successor Ernest-Théodore Hamy, and the development of an ethnographic approach to race and geography de-emphasized the polygenist mechanistic science of man. These two strands represent contradictory tendencies within the anthropological collection itself, one focused on pinpointing physical difference in human bodies, such as head form and pigment, and the other focused on a shared vitalism as the basis for the universality of mankind.[24] For vitalist thinkers, physical differences among human subjects were less indicators of genetic inferiority than cultural differences as encoded by race, to be transformed through a type of colonial interventionism, justifying the dogmatic imposition of educational and hygienic reform.

The story of Sarah Baartman, unlike that of Victor, the Wild Boy from the Caune Woods (discussed in chapter 1), is an illustration of how a mechanistic argument, such as that about the significance of the genital flap, points to an index of primitive morphological difference. As a fixed rather than dynamic category, structural morphology was an argument against the possibility of social or educational transformation. By this argument the search for the missing link between mankind and primates was localized on a differential anatomical polygenist map of difference. As a series of objects in the anthropological collection, fragments of the Hottentot Venus's body reinforced the authority and fixity of evolutionary and racial categories.

Krzysztof Pomian describes the process by which a series of objects is assembled and categorized and then enters the register of the visible through its materialization in a collection.[25] This assembly is directly linked to the exercise and manifestation of social hierarchies, thus safeguarding objects that exist outside an economic circuit of exchange to be periodically unveiled, allowing the status of these objects to shift. Although Pomian explains that the appearance of artifacts as part of a collection demonstrates their social location, he also asserts that subsequent presentations of the artifact herald its transformation from the realm of the invisible to the visible.

In the developing anthropological collection, anatomical parts replaced relics as scientific objects of contemplation and became part of study collections that rarely emerged into the public space of the museum. The desacralization of the relic in the scientific sphere was intimately connected with decentering the humanity of individual subjects. Although many scientists' brains were dissected, weighed, and analyzed upon their death, it was the body parts of unknown, racially distinct "others" that transformed the relic into the scientific artifact.[26] Significantly, the physical anthropologists who acquired, maintained, and described these artifacts acted as priestly figures mediating the significance of spatially and temporally distant worlds of geographic difference.

In my adaptation of Pomian's argument about the collection, the Musée d'Ethnographie du Trocadéro served as a significant site for secularization by redirecting the reliquary pilgrimage toward a scientific evolutionary faith in emancipating and forming the citizen-subject. With the continued acquisition of new objects following survey expeditions throughout the colonies, the quest to describe cultural forms as opposed to collecting and dissecting human remains created new categories that expanded the emerging geographic atlas of humankind.

Incorporating Regnault's chronophotographs into the historical record of French anthropology contributed to the revival of ethnology as the living museum of human history, which became closely allied with a coterie of Americanist and Pre-Columbian archaeologists from whose ranks Paul Rivet and Georges Henri Rivière emerged as important institutional figures who reimagined the Musée d'Ethnographie as the Musée de l'Homme. Two statements that Regnault made to the Parisian Anthropological Society in 1900 and 1912, along with Léon Azoulay's proposal for a sound archive, significantly expanded the parameters of the anthropological collection. In his first statement to the society, Regnault suggested that an array of evidentiary artifacts would allow ethnography to emerge as a more exact science, declaring that natural history museums should incorporate chronophotography and film because "it is simply not sufficient to possess a loom, a potter's wheel, javelins, [and other artifacts]; we must understand how they are used, which cannot be established without chronophotography [i.e., serial motion photography]."[27]

Regnault proposed that a print of all chronophotographs (and films) representing ethnographic scenes of a scientific nature be deposited and safeguarded at a national museum. He also proposed that they be held and protected by the state under the same statute that required editors to submit a copy of every new publication to the Bibliothèque Nationale. Regnault proclaimed that because chronophotography was a new instrument of vision beyond the reflex action of two eyes, it represented a step parallel to the invention of the telescope and the microscope, magnifying our vision in space.[28] As he wrote, "Cinema will become the instrument of the physiologist just as the microscope is to the anatomist, a new scientific tool of discovery."[29]

Choices of preservation are by no means neutral; they carry with them the institutional context that collects and catalogs the artifact. Ethnographic cinema began as a new museological form that attempted to preserve human cultures in danger of extinction as part of what Sally Price has called "the salvage paradigm," referring to the impulse of retrieving, restoring, and institutionalizing a receding cultural or social practice while claiming that the cultural producer's dynamic adaptations to the present are emptied of meaning and lack authenticity.[30] Regnault represents the institutional figure who makes the artifact visible in the archive. Further, an invention needs its proper archive in order to be named as such, and Pomian poses the question of how this transformation occurs by asking, "How does a man allotted the role of representing the invisible carry it out?"

Just as Marey's development of chronophotography as a scientific instrument was inscribed in the proceedings of the French Academy of Sciences (Académie des Sciences), Regnault and Azoulay's adaptation of an existing technology to anthropology was entered into the record of the Parisian Society of Anthropology. The close association between these institutional figures and officially sanctioned scientific bodies points to the indeterminacy of men and institutions, in which the scientific institution confers legitimacy on the work of individuals who embody institutional standards and practices. In answer to the question of how the representation of the invisible is carried out, Pomian writes that individuals who undertake this operation abstain from all utilitarian activities by distancing themselves by means of objects that are not simply things but semiophores, which primarily function in a symbolic system of meaning as opposed to having a use-value function. While the individual positions objects in the realm of the archive or the collection, the individual who undertakes the positioning is almost always already placed, archivized, and collected. Pomian terms these individuals "semiophore-men."[31] Men's act of making meaning in the archive points to the ritualization of institutional performance whose agents function as the ultimate purveyors of scientific knowledge.

By concentrating on gestures, Regnault's chronophotographs established a new context for scientific inquiry. Everydayness was reduced to articulations of micromotions in which cultural difference could be compartmentalized and objectified. The specificity of the chronophotograph depicting the Wolof potter lay in the deployment of scientific methods to reinscribe spirituality and the tactile by documenting an archaic form of production. Within the broader context of industrial and mechanical transformation during the latter half of the nineteenth century, the shifting terms of productive agency had wide-ranging effects; trains, automobiles, and airplanes served as the new perceptual vantage points from which to experience the temporal and spatial contingencies presented in motion pictures. A spiritual process of conversion was also implied by the reconfiguration of production techniques. The advent of a new perceptual environment transformed the Wolof potter into a moving picture of a reimagined living past, positioned as a historical memory fragment to be projected into a new order of mind, body, and gesture.

Regnault positioned an emerging technological matrix of knowledge gathering within an institutionally grounded French scientific community. The moving light-sensitive disk that recorded the gestures of the Wolof potter distilled them as an ethnographic object visible within a collection. Recording the molding of clay celebrated and preserved a preindustrial past that had been taken over by emerging forces of mechanization. Further, the exceedingly pliable image of luminous clay, as related to human evolution, could be turned against the forces of mechanization and the vitalist notion of "organic plasticity" and used instead to advance a vision of return.

In a well-known fragment from his 1939 *Cahier d'un retour au pays natal (Notebook of a Return to the Native Land)*, Aimé Césaire used the malleability of clay to celebrate the spirituality of the precolonial past overtaken by a new language of production bereft of spirituality. Near the conclusion of this poem, written while Césaire was staying on the coast of former Yugoslavia, he wrote of Europe as "twisted with a scream," a continent that "collects and proudly overrates itself."[32] For Césaire, the emerging discourse of négritude took "root in the red flesh of the soil," and called out:

> I protest the inequality of the sun is not enough for me
> wrap yourself, wind, around my new growth
> set yourself upon my measured fingers.

The sun, a reference to France and the Enlightenment, was no longer adequate; another form of emergence and growth was taking place. The inadequacy of the sun was to be reconsidered against the logocentrism implied by physical anthropological measurements. In asking the sun for a final embrace after it had bitten and infected us, he pointed to "our multicolored purities," which cannot be disentangled. He finally entreated the sun:

> Link me, link me, without remorse
> link me with your great vast arms to the luminous clay
> link my black vibration to the very navel of the world
> link me, link me, bitter brotherhood
> then strangle me with your lasso of clustered stars.[33]

"Luminous clay" came to be associated with the foundations of négritude, self-mastery, and a return to a previous state of affairs. The complex rendering of the sun as a force of domination went beyond colonial France into a register of knowledge and experience of the world. The register of the scientific thus revealed an emerging geographic tactility that could not be compartmentalized.

HUMAN GEOGRAPHY AND FILM

The consolidation of serial motion photography as cinema influenced how precinematic forms could be understood as the progenitor of a new way of not merely seeing but knowing, localizing, and identifying the particular context for the presentation of an event. The relationship between race and geographic location functioned metonymically, within a diffusionist paradigm of civilization. Colonial interventionism was grounded in a sociocultural environmental equation that was based on the discourse of racial mixing as the promise of evolutionary and social change.

In 1847, Gustave d'Eichthal, secretary of the Société d'Ethnologique (Ethnological Society), claimed that the "black race" could be uplifted by infusing it with white blood.[34] This approach to racial mixing reinforced the formation of a French *assimilé* culture initiated more than a century and a half earlier in North America, Réunion, Senegal, and the Caribbean, among other prerevolutionary French settlements. This perspective also suggests that the female Wolof potter whose image appears in the anthropological collection may function as a hybridizing agent, infusing it with a new dynamism and life force suggested by the semiotics of gestural movement, once again, against the static positioning of body parts in the anthropological collection.

As part of a broader interest in ethnography and the possibility of mapping social transformations, Paul Vidal de la Blache's notion of human geography was further developed with the publication of Jean Brunhes' *La Géographie humaine (Human Geography)* in 1910.[35] Brunhes' work elaborated the instrumental role of topography, soil, climate, hydrography, and plant and human life in relation to physical geography, mirroring the anthropological opposition between physical anthropology and ethnology. The study of human geography also expanded the study of geographic milieu and cultural practices in the context of what Lucien Febvre called *possiblisme,* the indeterminate relationship between society and environment.[36] Human geography repositioned "geographic milieu" in such a way that the synecdoche between the Hottentot Venus's body parts and the primitive state of African social organization was displaced by the possibility of social transformation associated with the Wolof potter, which was used to establish a fictional neolithic point of departure from which to measure the never-ending transformation of colonial subjects.

The movement from "physical geography" to "human geography" was part of a historical continuity within the diffusionist paradigm of civilization. Whereas physical geography focused on the morphology of rock formations as analogous to human head forms and bones, human geography focused on an atlas of cultural practices associated with Durkeimian sociology. In a quest for a functionalist science of the social, the agency of human actors allows them to shape their environment by asserting a form of free will. A new kind of inventory attempting to map the surface of the globe in relation to "the rhythm of life" developed through an emerging geographic humanism. Teresa Castro's evocation of the "atlas as *dispositif*," adapted from Christian Jacob's notion that the atlas reconciles totality and detail within an encyclopedic framework, serves to impose norms and forms through the processes of psychic projection that condition our encounter with these images.[37] It points to the scientific codification of mapping that conditions, and finally overdetermines, our encounter with images.

Luis Buñuel's 1933 film *Las Hurdes: Tierra sin pan (Land without Bread)* draws out a critique of determinist geographic forms, particularly given Buñuel's intellectual perspective on the aesthetically provocative art form. As Jordana Mendelson explains, the film was partially inspired by Maurice Legendre's 1927 study titled *Las Jurdes: Étude de géographie humaine* (The Hurdanos: A study in human geography), documenting the customs, living conditions, and religious practice of the Hurdanos. The study of "human geography," informed by the photographic illustrations in Legendre's work, was incorporated into the framing of several important sequences in *Las Hurdes*.[38] Originally a silent film that was typically presented with a live narrator using the same script,

FIGURE 61. Jean Brunhes (1869–1930). Autochrome portrait in Boulogne by Auguste Léon, September 11, 1922. Copyright Musée Albert-Kahn— Département des Hauts-de-Seine.

it came to be supplemented with recorded voice-overs read with ironic condescension in subsequent versions that describe the absolute depravity of the inhabitants of a mountainous region of Spain adjacent to Portugal known as Las Hurdes.[39]

Deploying conventions of the educational documentary film, such as maps and topographic wide-angle views of massive rock formations, Buñuel's use of parody remains a conundrum. On the one hand it can be read as a critique of physical geography; but, as James F. Lastra suggests, it might also be a critique of the ethnographic act itself.[40] By depicting Las Hurdes, with the highest rate of illness and a proliferation of goiters bulging from the necks of various inhabitants, Buñuel illustrated that this overdetermined geographic milieu had ultimately been primed to be made *dépaysé*, as a form of Surrealist disorientation.[41] When the narrator says that the inhabitants of the village eat meat if, and only if, a goat falls off a cliff, in spite of the puff of gunshot smoke that appears fleetingly onscreen, it becomes clear that their geographic milieu not only determines the ignorance of the inhabitants but also inhibits the goat's balance on a precipice. It has also been noted that before Buñuel made *Las Hurdes: Tierra sin pan*, the vicomte de Noailles asked him to accompany the 1931 Dakar–Djibouti expedition in order to make a documentary of it. Buñuel promptly refused because he believed that the notion of Africa as a geographic palimpsest existed within Spain itself, implying that traveling to "Africa" to make a documentary denied the point that the purported "otherness" of Africa was present within Europe itself.[42]

The Dakar–Djibouti expedition of 1931–33 was sponsored by the Musée d'Ethnographie and the Institut d'Ethnologie at the University of Paris. Some 3,500 objects were gathered, thirty languages or dialects were studied, Abyssinian painting and murals were collected, 300 manuscripts and Ethiopian amulets were acquired and later deposited at the Bibliothèque Nationale, a zoological collection that included living animals for the Muséum was secured, 6,000 photographs were taken, and 200 sound recordings were made.[43] Reportedly, thousands of feet of film footage were also shot over the course of the expedition and later incorporated into Marcel Griaule's 1935 film *Au Pays des Dogons* (In the land of the Dogon).[44] The relationship established between the institution of French cultural anthropology with the Dogon through this encounter and beyond became an ultimate point of reference for the rise of French cultural anthropology, and perhaps its ultimate reflection.[45] The artifacts collected were a means of renewing the ethnographic collection in preparation for the renovation and reorganization of the museum using new techniques of museum display pioneered by Rivet and Rivière.[46] Ethnographic film was integrated into this new vision of museological transparency by documenting native gestures, thus establishing a new form of scientific evidence alternating between colonial reform and exotic attraction.

The transformation from the Musée d'Ethnographie to the Musée de l'Homme was accomplished by infiltrating the anthropological collection with new objects, thus recoding previous objects and supporting the prospect for rapid evolutionary and social change in the colonies. It was none other than the Ministry of the Colonies that contributed to rebuilding the museum to showcase colonial reform as part of an educational project in France itself, where the accumulation of *connaissances* was conceived as the work of social solidarity, to use Sarraut's well-worn phrase. The contradictory forces at work in the transformation of the Musée de l'Homme's collections also demonstrated how colonization and modernity conspired to preserve cultural forms in danger of extinction by removing them from a local context and placing them in an institutional repository of meaning.[47] The institutional setting functioned as a contradictory site of colonial interventionism. An allegorical myth of origins was projected onto an atlas of geographic difference to assert mastery in order to foment and witness a process of colonial transformation.

ALBERT KAHN'S ARCHIVE OF THE PLANET

Albert Kahn's Archives de la Planète was an early French-based initiative that developed a collection of 72,000 Lumière still color autochromes, 4,000 stereographic plaques, and one of the first French documentary film collections.[48] From 1910 to 1930, Kahn orchestrated and financed the production of nearly 170,000 meters of film by a coterie of film operators that formed the basis for the early documentary cinema collection at the French National Film Archive, particularly in the area of early survey expeditions.[49] Kahn's internationalist vision projected a French republican-inspired discourse of civil and political rights that could be crystallized through the transformation of current events in the photographic image. On the basis of these images, Kahn prophesied that political decision makers, intellectuals, and inventors of the day would be able to expand the humanitarian spirit. This extension of the ethnographic impulse fractured the absolutism of polygenism with a spiritually inflected ethnographic spectacle to create a world picture of humanity.

During the interwar period, the Archives de la Planète became associated with international educational endeavors that promoted the rhetoric of humanitarianism instructed by the moving image as an ultimate form of unmediated truth. Brunhes and Bergson were Kahn's close intellectual allies who helped Kahn develop an archive and grant program that embodied principles derived from Brunhes' vision of human geography and Bergson's philosophical concepts of vitalist humanism. As Brunhes wrote, Kahn sought "to establish an archival repository of humanity taken in its full life, at the beginning of the twentieth century, serving as testimony to one of the most critical economic, geographic, and historical shifts witnessed in human history."[50]

It was during this period that Kahn built an archive that served as the basis for his interaction with influential politicians, intellectuals, artists, dignitaries, and policymakers of the day. Kahn's financial rise was linked to his penchant for influence peddling and access to investment opportunities during a period of successive investment booms associated with the discovery and large-scale excavations of natural resources throughout the European colonial domain. Gilles Baud Berthier explains that Kahn's fortune was initially amassed through speculating on gold mines in the Transvaal as an employee at the Goudchaux Bank.[51] These holdings were subsequently multiplied after he played an important role in introducing shares for the South African De Beers diamond mines onto the Paris stock exchange during the 1880s and 1890s. These activities were complemented by Kahn's specialization in state-financed loans. After establishing a loan program for the exploitation of minerals and precious metals in South Africa, he also played a leading role in securing loans for the Japanese war effort against Russia.

Kahn used his substantial personal fortune to finance extensive activities associated with the Archives de la Planète; a scholarship program known as Bourses du Voyage Autour du Monde, which sponsored French academic researchers' study of social phenomena in various parts of the world; and a series of weekly news journals edited by Kahn and members of the Cercle Autour du Monde.[52] These journals and weekly bulletins, such as *La Journée planétaire, Les Réalités, Les Possibilités, L'Orientation nouvelle,* and the *Comité National d'Études Sociales et Politiques* (CNESP), were a means

FIGURE 62. Albert Kahn (1860–1940), posing on the balcony of his apartment in Paris at 102 rue de Richelieu. Photographed by Georges Chevalier as part of the Paul Ducelier collection, 1914. Copyright Musée Albert-Kahn—Département des Hauts-de-Seine.

of circulating the research conducted by members of these groups as well as documenting the frequent conferences and presentations organized at Kahn's villa. Marcel Mauss, the eminent ethnologist and nephew of Emile Durkheim, presented his work on the evolution of race and nationality over the course of two meetings of the CNESP on the "Problem of Nationality."[53] At the meetings Mauss defined the notion of internationalism as the opposite of an anarchic "cosmopolitanism," which he branded as a perspective that seeks to destroy nations and dispenses with an all-important form of sovereign authority.[54] Internationalism does not deny the place of the national, he asserted, and it is the opposite of an isolating nationalism. This critical perspective on cosmopolitanism is a distinctly Jewish assimilationist perspective that claims the overarching dominance of the national.

As Mauss explained, "Internationalism is an amalgam of ideas, emotions, and rules as well as a collective assembly whose goal is to conceive and orchestrate relationships between nations and betwixt societies in general."[55] Mauss proposed a vision of internationalism as a Durkheimian collectivity of nations and minority groups that could be managed impartially through the newly founded League of Nations. Further, he described an emerging moral and economic interdependency that was based on a collective will against war, in which the League could serve as an impartial international body upholding the principle of arbitration as the best means by which to negotiate border disputes and manage conflict.

With a meticulously kept Japanese garden as a centerpiece, Kahn's Boulogne-Billancourt villa became a preeminent salon of its day. Certain of the more specialized meetings would feature autochromes, stereographs, films taken by one of Kahn's film operators, or footage purchased from Gaumont, Metro, or Pathé. These images served as a focal point for discussions of current world events. Mauss's discussion of internationalism, for example, evoked the instability of minority groups in the Balkans following the Treaty of Versailles, a subject that Brunhes had explored on one of his first expeditions as head of the Archives de la Planète, developing a catalogue of autochrome imagery documenting the life of communities in the region just prior to World War I.[56]

The use of the image as a geographic picture language established an atlas of current events in the emerging parameters of simultaneity. Just as early photography had mapped the exploration, prospecting, and overall development of the colonies, early cinema gave life to these overseas territories through a form of animated cartography. Kahn even sponsored a series of early ethnographic expeditions in search of still and moving imagery. On the first of these proto-ethnographic expeditions, Kahn traveled around the world with his chauffeur, Alfred Dutertre, who learned to develop still color autochromes and was trained as a cinematographer at Pathé.

Before Brunhes became director of the Archives de la Planète in 1912, Kahn commissioned still photographer Gervais Courtellemont to make a series of autochromes in Algeria and Auguste Léon to direct the work in Kahn's photocinematographic laboratory. The regimented scientific work of the Archives de la Planète under the direction of Brunhes began with a flurry of autochromes and filmmaking views by Stéphane

Passet in China as well as Léon Busy's work in Vietnam and Cambodia. While several film operators worked for Kahn during this period, Busy's military career, starting in the French navy and eventually ending in the Colonial Service as a lieutenant of the Supply Corps based in Hanoi, contributed to an intersecting iconographic history of photography and filmmaking in Indochina along with the Lumière operators Constant Girel and Gabriel Veyre prior to Albert Sarraut's 1918 Mission Photo-Cinématographique.[57]

Paul Castlenau, the geographer and filmmaker, also made films for Kahn in the Middle East (1917–19), immediately after working in the French Army Film Unit (SPCA) during World War I. Castelnau is perhaps better known for his later participation as director of the Citroën-sponsored *La Traversée du sahara* and the twelve-part travelogue *Le Continent mystérieux*. A member of the prestigious French Geographic Society, Castelnau also made a series of films on the African continent with a distinctively acute sense of physical and cultural geographic elements in the landscape, which I discuss in chapter 3 in relation to the Citroën-sponsored films.

Kahn's continued involvement with film operators and scientific expeditions locates his work in the development of French ethnographic film with significant government liaisons. Kahn contributed to the 1920 Charles Michel-Côte Expedition, which was initially commissioned as an official French government survey to study the potential for the development of railroad lines in Ethiopia, yet another iteration of the never completed Transsaharien project.[58] As part of a subsequent railroad survey expedition to Afghanistan in 1928, Kahn sponsored Michel Clemenceau's survey expedition along with the photographer and film operator Frédéric Gadamer's study for a proposed railroad project between India and Europe.[59] A few years later, Kahn extended funding to Father Francis Aupais of the Missions Africaines to document initiation ceremonies, seasonal celebrations, sacrifices, funeral processions, and dance sequences in Benin that were widely shown on his return in 1930 at the Musée d'Ethnographie and at numerous other venues. The films were subsequently withdrawn and finally censored by his own Catholic missionary order.[60] In addition to commissioning an extended series of films and autochromes, Kahn invited the well-known microcinematographer Jean Comandon, who began his work at the Pasteur Institute, to set up a biological laboratory to continue his work on the grounds of Kahn's villa in Boulogne.

The eventual inclusion of Comandon in Kahn's philanthropic endeavors as of 1929, just before Kahn's bankruptcy and the dissolution of the Archives de la Planète in 1931, suggests the hypnotic power invested in the magnification and rhetorical presentation of the microbe, as in Pasteur's immensely popular public demonstrations. Bruno Latour has traced the success of Pasteur's efforts to his uncanny ability to create a popular "theater of truth" tied to the public visual demonstration, which formed an arsenal of visual representation used to reveal an invisible structure of meaning.[61] Comandon's magnification of the microscopic served as the basis for visualizing the scientific basis of truth, revealing the unseen in the context of the geographically remote, which, in turn, animated a rhetoric of visual proof associated with Kahn's endeavors, including film footage depicting conflict, natural resources, and geographic survey material from around the world. These films were authoritative visual demonstrations of the current world political situation, to be interpreted by a select group of experts. The films and autochromes were primarily used at Kahn's villa in Boulogne but were also lent out for academic courses and scientific conferences throughout the world prior to the development of the educational film movement. The authority of the filmed image accompanied by a scientific lecture or conference was presented as having a privileged ontological bearing.

Kahn's planetary archive was primarily geared toward creating a foundation for debate and consensus in an international community of scientific, political, and social elites. Kahn's only book-length published work, *Des Droits et devoirs des gouvernements* (On the rights and duties of governments, 1918) is grounded in formulas of prediction and rationalism, where "science, stability, competence, and a spirit of community are the necessary conditions to guide the social collective, just as the mind guides an individual's existence."[62] Kahn's internationalist framing for his initiatives among decision makers anticipated the organization of the International Commission for Intellectual Cooperation (CIC) at the League of Nations, where Henri Bergson, an important adviser in Kahn's inner circle, also served as its first president.[63] Further, the interest in developing an increasingly scientific grounding for the image in the final years of the Archives de la Planète underscores a phenomenological approach to the image. In the shadow of a Bergsonian intuitive knowledge "of a cinematographic kind," André Bazin posited a reality that sees beyond the human eye and yet captures an *objectively beheld* spiritual truth, as a Personalist ontology of the photographic image.[64]

Bergsonian Duration and the League of Nations' Institute for Intellectual Cooperation

The attempt to forge consensus among decision makers at Kahn's villa through the instrumentality of the moving image had a significant impact on the use of film as a form of international educational cooperation at the League of Nations. At the CIC, Bergson encouraged various proposals concerning the integration of cinema into their work and even attempted to establish a French Educational Cinema Section under the CIC.[65] Established in 1922, the CIC was the last of the permanent organizations created under the League of Nations. It was initially proposed by the Belgian delegate to the Paris Peace Conference, Paul Hymans, and elaborated by French delegate Léon Bourgeois.[66] One of the first cabinet-level ministers of public health in France following the war, Bourgeois proposed "the creation of a Commission for the study of international questions of cooperation in education that would outline the measures to facilitate international intellectual exchange between peoples."[67] It was conceived as an early scientific and cultural complement to the political objectives of the League and served as the predecessor to UNESCO (the United Nations Educational, Scientific, and Cultural Organization).[68] Although Bourgeois's call for such a commission was accepted, the word "education" was struck from the project proposal so that the league's mission would not be misconstrued as that of coordinating an international educational center or making the French-inspired approach to education too explicit lest the league be construed as wielding a form of intra-European cultural hegemony. Instead, "education" was replaced with the more neutral and technical notion of "scientific intellectual cooperation."

Bergson explained that the goals of the commission were to "define the foundations for an organization of international cooperation" in the register of science while also pursuing a moral imperative, which he described as "the fostering of high ideals of brotherhood, human solidarity, and peace among men."[69] While this notion of scientific intellectual cooperation evokes the internationalist spirit of universalism, the moral goal is related to a philosophically grounded vision of intuition—that is, a notion of liberty and free will within a law-governed dynamism that privileges conscious and

FIGURE 63. Henri Bergson (1859–1941). Autochrome portrait taken in Boulogne by Auguste Léon, June 27, 1917. Copyright Musée Albert-Kahn—Département des Hauts-de-Seine.

voluntary choice.[70] Bergson's critique of a necessity-based determinism, elaborated in his early *Essai sur les données immédiates de la conscience* (*Time and Free Will*, 1889), emphasized a voluntary and conscious dynamism founded on action.

Bergson's elaboration of duration distinguishes between time as an interior concept proper to the functioning of an organism and the movement of this interiority toward a universal and interchangeable time. His notion of universal time has been variously interpreted, but had a direct bearing on culturally received notions that justified colonialism at the time as the only way to establish norms simultaneous with those in the West. The anthropological collection as a positivist compromise between physical anthropology and ethnology was finally breached by Bergson's antipositivist critique in the name of intuition, but this position was still based on an evolutionary grid of human history that rhymed with a hierarchy of mind. In *Matière et mémoire* (*Matter and Memory*, 1896), Bergson used an "African savage's" capacity to repeat a Catholic sermon as an example of "spontaneous memory."[71] The savage is able to use the same gestures as the priest, but can only incrementally understand their meaning because he is not yet able to organize recollections with acts.[72] Further, Bergson claimed that the "African savage" still exists in an oneiric state of consciousness, unable to correlate memory with distinct actions or transform memory into a higher form of conscious action.

In *Durée et simultanéité* (*Duration and Simultaneity*, 1922), Bergson drew on Einstein's special theory of relativity in the physical world in order to elaborate on its psychological and philosophical implications. The apprehension of interior time, Bergson claimed, can be attained only through indirect and allusive means—that is, intuition. It is in this sense that interiority is not simply a psychological concept, but belongs more properly in the metaphysical realm. It has been argued that Bergson misunderstood the twin paradox of Einstein, who claimed that twins would age at different rates if one remained in the same location and the other traveled around the world at close to the speed of light, beginning and ending at the same location. That is, time would slow down for the twin who traveled, but would further advance for the stationary one.

Bergson also asserted, however, that when the traveling twin's "phantasmatic" clock returned to the position of the stationary twin, it would return to the same time as that of the other twin. That is, the phantasmatic clock of the traveling twin would not be behind that of the stationary one on its return.[73] Bergson seemed to claim that there is one master clock—the immobile one—that is opposed to separate times that can never be wholly reconciled. As Peter Galison explains, the revolutionary aspect of Einstein's theory of relativity was that there is no master clock, thus no center for time, "upending the category of metaphysical centrality."[74] The violation of centrality, particularly in relationship to the emergence of synchronized clocks and the time zone debates at the turn of the century, animated Einstein's development of the special theory of relativity as an imaginative machine that interacts with others through the exchange of electromagnetic signals.[75]

Bergson's engagement with Einstein's concept of relativity has been understood primarily as his failure to understand the physics of relativity, which has since been positioned as the victory of "rationality" over "intuition."[76] This particular understanding of their debate has defined some broad parameters between the absolutism of scientific truths and the contextual nature of philosophical argumentation. Michael Biezunski has explained that Einstein's work was only marginally accepted and understood in the French physics community at the time, and that his theory of relativity generated more serious interest among mathematicians and engineers due to disciplinary incompatibilities within the French physics community.[77] The brief exchange between Einstein and Bergson in 1922 at the Société Française de Philosophie began with Bergson's complimentary introduction, in which he accepted Einstein's theory of relativity as a physical reality but not a philosophical one.[78] Their positions with regard to the role of philosophy in relation to science served as the basis for a disagreement that has remained a fault line between scientists and continental philosophers, culminating more recently with what has been called the "Science Wars."[79]

At the time of their discussion in April 1922, Bergson's work *Durée et simultanéité* had been completed but not yet printed, and his assertion that all did not end with relativity, or that a limited theory of relativity as a physical reality does not determine its philosophical meaning, became a contentious position, particularly given Einstein's strident disagreement. Their published interchange underscores the role of physical and psychological simultaneity in relation to relativity.[80] Bergson elaborated on the concept of relativity as a potential psychological state that demarcates interiority from the perception of simultaneous events. In their brief discussion, Bergson framed his interest in relativity as a search for a universal temporality and attempted to reconcile this vision with the existence of multiple temporalities. Einstein remained circumspect as he posed the question, "Is the concept of time in philosophy the same as that of the concept of time in physics?" He concluded that the philosophical and the physical frameworks are very different and added that there is not a clear notion of philosophical time, while there are distinctions to be made between psychological time and time in physics.[81]

Like Bergson, Einstein was a political figure engaged in world events who made a number of important statements about the nature of war and its technologies. He also became a member of the Anti-Imperialist League, led by the German communist leader Willi Münzenberg, until a resolution was adopted against Jewish construction efforts in Palestine.[82] Significantly, Einstein's position as a German Jew who renounced his citizenship at age sixteen made him more an antinationalist cosmopolitan citizen than a nationally grounded internationalist like Mauss, Kahn, and Bergson. Three months after his debate with Bergson, Einstein was invited by Gilbert Murray, a fellow member of the CIC, to serve as a representative of "German intellectual participation."[83] Einstein initially declined on the grounds that he did not consider himself or his work representative of German intellectual circles, but he claimed that he supported the commission's efforts and later reinstated his participation in spite of voicing doubts about the larger ambitions of the League of Nations itself.[84] Einstein's nomination to the CIC was an attempt to demonstrate the scientific universality of the commission, which was attempting to symbolically integrate German participation given its ambivalent relationship to interwar internationalism. It is in this sense that the CIC used "scientificity" to neutralize issues of nationality, overlaying political initiatives with the scientific prestige of its illustrious members. The slogan of "peaceful international cooperation" associated with the league's efforts served as a stabilizing form of political prophylaxis and was derived in part from Woodrow Wilson's formula of U.S. participation during World War I as "peace without victory."

Bergson's attempt to adapt Einstein's theory of relativity to a philosophical and psychological vocabulary—and especially to his own notion of duration—has some significant implications for an emerging vision of internationalism. While internationalism implies a simultaneity of (European) nations and the potential for cooperation, the intervention of a regulatory mechanism such as a master clock was imagined as a means to sublimate disparate destructive nationalisms. As Bergson wrote in the preface to *Durée et simultanéité,* "Our conception of duration translates direct and immediate experience. While we are not claiming the *necessary* existence of a universal concept of Time, duration harmonizes with this belief quite naturally."[85] With this emphasis on the spirit and intuition, Bergson attempted to create a universalism out of an interior vision of duration that would supersede the world of appearances. In Bergson's earlier elaboration of the cinematograph, it was presented at once as representative of an apparatus that marks interior time and as a universalizing mechanism capable of condensing and synthesizing multiple interior temporalities. As Bergson summarized in *L'Évolution créatrice (Creative Evolution),* "The mechanism of our ordinary knowledge is of a cinematographic kind."[86]

Bergson's cinematograph stood in for the perceptual parameters of human knowledge as a means of apprehending reality and a means of creating movement as does the human mind itself. He thus defined consciousness itself as the perception of objective movement with "personal attitudes." While Bergson likened the act of human perception to the action of a film camera, he saw the inscription of sensory data as analogous to the layering of memory traces, with imprinting the mind analogous to a form of registration and editing that condenses and structures temporal discontinuities.[87] Just as the cinema is used to parallel the act of human cognition in time, it is also a perceptual mechanism, and thus both a universal objective form of knowledge and a reflection of our lived adaptation. As Bergson noted in a well-known declaration about the nature of the cinematographic method as a discontinuous form of knowledge, "The cinematographic character of our knowledge of things is due to the kaleidoscopic character of our adaptation to them."[88]

The process of ordering the myriad forms of human adaptation is harnessed by Bergson's notion of cinematographic knowledge. In the same way that the camera selectively records discontinuous segments of time, the editing process implicitly structures and takes hold of time. Bergson's vision of cinema as a demonstration of human knowledge was relevant to the developing uses and form of the cinema. Bergson deployed "cinema" as a metaphor of mind in his philosophical writings, but did not elaborate on the uses of cinema as a narrative-producing semiotic machine. At the CIC, however, he encouraged various proposals concerning the future integration of cinema into the commission's work as a technical instrument by which to reintegrate education into the mandate of international cooperation.

A 1924 study commissioned by the CIC titled "Relations of the Cinematograph to Intellectual Life," written by Julien Luchaire, established a general framework for the expanding role of cinema in international educational endeavors.[89] Highlighting the impact of cinema on human consciousness, with nearly fifty thousand cinema halls worldwide, and comparing the epic spread of film productions to that of the Bible and the Koran, the report offered a number of proposals concerning the role of cinema in education, thus positioning it as an emergent form of international cooperation to be joined with the CIC. It conjugated film education as screen education in schools, emphasizing the role of the screen as a palimpsest of still and moving imagery. Luchaire's report also proposed the organization of an International Film Congress to further examine how cinema could be used to "exercise a fruitful influence on the development of culture," thus encouraging future international cooperative efforts. The report further recommended the creation of an international catalogue of scientific films for international distribution and the circulation and programming of scientific and educational films for international audiences.

Luchaire's report was a preliminary step in the creation of a series of film-related endeavors by the League of Nations, but a broader acknowledgment of cinema as a privileged international mechanism of intellectual cooperation began to emerge. In effect, the distribution and encouragement of educational film productions became a means of reintroducing education into the work of the CIC as a way to center the internationalist agenda. Cinema provided a technical means of managing and distributing an educational endeavor. In 1926 the International Cinema Congress established guidelines for a newly evolving international educational cinema that were first outlined at the 1923 meeting of the congress, issuing a statement that included resolutions inviting writers, filmmakers, producers, and distributors to promote an antiwar and antinationalist message using the cinema as an instrument of peaceful human coexistence.[90]

The guidelines included a series of practical resolutions supporting an educational and artistic cinema (against the American-led monopolies and trusts), international standards by which to display credit sequences, and the organization of international film competitions. Another resolution called for the production of films to mediate the relationship between East and West, invoking the transparency of film as an educational medium. This resolution described the cinema as an intermediary, such that "East and West might be brought into contact with one another, explaining different histories, customs, and traditions." The commission also recommended that films made in the West portray the history, culture, science, and industrial development of the West in a simple, romantic, ethical, and entertaining manner, as was only fitting for the West in its role as "the inheritor of humanity."[91]

The wording of this final resolution bears a striking resemblance to the mission of the first French film unit in Indochina after World War I, discussed in chapter 5, which sought to "make France known to Indochina and make Indochina known to France." But once again it integrates education as a kind of master clock in an exchange founded on cinema as a technology of synchronization that can assign positions in ordering of human history. Positioning the West as "the inheritor of humanity" and the East as the bearer of "ancient culture" and "[exotic] wonders" is a profoundly Eurocentric vision of cinematographic universalism in its role as a mediator of a time-based logistics. Just as the cinema can reveal cultural and geographic difference through editing, it offers an exchange of know-how for cultural authenticity. A time-based vision of education in relation to social and human progress transformed national constructions of otherness into an internationalist rhetoric of universal cinematographic knowledge, conceived of as an enlightened form of mastery in the register of an archival timekeeping machine.

As a potential tool of international educational initiatives, cinema was regarded as a positive source of pedagogy, a scientific demonstration, and a potentially regressive force. Part of this contradictory vision of the cinema can be traced to a time-based vision of educational progress and a positivist view of human development. Thus a humanist continuum was established between the metropolitan pupil and the colonized subject. These multiple interior temporalities, universalized as part of a Bergsonian concept of duration, was used to create the new unity of technical assistance in the name of the universal cinematographic apparatus—the ultimate machine of international cooperation.

The hegemonic nature of this paradigm is revealed through the distinction between the metropolitan pupil, who would become an adult, and the colonized subject, who was considered part of a historical evolutionary past; this rationale shows that it was thought that maturity and citizenship rights are not gained by attaining an individual chronological age but rather through a process of internalizing European norms of "civilization." Hence self-determination was deferred, remaining subject to European patterns of industrial development. In this regard, cinema was at once an educational master clock and a time machine, regulating norms by revealing difference.

THE INTERNATIONAL INSTITUTE FOR CINEMATOGRAPHIC EDUCATION

Time-based parameters, at once developmental and evolutionary, were also a means of establishing the educational role of cinema. A significant expression of a developing internationalist cinema movement was tied to the creation of the International Institute for Cinematographic Education (ICE), which was independent of the CIC. Directly supported by Benito Mussolini, it was led by a trusted ally, the Italian journalist Luciano de Feo. The ICE was maintained at Italy's expense on the grounds of

Mussolini's estate in Rome at Villa Falconieri de Frascati, but placed under the direction of the League of Nations. The Italian delegate, Count Cippico, submitted the proposal for the creation of an educational cinema institute to the Third Plenary Meeting of the League in 1927, outmaneuvering French efforts to establish a similar organization with neither the benefit of direct government subsidy nor the luxury of a rebuilt Roman villa, the site of Mussolini's most frequented estate. As Christel Taillibert explains in her comprehensive account of the ICE, the generous appointment of the facilities for the ICE represented Mussolini's attempt to remake Italy's image abroad, from that of a fascist state to that of a technologically advanced internationalist one.[92]

In the florid language of the proposal, Italy described its willingness and intent to create the institute with participation from all nations, "under conditions of perfect equality." Proclaiming the need for an international center for the promotion and cataloging of educational cinema, Count Cippico associated the ICE with "a real sense of the lofty and practical objectives with which it is possible to attain this new and important form of propaganda."[93] The potential of the institute, which was proposed as an international center for scientific study concerning the uses of cinema, was explained in the following manner: "[It] would be a center of information for the different problems of the cinema, giving the best opportunity for a mutual interchange and diffusion of every kind of film: scholastic, hygienic, historical, archaeological, artistic, and, in a general way, educational."[94] In the official language of the proceedings, educational cinema was defined as films that present objective and scientific information engaging the reflective capacity of spectators in a well-defined analytic sphere in order to develop the spirit and character of the spectator.[95]

One of the most significant forms of international legislation spearheaded by the ICE promoted the free circulation of educational film across national borders, defining cinema as a public utility contributing to the rhetoric of safeguarding the culture and traditions of European nations. Educational cinema was envisioned as a means of protecting and preserving national culture while also demonstrating the complementarity of national identities. But as Richard Maltby has persuasively argued, the dream of cultural resistance to the Americanization of cinema was transformed into a politically engineered form of acquiescence such that the activities of the ICE did not seriously endanger the interests of the Motion Pictures Producers and Distributors of America (MPPDA).[96] In spite of continued European rivalry over colonial possessions during the interwar period, films depicting Asia, Africa, and South America also served as an imagined realm for international cooperation. References to films that addressed the colonies, or what were described as "territories under mandate," served as a source of debate. The French delegate to the ICE, Henri Focillon, protested against the term "backward races" as an unacceptable way in which to describe those living under the European colonial mandate.[97] The compromise language of "mentalités diverses" ("people of diverse cultures") thus entered the register of ethnographic cinema, and in 1935 the ICE received a request from the secretary of the Anthropological and Ethnographic Congresses to coordinate an international archive of ethnographic film.[98]

In a debate on freedom of trade and tariff restrictions at the League of Nations, the French delegate, M. D. Serruys, pointed out that the circulation of films and cultural commodities was not merely an economic issue, but "spiritual in character."[99] Retaining the spirituality of the national through an emergent internationalist order meant establishing the phenomenal specificity of national film cultures while affirming their scientific complementarity. Echoing Ernest Renan's ascription of a spiritual principle to the nation, Serruys's invocation of the spiritual character of cinema referred to a vision of the national that is comprised of a shared historical legacy and a political climate of mutual consent.[100] As a public utility, the cinema was thus conceived as an extension of a European atlas of civilization.

The ICE also initiated an extensive series of surveys following Dr. F. Humbert's 1926 report "The Effect of the Cinematograph on the Mental and Moral Well-Being of Children,"[101] subsequently commissioning Maurice Rouvroy, a Belgian professor of psychiatric pedagogy, to study "the psychological *re-action* of the child and the adolescent to the *action* of the cinema."[102] Following the well-known Payne Fund Studies in the United States, a survey consisting of thirty-three questions was subsequently distributed to two hundred thousand Italian schoolchildren (as of June 1930) in order to determine their habits and opinions regarding cinema.[103] The responses to this questionnaire and subsequent surveys relating more generally to educational film holdings among member nations came to compose the backbone of *The International Journal for Cinematographic Education,* which began as an ambitious monthly multilingual journal in July 1928 and was distributed internationally.[104]

The journal published the results of survey-based research undertaken by the institute and its international correspondents in an overwrought style of exposition deploying a diplomatic language of internationalism in relation to positivist social scientific methods. With a rhetorical flourish it presented the cinema as the "universal heritage of humanity," claiming that it could be envisioned as "a powerful instrument of social peace, especially when considering the reach and scope of documentaries depicting the life, power, and general character of all nations."[105] Furthermore, the journal declared that the cinema could contribute to clarifying the spoken and written word, rectifying the univocal or inflammatory character so often falsely attributed to it, thus ushering in a more effective form of film in the service of propaganda.

This conception of cinema as a means of establishing the "truth" was tied to the institute's goal of maintaining current documentation concerning film education worldwide. The prestige associated with this endeavor carried with it an epistemological role of defining the relationship of film to the ideological construct of educating the public. The ICE claimed that one of its major tasks was to distinguish between "a purely educational cinema and a theatricalization of life and human action," which implies a politically neutral educational cinema. Attempting to distinguish an internationalist vision of facticity from the mythologizing forces that highlight the centrality of the nation, the opening editorial explained that cinema is "a persuasive means of educating and enlightening the masses." Further, it claimed that "the still-high levels of illiteracy throughout the world accentuate the role of cinema as a new instrument of civilization." The editorial also insisted that educational cinema "inspires human progress, emphasizing the values of science and know-how leading toward the greater good."[106]

Educational cinema as a field of international inquiry became a way to establish a discourse of education as a technical domain for internationally coordinated action. The evocation of "illiteracy" in opposition to "enlightenment" and "civilization" provided a dichotomy by means of which to insert the cinema into a "progressive" movement of European civilization extending from the invention of the printing press and photography to that of the cinema as the emerging arbiter of national political ambitions.

CONCEPTUALIZING THE FRENCH COLONIAL CINEMATOGRAPHIC GEOGRAPHIC TOTALITY

Félix Lampe, a Berlin-based professor of geography writing in the ICE journal, explained how the use of the cinematic close-up, aerial views, and montage create a mental continuity and dynamism essential to demonstrating geographic movements.[107] With the ability to see microscopic movements usually imperceptible to the human eye, as well as the capability of accelerating and slowing down hardly visible movement, the cinema is capable of refashioning geography as a constantly moving dynamic sphere.

Lampe also coined the notion of a geographic totality as a humanitarian supplement to Ernest Jünger's notion of total mobilization, witnessed during World War I.[108] Lampe defined geographic totality as the study of all phenomena that occupy geographic space in all its particularities, borrowing Brunhes' conception of human geography and approximating Marcel Griaule's notion of ethnographic totalization as a means of infiltrating the forbidden and secret dimension through multiple sites of observation.[109] As a constitutive element of an interdependent system, geographic change can be registered in the image and traced to historical shifts in space over time. Accordingly, Lampe wrote that "all of these elements can be shown in a geographic film through expeditions in the field, the use of maps, graphs, profiles, or animated illustrations."[110] While the creation of a geographic totality through the cinema represented a significant innovation in teaching geography, the cinema was also used to represent the possibility of a totalizing transparency revealing scientific truths in the natural world.

The totalizing transparency of the cinema served to justify a mission of enlightenment and civilization, which was precisely how the ICE described its mandate. It was in this way that a positivist vision of a cinematic international humanism was founded on a geographic form of orientation and description. Whether one considers a micro-cinematographic film by Jean Comandon, which reveals and orients a world of microorganisms, or documentary films such as the German film *Pori* (dir. A. von Dungen, Berlin, 1929), the American film *Trader Horn* (W. S. Van Dyke, MGM, 1931), the French-produced film *Au pays du scalp* (In the land of the head scalp, dir. Albert Cavalvanti,

1931), or the French film *Chez les buveurs du sang: Le Vrai visage de l'Afrique* (Among the blood drinkers: The true face of Africa, dir. Baron Gourgaud, 1931),[111] all of these films resulted from geographic expeditions, and all were presented as guides to an "unknown" geography, mapping a continuum of microbiological, human, zoological, and geographic difference.

The films presented at the ICE in Rome were reviewed in the institute's journal and illustrated a time-based evolutionary narrative through spatial and geographical visual signs. While the exploration narratives presented in these films were contiguous with the discussion of French colonial cinema, they also participated in an evolving geographic international picture language. As a means of piecing together a total picture of geographic phenomena, along the same lines as the notion of a Heideggerian mechanized "world picture" of humanity, an internationalist continuum ties geographic views from aerial and overland expeditions to more technical films focusing on human gesture in the anthropological collection and in the domains of worker productivity as well as social and medical hygiene. The permeability and transparency of a geographic totality for all the world to see served as a mainstay of scientific international cooperation.

As discussed throughout this chapter, the notion of a geographic totality illustrates a hierarchical evolutionary narrative of being that can be crystallized in a cinematic suturing synthesis. In chapter 5 I described the role of the 1931 Colonial Exhibition as a symbolic event that used film to illustrate the expanse and unity of empire where metropolitan France stood as the source of enlightenment and knowledge, shining forth over the colonial territories. This photocinematographic crystallization of colonialism simultaneously functioned within the rhetoric of cinematic internationalism. Just as the study of geography in France developed in relation to colonial expansion, the cinema unified and reduced geographic diversity to a political totality. The search for an internationally transparent form of communication was a means of penetrating cultural and geographic difference while seeking to preserve it. International cooperation was thus transformed into the reorganization of colonial domination as a moving image that "set in place" a mechanized world picture. Just as the moment of conquest was eclipsed, that which was already conquered was classified, identified, and hence transformed. This new realm, an empire to be integrated, was conceived and grasped as a representation, a "structured image" that was both objectified and capable of being reformed. At another level of abstraction, Heidegger aptly remarked that once the world stands at one's disposal as a conquered representation, the object within the representation rises up and is subjectively beheld, thus becoming human only when the world becomes a picture.[112]

The transformative process by which the world is conquered by a visual representation evokes humanism because resistance is to be found through the enframing of the image itself; the cinema thus becomes the ultimate instrument of an emergent form of internationalism. Adapting Heidegger's notion of the "world picture" *(Weltbilt)* to that of a "mechanized" image establishes cinema as an integral representational technology in an evolving technological matrix used to connect a geographically disparate colonial geography.[113]

International documentary cinema functioned as part of a universal geographic atlas that presented a visual landscape of international difference in an archive of human techniques, archaeological sites, and geographical phenomena. Albert Kahn's Archives de la Planète and the ICE functioned as archives, knowledge banks, and reservoirs of meaning set up to justify subsequent action. Michel Foucault's notion of discontinuity and continuity in the archive is, in fact, akin to Bergson's description of the cinematograph's assemblage of discontinuities accomplished by editing and creating its own chronology, which established a continuity between the child, as a developmental subject, and human civilizations hailing from a varying temporal order.

CONCLUSION

THE FRENCH COLONIAL MEDIA APPARATUS: NATURAL MAN AND THE DIALECTICS OF AMERICANIZATION

A geography of difference was fundamental to the origins and development of French colonial documentary cinema. It reinforced a time-based evolutionary framework and served as the basis for colonial humanitarian interventionism. Just as the study of bones, bodies, and gestures defined human difference within an evolutionary gradient, colonial documentary film used the rhetoric of photographic realism as a form of time travel to administer a remedy along a geographic continuum from the European present back into the colonial past. As a visual machine of wonder capable of bringing back moving images of civilizations lost in time and history, the cinematographic apparatus functioned as a humanitarian instrument used to rhetorically orchestrate their long march into the present.

A crucial question that arises in considering the expanded corpus of interwar colonial documentary films is whether the promise of European modernity was ever attainable for the colonial subject under observation. It was the workings of what I describe as the "French colonial media apparatus" that simultaneously displayed and distanced the increasingly assimilated colonial subject. The will to identify with the purity and virility of "natural man" provided the foundation for French national consciousness under the Third Republic as the regeneration of egalitarianism, against the church and the monarchy. The will to reform the colonial body, however, imposed a hierarchy of civilization in the name of asserting republican values. The original myth of difference, coded as spontaneity and attachment to the "natural" landscape, was a claim to authenticity that drew on instances of reforming the colonial subject as a body and a civilization without its own agency for change. Physical education thus became a contradictory site for remaking the French male body in relation to a representation of colonial authority and, as I will explain, a dialectical appropriation of black American authenticity in relation to the anonymity of Americanization.

Black American sporting culture in France was validated against fears of Americanization as an authentic response to the hegemony of industrial and time-based discipline perceived to annihilate sexual, social, geographic, and physical difference. During the interwar period, the positive side of natural man became associated with African American boxing and with the positioning of Jack Johnson and Panama Al Brown as "natural types." These black American figures were appropriated within a discourse of natural man and colonial humanitarianism because they represented a creative response to the institution of slavery. They could be celebrated within French performance culture because of their marginalized position within the American institution of slavery, not in spite of it. Their integration into the broader terms of a French colonial media apparatus reinforced a French colonial atlas of mankind, assimilating otherness against American norms of modernity, industry, and Protestant uplift.

GYMNASTIC TRAINING AND THE CODING OF THE MALE BODY

The history of gymnastic training in France is integral to the history of weights and measures initiated by Edme Regnier's invention of the dynamometer that François Péron deployed during Nicolas Baudin's expedition to Australia in 1800.[1] The same heritage of civilization and the measurable physical capacity of civilized man initiated by Péron entered into the discourse of French gymnastics when Colonel Francisco Amoros y Ondenao (1769–1848), a Spaniard who had risen through the ranks under Napoléon Bonaparte and known as the founder of French gymnastics, showed that many of the gymnasts whom he trained in the 1820s at the Gymnase Normal de Grenelle surpassed Regnier's predictive norms of strength in "ordinary men."[2] The advent of gymnastic training established objective techniques by which to measure and compare the physical capacity of able-bodied men. From individuating the worker as an agent of physical force in relation to draft animals, objectifying weights and measures evolved toward establishing statistical vanishing points for racial and geographic difference.

It was within the same register of rule-governed force that the body was theatricalized as part of an emerging culture of physical combat that displaced the duel, rearticulating a sense of justice as the exercise of force on the body. The shifting regimes of punishment, from the kidnapping of the heart *(rapt de séduction)* to a subsequent postrevolutionary conception focused on the kidnapping of the physical body itself *(viol de rapt),* privileged new forms of adjudication and marked a decisive epistemological break leading toward the modernization of violence.[3] This opposition was contingent on a secondary one between male honor and considering the effects of bodily force as a punishable offense.

Jean-Pierre Yahi identifies the shift toward a physical violation of the body as a punishable offense as early as 1794 with the formalization of savate, which was still considered suspect, but was referred to by 1854 as a more socially acceptable style of combat known as French (kick) boxing.[4] Derived from the traditions of the duel and fencing, formalized French boxing removed the use of knives in instances of honor-bound conflict, transforming it by 1894 into a form of rule-governed gymnastics that was eventually integrated into military training for French soldiers. Mastery over measurable acts and the advent of legal discourse for arbitrating them also hinged on the idea that violence could be kept in balance through techniques and mechanisms of self-defense under the control of the state. In this way the rule-governed spectacle of combat and the formalization of bodily training served as mainstays of national identity.

This vision of self-defense is elemental to a nation-state identity that links bodily movements to norms for education, ethics, and morality. The evolving terms of morality became closely associated with the development of physical education in France, beginning with Amoros and continued by the gymnastic promoter and savate enthusiast Eugène Paz. Training the body was integral to educational reform throughout Europe, beginning with Per Hendrik Ling's early nineteenth-century development of the Swedish method of physical education and continuing in Germany as *Turnverein* (gymnastic movement) by Friedrich Ludwig Jahn.[5] In France, gymnastic training began with the training of elite subjects associated with the 1852 founding of the École Normale at Joinville-le-Pont and was then incorporated into the national educational curriculum by government decree in 1854 and 1859.[6] Training the body in the spirit of national ideology served as the foundation for an emerging ethic of moral measurements congruent with the exercise of measurable force. In France, the continued emphasis on what Alain Ehrenberg has called "moralisation" was bound up in a relationship of discipline and the strict assertion of power by the master over the disciple based on silencing and retraining an undeveloped form of subjectivity.[7] Gymnastic training was legitimized by the discourse of medical hygienic reform during the second half of the nineteenth century and later served as the basis for attempts to recondition the French male body in the aftermath of the Franco-Prussian War.

In 1881, the Circle for Rational Gymnastics, established by Georges Demenÿ and Emile Corra, developed a program and a series of exercises for the development of physical education in France under the sway of physiological methods. In addition to launching their own publication, Demenÿ became a leading expert on international techniques of physical education. As discussed in chapter 1, Demenÿ served as Etienne-Jules Marey's assistant who managed the everyday projects and activities at the Physiological Station. It was thanks to Demenÿ's initiative that a series of chronophotographs of cadets from the École Normale at Joinville-le-Pont was used to illustrate a series of physical educational movements and training routines intended to normalize the scientific and moral authority of hygienic reform.

Georges Hébert, a disciple of Demenÿ and defender of his legacy in the aftermath of the Demenÿ–Marey controversy, was charged with reorganizing gymnastic training for the French navy in 1904.[8] He emphasized physical and moral training as the basis for a culture of virility among French males.[9] Hébert's multivolume *L'Education physique* is a detailed analysis of movements based on the analysis of walking, running, jumping, *quadrupédie* (exercises using all four limbs), climbing, balancing, lifting, throwing, defense, and swimming. The photographic plates integrated into the first volume begin with an etching from Jean-François de Galaup La Pérouse's late eighteenth-century *Voyage de La Pérouse autour du monde* (Voyage around the world, 1791–92).[10] It depicts the natural body types of men and women in a flow of movement displayed in front of Queen Tiné on the island of Tonga in the South Pacific. This reproduction is followed by a series of images depicting "primitive" poses among undifferentiated Southeast Asian Moï mountain people, the muscular body type of men from the Central African Republic and Senegal, and other colonial subjects in the act of hunting and boating, followed by images of Cameroonian women carrying water basins on their shoulders. If the underlying theme of evolutionary temporal displacement in the colonies was not already clear, the women carrying water basins were finally matched with a Roman bas relief of a similar scene. These images of native techniques serve as a prelude to "Exercises toward Virile Action," illustrated by French men.

Hébert's depiction of colonial bodies illustrates a geographically inscribed evolutionary atlas of bodies in action, based on a return to Rousseau's vision of natural man.[11] Hébert referred to civilization as a limiting form of social organization for the development of the human body that, in turn, justified the need to develop relevant exercises for physical and moral education. He privileged running as the most fundamental technique of physical education because of its relation to primitive man, who he claims is the basis for a natural state of being as not excessively muscular, but rather physically agile and infinitely adaptable.

HÉBERT, I.

Planche 1
17

UNE SCÈNE DE LA VIE PRIMITIVE AU XVIIIᵉ SIÈCLE

Indigènes de l'archipel des Amis (Océanie) exécutant une danse en présence de la Reine Tiné.
(Gravure extraite de l'Album du Voyage à la Recherche de La Pérouse. Années 1791-92.)

Dans cette gravure le dessinateur de la mission de recherche a reproduit la beauté sculpturale des jeunes hommes et des jeunes femmes avec le même souci d'exactitude que la maturité de la reine, ou que la flore tropicale, ou enfin que le costume d'un membre de la mission (à gauche).

FIGURE 64. Dance performance for Queen Tiné on the Island of Tonga. Etching from Jean-François La Pérouse, *Voyage de La Pérouse autour du monde* (Voyage around the world); reproduced in Georges Hébert, *L'Éducation physique, virile, et morale* (Paris: Librairie Vuibert, 1936), plate 1.

Hébert's notion of the "natural type" can be adapted to the reception of various boxing figures who made their way into French popular consciousness in interwar Paris and were celebrated by the Parisian avant-garde. The interrelated questions of racial and geographic displacement that I referred to earlier can be best understood through the challenge, and then adaptation, to this ideal type in the interwar remaking of French masculinity.

CARPENTIER VERSUS SIKI: NATURAL TYPE VERSUS COLONIAL TYPE

After World War I, the French boxer Georges Carpentier soon became the world light heavyweight champion by defeating Joe Beckett in London on December 4, 1919. The match became etched in the minds of French boxing enthusiasts because of Carpentier's easily identifiable local identity and what numerous commentators have called his "technically honest" style of boxing. Born in Liévin, a coal-mining region in Northern France, he became known as the Adonis of boxing in France for his good looks, working-class background, and sense of fitting into an artistic milieu, befriending and perhaps inspiring Francis Picabia in the cannibalistic phase of his literary and artistic production.[12] Carpentier's style of boxing also reinforced a sense of self-mastery aligned with the art of the gesture and virility developed through the legacy of French gymnastic training, demonstrating, at least temporarily, that the specter of emasculation could be vanquished through a regimen of physical education.

Unexpectedly, the perceived vitality of Carpentier's boxing style faltered in a boxing match held on September 24, 1922, when the almost unknown Senegalese boxer "Battling" Siki became an immediate international boxing sensation after knocking out Carpentier in the sixth round of a reputedly fixed fight.[13] Although Carpentier was to have won in the fifth round, Siki gained control of the fight by the third with what commentators have described as his "windmill" style of punching, in opposition to Carpentier's "civilized" movements. Poetic language was rarely used to describe Siki's boxing technique; instead, his gestures in the ring and his public flair registered as demonstrating a street fighter's sensibility. With Carpentier lying unconscious on the canvas, the referee attempted to disqualify Siki for tripping or hitting below the belt; but with the crowd in an uproar, the decision was reversed and Siki was declared the winner.

It might have been of some consequence that Blaise Diagne, leader of the French recruitment campaign for African troops from 1917 to 1922, was present during the fight. Diagne's presence, along with the shrapnel scars on Siki's legs, made the attempted disqualification a blatant form of injustice, given the colonial humanist commemorative politics that permeated the raucous undulations of the crowd—a crowd that made their displeasure known on hearing the initial attempt at disqualification.[14] Following the fight, Siki was denied the larger sum of the purse and the title of light heavyweight champion because his membership in the Fédération Français de la Boxe (French Boxing Federation, or FFB) was revoked. Diagne, the first African delegate to the French Chamber of Deputies, protested Siki's scurrilous treatment by the FFB and filed a motion in the chamber for Siki to be reinstated. Henri Paté, the sport's commissioner who later became instrumental in commissioning colonial documentary films for the 1931 Colonial Exhibition, promised an inquiry, but formal investigations were dropped when the chamber voted overwhelmingly against Diagne's motion. In spite of Diagne's persistence and Siki's statements, which continued to be published in the sports press, it was Siki's imputed disturbances in public that incrementally obscured his implied threat to the colonial humanist fiction of racial equality.[15]

Unlike black American figures in France during the interwar period, Siki, born Amadou M'barick Fall, was an in-between colonial subject, peculiarly assimilated to the norms of the street culture in Marseilles, where he had grown up, but a far cry from the *assimilé* ethos of West African or Antillean intellectuals and politicians such as Diagne or the novelist René Maran. Perhaps more analogous to the first- and second-generation *beur* and black youth who grew up in France after World War II, Siki suddenly became a public persona upon defeating Carpentier. Siki's presence in the Parisian public sphere provoked racial epithets in the popular press to which his own manager, Charlie Hellers, contributed by comparing him to a gorilla who lived in the jungle. Siki's victory was considered an aberration rather than an example of the

FIGURE 65. Siki knocks out Carpentier on September 24, 1922. Photograph courtesy of Peter Benson.

creative energy attributed to black American performers like Jack Johnson, "Panama" Al Brown, or Josephine Baker precisely because of his French proletarian colonial origins. Though born in St. Louis, Senegal, Siki had moved to France as a teenager and had been abandoned by the person who had taken him there. Just as the details of Siki's arrival in France remain uncertain, so do the exact circumstances surrounding his 1925 murder in New York.

Peter Benson's definitive biography of Siki specifies that he was at least ten years old in 1908 on arriving in Marseilles, and he struggled to make a living. He started to box as a teenager at the Premiereland Boxing Club, then left for Toulon, where he was trained by Honoré de Bruyère and was entered on the Bordeaux boxing lists in 1913.[16] After a series of fights, he was recognized as a talented fighter and fought some of the best French middleweight fighters of the period. Siki learned to box professionally only after enlisting during World War I when he gained access to the American Expeditionary Force Camps in the South of France. From the numerous accounts that Benson cites, along with various clippings about Siki, it remains unclear whether he was integrated into a section of the Tirailleurs sénégalais or merely enlisted as part of a colonial regiment, serving with the *Français de souche* (Frenchmen of white European origin), for whom he reputedly fought on every front as part of the Eighth Colonial Regiment from Toulon. Siki learned to train and box professionally while stationed in a heavy artillery unit attached to American gunners, for whom boxing was an important form of military training and one of the ways in which segregated black and white American regiments interacted with one another—yet another means of regulating racial antagonism.

The Siki–Carpentier fight sheds light on French perceptions of racially marked otherness. Neither Siki's boxing style nor his public appearance was taken up as a symbol of the aspirations of the Parisian avant-garde as were those of Jack Johnson or Georges Carpentier. Instead, Siki's participation in World War I (for which he received the Croix de Guerre in commemoration of his single-handed capture of a German tank) evoked the myth of Mamadou Diarra and the ambivalent portrayal of the Tirailleur sénégalais as a physically powerful specimen in the midst of a French-led civilizing process. Following his 1922 defeat of Carpentier, a flurry of fight contracts were offered in the United States, but the terms slowly shifted until he was matched with Kid McTigue in 1923, losing a twenty-round decision, and later he lost two other fights, one to Emile Morelle and another to Kid Norfolk, the latter on November 23, 1923.

A generation later, Siki was transformed into a calligram in the New York–based Surrealist literary journal *View*, where Paul Eaton Reeve wrote, "*Siki had an estimated vocabulary of 96 words,* poetry in itself . . . he reduced complexities to nerve-explosions, gestures without symmetry, ceremonies of love to which the god declines the invitation."[17] This poetic rendition seventeen years after Siki died might have been misconstrued as reference to an obituary appearing in the *New York World* newspaper claiming that Siki could "speak nine languages, and his total vocabulary . . . was said to be 157 words, counting profane expletives."[18] Though this was short of the 850 words at the core of Charles K. Ogden's soon-to-be-published *Basic English,*[19] Siki was defamiliarized.

He was transformed into a mirror image of the African American on the other side of the Atlantic as a Francophone African in America who was displayed and finally transformed into another victim of gang-related violence on the streets of New York. Siki was shot twice in the back at close range near Times Square, but the investigation into his murder remained inconclusive. The marriage between boxing culture, gang violence, and gambling made it likely that he was killed by a hit man. Attempts to reconstruct his evening activity led Ocania Chalk to claim in Niek Koppen's documentary film *Siki* (1992) that Siki was walking home alone late at night after spending a night out drinking with friends, including the well-known welterweight fighter "Panama" Al Brown, with whom he discussed the prospect of returning to Europe.[20]

"PANAMA" AL BROWN, ETHNOGRAPHIC DISPLAY, AND MASQUERADE

Siki and "Panama" Al Brown were part of an intersecting circuit of boxers, promoters, bookmakers, and other sportsmen who often congregated at Villepontoux's bistro on Forty-seventh Street in New York City.[21] With Siki's career in decline, "Panama" Al Brown was a rising star and a local favorite among boxing enthusiasts in New York for his skeletal build and lithe movements in the ring. Unlike Siki, who was shunned by the Parisian avant-garde as less than an authentic example of enlightened primitive display, Al Brown soon became part of a circle of French artists and literary figures associated with colonial ethnography and Surrealism. The son of an American construction worker who had grown up in Panama, Alfonso Theofil Brown passed through the gauntlet of American racialized immigrant boxing culture to become an indispensable point of reference for a black male physical aesthetic in French literary circles, which existed on a continuum with Josephine Baker's sexual appeal. For Jean Cocteau, Al Brown's boxing style, particularly his signature footwork, was an innovative form of dance.

Just as Siki was vanishing from the boxing scene, "Panama" Al Brown became the undisputed world bantamweight champion during the middle to late 1920s, living on and off in Paris until the late 1930s. A close friend of Georges Henri Rivère and Michel Leiris, Al Brown was asked to appear in one of two exhibition matches used to raise money for the 1931–33 Dakar–Djibouti expedition led by Marcel Griaule. At a time when the public and museums were eager for a more aestheticized commodity, the boxing match was indeed a peculiar mix of colonial objectives submerged in the Parisian avant-garde's celebration of African American aesthetics as neither colonialism nor slavery.[22]

The Dakar–Djibouti expedition was firmly tied to the ethnographic Surrealism of the early 1930s, with the second issue of *Le Minotaure* devoted to the expedition. Al Brown appeared at the Cirque d'Hiver in an exhibition match as reigning international champion against Roger Simendé, the French bantamweight champion. After a brief intermission, this ten-round match was followed by a twelve-round middleweight fight featuring Marcel Thil against Emile Lebrize. The organizers raised more than 100,000 francs, which was used to purchase a boat for the expedition. In a short speech delivered in English the evening of the gala, Brown announced that he was going to donate the proceeds of the match to the anthropological expedition for the cultural development and gathering of knowledge about Africa. Likewise, the invitation to the gala and match reads, "As a token of generosity, Al Brown and his manager David Lumi-enski dedicate the proceeds of a boxing match as a symbolic act of good will. Their encouragement and participation demonstrates how ethnography, a science so long relegated to dry and dusty settings, can reconcile itself with the living." The transformation of a physical anthropological point of reference to a living ethnographic spectacle was part of the same totalizing framework that Griaule had developed for the ethnographic event. As Jean Jamin describes, a guard was positioned at each of the four corners of the ring, standing in for Griaule's multiple ethnographic observers.[23]

Also on the invitation to the match, Griaule thanks Al Brown "for putting his fists at the service of the ethnographic mission of a universal and scientific nature to facilitate a deeper and more profound understanding of colonized peoples while allowing for a more fruitful collaboration to be exercised on a less brutal and more rational trajectory."[24] The primitive display of the exhibition match adopted museology as the enlightened evolutionary approach to classifying the spirit of socialist humanitarian values. The final statement on the invitation parallels an editorial statement in *Le Minotaure,* "affirm[ing] the will to rediscover, reunite, and synthesize elements that have constituted the spirit of modern artistic movements that extend and are attached to the clearing of an artistic space that attributes artistic creation to its flourishing universality."[25] These two statements tend to focus on the universality of artistic creation and science as a privileged means by which to discover such universal structures, exemplifying a colonial humanist compromise of the interwar period.

Correspondence written by Michel Leiris during the Dakar–Djibouti expedition as well as his more intense and better-documented relationship with Jean Cocteau established Brown as an artistically authenticated black American presence. Cocteau finally served as Brown's boxing manager following the loss of his title as world champion to Baltasar Sangchilli. With the financial backing of Coco Chanel, Cocteau helped Brown regain his title as the bantamweight champion of Europe. Brown's technique was considered unique to the boxing arena; he had a distinctive style of dance celebrating speed, virtuosity, and grace.[26] After he regained his title in 1938, Cocteau wrote an open letter that appeared in the newspaper *Ce soir* in which he urged Brown to retire from boxing.[27] Brown did retire from the ring after one more match, and for a time the Médranos theater featured him in its circus in a shadow-boxing dance act set to jazz played by black musicians.

Francis Steegmuller, Cocteau's best-known biographer, has written that "Brown entered the circus ring clad in the long dressing gown he had worn the night of his famous fight, then dropped it to reveal an elegant all-white tail-suit."[28] As world champion, or "ondumonde" as E. E. Cummings called him in an anagrammatic poem that also refers to the declining world champion as "ahlbrohoon," Al Brown might have finally lost his title, but the underlying tensions of his dual African American identity positioned him in a Parisian vernacular that Cummings mimicked when he wrote in the same poem "Qu'est-ce que tu veux . . . il est trop fort le nègre" (What do you want? This *nègre* is just too strong) as part of a popular self-assured French stereotyped imagination.[29] As the powerful but less than muscularly bulky *nègre,* Brown embodied the positive features associated with natural man while also being representative of phrenological stereotypes, particularly within the measurable parameters of the boxing ring. As a close observer in the stands, Cummings offered a commentary on the universality of racial myths that refers to the reaction formation of white masculinity under threat, which the late nineteenth-century discourse of physical education was developed to address.

With the decline in Brown's boxing career, the transformation of his costume from the long dressing gown used in the fight arena to an elegant white suit situated him as a black entertainer, analogous to a music or dance performer, who combined the specter of sexual and racial alterity. Under Cocteau's watchful eye, Brown performed as late as 1938 in the Médranos theater, where he appeared alongside an act by the performer Lady Antonia that paid homage to the well-known trapeze artist cum female impersonator Barbette.[30] Barbette (born Vander Clyde in Round Rock, Texas) appeared in several aerial acts before becoming a star attraction in North America on the Orpheum Circuit.[31] Featured on Broadway in 1923 and then sent to England and France by the William Morris Agency, he became an international sensation.

Parallel to Brown's surprising transformation from a shadow-boxing figure in a long dressing gown to a black entertainer clad in white, Barbette initially appeared on stage wearing an elaborate ball gown and ostrich feather hat that he would subsequently remove as part of a striptease during the trapeze act itself in which he stripped down to his tights and leotard by the middle of the performance. The feminine allure that Barbette projected, in spite of the muscular activity required by the trapeze, made the final gesture of removing his wig all the more uncanny. In his well-known essay "Le numéro Barbette," Cocteau claimed that Barbette was the harbinger of a new aesthetic form in which a supernatural expression of sexuality emerged. As Cocteau explained, "Just as cinema has displaced realist sculpture, Barbette reveals that the [idealized feminine] statue transforms even when we think we know it, and remains elusive. What appears to be a bronze sculpture, a wax figure, is in fact a living being draped and transformed on Robert Houdin's magic pedestal."[32] Evoking Condillac's inanimate statue, which came to life once endowed with human qualities, the power of Barbette's trapeze work was the magical performance of the feminine as well as the masculine. As Cocteau emphasized, its power came not merely from the fact that Barbette removed his wig but from the way he readjusted his shoulders, extended his hands, flexed his muscles, and exaggerated his posture as if he were a golfer, demonstrating a final masculine presence in stark opposition to the feminine grace that had preceded it.

Barbette performed sexuality in the context of a circus act, thereby revealing the illusion of stagecraft through the sexualization of the performer as both feminine and masculine. It was this very same quality of masquerade that Cocteau cultivated in Al Brown's performances, showing him as virile natural man on the one hand, covered from head to toe, and then revealing him as just another black entertainer dressed in white, which, in turn, reflects his blackness back onto the spectators in an expression of showmanship. Through the illusionism of theatrical display, sexual and racial terms were exposed as constructed categories, fictionalized within the ropes of the boxing ring or, magically, in the air, on the perilous tightrope.

Repositioning racial and sexual difference was part of an ascendant discourse of medical and hygienic reform. Hébertisme supported a scientific approach to bodily training and physical display that was adapted to a strand of circus training, particularly for the development of such skills as maintaining equilibrium and juggling.[33] The staging of circuslike implements including rings, bars, and balancing equipment became the basis for constructing the popularly staged illusion as the contest or balance of measurable force. Whereas mid-nineteenth-century French gymnastic techniques were considered too specialized, showcasing the equipment allowed them to serve as rational parameters for the measurement of physical achievement. In other words, it provided the ultimate mise-en-scène for the masquerade of civilized technique in relation to natural man.

THE DIALECTICS OF AMERICANIZATION AND BLACK AMERICAN PERFORMANCE IN FRANCE

In response to the multiple facets of Americanization, a black American cultural aesthetic was celebrated by the Parisian avant-garde as an authentically creative response to the "primitive" nature of American social norms of racial inequity and a Protestant ethic of rationalized scientific industrial reform. The rationalization of labor under the sign of scientific industrial management found expression as recorded spectacle. Local and international antagonisms could thus be symbolically adjudicated in the boxing arena. As the preeminent international sport spectacle at the beginning of the twentieth century, boxing served as a primary site for the popular exhibition of class-based, racial, and national difference. The rule-governed display of physical violence in the ring served as a site of artistic reflection and excess for the European avant-garde. As a symbolic form of popular resistance, boxing was reconfigured as a palette for a physical poetry of action and retribution.

The codification of boxing as an international sport and part of a science of bodily training is indebted to the science of human measurement rooted in the ambivalent relationship between physical anthropology and ethnology. As a supplement to nineteenth-century anthropometrics, the boxing ring often served as the testing ground for moral, racial, and physical difference. Conceptions of racial categories were derived from a rule-governed calculus of combat. In colonial Australia, where Péron transformed early anthropometric and dynamometric measurements into an attack on the superiority of Rousseau's vision of natural man, Jack Johnson, the black American heavyweight champion, won his first international boxing title in 1908 by defeating the Canadian-born Tommy Burns.

In the context of the rough-and-tumble convict surroundings of Sydney, the Burns-Johnson fight was staged within a British colonial culture of Victorian values that was fascinated yet repelled by the interracial boxing encounter. The staging of this fight in colonial Australia also dipped into a prevailing physical culture of masculinity and civilization, which was presumably threatened by Johnson's physical mastery and verbal taunting.[34] While the boxing match drew more than twelve thousand spectators, the filmed version of the fight was especially popular in North America, precisely because of the racial anxiety so many whites felt about Johnson's physical presence and his resounding victory. As the novelist Jack London proclaimed while reporting for the *New York Herald* in Sydney, it was an "Armenian massacre" or "hopeless slaughter" in which an "Ethiopian giant's thunderbolts" were met by mere "butterfly flutterings," thus contributing to a racially marked evolutionary context for Burns's defeat.[35]

As an early form of filmed spectacle, boxing was an international popular attraction with an easily understood set of rules and setting. The establishment of the Marquise of Queensbury Rules in 1891 internationalized Anglo-American boxing as a popular attraction that displaced French boxing, which became increasingly associated with French military training techniques. Anglo-American boxing was understood as a sport advocating the spirit of "fair play," in which parameters for weight categories, rules of combat, use of boxing gloves, dimensions of the ring, and arbitration by a referee rationalized it as a genre-specific semiotic spectacle.[36] Eugenic mythologies of ethnic blood as a source of evolutionary superiority were tested in the ring; the extent to which physical education could transform the subaltern subject likewise became a source of popular fascination. Rule-governed Anglo-American boxing captivated the social imagination in the name of transforming class conflict into an international spectacle of bodily techniques.

Boxing was among the earliest filmed subjects. The boxing spectacle was an attraction around which the recording of motion existed in a matrix of newly emerging devices for the recording, projection, and transmission of an event. The July 4, 1910, boxing match held in Reno, Nevada, between Jack Johnson and Jim Jeffries was promoted as a national response on racial grounds to Johnson's resounding defeat of Tommy Burns. Staging the fight on Independence Day was a means of defensively positioning white masculinity against the assertion of black power. Jim Jeffries, the former heavyweight champion, came out of retirement as the Great White Hope with encouragement from Jack London and other journalists who had witnessed Burns's defeat in Australia. Tex Ricard, the preeminent boxing promoter of the period, orchestrated the event. He arranged for the filming of the fight and, more significantly, for the use of the recently patented wireless telegraph to relay news of the fight to major cities across the country simultaneously.

The match symbolically positioned the black race against white hegemony with an unfamiliar immediacy; the outcome was reported in the next morning's headlines around the nation. Johnson verbally taunted Jeffries throughout the fight and easily defeated him, knocking him out in the fifteenth round. Johnson's decisive defeat of Jeffries provoked race riots in all major cities in the South as well as the North at a time when nearly 90 percent of all African Americans lived south of the Mason-Dixon Line. Eldridge Cleaver, a member of the Black Panthers who went into exile in Algiers during the 1970s, has written that "the boxing ring is the ultimate focus of masculinity in America, the two-fisted testing ground of manhood, and the heavyweight champion, as a symbol, is the real Mr. America."[37] Johnson's public persona as physically powerful and sexually appealing to white women directly challenged the virulent American Jim Crowism during this period of the Great (Black) Migration to urban areas.

Johnson's arrival in France in 1911 was precipitated by a yearlong prison sentence for his involvement with and marriage to a white woman under the White Slave Act, which forbade the transportation of women in interstate or foreign commerce "for the purpose of prostitution or debauchery, or for any other immoral purpose."[38] His temporary relocation to Paris and exhibitions throughout Europe on stage, in music halls, in wrestling stadiums, and the ring influenced the revival and privileging of natural man in avant-garde movements throughout Europe, especially in Paris. However the connection between French colonial hierarchies and American racism was typically disavowed: whereas the African continent was in need of European colonial patronage, African Americans were considered the secondary victims of an Anglo-Protestant settler culture that had exterminated the heritage of the American Indian, who was considered the original French archetype of the pure, uncorrupted eighteenth-century vision of the "noble savage." By proxy and through intermarriage, black Americans became the inheritors of this uncorrupted European heritage. Though racially marked as descendants of the West African slave trade, they remained tied to a proto-European American Indian genealogical legacy, in opposition to European white settler culture.

As yet another iteration of a "socially progressive" French colonial hierarchy of being, the authenticity associated with African American performance also positioned them as the conscience of and the creative response to Anglo-Protestant settler culture. The valorization of African American cultural forms by the Parisian avant-garde existed alongside a universal colonial consciousness. In fact, the embrace of African American cultural forms suggests that the exclusionary effects of slavery created conditions analogous to those of an accelerated and distorted colonial time machine in which the Taylorist strain of Protestant moral uplift in American culture, allied with racism, led to a dynamic sense of cultural and physical resistance.

In France, Jack Johnson embodied black American authenticity associated with *l'art nègre*—an open-ended field of artistic expression that valorized uninhibited display in opposition to self-conscious aesthetic constructions. The *délire du combat* was associated with boxing in interwar Paris; it referred to the pathos in the ring as a trance dance of movement inflected by the gestures of work discipline but then condensed and imagined as the poetry of movement. The boxing match itself illustrated rhythms of resistance and disciplined muscular movements seen at the docks and in the physical trades that were so closely allied with the ascendant French myth of Americanization as a blend of brutality and pragmatism. The transformation of these work gestures into rule-governed events created a sense of aesthetic spectacle. After publishing an auto-biographical account as early as 1914 in French, Johnson later contributed a series of translated articles to the French boxing magazine *La Boxe et les boxeurs,* testifying to his renown among French sport enthusiasts who embraced an internationalist ethic of sporting culture.[39]

The culture of sports journalism in France began when daily newspapers staged cycling and automobile events to enhance circulation. Fears of degeneration, pathology, and neurasthenia were contravened by an emphasis on conditioned reflexes and willpower that could be celebrated in the public space.[40] In addition to boxing, cycling and automobile races had a mass appeal as other illustrations of competition among athletes using their bodies and machines in a match of comparable measurable force. An internationalist spirit of competition in France, represented by Pierre de Courbertin and his efforts in initiating the Olympic movement, integrated African American sports figures such as the Indianapolis-born African American cyclist Major Taylor, who regularly competed at the Vélodrome de Paris as early as 1901.[41]

For those in the Parisian literary and artistic milieu, however, "being American" was associated with emerging American industrial practices and the uninhibited authentic responses of black American cultural forms including dance, sports, and music. The cakewalk became a popular sensation when it was paired with ragtime idioms and New Orleans–style jazz, which made its popular debut with the 369th Regiment of black recruits in France during World War I. The cakewalk was introduced into Parisian music hall culture around 1900, and its stripped-down gestures were rooted in a vernacular satire of the "uppity" manners of white plantation owners that immediately became a symbol of the Jazz Age.[42] Initiated as the performance of mimicry, it was soon transformed into modernist spectacle through its popularization in Lumière's *Le Cake-walk au nouveau cirque* (The cakewalk at the new circus, 1902), Pathé's *Le Cake-walk chez les nains* (The dwarf's cakewalk, 1903), and Georges Méliès's *Le Cake-walk infernal* (Infernal cakewalk, 1903) while entering the repertoire of well-known French music hall performers, and was finally codified as a dance form in music hall competitions.

Prior to Jack Johnson's arrival in Paris, several black American boxers such as Sam MacVea (aka The Colored Globetrotter), Frank Craig (aka The Harlem Coffee Cooler), and Sam Langford had made Paris their home. Among the best-known early black American boxing spectacles that captivated the Parisian imagination was the 1909 forty-nine-round, four-hour-long fight between Joe Jeannette and Sam MacVea. The subsequent arrival of Jack Johnson was important for the beginnings of the Dada movement in France, especially because Johnson became an obsession of the proto-Dada figure Arthur Cravan, best known for his writings in the short-lived literary journal *Maintenant.* The nephew of Oscar Wilde and the short-lived spouse of the British Imagist poetess Mina Loy, Cravan was also an amateur boxer. After becoming a boxing instructor in Barcelona for a brief stint, he managed to film a seven-round exhibition match featuring Jack Johnson.[43] The fight itself was a form of early performance art in which there was no contest, but the event itself justified Cravan's self-fashioned literary embrace of a Johnson-inspired sense of black American dandyism. For Cravan and a new generation of European artists, the question was "To be or not to be American?"[44] Being American, however, was to be a black American, inflected by jazz musical idioms and indebted to a gestural economy based on the cakewalk and boxing.

FIGURE 66. Poster for an exhibition match of Jack Johnson versus Arthur Cravan held on April 23, 1916, in Barcelona, Spain. Copyright Collection Galerie 1900–2000, Paris.

Collection Fabienne Bénédict.

African American boxers were a provocation to an established order of high-brow artistic aesthetics that writers such as Cravan, Blaise Cendrars, and Colette as well as painters (Francis Picabia, Sonia Delaunay, and Kees van Dongen) were quick to incorporate in their own pursuits, so depicting provocative subjects became associated with artistic strategies of defamiliarization. The enduring legacy of natural man as the positive image of the African American subject in France continues to stand in opposition to Americanization in the still-operative colonial media apparatus.

THE COLONIAL MEDIA APPARATUS

Contemporary iterations of physical culture point to the residual power of colonial mythologies of the self and the other. The mise-en-scène in the French colonial documentary films discussed throughout this work functioned as a backdrop for the reinvention of natural man in relation to French masculinity. The intrusion of new techniques and the continued elaboration of a visual media apparatus nominated difference as a vehicle for the transformation of French national identity. Condillac's marble statue endowed with human qualities served as the basis for the successive elaboration of a French colonial media apparatus as a sensory order that was then mapped onto the expanding physiological and geographic body. Investing the geographically inanimate being with human qualities was a structuring element in the colonial narrative of education and hygienic reform under the Third Republic. The additive and subtractive qualities associated with the civilizing process became consolidated as part of a series of representative scientific techniques in the history of statistical measurement, photography, and cinema.

An elemental scene present in so many of the colonial documentary films under discussion depicts the interaction between the native subject and techniques of modernity. Embodied by machines, such as the moving picture camera in *Chez les mangeurs d'hommes,* and methods, such as Eugène Jamot's army of Tirailleurs médicaux injecting Cameroonians with an arsenic compound used against trypanosomiasis, colonial humanitarianism became a metonym for modernity. The broader humanitarian context for French colonialism was finally folded into the reengineering of the French body through the historically dislocated and untrammeled evolutionary colonial landscape.

Finally, the colonial media apparatus is at once a corpus of films and a sensory machine. It shifts the cinematographic apparatus, as a discourse, away from origins and vanishing points. Instead of focusing exclusively on the analytic parameters of the camera, perspective, and the invention of cinema, colonial imagery and myths continue to be recycled as media representations that enact the structure of distorted political objectives, encoding otherness as new forms of technological illusionism.

Acknowledgments

Many people contributed to this book, and the final text has been the result of a series of friendships, of teaching, and of conference presentations. Over the past few years, Steve Ungar has been a careful and interested reader who has helped me maintain a sense of confidence in this project; he has always been willing to listen and give his generous and well-considered advice. His involvement has been crucial to my rethinking of the organization and organizing principles of the book. I am also greatly indebted to Andrea Kleinhuber, who first acquired this project for the University of Minnesota Press, and Richard W. Morrison, for embracing it with a generosity of spirit. Adam Brunner, Marilyn Martin, and Nancy Sauro at the Press have also contributed in important ways to its final form. During the initial dissertation phase of this project, my former advisers, Bennetta Jules-Rosette and Teshome H. Gabriel, provided unfailing support, guidance, and friendship, when it first came to life—and ever since. Janet Bergstrom and Peter Wollen were also critical in seeing this project through its initial phase of completion as a dissertation.

During the past four years, my colleagues at the University of California–Santa Barbara (UCSB) have provided me with a new context for my work. In the film and media studies department, Kathryn Carnahan, Flora Furlong, and Joe Palladino have facilitated much of my activity there. Charles Wolfe commented on and engaged with several of the chapters in insightful ways; Cristina Venegas served as a witness upon its first phase of completion; and Edward Branigan, Anna Everett, Cynthia Felando, Dick Hebdige, Lisa Parks, Constance Penley, Bhaskar Sarkar, and Janet Walker have been important allies in fun, abreactive faculty meetings and analytic thinking. David Marshall, dean of humanities and fine arts, has been very supportive of my research and integration at UCSB. Also at UCSB, Catherine Cole, Tim Cooley, Susan Derwin, Colin Gardner, Bishnupriya Ghosh, Jocelyn Holland, Yunte Huang, Sydney Lévy, Anne Beate Maurseth, Stephan Miescher, Catherine Nesci, Sylvester Ogbechie, Michael A. Osborne, and Elisabeth Weber have been crucial to my intellectual and emotional equilibrium. Several students also contributed to this work in significant ways, including Aaron Ansel, Lachelle R. Hannickel, James J. Hodge, Melissa Mabie, Philipp Schmerheim, Amitabh Virmani, and Colin Williamson.

An extended community of friends in California has been important to extending the intellectual context for this work. Some just passed through for a limited period of time, such as Marie-Luise Angerer, Ian Balfour, Sara Danius, Yannis Hamilakis, Thomas Y. Levin, and Angela Windholz. Others live here: Andrew Apter, Ivan Baez, Sarah Minwalla-Baez, Marjorie Beale, Ali Behdad, Barbara Boyle, Lisa Cartwright, Lane Clark, Raul Fernandez, David Theo Goldberg, Brian Goldfarb, Albrecht Gumlich, Betti-Sue Hertz, Jan-Christopher Horak, Segolen Koschu, Anne Lacoste, Tamara Levitz, Akira Lippit, Kathleen Louw, Ghislaine Lydon, Bill Meyeroff, Carrie Noland, Panivong Norindr, Christel Pesme, Nella Poggi, Warren R. Procci, Bérénice Reynaud, Fatimah Tobing Rony, Vanessa Schwartz, Allan Sekula, Dominic Thomas, Denice Tousche, Margaret Waller, Gary Wilder, James Wiltgen, and Billy Woodberry. In New York, Jung Bong Choi, Stathis Gourgouris, and Neni Panourgià have been close friends and allies in thinking through the relationship between the emotional and the writing self.

While I was at Indiana University–Indianapolis from 2001 to 2003, Darrell L. Bailey, Dennis Bingham, Ken Davis, Paul and Nancy Dubin, Jane Goodman, John Hansen, Kelly Hayes, Christian Kloesel, Nadia Lozovsky, Michael Maitzen, James O. Naremore, Larbi Oukada, Jane Schultz, Michael Snodgrass, Rachael Stoeltje, and William Touponce helped me integrate into the teaching environment and rearticulate my own interests and research to the students in this new context. My encounters with Didier Gondola, Maria Grosz-Ngate', and William Schneider, who remain friends and intellectual compatriots, have contributed to the elaboration of themes in this work. While I was between Davis and San Francisco as a UC President's Postdoctoral Fellow at UC–Davis from 1997 to 1999, Dean and Juliet MacCannell opened their world to me; working with Dean in particular was an important experience in rethinking this work. Craig Baldwin, Bernard Lubell, Lydia Matthews, and Wayne Vitale were supportive friends in the Bay Area during this transitory period.

In France, many people were important to the development of this project. In the intersecting realm of friends, Bolya Baenga, Paul Belopolsky, Abdelkader Benali, Pascal Blanchard, Michel Caffarel, Jean-Pierre Dieterlen, Anne Doquet, Youssef el Ftouh, Antoine Garapon, Michel Garcin, David Gardner, Catherine Hodeir-Garcin, Catherine Jami, Michel Jaoul, Vincent Jarreau, Floréal Jiminez, Anna de Kisiel, Linda Koike, Alexandre Kostka, Nadia Meflah, Anne Marie Moulin, Simon Njami, Annick Opinel, Manuel Pinto, Emilie Py, Jean-Baptiste Tiemélé, Françoise Vergès, and Martine van Woerkens were decisive forces. In various locales, Richard Abel, Dudley Andrew, Emily

Apter, Filip de Boeck, Robert Bramkamp, Marta Braun, Louis Chude-Sokei, James Clifford, Kelly Conway, Mamadou Diouf, Sylvie Durmelat, Christopher Faulkner, Ulf B. Goebel, Donna Hunter, Anton Kaes, Richard Keller, Herman Lebovics, Babette Mangolte, Hudita Mustafa, Hamid Naficy, Béatrice de Pastre, Charles Piot, Dana Polan, Donald Presziosi, Cathy Schneider, Ann Laura Stoler, Charles Tshimanga-Kashama, Joan Wargo, Samuel Weber, Susanne Weirich, Richard Werbner, Donald Dean Wilson Jr., and Chantal Zabus have contributed to this work. At the Getty Research Institute in Los Angeles (a remarkably welcoming place), Frances Terpak has been extremely generous in her support of this work, revealing archival treasures that have shaped my understanding of the relationship between French colonial iconography and the photo-mechanical arts.

The screenings at the Archives du Film–Bois D'Arcy form the foundation for much of the work presented here. I would like to especially thank Michèle Aubert, Eric Le Roy, Daniel Courbet, Sylvie Bourcier, and Emma Cliquet, who facilitated much of my film research there. I thank Christine Menat at the Etablissements Cinémato-graphique et Photographiques de l'Armée at Fort D'Ivry, now ECPAD; Anne-Marie Michel, André Souchet, and Alain Nougaret at Citroën; Dominique Taffen at the former Musée des Arts D'Afrique et d'Océanie; Thierry Rolland at Pathé Télévision; Brigitte Berg at Les Documents Cinématographiques; Elisabeth Rabut and Serge Dubuisson at the Centre des Archives d'Outre-mer in Aix-en-Provence; Jeanne Beausoleil and Flore Hervé at the Collection Albert Kahn; Laurent Mannoni at the Cinémathèque Française; Peter Westervoorde at the Nederlands Filmmuseum in Amsterdam; Jens Boel at the United Nations Educational, Scientific, and Cultural Organization in Paris; Alfred Guindi at the League of Nations Archive in Geneva; and the late Jean Rouch and Françoise Foucault at the Comité du Film Ethnographique in the Musée de l'Homme. Thanks also to Claudine Salmon for help with identifying films at Pathé Télévision. I would like to acknowledge the support and guidance of Michel Fabre, director of the Centre d'Etudes Afro-américaines at the Université de Paris III; Michel Maffesoli, director of the Centre d'Etudes des Activités Quotidiennes at the Université de Paris V; François Chevaldonné at Université de Aix-en-Provence; Jean-Dominique Lajoux, director of research at Centre National de la Recherche Scientifique (CNRS); and Jean Jamin, at the École des Hautes Etudes en Sciences Sociales and CNRS, who is perhaps the most influential guiding intellectual presence in this work. The Asso-ciation des Connaissances de l'Histoire de l'Afrique Contemporaine, under the lead-ership of Pascal Blanchard along with Nicolas Bancel, Armelle Chatelier, and Stéphane Blanchion, encouraged me to present my work and facilitated contact with a wide variety of scholars working on questions of French colonial history.

The defining friendships of Alessandro Angulo, Abderrahim Benkirane, Samuel Borinsky, Katherine J. Hagedorn, Corinne Castellano Ionescu, Kazuyo Kamiya, Léa Nash, Alexandre Scharl, and Jean Robert François Tousche-Lecourt have been an important part of this project. I would like to dedicate the discussion of "Panama" Al Brown in the conclusion to my late grandfather Herman Bloom, whose memory of

Al Brown's fights were crystal clear when he could barely remember who I was. The intellectual and emotional camaraderie of my sister, Lisa Bloom, and her partner, Roddey Reid, has helped me better understand the context for my work and has kept me moored in California in spite of changing circumstances. Throughout this very long process, the unconditional love, support, and encouragement of my parents, Flora and Elliott Bloom, have made the essential difference. These people, among others, have left their mark on this work, but I alone bear the brunt of the text's errors and excesses.

APPENDIX
ARCHIVES AND FILM AND MEDIA REFERENCES

This appendix lists first film archives, then document and image archives; these were the major archives where I undertook much of the research for this book in addition to the libraries at the University of California (UC)–Los Angeles, UC–Berkeley, UC–Santa Barbara, and Indiana University. I then present film and media references organized by chapter, providing filmographic information for titles mentioned in the text and also including an extended corpus of films of the same historical period discussed in that chapter as well as contemporary documentaries and media exploring related themes. The films and media included here are primarily derived from French sources, but I indicate availability in English and in DVD or VHS format whenever possible. The abbreviations given are those of the archives where they may be found.

FILM ARCHIVES

Amateur Athletic Foundation Sports Library (AAFSL)
2141 W. Adams Blvd.
Los Angeles, Calif. 90018
http://www.aafla.org/4sl/over_frmst.htm

   Houses American and French boxing films.

Archives du Film (AF) (French National Film Archive)
Centre National du Cinématographie (à Bois D'Arcy)
Direction du patrimoine cinématographique
7 bis rue Alexandre Turpault
78390 Bois d'Arcy
http://www.cnc.fr/

Houses the largest film collection in France; serves as the legal copyright film archive in France; also maintains the largest nitrate film collection in France.

William Cayton's Big Fights Boxing Collection (BFBC)

Houses original boxing films; known to be the largest boxing collection. Uncertain conditions of access. Formerly managed by Jim Jacobs in New York City; sold to ESPN Classic in 1998.

Centre National de la Recherche Scientifique–Images (CNRS–Audiovisuel)
1, place Aristide Briand
92190 Meudon
http://www.cnrs.fr/cnrs-images/

Houses English versions of French documentaries that are available for rental and purchase.

La Cinématheque Française (CF)
51 rue du Bercy
75012 Paris
http://www.cinematheque.fr/fr/nosactivites/collections-cinema.html

One of the largest film collections in France; examples from early cinema include films by Marey and Demenÿ and chronophotography.

Le Comité du Film Ethnographique (CFE)
Musée de l'Homme
16 Place du Trocadero
75116 Paris
http://www.comite-film-ethno.net/

Known for the Bilan du Film Ethnographique (ethnographic film festival); associated with Jean Rouch's legacy.

L'Etablissement de Communication et de Production Audiovisuelle de la Défense (ECPAD) (Formerly known as Etablissements Cinématographiques et Photographiques des Armées à Fort d'Ivry, or ECPA)
2 à 8 Route du Fort
94205 Ivry-sur-Seine
http://www.ecpad.fr

Houses films related to the Missions Cinématographiques des Armées and colonial educational films.

Forum des Images (FDI); formerly known as the Videothèque de Paris
Forum des Halles, porte Saint-Eustache, Place Carrée
Paris 75001
http://www.forumdesimages.net/fr/alacarte/comment.php (to find a film)

Houses contemporary documentary film and video; offers public access.

Gaumont-Pathé Archives (GPA)
4 rue du Docteur Bauer
93400 Saint-Ouen
http://www.gaumont-pathe-archives.com/

Houses early hygiene films, industrial films made in the colonies, and Indochina documentary footage.

Library of Congress (LC)
Motion Picture, Broadcasting and Recorded Sound Division
101 Independence Avenue Southeast
James Madison Building, LM 336
Washington, D.C. 20540-4690
http://www.loc.gov/rr/mopic/

La Mediathèque des Trois Mondes (G3M)
63 bis rue du Cardinal Lemoine
75005 Paris
groupe3mondes@wanadoo.fr

Distributor of French audiovisual media.

Musée Départemental Albert Kahn (AK)
14 rue du Port
92100 Boulogne-Billancourt

Houses films by Albert Kahn, Archive of the Planet, autochromes, and film.

Nederlands Filmmuseum (NFM)
Het Filmmuseum
PO Box 74782
1070 BT Amsterdam
http://www.filmmuseum.nl/

Houses an early European documentary cinema collection. Its archive and lab are located in Overveen.

PSA Peugeot Citroën Archives (PSA)
http://www.psa-peugeot-citroen.com/en/afternoon.php

> Its public relations office has information about Citroën and Peugeot crossing films.

DOCUMENT AND IMAGE ARCHIVES

Académie des Sciences d'Outre-Mer
14 rue de la Pérouse
75016 Paris
http://www.academiedoutremer.fr/

> Houses French colonial archival documents and journals.

Bibliothèque de l'Académie Nationale de Médecine
16 rue Bonaparte
75006 Paris
http://www.academie-medecine.fr/bibliotheque.asp

> Houses nineteenth-century French psychiatric and psychology journals and French colonial psychiatry sources.

Bibliothèque du Cinema François Truffaut (formerly Bibliothèque André Malraux)
Forum des Halles
Avenue de Cinéma
75001 Paris
http://www.paris.fr/portail/Culture/Portal.lut?page_id=7714

> A public lending library with an important collection of early French film books and journals from the André Malraux film library.

Bibliothèque du Film (BiFi)
Le Service d'Informations à Distance
51 rue de Bercy
75012 Paris
http://www.bifi.fr/public/index.php

> An extensive photo archive on this history of French cinema from the Archives du Film among other sources.

Bibliothèque Interuniversitaire de Médecine et d'Odontologie
2 rue de l'Ecole de Médecine
75006 Paris
http://194.254.96.19/histmed/hm_cat.htm

> Houses works on the history of medicine in France and works by Raphaël Blanchard.

Bibliothèque Littéraire Jacques Doucet
8–10 place du Panthéon
75005 Paris
http://www2s.biglobe.ne.jp/~sug/Doucet.html

Houses works by Henri Bergson and examples of surrealism; also houses the Arthur Cravan Archival Holdings.

Bibliothèque Nationale de France
Bibliothèque de l'Arsenal (houses the Rondel Collection, examples of early cinema, and a music hall)
Département Estampes et Photographie (houses early sports photos)
Le Département des Cartes et Plans (houses works on colonial expeditions)
Le Département Philosophie, Histoire, Sciences de l'Homme
http://www.bnf.fr/pages/bibliotheque.htm

Le Centre des Archives d'Outre-Mer (CAOM) (The French National Colonial Archives in Aix-en-Provence)
29 Chemin de Moulin Detesta
13090 Aix-en-Provence
http://www.archivesnationales.culture.gouv.fr/caom/fr/

The most extensive archive of documents from Agences Économiques de l'Indochine; houses the archives of the Agences Économiques and French colonial administrative offices, a collection of post-1945 colonial films, still imagery, and maps.

The Getty Research Institute (GRI)
1200 Getty Center Drive, Suite 1100
Los Angeles, Calif. 90049-1688
http://www.getty.edu/research/institute/

Houses an important collection of French colonial iconography and printed matter from 1880 to ca. 1975 known as the ACHAC (Association Connaissance de l'Histoire de l'Afrique Contemporaine) Collection.

Institut Pasteur (IP)
Service des Archives
28 rue du Dr Roux
75724 Paris cedex 15
http://www.pasteur.fr/externe

Houses works on the history of colonial medicine, Louis Pasteur, and the Pastorians.

League of Nations Historical Archives and Collections
Palais des Nations
8–14 avenue de la Paix
CH-1211 Geneva 10
http://www.unog.ch/library

> Houses the Intellectual Cooperation and International Bureaux Section Archives (1919–46).

Du Musée Pédagogique au Musée National de l'Education
39 rue de la Croix Vaubois
76130 Mont Saint-Aignan
http://www.inrp.fr/musee/page3.php?version=francais&rubrique=MNE_1

> Houses early educational magic lantern slide and early cinema texts and L'Ancien Fond du Musée Pédagogique.

The Rockefeller Archive Center
15 Dayton Avenue
Sleepy Hollow, New York 10591
Fax: (914) 631-6017
http://archive.rockefeller.edu/

> Houses works used for mobile media hygiene campaigns and American hygiene films.

United Nations Educational, Scientific, and Cultural Organization (UNESCO)–Service des Archives
7 Place de Fontenoy
75352 Paris
http://www.unesco.org/general/eng/infoserv/archives/guide.shtml

> Houses the Institute for Cinematographic Education Paper Archives.

FILM AND MEDIA REFERENCES

Chapter 1. Tupi or Not Tupi

Chez les mangeurs d'hommes (Land of the Cannibals), dir. André-Paul Antoine and Robert Lugeon, France, 1928. (AF)
Como era gostoso o meu Francês (How Tasty Was My Little Frenchman), dir. Nelson Peirera dos Santos, Brazil, 1971. Distributed by New Yorker Films. (DVD–U.S.)
L'Enfant sauvage (The Wild Child), dir. François Truffaut, France, 1970. Distributed by New Yorker Films. (DVD–U.S.)

Related titles:

L'Exposition coloniale et la mode (The Parisian Colonial Exposition and fashion), dir. Henri de Turenne and Jean-Noël Delamarre, France, 1988. 3'. (FDI)

La Naissance du cinéma (The birth of cinema), dir. Roger Leenhardt, 1946. (CF)

Les Noirs des blancs (The blacks of whites), dir. Youssef el Ftouh, France, 1995 (video). 26'. (FDI retrospective)

Nos Oeuvres en 1931 (Our work in 1931), dir. unknown, 1931. 13'. (FDI)

Origins of Scientific Cinema: The Pioneers, dir. Virgilio Tosi, 1989. 53'. With English voice-over (CNRS–Audiovisuel). The history of chronophotography is featured with original material.

Préambule au Cinématographe: Etienne-Jules Marey (Preamble to the motion picture machine), dir. Jean Dominique Lajoux, 1995. 13'. Distributed by Cinédoc-Paris. (CNRS–Audiovisuel)

Village noir au Jardin d'Acclimatation de Paris (African village at the Jardin d'Acclimatation in Paris), dir. Louis and Auguste Lumière, 1896 (short film). 2'. (AF, FDI retrospective)

Chapter 2. Mythologies of the Tirailleurs Sénégalais

L'Aide des colonies à la France (Aid to France from the colonies), dir. Henri Desfontaines, 1918. 19'. (ECPAD)

Le Camp de Thiaroye (The Camp at Thiaroye), dir. Ousmane Sembene, Senegal, 1988. 148'. (VHS–U.S.; DVD–France)

La France est un empire (France is an empire), dir. Gaston Chelle, Hervé Missir, Georges Barrois, Raymond Méjat, and André Persin, France, 1939. 90'. (AF)

Der Golem (The Golem), dir. Carl Boese and Paul Wegner, Germany, 1921. (DVD–U.S.)

Les Maîtres fous (The crazy masters), dir. Jean Rouch, France, 1954. 35'. (VHS–U.S.)

Die Schwarze Schmach (The black shame), dir. Carl Boese, Germany, 1921. (Not located)

Les Sentinelles de l'empire (Sentinels of empire), dir. Jean D'Esme, France, 1938. 58'. Franfilmdis (Gaumont). (AF)

Tirailleurs sénégalais en Alsace (Senegalese Sharpshooters in Alsace), prod. Service Cinématographique des Armées, 1917. 15'. (ECPAD)

Related titles:

L'Ami y'a bon (The *y'a bon* buddy), dir. Rachid Bouchareb, France–Germany, 2004. 35mm, 9'. (FDI retrospective)

C'est nous les Africains eux aussi ont libéré l'Alsace (We, Africans, also liberated Alsace), dir. Pétra Rosay and Jean-Marie Fawer, France, 1994. 26'. (FDI retrospective)

Les Combattants africains de la Grande Guerre (African combatants in the Great War), dir. Laurent Dussaux, France, 1984. 16mm, 82'. (FDI retrospective)

Dans les tranchées, l'afrique, l'aventure ambigüe (In the trenches, Africa, the ambiguous adventure), dir. Florida Sadki, France, 2004 (video). 52'. (FDI retrospective)

Devoir de mémoire (The work of memory), dir. Cheick Tidjane N'Diaye, Senegal (video). 26'. (FDI retrospective)

Emitaï, dieu du tonnerre (Emitai, God of Thunder), dir. Ousmane Sembene, Senegal, 1971 (video). 101'. Distributed by New Yorker Films. (VHS–U.S.; DVD–France)

Histoire oubliée: Soldats noirs (Forgotten history: Black soldiers), dir. Eric Deroo, France, 1985. 16mm, 54'. (DVD–G3M)

Indigènes (Days of glory), dir. Rachid Bouchareb, 2005. (DVD–U.S.)

Les Parachutistes indochinois (The Indochinese parachutists), dir. Eric Deroo, France, 1992 (video). 59'. (FDI retrospective)

Tasuma, le feu (Tasuma, the fire), dir. Daniel Kollo Sanou, Burkina Faso, 2003. 35mm, 90'. (DVD–G3M)

Les Tirailleurs d'ailleurs (Sharpshooters from elsewhere), dir. Imunga Ivanga, Gabon, 1996 (video). 27'. (FDI retrospective)

Les Tirailleurs malgaches (The Malagasy Sharpshooters), dir. Bernard Simon, France, 2003 (video). 54'. (FDI retrospective)

Les Troupes africaines ont cent ans (The hundredth anniversary of African troop contingents), prod. Service Cinéma des Armées, 1957. 13'. (ECPAD)

Chapter 3. The Trans-Saharan Crossing Films

L'Atlantide (Atlantis), dir. Jacques Feyder, 1921. 165'. (AF, DVD–France)

The Champagne Safari, dir. George Ungar, 1995. 94'. (DVD–U.S.)

Le Continent mystérieux (The mysterious continent), dir. Paul Castelnau, Première Mission Haardt–Audouin–Dubreuil, 1923 (in twelve parts). 100'. (PSA)

La Croisière blanche (The White Cruise) (aka *The Bedeaux Sub-Arctic Expedition*), dir. Charles E. Bedeaux, 1934. Never completed; outtakes at the Canadian Film Archive in Ottawa.

La Croisière jaune (The Yellow Cruise), dir. Léon Poirier, 1932. 90'. (PSA)

La Croisière noire (The Black Cruise), dir. Léon Poirier, 1925. 100'. (CF, PSA)

Images d'afrique, dir. Joseph Barthes and Jean Vallée, Mission Proust-Peugeot, 1926/1930. 31'. (AF)

Lève africaine (African awakening), dir. Léon Poirier, France, 1925. 22'. (PSA)

Les Mystères du continent noir (Mysteries of the dark continent), dir. unknown, Mission Gradis-Delingette, France, 1926. (NFM)

Peaux noires: Film de l'expédition Jean d'Esme à travers l'Afrique Equatoriale Française (Black skins: The Jean D'Esme expedition through Equatorial French Africa), dir. René Moreau, Mission Jean D'Esme, 1932. 61'. (AF)

Sables de feu (Sand of fire), dir. Jean d'Esme, France, 1936. 15'. (AF)

Le Transsaharien, dir. [General] Louis-Dominque-Achille Aubier, 1922. (Not located)

La Traversée du Sahara en autochenilles (Traversing the Sahara in half-track vehicles) (aka *La Première traversée du Sahara en autochenilles*), dir. Léon Poirier, 1923. 49'. (AF, PSA)

Related titles:

Amours exotiques (Exotic love), dir. Léon Poirier, 1925. 35'. (AF)

À propos du Transsaharien (Concerning the Trans-Saharan), dir. Etienne Lallier, 1935. 3'. (Atlantic Film–Paris)

L'Atlantide (Atlantis), G. W. Pabst, France–Germany, 1932 (sound). 89'. (DVD–France)

Autochenilles (Half-track vehicles), prod. Citroën, 1921. 15'. (PSA)

Colomb-Béchar, prod. Service Cinématographique du Governement Général de l'Algérie, prod. Éclair. 5'. (AF)

Au Congo Belge (In the Belgian Congo), dir. Léon Poirier, Expedition Citroën-Centre-Afrique, Second Haardt–Audoin–Dubreuil Expedition, 1923. 22'. (PSA)

Kaïma, danseuse Ouled Naïl (Kaïma, Nailiyat dancer), dir. Marc de Gastyne, 1953. 17'. Franfilmdis (Gaumont). (AF)

Oasis Saharienne: En marge de la Croisière noire (Saharan oasis), dir. Georges Sprecht, 1928. 17'. (PSA)

Aux pays des sultans noirs (In the land of black sultans), camera: Georges Sprecht (?), 1925. 10'. (AF)

Le Sol saharien (The Saharan soil), dir. Paul Castelnau, First Haardt–Audoin–Dubreuil Expedition, 1923. (PSA)

Chapter 4. Diagnosing Invisible Agents

Black and Tan Fantasy, dir. Dudley Murphy, starring Duke Ellington and Fredi Washington, United States, 1929. 20'. (RKO, DVD–U.S.)

La Chasse au lion à l'arc (The lion hunters), dir. Jean Rouch, 1965. 77'. (DVD–France)

Conte de la mille et une nuits (Tale of a thousand and one nights), prod. Jean Benoît-Lévy, illustrated by Albert Mourlan, 1929. (AF)

Itto, dir. Jean Benoît-Lévy and Marie Epstein, 1934 (sound). 117'. (AF)

Les Magiciens de Wanzerbe (The magicians of Wanzerbe), dir. Marcel Griaule and Jean Rouch, 1949. (CNRS–Audiovisuel)

Les Maladies vénériennes (Venereal disease), dir. Jean Benoît-Lévy and Marie Epstein, 1925. (Les Documents Cinématographiques)

La Maternelle (The children of Montmartre), dir. Jean Benoît-Lévy and Marie Epstein, 1933 (sound). 83'. (DVD–U.S.)

Mission en AEF (Mission in French Equatorial Africa), 1920. (Not located)

La Mouche bleue de la viande (The parasitic bluebottom fly), prod. Gaumont, 1917. (GPA)

La Mouche domestique (The housefly), prod. Pathé, 1917. (GPA)

Les Mouches (Flies), prod. Eclipse–Urbanorama, 1913. (NFM)

Nosferatu: Eine Symphonie des Grauens (Nosferatu: A symphony of terror), dir. F. W. Murnau, 1922. 94'. (DVD–U.S.)

Pasteur, dir. Jean Epstein, 1922. (CF)

Peaux noires (See list for chapter 3)

Promenade en AEF (A stroll through French Equatorial Africa), dir. J. K. Raymond-Millet, 1931. 20'. (AF)

Le Réveil d'une race au Cameroun (The awakening of a race in Cameroon), dir. Alfred Chaumel, France, 1930 (in five parts). (AF)

Trypanosoma gambiense: Agent de la maladie du sommeil (Gambian trypanosomiasis: The agent of sleeping sickness), dir. Jean Comandon, 1924. (AF)

Le Vampire (The vampire), dir. Jean Painlevé, France, 1945. (DVD–U.S.)

Les Vampires (The Vampires), dir. Louis Feuillade, France, 1914 (serial). 399'. (DVD–U.S.)

Voyage au Congo (Travels in the Congo), dir. Yves Allégret (with André Gide), France, 1925. 79'. (AF, VHS–France)

Related titles:

L'Alcool engendre la tuberculose (Alcohol leads to tuberculosis), dir. Ferdinand Zecca, 1906. 4'. (AF)

Le B.C.G. (Comité National de Défense Contre la Tuberculose). 7'. (AF)

La Contagion par la poussière (Contagion by dust), dir. Jean Benoît-Lévy, 1925–30. 2'. (AF)

Hémolyse: Action de l'eau sur le sang (Hemolysis: Water in the blood), dir. Jean Comandon and P. de Fonbrune, n.d. 12'. (AF)

L'Homme du Niger (The Man from Niger), dir. Jacques de Baroncelli, 1939. 102'. (DVD–France, AF)

Leçon du docteur Louis Chauvois (Lesson by Doctor Louis Chauvois), aka *La Machine humaine enseignée par la machine automobile* (The human machine instructed by the automobile), dir. Jean Benoît-Lévy, 1930 or 1932. 10'. (AF)

Serums et vaccin (Serums and vaccines), dir. Henri Nozet, prod. Éclair, Ministère de l'éducation nationale. 19'. (IP)

Chapter 5. Infiltrate the Crowd with an Idea!

L'Arabe (The Arab), dir. Rex Ingram, 1924. (Gosfilmofond, Moscow Region, Russian Federation)

Arsène Lupin, dir. Jack Conway, starring John Barrymore and Lionel Barrymore, 1932. 84'. (Turner Entertainment) (VHS–U.S.)

Le Bled (The outback), dir. Jean Renoir, Société des Films Historiques, 1929. 60'. (CF)

Le Fils du soleil (The child of the sun), dir. René Le Somptier, 1924 (eight-part serial). (AF)

La France est un empire (France is an empire), dir. Gaston Chelle, Hervé Missir, Georges Barrois, Raymond Méjat, and André Persin, France, 1939. 90'. (AF)

L'Histoire de la Plus Grande France (The history of Greater France), n.d. (not located).

Le Jardin d'Allah (The Garden of Allah), dir. Rex Ingram, 1927. 96'. (Turner Entertainment)

Kim Van Kieu (New accents of a heart-rending song), dir. E. A. Famechon, la Société Indochine Films et Cinémas, 1924. (No known existing print)

La Marche vers le soleil (Marching toward the sun), dir. René Le Somptier, 1928. (BiFi, AF; no known existing print)

The Mark of Zorro, dir. Fred Niblo, starring Douglas Fairbanks, 1920. 80'. (DVD–U.S.)

Melodie der Welt (Melody of the world), dir. Walther Ruttman, 1928/1929. 50'. Distributed by the Museum of Modern Art.

L'Oeuvre de la République: Au service de la Plus Grande France (The creation of the Republic: In the service of Greater France), prod. S.C.P.A., 1935 (silent). 35 mm, 9'. (ECPAD)

Promenade en AEF (A stroll through French Equatorial Africa), dir. J.-K. Raymond-Millet, 1931. 20'. (AF)

La Sultane de l'amour (The sultan of love), dir. René Le Somptier and Charles Burguet, prod. Louis Nalpas, 1919. (AF)

[Le Vrai visage de l'Afrique:] Chez les buveurs du sang (The true face of Africa: Among the blood drinkers), dir. Baron Napoléon Gourgaud, 1930 (silent version). 57'. (AF)

Related titles:

Boma-Terverun, The Journey, dir. Francis Dujardin, 1999 (with English subtitles). 54'. Distributed by ArtMattan Productions. (VHS–U.S.)

Le Continent noir (Sortilège exotique) (The black continent), dir. Alfred Chaumel and Geneviève Chaumel-Gentil, 1942. 20'. Franfilmdis (Gaumont). (AF)

Exposition Colonial 1931, dir. Ladislas Tellier, 1931. 7'. (AF)

Histoire de l'expansion coloniale française (History of French colonial expansion), prod. Section Photo-Cinéma des Armées, 1930. 37'. (ECPAD)

En Indochine Française: Une excursion en baie de Halong (In French Indochina: Along the Halong Bay), prod. Pathé, n.d. 3'. (AF)

Institut Pasteur à Nhatrang, 1927 (outtakes). (IP)

Laghouat, prod. Éclair, Service Cinématographique du Gouvernment Général de l'Algérie, 1930. 5'. (AF)

Lyautey, bâtisseur d'empire (Lyautey, builder of empire), dir. René Lucot and Georges Maurice, 1947. 40'. (CF)

Les Manoeuvres aériennes d'outre-mer (Aerial maneuvers overseas), prod. Section Photo-Cinéma des Armées, 1937. 11'. (ECPAD)

L'Oeuvre de la République: Evocation de la conquête du Sahara (The creation of the Republic: The conquest of the Sahara), prod. Section Photo-Cinéma des Armées, 1931. 35'. (ECPAD)

Au Tonkin, prod. Section Photo-Cinéma des Armées, 1920. 20'. (ECPAD)

Vues de l'Exposition Coloniale de 1931 (Views of the Colonial Exposition of 1931), prod.

Pathé–Nathan, camera: Benoit, assisted by Pierre Levent, Dr. Chrétien's Hypergonar process, 1931. (AF)

Chapter 6. Humanitarian Visions and Colonial Imperatives

Chez les buveurs du sang: Le Vrai visage de l'Afrique (Among the blood drinkers: The true face of Africa), dir. Baron Napoléon Gourgaud, 1931 (sound version of *Le Vrai visage de l'Afrique*). 57'. (AF)

Ethiopie–Soudan, Mission Charles Michel-Cote, 1920. (AK)

Las Hurdes: Tierra sin pan (Land without Bread), dir. Luis Buñuel, 1933. 26'. (VHS–U.S.)

The Life and Times of Sarah Baartman: The Hottentot Venus, dir. Zola Maseko, South Africa, 1998. 52'. Distributed by First Run Icarus.

Missions africaines, Francis Aupais expedition, 1930. (VHS compilation on site, AK)

Origins of Scientific Cinema: Early Applications, dir. Virgilio Tosi, 1993. 27'. Distributed by CNRS–Audiovisual with English voice-over). Includes animated chronophotography by Félix-Louis Regnault.

Aux pays des buveurs du sang (In the country of the blood drinkers), dir. J. R. Barthes, 1943. 22'. (Films de Cavaignac, AF)

Au pays des Dogons (In the land of the Dogon), dir. Marcel Griaule, 1935. 16 mm, 15'. (CFE)

Au pays du scalp (In the land of the head scalp), dir. Albert Cavalvanti, 1931. (Not located)

Pori, dir. Adolphe von Dungern, 1928 Von Gontard–Kluge expedition, Berlin, 1929. (Not located)

The Return of Sarah Baartman, dir. Zola Maseko, South Africa, 2005. 55'. Distributed by First Run Icarus. (DVD–U.S.)

Related titles:

Aimé Césaire: Une voix pour l'histoire (Aimé Césaire: A voice for history), dir. Euzhan Palcy, 1994. 3 × 50' (150'). Distributed by California Newsreel. (DVD–U.S.)

On Cannibalism, dir. Fatimah Tobing Rony, 1994. 6'. Distributed by Women Make Movies.

Maroc 1912–1926. (VHS compilation, AK)

Zoos humaines (Human zoos), dir. Pascal Blanchard and Eric Deroo, France (documentary). 52'. Distributed by Films du village, village@noos.fr.

Conclusion: The French Colonial Media Apparatus

Le Cake-walk au nouveau cirque (The cakewalk at the new circus), dir. Auguste and Louis Lumière, 1902. (AF)

Le Cake-walk chez les nains (The dwarf's cakewalk), prod. Pathé, 1903. (National Film and Television Archive, London)

Le Cake-walk infernal (Infernal cakewalk), dir. Georges Méliès, 1903. (LC)

Georges Carpentier vs. Battling "Siki," 1922 (with English voice-over). (AAFSL)

Jack Johnson: The Big Fights, dir. William Cayton, United States, 1970. 90'. (VHS–U.S.)

Jack Johnson vs. Arthur Cravan, 1916, Spain–France, Gallerie 1900–2000, Paris. 35 mm.

Siki, dir. Niek Koppen, 1992. 62'. (NFM)

Related titles:

Georges Demenÿ et les origines "sportives" du cinéma (Georges Demenÿ and the "sports-related" origins of cinema), dir. André Drevon, 1995 (with English subtitles). 23'. (CNRS–Audiovisuel)

Unforgivable Blackness, dir. Ken Burns, United States, 2004. 220'. (DVD–PBS Home Video)

NOTES

INTRODUCTION

1. Adi Ophir, "The Contribution of Global Humanitarianism to the Transformation of Sovereignty," paper presented as part of the humanitarian workshop On Catastrophes in the Age of Global Capitalism, Neve Ilan, Israel, January 2003, 1, http://www.round table.kein.org/node/123 (accessed May 16, 2007).

2. Giorgio Agamben, *Homo Sacer: Sovereign Power and Bare Life,* trans. Daniel Heller-Roazen (Stanford, Calif.: Stanford University Press, 1998 [1995]), 124–25.

3. Ibid., 133, cited by Ophir, "The Contribution of Global Humanitarianism," 14.

4. Louis Althusser, "Ideology and Ideological State Apparatuses (Notes towards an Investigation)," in *Lenin and Philosophy and other Essays,* trans. Ben Brewster (New York: Monthly Review Press, 1971), 127–85; Jean-Louis Baudry, "The Apparatus," trans. Jean Andrews and Bertrand Augst, *Camera Obscura* 1 (Fall 1976): 104–26; Jean-Louis Comolli, "Technique and Ideology: Camera, Perspective, Depth of Field," *Film Reader* 2 (January 1977): 128–40; Stephen Heath, "Notes on Suture," *Screen* 18, no. 4 (Winter 1977–78): 48–76.

5. The most relevant of the numerous books edited by the ACHAC Collective relative to this work include *Images et colonies: Nature, discours, et influence de l'iconographie coloniale,* ed. Pascal Blanchard and Armelle Chatelier, proceedings of a conference held at the Bibliothèque nationale, January 20–22, 1993 (Paris: Achac–Syros, 1993); *Images et colonies: Iconographie et propagande coloniale sur l'Afrique française de 1880 à 1962,* ed. Nicolas Bancel, Pascal Blanchard, and Laurent Gervereau (Paris: BDIC–Achac, 1993); *L'Autre et nous: "Scenes et types,"* ed. Pascal Blanchard, Stéphane Blanchoin, Nicolas Bancel, Gilles Boëtsch, and Hubert Gerbeau (Paris: Achac–Syros, 1995); and *Zoos humaines: De la Vénus hottentote au reality shows,* ed. Nicolas Bancel, Pascal Blanchard, Gilles Boëtsch, Éric Deroo, Sandrine Lemaire (Paris: La Découverte, 2002).

6. Eric Le Roy, "Le Fonds cinématographique colonial aux Archives du film et du depot légal du CNC (France)," *Journal of Film Preservation* 93 (October 2001): 55–59.

7. The indexical works in this area include Georges-Michel Coissac, "Le Cinéma au service de la civilisation et de la propagande," *Le Tout-cinéma 1931–1932* (Paris: Publications "Filma," August 7–31, 1931): 53–80; Pierre Leprohon, *L'Exotisme et le cinéma: Les Chasseurs d'images à la conquête du monde* (Paris: J. Susse, 1945); André Francis Liotard, Samivel (pseud.), and Jean Thévenot, *Cinéma d'exploration: Cinéma au long cours* (Paris: Chavane, 1950); Maurice-Robert Bataille and Claude Veillot, *Caméras sous le soleil* (Alger: SNED, 1956); Pierre Boulanger, *Le Cinéma colonial* (Paris: Seghers, 1976); Abdelghani Meghrebi, *Les Algeriens au miroir du cinéma colonial: Contribution à une sociologie de la décolonisation* (Alger: SNED, 1982); Abdelkader Benali, *Le Cinéma colonial au maghreb: L'Imaginaire en trompe l'oeil* (Paris: Éditions du Cerf, 1998); and David Henry Slavin, *Colonial Cinema and Imperial France, 1919–1939: White Blind Spots, Male Fantasies, Settler Myths* (Baltimore, Md.: Johns Hopkins University Press, 2001).

1. TUPI OR NOT TUPI

1. François Péron, "De la force physique des sauvages," in *Aux origines de l'anthropologie française,* ed. Jean Copans and Jean Jamin (Paris: Éditions Jean-Michel Place, 1994), 179–200. This short notice was taken from the larger work titled *Voyage de découvertes aux terres australe executé sur les corvettes, le géographe, le naturaliste . . . pendant les années 1800 . . . [à] . . . 1804,* vol. 1 (Paris: Imprimerie impériale, 1807). The most extensive summary in English can be found in Norman J. B. Plomley, *The Baudin Expedition and the Tasmanian Aborigines, 1802* (Tasmania, Australia: Blubber Head Press, 1983).

2. Copans and Jamin, *Aux origines de l'anthropologie française,* 182–83. See Armand de Quatrefages, *Hommes fossiles, hommes sauvages* (Paris: Jean-Michel Place, 1986 [1894]), 325. De Quatrefages describes the conditions surrounding Péron's use of the dynamometer on the Timorians and Tasmanians in Australia. He notes that the Tasmanians, in particular, are hunters and often go without food for several days at a time. This question of irregular and insufficient nutrition, de Quatrefages claims, might be considered the cause for their ill physical health at the time of Péron's findings. Further, the broader argument of de Quatrefages also sought to dislodge the simplistic association between civilization and physical force.

3. For further discussion of this concept, see Jean-Patrick Lebel's articles in *La Nouvelle Critique* on ideology and cinema. See the collection of his articles in Jean-Patrick Lebel, *Cinéma et idéologie* (Paris: Éditions Sociales, 1971). See also Jean-Louis Comolli, "Technique and Ideology: Camera, Perspective, Depth of Field," *Film Reader* 2 (January 1977): 128–40.

4. Immanuel Kant, *Anthropology from a Pragmatic Point of View,* ed. and trans. Robert B. Louden (Cambridge: Cambridge University Press, 2006 [1797]).

5. The term *idéologues* was intended by the emperor Napoléon Bonaparte as a pejorative description of a group of oppositional intellectuals who supported the coup d'état of the eighteenth Brumaire and sought to submit Bonaparte's ambitions to the laws of analytic reason. Although this group was said to have identified themselves under the less dogmatic term *idéologistes,* they became known (and still remain known) as the idéologues. The idéologues were part of a second wave of French Enlightenment thinkers. Figures of the first wave, such as D'Alembert (1717–83), Rousseau (1712–80), Diderot (1713–84), and Condillac (1715–80), were in their forties when men such as Degérando (1772–1842), Cabanis (1757–1808), and Destutt de Tracy (1754–1836) were born. Jean Jamin, "Naissance de l'observation anthropologique: La Société des Observateurs de l'Homme (1799–1805)," *Cahiers internationaux de sociologie* 67 (1979): 318 (313–35).

6. As John Yolton explains, this tradition of French materialist thought stresses sensation as the origin of ideas, which has been taken as a response to an empiricist reading of John Locke's *Essay concerning Human Understanding.* Abbé de Condillac, however, gave prominence to Locke's sensory aspects of the origins of human knowledge. See John W. Yolton, *Locke and French Materialism* (Oxford: Oxford University Press, 1991), 4.

7. Brian William Head, *Ideology and Social Science: Destutt de Tracy and French Liberalism* (Dordrecht: Kluwer Academic Publishers, 1985), 38.

8. Etienne Bonnet, Abbé de Condillac, *Traité des sensations* (Paris: Librairie Arthème Fayard, 1984 [1754]), 89–90.

9. Marta Braun, *Picturing Time: The Work of Etienne-Jules Marey (1830–1904)* (Chicago: University of Chicago Press, 1992), 223. Braun's book is the most extensive study of Marey's oeuvre available in English. For more on the history of the Institut Marey, see Louis Olivier, "L'Institut Marey," *Revue générale des sciences pures et appliqués* 4 (February 28, 1902): 193–99. The Institut Marey was located on the Parc-des-Princes, which is now the site of a large soccer stadium.

10. Louis-François Jauffret, "Introduction aux Mémoires de la Société des Observateurs de l'Homme," in *Aux origines de l'anthropologie française,* ed. Copans and Jamin. See also Jean Jamin, "Faibles sauvages . . . corps indigènes, corps indigents: Le Désenchantement de François Péron," in *Le Corps enjeu,* ed. Jacques Hainard and Roland Kaehr (Neuchâtel, Switzerland: Musée d'Ethnographie, 1983), 45–76.

11. Elizabeth A. Williams, *The Physical and the Moral: Anthropology, Physiology, and Philosophical Medicine in France, 1750–1850* (Cambridge: Cambridge University Press, 1994), 88.

12. Albrecht von Haller, "A Dissertation on the Sensible and Irritable Parts of Animals (1753)," *Bulletin of the Institute of the History of Medicine* 4, no. 7 (July 1936): 661–99. (This is a reprint of a 1755 English translation introduced by Oswei Temkin.) In his introduction Temkin notes that considerations of sensation rather than considerations of the soul were beyond the pious concerns of Haller himself. For a more detailed history of the constitution of physiology as a science, see Georges Canguilhem, "La Constitution de la physiologie comme science," in *Etudes d'histoire et de philosophie des sciences concernant les vivants et la vie,* 7th ed. (Paris: J. Vrin, 1994 [1968]), 226–73.

13. Michel Foucault, *The Order of Things: An Archaeology of the Human Sciences,* trans. Alan Sheridan (New York: Vintage Books, 1973), 241.

14. Jean Copans and Jean Jamin, "Présentation," in *Aux origines de l'anthropologie française,* 14.

15. Itard's two monographs on Victor (1801 and 1806) have been re-edited by Lucien Malson. See Lucien Malson and Jean Itard, *Wolf Children and the Wild Boy of Aveyron,* trans. Edmund Fawcett, Peter Ayrton, and Joan White (London: New Left Books, 1972). For further commentary, some of which I have used here, see the well-crafted essay by George W. Stocking Jr., "French Anthropology in 1800," in *Race, Culture, and Evolution: Essays in the History of Anthropology* (Chicago: University of Chicago Press, 1982 [1968]), 13–41. For reprints of some of the original articles about Victor, see Thierry Gineste, *Victor de l'Aveyron, dernier enfant sauvage, premier enfant fou* (Paris: Hachette, 1993 [1981]).

16. See Philippe Pinel, "Rapport fait à la Société des Observateurs de l'Homme sur l'enfant connu sous le nom de sauvage de l'Aveyron," in *Aux origines de l'anthropologie française,* ed. Copans and Jamin, 127–46. Roche-Ambrose Sicard became the second director of the institute following the death of L'Abbé de l'Epée.

17. Georges Gusdorf, *La Conscience révolutionnaire: Les Idéologues,* vol. 8 of *Les Sciences humaines et la pensée occidentale* (Paris: Payot, 1978), 502–3.

18. Jean Baptiste Lamarck, "Zoological Philosophy," in *This Is Race,* ed. Earl W. Count (New York: Henry Schuman, 1950), 40–44.

19. Taken from Gusdorf, *La Conscience révolutionnaire,* 503.

20. Joseph-Marie Degérando, "Présentation du rapport de J. M. G. Itard sur l'enfant sauvage de l'Aveyron," in *Aux origines de l'anthropologie française,* ed. Copans and Jamin, 152.

21. Roch-Ambrose Sicard, *Cours d'instruction d'un sourd-muet de naissance, pour servir à l'éducation des sourds-muets, et qui peut être utile à celle de ceux qui entendent et qui parlent* (Paris: Chez Le Clere, 1800), ix.

22. Joseph-Marie Degérando, *De l'éducation des sourds-muets de naissance* (Paris: Chez Mequignon L'Aîné Père, 1827), 133.

23. Denis Diderot, "Lettre sur les sourds et muets, à l'usage de ceux qui entendent et qui parlent (1751)," in *Diderot premières oeuvres 2,* ed. Norman Rudich and Jean Varloot (Paris: Éditions sociales, 1972), 121. This discussion of the deaf-mute was complemented by an earlier essay on the blind, "Lettre sur les aveugles" (1749), featuring the case of the blind mathematician Nicholas Saunderson. Saunderson made the claim for a tactile geometry in which touch can serve to anchor universal truths. See also Jonathan Crary, *Techniques of the Observer* (Cambridge, Mass.: MIT Press, 1991), 59–60.

24. Georges Demenÿ, "La Photographie de la parole," *Paris-photographe,* October 25, 1891, 2.

25. Braun, *Picturing Time,* 176. See Laurent Mannoni's discussion of Demenÿ's split with Marey as a result of patenting the Phonoscope: Laurent Mannoni, *The Great Art of Light and Shadow* (Exeter, England: Exeter University Press, 2000), 320–63. See also *Georges Demenÿ et les origines "sportives" du cinéma* (Georges Demenÿ and the "sports-related" origins of cinema), dir. André Drevon, 1995, 23', distributed by CNRS–Audiovisuel.

26. Mannoni, *The Great Art of Light and Shadow,* 354–63.

27. Georges Demenÿ, "Les Photographies parlantes," *La Nature: Revue des sciences* 20 (April 20, 1892): 311–15. The plates from this series initially appeared in *La Nature* and have been reprinted elsewhere.

28. Ibid., 314.

29. François Dagognet, *Etienne-Jules Marey: A Passion for the Trace,* trans. Robert Galeta with Jeanine Herman (New York: Zone Books, 1992), 41–42.

30. Walter Benjamin, "The Work of Art in the Age of Mechanical Reproduction," in *Illuminations,* ed. Hannah Arendt, trans. Harry Zohn (New York: Schocken Books, 1968), 248–49, n. 14.

31. Malson and Itard, *Wolf Children and the Wild Boy of Aveyron,* 84.

32. Louis Olivier, "Le Microphonographe et ses application à l'éducation des sourds-muets, à la téléphone et à la cinématographie," *Revue générale des sciences pures et appliqués* 8 (1897): 1005.

33. Angelo Mosso, *La Fatigue intellectuelle et physique,* trans. P. Langlois (Paris: Félix Alcan, 1894 [1891]), 52.

34. Mosso also worked with Marey at the Physiological Station earlier in his career and was a member of the commission that established the Institut Marey. See in particular the "Statuts de l'Institut Marey" in Olivier, "L'Institut Marey," 198–99.

35. Braun, *Picturing Time,* 327.

36. Georges Ribeill, "Les Débuts de l'ergonomie en France," *Le Mouvement social* 113 (October–December 1980): 3–36. Ribeill also notes that the term *ergonomics* is a recent invention and was grounded more specifically in the study of fatigue.

37. Anson Rabinbach, *The Human Motor* (Berkeley: University of California Press,

1992), 48–51. See the discussion of *kraft* in chapter 2, "Transcendental Materialism." Overall, this is a brilliant work on the history of fatigue in the European fin-de-siècle and interwar imagination. For a more complete treatment of related issues in Germany see Frederick Gregory, *Scientific Materialism in Nineteenth-Century Germany* (Dordrecht: D. Reidel, 1977).

38. For a more detailed historicization of Ludwig's kymograph, see H. E. Hoff and L. A. Geddes, "Graphic Registration before Ludwig: The Antecedents of the Kymograph," *Isis* 50, part 1, no. 159 (March 1959): 5–21; see also H. E. Hoff and L. A. Geddes, "The Beginnings of Graphic Recording," *Isis* 53, no. 173 (1962): 287–324. While the search for the origin of a technique can never be conclusive by any means, Hoff and Geddes trace the origins of the German school of physiology back to France and relate Ludwig's kymograph to the eighteenth-century ballistic galvanometer developed by Claude Servais Pouillet.

39. Rabinbach, *The Human Motor,* 339.

40. Auguste Chauveau, "Du travail physiologique et de son équivalence," *Revue scientifique* (Paris: Administration des deux revues, 1888): 3.

41. Etienne-Jules Marey, *La Machine animale* (Paris: Librairie Germer Baillière, 1873), 12.

42. Jules Gavarret, "Chaleur animale," in *Dictionnaire encyclopédique des sciences médicales,* vol. 15 (CHA–CHE), ed. Raige-Delorme and A. Dechambre (Paris: P. Asselin and G. Masson, 1874), 82.

43. Ibid.

44. Marey, *La Machine animale,* 12.

45. Jules-Etienne Marey, "Des lois de la mécanique en biologie," *Revue scientifique,* 3d ser., no. 1 (July 3, 1886): 5.

46. Jules-Etienne Marey, "Recherches expérimentales sur la morphologie des muscles," *Comptes rendus des séances de l'Académie des Sciences* 55 (September 12, 1887): 3.

47. M.-N. Bouillet, "Nègres," in *Dictionnaire universel d'histoire et de géographie* (Paris: Librairie de L. Hachette et Cie., 1867 [1842]), 1335.

48. For an excellent study of Gall's work, see Georges Lanteri-Laura, *Histoire de la phrenologie: L'Homme et son cerveau selon F. J. Gall* (Paris: Presses Universitaires de France, 1970).

49. R. J. Cooter, "Phrenology: The Provocation of Progress," *History of Science* 14, no. 4 (1976): 211–34. This article provides an overview of phrenology in the nineteenth century, but mostly focuses on the Victorian phrenological debates, though some references are made to the French case.

50. Oswei Temkin, "Gall and the Phrenological Movement," *Bulletin of the History of Medicine* 21, no. 3 (May–June 1947): 275–321.

51. Joseph Deniker, "Introduction: Ethnic Groups and Zoological Species," excerpted from *The Races of Man* (1900), in *This Is Race,* ed. Earl. W. Count (New York: Henry Schuman, 1950). Virey was also among the sixty members of the Société des Observateurs de l'Homme.

52. See Commandant V. Legros's preface to Angelo Mosso, *L'Éducation physique de la jeunesse,* trans. J. B. Bahar (Paris: Félix Alcan, 1895), xx.

53. Alain Ehrenberg, *Le Corps militaire: Politique et pédagogie en démocratie* (Paris: Aubier Montaigne, 1983), 116.

54. Jean-Marie Lahy, "La Psychologie du combattant dans la guerre de tranchées et dans le combat corps à corps," *La Grande revue* (May 1915): 317–55. For a brief overview of Lahy's work in English, see William H. Schneider, "The Scientific Study of Labor in Interwar France," *French Historical Studies* 17, no. 2 (Fall 1991): 410–46. Schneider discusses Lahy's work in relation to the development of psychophysiology in France (423–28).

55. Ehrenberg, *Le Corps militaire,* 111.

56. Shelby Cullom Davis, "Reservoirs of Men: A History of Black Troops of French West Africa" (Ph.D. diss., University of Geneva, 1934), 68.

57. Capitaine Hippolyte-Victor Marceau, *Le Tirailleur soudanais* (Paris: Berger-Levrault, Éditeurs, 1911), 31.

58. Jacques Ulmann, *De la gymnastique aux sports modernes: Histoire des doctrines de l'éducation physique* (Paris: Presses Universitaires de France, 1965), 317.

59. Christian Pociello, "Physiologie et education physique au XIXe siècle: J.-E. Marey et G. Demenÿ," (Ph.D. diss., University of Paris VII–Jussieu, 1974), 145.

60. J. Baills (Frigate Captain in the French Navy), "Théorie mécanique de la marche et de la course," *Revue maritime et coloniale* 118 (Paris: Ministère de la Marine, Librairie Militaire de L. Badoin, 1893): 81–97. Thanks to Frances Terpak for this citation.

61. Regnault notes that Commandant de Raoul had been developing the flexioned gait as a less tiring form of walking and running since 1872. Félix Regnault, "Des divers méthodes de marche et de course," *L'Illustration* 2765 (February 22, 1896): 155.

62. For further discussion of Manouvrier's position see L. Manouvrier, "Étude sur la rétroversion de la tête tibia et l'attitude humaine à l'époque quaternaire," *[Bulletins et] Mémoires de la Société d'Anthropologie de Paris* 4, no. 1 (1889): 219–64.

63. Félix Regnault, "La Locomotion chez l'homme," *Journal de physiologie et de pathologie générale* 15, no. 1 (January 1913): 51–52 (46–61).

64. Ibid., 60.

65. Félix Regnault, "Des divers genres de marche," *Biologica: Revue scientifique du médecin* 3, no. 35 (1913): 348 (346–48).

66. Stephen Jay Gould, *The Mismeasurement of Man* (New York: W. W. Norton, 1981), 129. Citation from Cesare Lombroso, "Histoire des progrès de l'anthropologie et de la sociologie criminelles pendant les années 1895–1896," in *Travail du Quatrième Congrès d'Anthropologie Criminelle* (Geneva, 1896), 187–99.

67. Félix Regnault, "Le Grimpeur," *Revue encyclopédique* (1897), 904–5.

68. Joy Dorothy Harvey, "Races Specified, Evolution Transformed: The Social Context of Scientific Debates Originating in the Société d'Anthropologie de Paris, 1859–1902" (Ph.D. diss., Harvard University, 1983), 165. As Harvey explains, "a forest of trees" was a term that Armand de Quatrefages used to describe an evolutionary paradigm established by Carl Vogt. However, de Quatrefages himself was a firmly committed monogenist.

69. Albert Messimy, *Notre oeuvre coloniale* (Paris: Émile Larose, 1910), 44.

70. Regnault, "Le Grimpeur," 905.

71. Edward Said, *Orientalism* (New York: Vintage Books, 1978), 95–97.

72. Georges-Michel Coissac, "Au service de la civilisation," *Cinéopse* 140 (April 1, 1931): 176 (175–77).

73. Emilie de Brigard, "Historique du film ethnographique," in *Pour une anthropologie visuelle,* ed. Claudine de France (Paris: Mouton de Gruyer, 1979), 30 (21–51). In an earlier book Titaÿna explains that the film was shot on plantations that she knows well and that the roles of cannibals were played by plantation workers to please the Americans. Titaÿna (pseud.), *Chez les mangeurs d'hommes* (Paris: Éditions Duchartre, 1931), 11.

74. Jean-Jacques Rousseau, *Discourse on the Origin of Inequality,* trans. Donald A. Cress (Indianapolis: Hackett Publishing, 1992 [1755]), 50. I have abbreviated the original title, *Discours sur l'origine et les fondements de l'inégalité parmi les hommes,* as *De l'inégalité parmi les hommes* throughout the text.

75. The Brazilian avant-garde poet Oswaldo de Andrade initiated a series of reflections on anthropophagi with his influential *Anthropophagic Manifesto* (1928) as the first issue of the short-lived Brazilian avant-garde literary journal *On Anthropophagy.*

76. "Tupi" refers to the sixteenth-century ritualistic cannibalism of the Brazilian Tupi-namba. Oswald de Andrade, *Anthropophagies,* trans. Jacques Thiériot (Paris: Flammarion, 1982), 267. See Francis Picabia, "Manifeste cannibale," *Dadaphone* 7 (March 1920): 3; reprinted in *Dada: Réimpression intégrale et dossier critique de la revue publiée de 1916 à 1922 par Tristan Tzara,* intro. Michel Sanouillet, vol. 1 (Nice: Centre du XXe siècle, 1976), 113. See also *Cannibale: Revue mensuelle sous la direction de Francis Picabia avec la collaboration de tous les dadaïstes du monde.* Only two issues were printed, no. 1 (April 25, 1920) and no. 2 (May 25, 1920).

77. Raoul Girardet, *L'Idée coloniale en France de 1871 à 1962* (Paris: Hachette, 1972), 137–38.

78. Jamin, "Faibles sauvages . . . corps indigènes, corps indigents," 62.

79. Georges Hébert, *La Culture virile et les devoirs physiques de l'officier combattant* (Paris: G. Codin et Cie, 1913), xi. Hébert served as a Navy Lieutenant at the time.

2. MYTHOLOGIES OF THE TIRAILLEURS SÉNÉGALAIS

1. I translate *Tirailleur sénégalais* as the Senegalese Sharpshooter associated with World War I, partly to evoke the sense that their vision was purposefully obscured and focused on particular targets. I use *Tirailleurs sénégalais* and *Senegalese Sharpshooters* interchangeably throughout this chapter. *Tirailleurs* may also be translated as "artillerymen" or "riflemen." Further, the Senegalese Sharpshooters were not necessarily from Senegal, but from a wide variety of geographic areas in French West and Equatorial Africa.

2. Roland Barthes, "Myth Today," in *Mythologies,* trans. Annette Lavers, 20th printing (New York: Hill and Wang, 1987 [1957]), 116. The cover photo appears in *Paris-Match* 326 (June 25–July 2, 1955).

3. Carl Jung first used the term *imago* in place of the Freudian term *complex* in order to "*invest* this psychological condition" (emphasis in the original). See Carl G. Jung, *Psychology of the Unconscious,* trans. Beatrice M. Hinkle (New York: Moffat, Yard, and Company, 1974 [1916]), 49. My discussion of the imago more closely approximates Laplanche and Pontalis's notion of the imago as an "unconscious representation." See Jean Laplanche and Jean-Baptiste Pontalis, *The Language of Psychoanalysis,* trans. Donald Nicholson-Smith (New York: W. W. Norton, 1973), 211.

4. Thanks to Pascal Blanchard for examining this image and suggesting the reference to the Boy Scout uniform.

5. As cited by Terence Ranger, "The Invention of Tradition in Colonial Africa," in *The Invention of Tradition,* ed. Eric Hobsbawm and Terence Ranger (Cambridge: Cambridge University Press, 1983), 224. For the details regarding miniature equipment Ranger cites a conference paper by Sylvanius Cookey.

6. J. Malcolm Thompson, "Colonial Policy and the Family Life of Black Troops in French West Africa, 1817–1904," *International Journal of African Historical Studies* 23, no. 3 (1990): 425–26.

7. Zouaves were Algerian infantry contingents created by France in 1830 and dissolved in 1962. Originally composed of members from the Kabyle tribe, known as Zouavas, they traditionally provided troops to the Ottomans prior to the French conquest. The Zouaves were deployed by France in Europe, Indochina, North Africa, and the Crimea.

8. Shelby Cullom Davis, *Reservoirs of Men: A History of the Black Troops of French West Africa* (Geneva: Librairie Kundig, 1934), 40.

9. Gum arabic is conventionally known as a tree extract that is used in glue, incense, and soft drinks. More precisely it is "a water-soluble, dried, gummy exudation obtained

from the stems and branches of *Acacia Senegal* and other species of *acacia:* used as a food thickener, an emulsifier, in inks, textile printing, and in pharmaceuticals as an excipient for tablets." *The Random House Dictionary of the English Language: The Unabridged Edition* (New York: Random House, 1983), 630. Senegal and the surrounding area of present-day Mali and Niger were considered a primary source of gum arabic until the beginning of the nineteenth century, when it was more successfully harvested in Kordofan, Sudan, where it is still found today.

10. St. Louis, Rufisque, Dakar, and Gorée Island were the four municipalities located in present-day Senegal that later became known as the Four Communes. They were initially settled under the ancien régime. Other parts of sub-Saharan Africa colonized by France were largely established under the Third Republic, or after 1870. A well-established bourgeoisie developed in the Four Communes because each of these municipalities was successively granted rights—a locally elected administration as well as civil rights—equivalent to those of municipalities in France as of 1871 (in St. Louis and Gorée), 1880 (in Rufisque), and 1887 (in Dakar). For further details see Alice M. Conklin, *A Mission to Civilize: The Republican Idea of Empire in France and West Africa, 1895–1930* (Stanford, Calif.: Stanford University Press, 1997), 151.

11. See Mamadou Diouf, *Le Kajoor au XIXe siècle: Pouvoir ceddo et conquête coloniale* (Paris: Karthala, 1990). See also Abdoulaye Bathily, "Aux origins de l'Africanisme: Le Role de l'oeuvre ethno-historique de Faidherbe dans la conquête française du Sénégal," in *Le Mal de voir* [Cahiers Jussieu no. 2, Université de Paris VII] (Paris: 10/18 Union Générale d'Éditions, 1976), 77–107.

12. The Mission Crampel, led by Paul Crampel, was sanctioned by the French Colonial Lobby to establish a French presence in Equatorial Africa. This expedition ended in disaster when Crampel and his chief medical officer, Mohammed Said, were killed in combat in Dar Kouti, Chad.

13. The Voulet–Chanoine Expedition, also known as Mission Afrique Centrale, was commissioned by the French government to pass through Chad and Niger and establish a French foothold in Eastern Nigeria, finally meeting up with other French forces in the region. When the increasingly mentally unstable leaders of this expedition, Voulet and Chanoine, were refused six steers in the Niger village of Birni N'Konni, they instructed their squadron of Senegalese Sharpshooters to destroy and massacre the whole village, estimated at 15,000 people. After word of this reckless massacre reached Paris, Voulet and Chanoine were pursued by Colonel Klobb, who was fired upon and killed on Voulet and Chanoine's command. Finally, the Senegalese Sharpshooters mutinied and killed Voulet and Chanoine. From all reports, Voulet and Chanoine's ambition was to establish their own personal African empire. See Jean Martin, *Lexique de la colonisation française* (Paris: Dalloz, 1988), 387–88.

14. Marc Michel, *L'Appel à l'Afrique: Contributions et réactions à l'effort de guerre en A.O.F., 1914–1919* (Paris: Publications de la Sorbonne, 1982), 16.

15. Myron Echenberg, *Colonial Conscripts: The Tirailleurs Sénégalais in French West Africa, 1857–1960* (Portsmouth, N.H.: Heinemann, 1991), 15.

16. Jean Garrigues, *Banania, histoire d'une passion française* (Paris: Du May, 1991), 16–18. See also, more generally, Raymond Bachollet, Jean-Bathélemi Debost, Anne-Claude Lelieur, and Marie-Christine Peyrière, *Négripub: L'Image des noirs dans la publicité* (Paris: Somogy, 1992).

17. Mireille Rosello, *Declining the Stereotype: Ethnicity and Representation in French Cultures* (Hanover, N.H.: University Press of New England, 1998).

18. Léopold Sédar Senghor, "Hosties noires," in *Poèmes* (Paris: Seuil, 1971 [1948]), 55.

19. Gilbert Meynier, following official sources, estimates that the number of colonial soldiers who fought in the war was between 535,000 and 607,000, not including 73,000 French Algerians or the cadre of colonial laborers (approximately 310,000 men, of which one-third were Algerian [50 percent were North African], one-sixth Annamite, and one-seventh Chinese). In total, at least 800,000 to 900,000 soldiers and workers were recruited from the colonies for the war. For a more detailed breakdown, see Gilbert Meynier, "Guerre et pouvoir colonial: Continuités et adaptations," in *Histoire de la France Coloniale: 1914–1990*, ed. Jacques Thobie et al. (Paris: Armand Colin, 1990), 78–79.

20. Michel, *L'Appel à l'afrique*, 408.

21. Ibid., 407.

22. The first few months of battle were at Ypres, Picardie, Dixmude, Artois, Champagne, and in the Dardanelles.

23. The *originaires* were those people indigenous to the Four Commune region of Senegal who enjoyed the rights of French citizenship. They were predominantly Muslim, poor, and outside of the French cultural and educational orbit. However, a small subset of the *originaires,* known as *métis* or *assimilé,* were identified with the Catholic bourgeois elite. They were the progeny of mixed marriages. Particularly after World War I, a new generation of French-educated Muslim clerks, managers, and returning soldiers, initially known as *lettrés* and later identified as *évolués,* began to emerge who were not necessarily Catholic or from mixed marriages. Further, the *originaires* were typically opposed to the *indigènes,* those who did not enjoy the same rights of French citizenship. Marc Michel writes that during the West African recruitment effort between 1914 and 1918, 7,200 *originaires* were recruited as opposed to 161,000 *indigènes.* See Michel, *L'Appel à l'afrique,* 410.

24. For a comprehensive discussion of the trench newspaper phenomenon, see Stéphane Audoin-Rouzeau, *Men at War, 1914–1918: National Sentiment and Trench Journalism in France during the First World War,* trans. Helen McPhail (Providence, R.I.: Berg, 1992).

25. Annabelle Melzer, "Spectacles and Sexualities: The 'Mise-en-Scène' of the 'Tirailleur Sénégalais' on the Western Front, 1914–1920," in *Borderlines: Genders and Identities in War and Peace, 1870–1930,* ed. Billie Melman (New York: Routledge, 1998), 218 (213–44).

26. Ibid., 228; Michel, *L'Appel à l'afrique,* 390; Charles Regismanset, "La croisade coloniale," in *Questions Coloniales* (Paris, 1917), 57.

27. Keith L. Nelson, "The 'Black Horror on the Rhine': Race as a Factor in Post-War Diplomacy," *Journal of Modern History* 42, no. 4 (December 1970): 612–13. See Nelson's remarkably complex note 31 for further discussion of this perspective.

28. Some mixed-race children were born as a result of the occupation, and the Senegalese were generally liked by the local population, particularly by the women, as Sally Marks notes. In fact, of the mixed-race relationships from which 53 children were born in 1919 and 105 children in 1920, there was only one case in which a rape was reported by one of the mothers. These children, who became known as "Rhineland bastards" under Hitler, became a source of virulent propaganda that made its way into *Mein Kampf.* See Sally Marks, "Black Watch on the Rhine: A Study in Propaganda, Prejudice and Prurience," *European Studies Review* 13, no. 3 (July 1983), 297–334. See also Marc Michel, *Les Africains et la Grande Guerre* (Paris: Editions Karthala, 2003), 238.

29. Marks, "Black Watch on the Rhine," 299.

30. Joe Lunn, "'Les Races Guerriers': Racial Preconceptions in the French Military about West African Soldiers during the First World War," *Journal of Contemporary History* 34, no. 4 (1999): 12, note 19 (517–36).

31. Cited in Michel, *Les Africains et la Grande Guerre,* 235. See also Edmund D. Morel, "The Horror on the Rhine," *Daily Herald,* April 6, 1920; Robert C. Reinders, "Radicalism

on the Left: E. D. Morel and the 'Black Horror on the Rhine,'" *International Review of Social History* 13 (1968): 1–28.

32. The film was produced by the Munich-based production company Bayerische Film–Gesellschaft Fett & Wiesel and was cowritten by John Freden and Heinrich Distler. For a catalogue record of this film see http://www.deutsches-filminstitut.de/filme/f011996 .htm. See Tobias Nagl, "'Die Wacht am Rhein': 'Rasse' und Rassismus in der Filmpropaganda gegen die 'schwarze Schmach' (1921–1923)," in *Kultur, Macht, Politik: Perspektiven einer kritischen Wissenschaft* (Berlin: Karl Dietz, 2003), 135–54.

33. Marks, "Black Watch on the Rhine," 315–16.

34. The film unit and the photography unit were actually separate sections until January 1917, when they became unified under one heading, SPCA.

35. Laurent Véray, "La représentation de la guerre dans les actualités françaises de 1914 à 1918," *1895* 17 (December 1994): 3 (3–52).

36. Etablissements de Communication et de Production Audiovisuelle de la Défense (ECPAD), *Tirailleurs sénégalais en Alsace*, 1917, 8'. This film was subtitled in French and English for international distribution, including Germany.

37. Jean-Louis Croze, "Reportage," in *Le Cinéma des origines à nos jours,* with a preface by Henri Fescourt but no editor named (Paris: Editions du Cygne, May 1932), 325–30. Croze was the first director of the SCA.

38. ECPAD, *L'Aide des colonies à la France* (dir. Henri Desfontaines, 1918, 19'). René Jeanne and Charles Ford name Henri Desfontaines as the filmmaker in their *Le Cinéma et la presse, 1895–1960* (Paris: Armand Colin, 1961), 204.

39. For a detailed description of Diarra's accomplishments and those of other Tirailleurs sénégalais at La Maisonnette, see "Les Héros blancs et noirs," http://perso.wanadoo .fr/grande.guerre/somme.html (accessed May 15, 2006).

40. Jeanne and Ford, *Le Cinéma et la presse,* 202.

41. Marcel Pierre, *Les Cent visages du cinéma* (Paris: Éditions Grasset, 1948), 124.

42. Charles Samuel Myers, *Shell Shock in France, 1914–1918: Based on a War Diary Kept by Charles S. Myers* (Cambridge: Cambridge University Press, 1940), 3.

43. Martin Stone, "Shellshock and the Psychologists," in *The Anatomy of Madness: Essays in the History of Psychiatry,* ed. W. F. Bynum, Roy Porter, and Michael Shepherd, vol. 2 (London: Tavistock Publications, 1985), 258.

44. Joseph Babinski and J. Froment, *Hysteria or Pithiatism and Reflex Nervous Disorder in the Neurology of the War,* trans. J. D. Rolleston, M.D. (London: University of London Press, 1918).

45. H. Reboul and E. Régis, *L'Assistance des aliénés aux colonies* (Paris: Masson et Cie., 1912). This report was presented at the Congrès des Médecins Aliénistes et Neurologistes de France et des Pays de Langue Française, 22nd session, Tunis, April 1–7, 1912. The quotation is taken from François Cazanove, Régis's former student, who served as *médecin-major* of colonial troops. See Cazanove's important article on French colonial psychiatry, "Memento de psychiâtrie coloniale Africaine," *Bulletin du Comité d'Études Historiques et Scientifiques de l'Afrique Occidentale Française* 10, no. 1 (January–March 1917): 161 (133–77).

46. René Collingnon, "Pour une histoire de la psychiatrie coloniale française: A partir de l'exemple du Sénégal," *L'Autre, cliniques, cultures, et sociétés* 3, no. 3 (2002): 475 (455–80).

47. Charles-Marie-Emmanuel Mangin, *Troupes noires* (Coulommiers: Impr. P. Brodard, 1909), 21.

48. Davis, *Reservoirs of Men,* 94–95.

49. Anne Harrington, "Hysteria, Hypnosis, and the Lure of the Invisible: The Rise of Neo-Mesmerism in Fin-de-Siècle French Psychiatry," in *The Anatomy of Madness: Essays*

on the History of Psychiatry, ed. W. F. Bynum, Roy Porter, and Michael Shepherd, vol. 3: *The Asylum and Its Psychiatry* (New York: Routlege, 1988), 234 (226–46). See also J. Babinski, *Recherches servant à établir que certaines manifestations hystériques peuvent être transferees d'une sujet à une autre sous l'influence de l'aimant* (Paris: A. Delahaye and E. Lecrosnier, 1886).

50. Gabriel Tarde, *Les Lois de l'imitation* (Paris: Éditions Kimé, 1993 [1890]), 84; Gustave Le Bon, *Psychologie des foules* (Paris: Quadridge, 1995 [1895]), 17.

51. J.-M. Charcot, "Sur les divers états nerveux determines par l'hypnotisation chez les hystériques," *Comptes-rendus hebdomadaires de l'Académie des Sciences* 94 (1882): 403–5. As cited by Harrington, "Hysteria, Hypnosis, and the Lure of the Invisible," 226.

52. Duchenne de Boulogne was also known as Guillaume Benjamin Amand Duchenne. For further details on Duchenne de Boulogne's work related to techniques of electrical faradizations, see Guillaume-Benjamin Duchenne de Boulogne, *De l'électrisation localisée et son application à la pathologie et à la thérapeutique* (Paris: Ballière, 1872).

53. Stone, "Shellshock and the Psychologists," 253 and 269–54.

54. Claude Bernard, *Introduction à l'étude de la médecine expérimentale* (Paris: Librairie Charles Delagrave, 1898 [1865]), 27–28.

55. George W. Stocking, "Fieldwork in British Anthropology," in *Observers Observed: Essays on Ethnographic Fieldwork,* ed. George W. Stocking Jr. (Madison: University of Wisconsin Press, 1983), 80.

56. Alison Griffiths, *Wondrous Difference* (New York: Columbia University Press, 2002), 131.

57. Ruth Leys, "Traumatic Cures: Shell Shock, Janet, and the Question of Memory," *Critical Inquiry* 20 (Summer 1994): 627. See also William Brown, "The Revival of Emotional Memories and Its Therapeutic Value," *British Journal of Medical Psychology* 1 (October 1920): 16–33.

58. In addition to discussions of Freud's work by Brown, Myers, and McDougall, W. H. R. Rivers incorporates Freud's vocabulary into his discussion. See W. H. R. Rivers, "War Neurosis and Military Training," *Mental Hygiene* 2, no. 4 (October 1918): 513–33.

59. Stone, "Shellshock and the Psychologists," 255.

60. Leys, "Traumatic Cures," 636.

61. Brown, "The Revival of Emotional Memories," 17.

62. Henri Bergson, *Creative Evolution,* trans. Arthur Mitchell (Lanham, Md.: University Press of America, 1983 [1911]), 72–74.

63. *Working-through* refers to Sigmund Freud, "Remembering, Repeating, and Working-Through (1914)," in *The Standard Edition of the Complete Psychological Works of Sigmund Freud,* ed. and trans. James Strachey, vol. 12 (London: Hogarth Press, 1958), 145–56.

64. Laplanche and Pontalis, *The Language of Psychoanalysis,* 73.

65. Jung, *Psychology of the Unconscious,* 49.

66. Laplanche and Pontalis, *The Language of Psychoanalysis,* 211.

67. Cited from Christopher Lane, "Psychoanalysis and Colonialism Redux: Why Mannoni's 'Prospero Complex' Still Haunts Us," *Journal of Modern Literature* 25, no. 3–4 (Summer 2002): 145 (127–50). See also Leo Bersani, "Against Monogamy," in "Beyond Redemption: The Work of Leo Bersani," special issue, *Oxford Literary Review* 20 (1998): 20.

68. Philippe David, "La carte postal sénégalaise de 1900 à 1960: Production, édition, et signification: Un bilan provisoire," *Notes Africaines* 157 (1978): 10 (3–12).

69. Ibid., 5.

70. David Prochaska, "Fantasia of the *Photothèque:* French Postcard Views of Colonial Senegal," *African Arts* 24, no. 4 (October 1991): 43 (40–47 and 98, notes).

71. Lunn, "'Les Races Guerriers,'" 529.

72. Capitaine Hippolyte-Victor Marceau, *Le Tirailleur soudanais* (Paris: Berger–Levrault, Éditeurs, 1911).

73. Paul Borreil, *Considerations sur l'internment des aliénés Sénégalais* (Montpellier: Imp. Gustave Firmin, Montane et Sicardie, 1908), 43.

74. Ibid., 7.

75. Collingnon, "Pour une histoire de la psychiatrie coloniale française," 457.

76. Ibid., 461.

77. The name of the Senegalese rap group Wa BMG 44 refers to the 1944 massacre and the words "Wa bokk menmen guestu," which means "All together to better understand." The group is based in Thiaroye. Thiaroye is now known as a neighborhood with a high crime rate. See the group's track *"44,"* on *African Underground,* vol. 1 of the *Hip Hop Senegal* CD (Dakar: Sacre Keur Community Center, 2001).

78. Mannoni's approach is derived from the work of Alfred Adler, who was an early associate of Sigmund Freud but later broke with him. Octave Mannoni, *Prospero and Caliban: The Psychology of Colonization,* trans. Pamela Powesland (New York: Frederick A. Praeger, 1950).

79. Jock McCulloch, *Colonial Psychiatry and the African Mind* (Cambridge: Cambridge University Press, 1995), 122.

80. Frantz Fanon, *Black Skin, White Masks,* trans. Charles Lam Markham (New York: Grove Press, 1967 [1952]), 106.

81. The original title of the work was *La Psychologie de la colonisation.*

82. Octave Mannoni, "The Decolonisation of Myself," *Race: The Journal of the Institute of Race Relations* 7, no. 4 (April 1966): 331 (327–35).

83. René Collignon, "Vingt ans de travaux en psychiatrie et santé mentale au Sénégal (1979–1999): Essai de bibliographie annotée," *Psychopathologie africaine* 30, no. 1–2 (2000): 3–185.

84. Jean Rouch, "On the Vicissitudes of the Self: The Possessed Dancer, the Magician, the Sorcerer, the Filmmaker, and the Ethnographer," in *Ciné-Ethnography: Jean Rouch,* ed. and trans. Steven Feld (Minneapolis: University of Minnesota Press, 2003), 100 (87–101).

85. Albert Cervoni, "Une confrontation historique en 1965 entre Jean Rouch et Sembène Ousmane: 'Tu nous regardes comme des insectes,'" *CinémAction* 17 (1982): 77–78.

86. Marcel Mauss, "Techniques du corps," *Journal de psychologie normale et pathologique* 3–4 (March 15–April 15, 1935), 271–93. A translation of this essay, by Ben Brewster, appears in *Incorporations: Zone 6,* ed. Jonathan Crary and Sanford Kwinter (Cambridge, Mass.: MIT Press, 1992), 455–77.

87. Hervé Mbouguen, "Y'a bon banania, le retour!" http://www.grioo.com/opinion 3897.html (accessed January 2005).

88. The slogan "Y'a bon Banania" was finally abandoned by the multinational company Nutrimaine as of March 2006. See Laurence Girard, "Le Slogan 'Y'a bon Banania' est définitivement abandonné," *Le Monde* (March 2, 2006), no page number cited. Thanks to Steve Ungar for this reference.

89. Roland Barthes, "Change the Object Itself: Mythology Today," in *Image–Music–Text,* trans. Stephen Heath (New York: Noonday Press, 1977), 168.

3. The Trans-Saharan Crossing Films

1. Throughout this chapter I refer to *autochenilles* as half-track vehicles.

2. The full title of the film varied between *La Traversée du Sahara en autochenilles* and *La Traversée du Sahara en automobiles.* I refer to this film as *La Traversée du Sahara*

throughout the text. The Gaumont release featured the title ending in "autochenilles," which was also prominently featured in poster art for the film.

3. A fourth Citroën film titled *La Croisière blanche* (aka *The Bedeaux Sub-Arctic Expedition,* dir. Charles E. Bedeaux, 1934) was commissioned, but never completed, about a journey across Canada. The film is held at the Canadian Film Archive in Ottawa. Charles E. Bedeaux was a scientific industrial engineer who led chronometric studies at the Citroën factories during the 1920s. The Canadian filmmaker George Ungar used outtakes from *La Crosière blanche* in his 1995 documentary about Bedeaux titled *The Champagne Safari.*

4. Jean de Tallis, *Le Tourisme automobile en Algérie-Tunisie: Guide Dunlop* (Paris: Éditions des Guides du Tourisme Automobiles, 1923), 30–31.

5. Because of the enormous popularity of Feyder's *L'Atlantide,* a sound remake was directed by G. W. Pabst in 1932. For further discussion of the two films, see Abdelkader Benali, *Le Cinéma colonial au maghreb: L'Imaginaire en trompe l'oeil* (Paris: Editions du Cerf, 1998), and David H. Slavin, *Colonial Cinema and Imperial France, 1919–1939: White Blind Spots, Male Fantasies, Settler Myths* (Baltimore, Md.: Johns Hopkins University Press, 2001).

6. Benali, *Le Cinéma colonial au maghreb,* 105.

7. In a number of accounts, the French linguist Georges Hanoteaux was credited with suggesting the idea of the Transsaharien sometime before Duveyrier. See Camille Guy, *Les Colonies françaises: La Mise-en-valeur de notre domaine colonial* (Paris: Augustin Challamel, 1900), 532–39. Henri Duveyrier (1840–92), son of well-known Saint-Simonist Charles Duveyrier, went to study Arabic in Germany before traveling to Algeria. Further, the Saint-Simonists were among the most ardent supporters of railroad construction, holding a utopian socialist view that the railroad embodied the potential for progressive social reform. See René Pottier, *Henri Duveyrier: Un prince saharien méconnu* (Paris: Plon, 1938).

8. Adolphe Duponchel, *Le Chemin de fer trans-saharien, jonction coloniale entre l'Algérie et le Soudan: Études préliminaries du project et rappart de mission, avec cartes générale et géologique* (Montpellier: Coulet, 1879).

9. Fernand Foureau, *Mission chez les Touareg: Mes deux Itinéraires sahariens d'octobre 1894 à mai 1895* (Paris: Augustin Challamel, 1895).

10. Duponchel, *Le Chemin de fer Trans-Saharien,* 218–26.

11. Le Raid Citroën was the name of the expedition on which *La Traversée du Sahara* was filmed.

12. Georges-Marie Haardt and Louis Audouin-Dubreuil, *Le Raid Citroën: La Première traversée du Sahara en automobile: De Touggourt à Tombouctou par l'Atlantide* (Paris: Librairie Plon, 1923), 139.

13. Le Général Charles Philebert and Geroges Rolland, *La France en Afrique et le Transsaharien* (Paris: Augustin Challalmel, 1890).

14. Siegfried Zielinski, *Audiovisions: Cinema and Television as Entr'actes in History,* trans. Gloria Custance (Amsterdam: Amsterdam University Press, 1999), 74.

15. Eugene S. Ferguson, "Kinematics of Mechanisms from the Time of Watt," in *Contributions from the Museum of History and Technology,* United States National Museum bulletin 228, paper 27, Smithsonian Institution (Washington D.C.: U.S. Government Printing Office, 1962), 186 (186–230).

16. I am referring to Martin Bernal's critique of the "Aryanist model" here, but I use it as a critique of the colonial paradigm. The primary work that elaborates this thesis is in the first volume of Martin Bernal's *Black Athena.* Martin Bernal, *Black Athena,* vol. 1: *The Fabrication of Ancient Greece, 1785–1985* (New Brunswick, N.J.: Rutgers University Press, 1989). A sharp critique of Bernal's discussion of the "Arayanist model" and his argument

for a "Revised Ancient model" was undertaken by Mary Lefkowitz, but it does not include a response from Bernal himself. See *Black Athena Revisited,* ed. Mary R. Lefkowitz and Guy MacLean Rogers (Chapel Hill: University of North Carolina Press, 1996). Bernal did respond to these criticisms and his critics in a more recent volume titled *Black Athena Writes Back: Martin Bernal Responds to His Critics,* ed. David Chioni Moore (Durham, N.C.: Duke University Press, 2001).

17. Sylvie Schweitzer, *Des Engrenages à la chaîne: Les Usines Citroën, 1915–1935* (Lyon: Presses Universitaires de Lyons, 1982), 66–79. There is an extended discussion of Ernest Mattern's career at Citroën, particularly his impact on developing procedures for assembly line production and the introduction of the chronometer.

18. For more information about the history of French nuclear testing, see Bruno Barrillot, *Les Essais nucléaires français, 1960–1996* (Lyon: Centre de Documentation et de Recherche sur la Paix et les Conflits, 1990).

19. De Tallis, *Le Tourisme automobile en Algérie-Tunisie,* 219.

20. Ellen Furlough, "Une Leçon des choses: Tourism, Empire, and the Nation in Interwar France," *French Historical Studies* 25, no. 3 (2002): 441–73.

21. See André Citroën's introduction in Haardt and Audouin-Dubreuil, *Le Raid Citroën,* 5–24.

22. Marius Leblond, *L'Empire de la France: Sa grandeur, sa beauté, sa gloire, ses forces* (Paris: Editions Alsatia, 1944), 129–30. A journalist writing for the film journal *Le Cinéopse* wrote that a film titled *Le Transsaharien* (dir. [General] Louis-Dominque-Achille Aubier, 1922) was produced by the French military and presented at the 1922 Colonial Exhibition in Marseilles. See Jehane de Vimbelle, "Chronique du cinéma éducateur," *Le Cinéopse* 40 (December 1, 1922): 977.

23. Jeremy Keenan, *The Tuareg: People of Ahaggar* (London: Allen Lane Penguin Books, 1977), 87–88.

24. Georges Ferré, *Le Sahara sur quatre roues* (Paris: Éditions de la Nouvelle Revue, 1931), 28.

25. Alison Murray writes that General Laperrine was the first to undertake the journey from Ouargla to In Salah in 1916. See her informative article for further detail about the Citroën tourism agenda. Alison Murray, "Le Tourisme Citroën au Sahara (1924–1925)," *Vingtième siècle: Revue d'histoire* 68 (October–December 2000): 97 (95–107).

26. Gaston Gradis, *A la recherche du Grand-Axe: Contribution aux études Transsahariennes* (Paris: Librarie Plon, 1924), 12.

27. *L'Automobile à la conquête de l'Afrique (1898–1932),* ed. Centre des Archives d'Outre-Mer [CAOM] and Association des Amis des Archives d'Outre Mer (Aix-en-Provence: CAOM, 1988), 30.

28. The full title of the film is *Raid Citroën: La Première Traversée du Sahara en auto-chenilles; Première Mission Haardt–Audouin–Dubreuil; De Touggourt–Tombouctou–Touggourt* (dir. Paul Castelnau, 1923).

29. *Le Continent mystérieux, Part IV: Méharistes et Touareg* (dir. Paul Castelnau, 11', 1923).

30. Terence Ranger, "The Invention of Tradition in Colonial Africa," in *The Invention of Tradition,* ed. Eric Hobsbawm and Terence Ranger (Cambridge: Cambridge University Press, 1992 [1983]), 223.

31. The sequences from Niger to Gao on the return trip were filmed by de Céris, who was part of the support team for the expedition.

32. Jean-Gabriel Jeudy, "Rétrospective: Kégresse et le Système Semi-Chenillé, 1er Partie," *4×4 Magazine* 93 (June 1989): 93 (92–94).

33. Flossie was, in fact, Haardt's white-coated Sealyham terrier, who later became immortalized as Milou, the canine adventuress in Hergé's celebrated *Tintin* comic strip. See John Reynolds, *André Citroën: The Henry Ford of France* (New York: St. Martin's Press, 1996), 95.

34. Léon Poirier, *Vingt-quatre images à la second: Du studio au désert, journal d'un cinéaste pendant quarante-cinq années de voyages à travers le pays, les événements, les idées, 1907–1952* (Tours: Maison Mame, 1953), 63.

35. Léon Poirier writes that Georges Sprecht, his film operator during the making of *La Croisière noire,* took over the editing of *La Traversée du Sahara* upon Castelnau's return to Paris.

36. Achille Mbembe, *On the Postcolony* (Berkeley: University of California Press, 2001), 27.

37. Pierre Leprohon, *L'Exotisme et le cinéma* (Paris: J. Susse, 1945), 65.

38. Marnia Lazreg, *The Eloquence of Silence: Algerian Women in Question* (New York: Routledge, 1994), 29–33.

39. Malek Alloula, *The Colonial Harem,* trans. Myna Godzich and Wlad Godzich (Minneapolis: University of Minnesota Press, 1986).

40. Leïla Sebbar and Jean-Michel Belorgey, *Femmes d'Afrique du Nord: Cartes postales (1885–1930)* (Saint-Juste–la-Pendue, France: Bleu Autour, 2002), 11.

41. Lazreg, *The Eloquence of Silence,* 55–59.

42. Todd Porterfield, *The Allure of Empire: Art in the Service of French Imperialism, 1798–1836* (Princeton, N.J.: Princeton University Press, 1998).

43. Georges Onclincx, "Milieux coloniaux et cinématographie à l'Exposition Internationale de Bruxelles de 1897," *Cahiers Bruxellois* 3, no. 4 (October–December 1958): 287–309.

44. See the official catalogue for the 1897 Tervueren International Colonial Exhibition, *Bruxelles-Exposition: Organe Officiel de l'Exposition International de Bruxelles* (Brussels, 1897), 189–90.

45. Emmanuelle Toulet, "Cinema at the Universal Exposition, Paris, 1900," trans. Tom Gunning, *Persistence of Vision* 9 (1991): 18 (10–36).

46. The Mission Marchand was a French expeditionary force that arrived at Fachoda from Brazzaville three months prior to being forced to retreat by Kitchener's Anglo-Egyptian force.

47. Toulet, "Cinema at the Universal Exposition, Paris, 1900," 20.

48. Paul Rabinow, *French Modern: Norms and Forms of the Social Environment* (Cambridge, Mass.: MIT Press, 1989), 70–72.

49. Charles Musser, *The Emergence of Cinema: The American Screen to 1907* (Berkeley: University of California Press, 1990), 429.

50. Lauren Rabinovitz extends an analysis of the Hale's Tours exhibition to a sophisticated discussion of early film and amusement park experiences, which she describes as "body genres," an enduring legacy of the cinema. See Lauren Rabinovitz, "From *Hale's Tours* to *Star Tours,*" in *Virtual Voyages: Cinema and Travel,* ed. Jeffrey Ruoff (Durham, N.C.: Duke University Press, 2006), 42–60.

51. This was the first of two expeditions led by Gaston Gradis using three specially equipped, large, six-wheeled, double-tired Renault vehicles. In addition to the Estienne brothers, the Renault engineer M. Schwob and three mechanics accompanied them on the voyage. It departed from Colomb-Béchar on January 25, 1924, achieved their destination of Dahomey (now Niger) south of the Sahara, and returned to Colomb-Béchar on March 1, 1924. Gradis, *A la recherche du Grand-Axe.*

52. Georges-Michel Coissac, "Le Cinéma au service de la civilisation et de la propagande," *Le Tout-cinéma 1931–1932* (Paris: Publications "Filma," August 7–31, 1931): 61 (53–80).

53. This is a Dutch print of the French film held by the Nederlands Filmmuseum. Thanks to Nico deKlerk for his assistance with this print of *Les Mystères du continent noir* (1926). No director or cameraman is mentioned.

54. Coissac, "Le Cinéma au service de la civilisation et de la propagande," 61. Although I have not been able to locate this film or verify its existence, it is likely that it was filmed during the first Mission Gradis if, as Coissac asserts, the film was released in 1924. The second Mission Gradis–Delingette was undertaken from November 15 to December 11, 1924, and then continued with Mme. Delingette toward Capetown, South Africa. See Henri de Kerillis, *De l'Algérie au Dahomey en automobile: Voyage effectué par la seconde Mission Gradis à travers le Sahara, le Soudan, le Territoire du Niger, et le Dahomey* (Paris: Librairie Plon, 1925).

55. James M. Laux, *The European Automobile Industry* (New York: Twayne, 1992), 9–10.

56. CAOM (Centre des Archives d'Outre-Mer), "Algérie: Territoires du Sud: Questions administratives et economiques," file no. 24H17 (16), Transports Autos.

57. Jacques Wolgensinger, *André Citroën* (Paris: Flammarion, 1991), 159.

58. Alison Murray describes in great detail the events surrounding the CITRACIT project, its history, and its abandonment. Murray, "Le Tourisme Citroën au Sahara (1924–1925)."

59. Alain Frèrejean, "Citroën et Renault, précurseurs du Paris–Dakar," *Historia* 616 (April 1998): 79 (74–79).

60. Ibid., 77.

61. Ibid., 79.

62. Georges-Marie Haardt and Louis Audouin-Dubreuil, *La Croisière noire: Expédition Citroën Centre-Afrique* (Paris: Libriarie Plon, 1927), v.

63. Some of these venues included the Belgian royal court and the Théâtre de la Monnaie in Brussels; in Paris, it was shown regularly at Théâtre Marivaux, but also at the Sorbonne and the Grand Amphitheater of the Muséum Nationale d'Histoire Naturelle. See *Bulletin Citroën* (1926), 292–94.

64. Gilbert Meynier, "Guerre et pouvoir colonial: Continuités et adaptations," in *Histoire de la France coloniale, 1914–1990,* vol. 2, L'apogée, 1871–1931, ed. Jacques Thobie et al. (Paris: Armand Colin, 1991), 379–418.

65. See *Alexandre Iacovleff: Itinérances,* ed. Pascal Blanchard, Emmanuel Bréon, Ariane Audouin-Dubreuil, and Blandine Chavanne (Paris: Somgy, 2005). Thanks to Steve Ungar for this citation.

66. *Bulletin Citroën* (1926), 397–405.

67. Reynolds, *André Citroën,* 81.

68. *Bulletin Citroën* (1926), 262.

69. Christraud M. Geary, "Nineteenth-Century Images of the Mangbetu in Explorers' Accounts," in *The Scramble for Art in Central Africa,* ed. Enid Schildkrout and Curtis A. Keim (Cambridge: Cambridge University Press, 1998), 147 (133–68).

4. Diagnosing Invisible Agents

1. For one of the earliest overviews of the French colonial novel, see Roland Lebel, *La Littérature coloniale* (Paris: Larose, 1931).

2. Maryinez Lyons, *The Colonial Disease: A Social History of Sleeping Sickness in Northern Zaire, 1900–1940* (Cambridge: Cambridge University Press, 1992), 42.

3. The Republic of Gambia remains a territorial wedge of a country within present-day

Senegal that owes its existence to its territorial envelopment of the Gambian River. Bathurst was renamed Banjul in 1973 and remains the capital of The Gambia.

4. A. Laveran and F. Mesnil, *Trypanosomes et trypanosomiasies* (Paris: Masson, 1912), 675.

5. Spirochetes are any of the several spiral-shaped bacteria of the order Spirochaetales, certain species of which are pathogenic for man and animals, others being free-living, saprophytic, or parasitic. See *The Random House Dictionary of the English Language: The Unabridged Edition* (New York: Random House, 1983), 1372.

6. Jean Painlevé, *Les Pionniers du cinéma scientifique: Jean Comandon* (Bruxelles: Hayez [in collaboration with the Cinémathèque Internationale in Bruxelles], 1967), 5.

7. Isabelle Do O'Gomes, "L'Oeuvre de Jean Comandon," in *Le Cinéma et la science,* ed. Alexis Martinet (Paris: CNRS Éditions, 1994), 82–83 (78–85).

8. See Painlevé, *Les Pionniers du cinéma scientifique,* 35. See also Brigitte Berg, "Contradictory Forces: Jean Painlevé, 1902–1989," in *Science Is Fiction: The Films of Jean Painlevé,* ed. Andy Masaki Bellows and Marina McDougall with Brigitte Berg, trans. Jeanine Herman (Cambridge, Mass.: MIT Press, 2000), 35.

9. *Dracula* was first translated into French by Éve and Lucie Paul-Marguerite under the title *Dracula: L'Homme de la nuit,* Collection littéraire des roman étrangers (Paris: L'Édition française illustrée, 1920). Subsequent editions of the same translation were published in 1924 , 1932, and 1946. See La Librairie Compagnie, "Cette Saison irlandaise: Les Écrivains irlandais du XIXe siècle à nos jours," http://www.librarie-compagnie.fr/irlande/auteurs/stoker.htm (accessed July 12, 2005).

10. Alexandra Warwick develops this point in some detail with regard to the British case. Alexandra Warwick, "Vampires and the Empires: Fears and Fictions of the 1890s," in *The Cultural Politics at the Fin de Siècle,* ed. Sally Ledger and Scott McCracken (Cambridge: Cambridge University Press, 1995), 202–20.

11. Robert A. Nye, *Masculinity and Male Codes of Honor in Modern France* (New York: Oxford University Press, 1993).

12. Ronald Genini, *Theda Bara: A Biography of the Silent Screen Vamp, with a Filmography* (Jefferson, N.C.: McFarland, 1996).

13. Hélène Hazera and Dominique Leglu, "Jean Painlevé Reveals the Invisible," interview with Jean Painlevé, in *Science Is Fiction: The Films of Jean Painlevé,* ed. Andy Masaki Bellows and Marina McDougall with Brigitte Berg, trans. Jeanine Herman (Cambridge, Mass.: MIT Press, 2000), 176–77.

14. Ibid., 177.

15. Ian Thomson, "How Do You Like Your Stake?" review of *From the Shadow of Dracula: A Life of Bram Stoker* by Paul Murray (London: Jonathan Cape, 2004), *Guardian Weekly* 171, no. 7 (August 6–12, 2004): 25.

16. Luise White, *Speaking with Vampires: Rumor and History in Colonial Africa* (Berkeley: University of California Press, 2000), 213, 233.

17. T. K. Biaya, "La Culture urbaine dans les arts populaires d'Afrique: Analyse de l'ambiance zaïroise," in *Canadian Journal of African Studies* 30, no. 3 (1996): 354, 355 (345–70).

18. Georges-Michel Coissac, "Le Cinéma au service de la civilisation et de la propagande," *Le Tout-Cinéma 1931–1932* (Paris: Publications "Filma," August 7–31, 1931): 58–59 (53–80). Francis Lacassin's biography of Machin explains that Machin's first expedition to the African continent began with the premiere of *Les Grandes chasses africaines: Une expédition cinématographique* in 1908. See Francis Lacassin, *Alfred Machin: De la jungle à l'écran* (Paris: Dreamland Éditeur, 2001).

19. The Songhay are an ethnic group with historical roots in Timbuktu and nearby

villages along the Niger River. They were later immortalized in Jean Rouch's films *Les Magiciens de Wanzerbe* (The magicians of Wanzerbe, 1949), *Jaguar* (1954), and *La Chasse au lion à l'arc* (The lion hunters, 1964). The Songhay became associated with important themes in French anthropology, such as migration patterns, indigenous oral history, and spirit possession. Marcel Griaule was among the first of the French anthropologists to study the Songhay. For further information on Rouch's films, see Paul Stoller, *The Cinematic Griot: The Ethnography of Jean Rouch* (Chicago: University of Chicago Press, 1992).

20. D. Scott, "The Epidemic of Sleeping Sickness," in *The African Trypanosomiasis,* ed. H. W. Mulligan with W. H. Potts (London: Allen and Unwin, 1970), 640, as quoted by Mario Joaquim Azevedo, "Epidemic Disease among the Sara of Southern Chad, 1890–1940," in *Disease in African History,* ed. Gerald W. Hartwig and K. David Patterson (Durham, N.C.: Duke University Press, 1978), 126.

21. Michael Worboys, "The Emergence of Tropical Medicine: A Study in the Establishment of a Scientific Specialty," in *Perspectives on the Emergence of Scientific Disciplines,* ed. Gerard Lemaine, Roy MacLeod, Michael Mulkay, and Peter Weingart (The Hague: Mouton, 1976), 81.

22. Dr. H. Dupont, "Contribution à l'étude de la maladie du sommeil," *Le Caducée* 8 (1904): 103 (103–8).

23. Dr. H. Dupont was a Belgian military doctor formerly stationed in the Congo and professor at the Antwerp School of Business.

24. Dr. H. Dupont, "Contribution à l'étude de la maladie du sommeil (suite)," with an introductory text by the editors of the journal, *Le Caducée* 10 (1904): 131 (131–32).

25. Gustave Martin and Georges Ringenbach, "Troubles Psychiques dans la maladie du sommeil," *L'Encéphale* 1, no. 6 (June 10, 1910): 625–71. French Soudan consisted of present-day Mali, as well as parts of Burkina Faso, Senegal, and Niger. It was integrated into French West Africa (Afrique Occidentale Française) in 1895 and was subject to numerous reorganizations and territorial amputations until 1960. For further discussion, see Jean Martin, *Lexique de la colonisation française* (Paris: Dalloz, 1988), 342–43.

26. Richard von Krafft-Ebing, *Psychopathia Sexualis,* trans. F. J. Rebman (Burbank, Calif.: Bloat Books, 1999 [1903]).

27. "XXe Congrès des Aliénistes de France," *Revue de psychiatrie* 14, no. 8 (1910): 320.

28. Dr. E. Brumpt, "Maladie du sommeil: Distribution géographique, étiologie, prophylaxie," in *Archives de Parasitologie* 9 (1905): 205 (205–24).

29. La Ligue Sanitaire Française contre la Mouche et le Rat was established in 1914 under the Ministry of Public Health. For more information on the organization, which came to be known as LSF, see the founding statutes of the organization. "Statuts, règlements, constitution, et renseignements divers," *[Bulletin de la] Ligue Sanitaire Française contre la Mouche et le Rat* 1 (Paris: Au Secrétariat Général, April 1914): 9–11.

30. Thierry Lefebvre, "Louis-Ferdinand Céline, Raphaël Blanchard et les mouches," *1895* 8 (Summer 1995): 99.

31. These examples are drawn from another film of the same period, *Les Mouches* (The flies, undated). Though undated, this film was also a compilation of sequences, some from the original L'Eclipse/Urborama–produced film, also entitled *Les Mouches* (1913). As Thierry Lefebvre reports, a hand-colored print of this film is available at the Nederlands Filmmuseum in Amsterdam. Lefebvre, "Louis-Ferdinand Céline, Raphaël Blanchard et les mouches," 99.

32. Éclair produced a series of scientific films from 1911 to 1914 under the heading of Scientica productions, which were focused on the popularization of science. See Theirry Lefebvre, "The Scientica Production (1911–1914): Scientific Popularization through Pictures," *Griffithiana: Journal of Film History* 16, no. 47 (May 1993): 137–53.

33. Edouard Herriot, "La Mouche et le rat," in [Bulletin de la] *Ligue Sanitaire Française contre la Mouche et le Rat* 2 (July 1914): 13.

34. Raphaël Blanchard and Henri G. Richter, "Projet de campagne contre la mouche," in [Bulletin de la] *Ligue Sanitaire Française contre la Mouche et le Rat* 4 (August 10, 1915): 17.

35. Ibid., 18.

36. Raphaël Blanchard, "La Propagande hygiénique par l'affiche et le cinématographe," in *Compte rendu des séances: Conseil d'Hygiène Publique et de Salubrité: Seine* 18 (1916): 318 (317–20).

37. Upon screening *Trypanosoma gambiense: Agent de la maladie du sommeil* at Les Archives du Film–Bois D'Arcy, another copy of this film with Dutch subtitles appeared on a second reel in the same storage box.

38. Lucien Viborel, *La Technique moderne de la propagande d'hygiène sociale* (Paris: Éditions de "La Vie Saine," 1932), 407.

39. "Création à Paris d'un Institut de Médecine Coloniale," *Archives de parasitologie* 4 (1901): 414–74.

40. As indicated by Gustave Martin, Maurice Leboeuf, and Émile Roubaud in *Rapport de la mission d'étude de la maladie du sommeil au Congo Français, 1906–1908* (Paris: Masson, 1909), iii. Prior to Winterbottom, John Atkins first identified the disease in his travels along the Guinea coast in 1721 according to Mario Joaquim Azevedo and Kirk Arden Hoppe. Azevedo cites Reinhard Hoeppli, *Parasitic Diseases in Africa and the Western Hemisphere* (Basel: Verlag für Recht und Gessellschaft, 1969), 215. See Kirk Arden Hoppe, *Lords of the Fly: Sleeping Sickness Control in British East Africa, 1900–1960* (Westport, Conn.: Praeger, 2003), 50.

41. Mario Joaquim Azevedo cites K. R. S. Morris's work and explains that Ibn Khaldun mentioned symptoms analogous to sleeping sickness in the fourteenth century. He also notes that the King of Mali, Mansa Djata, reportedly died from the disease in 1374. Azevedo, "Epidemic Disease among the Sara of Southern Chad," 121. For more information on early sources of sleeping sickness, see K. R. S. Morris, "The Spread of Sleeping Sickness across Central Africa," *Journal of Tropical Medicine and Hygiene* 66 (March 1963): 159–76.

42. Thomas Masterman Winterbottom, *An Account of the Native Africans in the Neighbourhood of Sierra Leone: To Which Is Added an Account of the Present State of Medicine among Them*, vol. 2 (London: C. Whittingham, 1803), 29, 30.

43. Brumpt, "Maladie du sommeil," 205.

44. Mareyinez Lyons, "Sleeping Sickness Epidemics and Public Health in the Belgian Congo," in *Imperial Medicine and Indigenous Societies*, ed. David Arnold (Manchester, England: Manchester University Press, 1988), 105.

45. Hoppe, *Lords of the Fly*, 1, 13. See also Mulligan, *The African Trypanosomiasis*, xlix.

46. Russell West, "Sleepers Wake: André Gide and Disease in Travels in the Congo," in *Pathologies of Travel*, ed. Richard Wrighley and George Revill (Amsterdam: Rodopi, 2000), 304 (299–316).

47. Lucien Viborel, "L'effort de propagande d'hygiène sociale par le cinématographe en France," *Revue internationale du cinéma éducateur* 4 (April 1932): 313.

48. Thierry Lefebvre, "Les films diffusés par la mission américaine de prévention contre la tuberculose (Mission Rockfeller, 1917–1922)," *1895* 11 (December 1991): 101–6.

49. Jane Ellen Crisler, "'Saving the Seed': The Scientific Preservation of Children in France during the Third Republic" (Ph.D. diss., University of Wisconsin–Madison, 1984), 241. These statistics are excerpted from the classic work about the Rockefeller campaign in France from the perspective of one of the French participants, Alexandre Bruno. Alexandre

Bruno, *Contre la tuberculose: La Mission américaine en France et l'effort français* (Paris: Société Moderne d'Impression et d'Édition, 1925), 142–43.

50. Claude Bonnefoy, "Dernier adieu à sa jeunesse: Quelques semaines avant sa mort, L.-F. Céline a raconté l'histoire de ses vingts ans," *Arts* 832 (August 1961): 5. Originally cited by Thierry Lefebvre, "Louis-Ferdinand Céline, Raphaël Blanchard et les mouches," *1895* 8 (Summer 1995): 98–99.

51. André Touzet, *Une oeuvre de guerre et d'après-guerre: La Mission cinématographique du gouvernement général de l'Indochine* (Hanoi–Haiphong: Impr. d'Extrême–Orient, 1919), 37.

52. Bruno Latour, *The Pasteurization of France,* trans. Alan Sheridan and John Law (Cambridge, Mass.: Harvard University Press, 1988), 86.

53. The second official Pasteur Institute outside of France was established in Saigon (1890) in a portion of a military hospital after the first one had been set up by Pasteur's nephew and assistant, Adrien Loir, in Australia. See Jean Chaussivert, "L'Institut Pasteur en Australie," in *L'Institut Pasteur: Contributions à son histoire,* ed. Michel Morange (Paris: Editions de la Découverte, 1991), 242–52.

54. This well-known turn of phrase is attributed to the Italian futurist Filippo Marinetti, "Geometrical and Mechanical Splendor and the Numerical Sensibility" (1914), in *Let's Murder the Moonshine: Selected Writings, F. T. Marinetti,* trans. R. W. Flint (Los Angeles: Sun and Moon Classics, 1972), 105–11. See also Stephen Kern, *The Culture of Time and Space: 1880–1918* (Cambridge, Mass.: Harvard University Press, 1983), 298.

55. Claire Salomon-Bayet, "Penser la révolution pastorienne," in *Pasteur et la révolution pastorienne,* ed. Claire Salomon-Bayet (Paris: Payot, 1986), 53 (17–64).

56. Anne Marcovich, "French Colonial Medicine and Colonial Rule: Algeria and Indochina," in *Disease, Medicine, and Empire,* ed. Roy MacLeod and Milton Lewis (New York: Routledge, 1988), 110 (103–17).

57. Anne-Marie Moulin, "Patriarchal Science: The Network of the Overseas Pasteur Institutes," in *Science and Empires: Historical Studies about Scientific Development and European Expansion,* ed. Patrick Petitjean, Catherine Jami, and Anne-Marie Moulin (Dordrecht: Kluwer Academic Publishers, 1992), 318 (307–22).

58. P. Richet, "Eugène Jamot: Son Oeuvre," *Médecine tropicale: Revue française de pathologie et de santé publique tropicales* 39, no. 5 (September–October 1979): 485–93.

59. Quoted from Jean-Pierre Dozon, "Quand les pastoriens traquaient la maladie du sommeil," *Sciences sociales et santé* 3, nos. 3–4 (November 1985): 39 (27–56).

60. *Mission en AEF* (Mission in French Equatorial Africa, 1920) is an educational documentary that was commissioned by Governor Generals Engoulavant and Sarraut. It traces a voyage from Cameroon through Ubangi-Chari to Gabon. See "Le cinématographe utilisé comme propagande aux colonies," *Le Cinéopse* 14 (October 1920): 414.

61. L. Sanner, "Eugène Jamot: L'homme (1879–1937)," *Médecine tropicale: Revue française de pathologie et de santé publique tropicales* 39, no. 5 (September–October 1979): 479–86. See also Marcel Bebey-Eyidi, "La Vie et l'oeuvre médico-sociale en afrique intertropicale française d'Eugène Jamot (1879–1937)" (medical thesis, University of Paris, 1950).

62. It is likely that similar cases occurred in other zones of Cameroon; it was not widely known at the time that high dosages of the vaccine (which is based on an arsenic compound) could cause blindness and death. As Dr. Sanner reported in an essay commemorating Jamot's contribution to tropical medicine on the centennial of Jamot's birth, "While the ocular toxicity of tryparsamide (the vaccine for sleeping sickness) is widely known today, instances of visual impairment occur fifteen percent of the time at dosages slightly under those used by the medical unit (i.e., four to six centigrams per human kilo)." Bebey-Eyidi, "La Vie et l'oeuvre d'Eugène Jamot," 482.

63. D. Doumergue, "La lutte contre la trypanosomiase en Côte d'Ivoire, 1900–1945," *Journal of African History* 22 (1981): 65 (63–72).

64. Lyons, "Sleeping Sickness Epidemics and Public Health," 105–24.

65. Dozon, "Quand les pastoriens traquaient la maladie du sommeil," 39.

66. Alan Williams, *Republic of Images: A History of French Filmmaking* (Cambridge, Mass.: Harvard University Press, 1992), 122. For more on Marie Epstein's collaboration with Benoît-Lévy, see Sandy Flitterman-Lewis, *To Desire Differently: Feminism and the French Cinema* (Urbana: University of Illinois Press, 1990).

67. Jean Epstein and his sister, Marie Epstein, worked as a team. They initially collaborated with Jean Benoît-Lévy, but when Jean Epstein began working for Pathé–Consortium–Cinéma, Marie Epstein continued working with Benoît-Lévy. She remained Benoît-Lévy's partner throughout the rest of her career.

68. Jean Benoît-Lévy, *The Art of the Motion Picture,* trans. Theodore R. Jaeckel (New York: Coward–McCann, 1946), 39–40.

69. Marcel Huret, *Ciné actualités: Histoire de la presse filmée, 1895–1980* (Paris: Henri Veyrier, 1984), 46.

70. Marcovich, "French colonial medicine and colonial rule," 113.

71. Several national public health leagues were established by 1931. For a full discussion of the uses of cinema in the various health leagues consult Lucien Viborel, *La Technique moderne de la propagande d'hygiène sociale* (Paris: Éditions de "La Vie Saine," 1931), 401–52. Viborel described sixteen major film categories available for rent, including general hygiene films and more specific films treating targeted social diseases, such as tuberculosis, venereal disease, alcoholism, diphtheria, and malaria.

72. Benoît-Lévy, *The Art of the Motion Picture,* 28.

73. Pierre Boulanger, *Le Cinéma colonial* (Paris: Éditions Seghers, 1975), 116. According to Boulanger, the story of *Itto* was based on the life of Dominique Reznikoff, a former television producer living in France.

74. Yvonne Turin, *Affrontements culturels dans l'Algérie coloniale* (Paris: Maspero, 1971).

75. Boulanger, *Le Cinéma colonial,* 116.

76. Marie-Paule Laberge, "Les Instituts Pasteur du Maghreb: La recherche scientifique médicale dans le cadre de la politique coloniale," *Revue française d'histoire d'outre-mer* 74, no. 274 (1987): 31 (27–42). The work of the Pasteur Institute in Morocco, which began as early as 1913 in Tangier, followed an agreement with the Paris-based Pasteur Institute. Beginning with the preparation of vaccines against rabies and smallpox as well as the establishment of veterinary and bacteriological research laboratories, the presence of the Pasteur Institutes was later expanded to include a broader research agenda.

77. Frantz Fanon, *Black Skin, White Masks,* trans. Charles Lam Markham (New York: Grove Press, 1967), 142.

5. INFILTRATE THE CROWD WITH AN IDEA!

1. *L'Oeuvre de la République: Au service de la Plus Grande France* (The creation of the Republic: In the service of Greater France, prod. SCPA, part 1, silent, 35mm, 9').

2. Patricia A. Morton, *Hybrid Modernities: Architecture and Representation at the 1931 Colonial Exposition, Paris* (Cambridge, Mass.: MIT Press, 2000), 71.

3. Charles-Robert Ageron, "Exposition coloniale de 1931: Mythe républicain ou mythe imperial?" in *Les Lieux de mémoire,* ed. Pierre Nora, vol. 1, *La République* (Paris: Gallimard, 1984), 577 (563–91). See also Catherine Hodeir and Michel Pierre, *L'Exposition coloniale* (Paris: Éditions Complexe, 1991); and Catherine Coquery-Vidrovitch, "L'Apogée: L'Exposition

Coloniale Internationale," in *Histoire de la France Coloniale III: Le Déclin, 1931 à nos jours*, ed. Charles-Robert Ageron and Catherine Coquery-Vidrovitch (Paris: Armand Colin, 1991), 9–140. I refer to the "1931 Colonial Exhibition" alternatively as the "Parisian Colonial Exhibition" and "the exhibition."

4. Herman Lebovics, *True France: The Wars over Cultural Identity, 1900–1945* (Ithaca, N.Y.: Cornell University Press, 1992), 94.

5. Georges-Michel Coissac, "Le Cinéma au service de la civilisation et de la propagande," *Le Tout-Cinéma 1931–1932* (Paris: Publications "Filma," August 7–31, 1931): 62 (53–80).

6. For further discussion of Sarraut's legacy see Clifford Rosenberg, "Albert Sarraut and Republican Radical Thought," *French Politics, Culture, and Society* 20, no. 3 (Fall 2002): 97–116.

7. "L'Objet d'un arrêté du 11 mai 1918," in *Congrès National d'Action et de Propagande Coloniales* (Paris: Éditions de l'Institut Colonial Français, 1931), 58. The extended title of this document reveals that it is a transcription of lectures, meetings, and discussions *(Compte-rendu des séances)* that took place May 11–12, 1931, as part of the Parisian Colonial Exhibition.

8. Paul Bourdarie, "Une politique coloniale française et rapport de M. Albert Sarraut sur un 'Project de loi portant fixation d'un programme général de mise en valeur des colonies françaises,'" in *Revue indigène: Organe des intérêts des indigènes aux colonies et pays de protectorat* 16 (1921): n.p. This periodical was published in Paris from 1906 to 1932 under the direction of Paul Bourdarie. This article appears in the press clippings file at the French National Colonial Archives in Aix-en-Provence, which I subsequently refer to as CAOM for Centre des Archives d'Outre-Mer à Aix-en-Provence. See CAOM, Agence FOM, carton 248, dossier 363.

9. CAOM, correspondence from Tony Jourdan, Film Colonial, to the minister of the colonies, January 22, 1930, Affairs politiques documents, file 859. Seven million francs in 1930 was roughly equivalent to 2.9 million euros today (about US$4 million), but this calculation does not clearly reflect the shifting mode of production for filmmaking activities, which is much more expensive today.

10. "Mission Cinématographique à la Guyane," *La Presse coloniale* 2415 (January 14, 1931): n.p.

11. "Un film officiel sur le Maroc," *Ciné-miroir* 232 (September 13, 1929): 588. In the article the novel is referred to as *Epopée africaine*. However, it refers more specifically to *Le Maître des cités: Épopée africaine*, which was supposedly written by Élissa Rhaïs (aka Rosine Boumendil). The adaptation project was undertaken at the peak of her fame in French literary circles and prior to revelations that she not only was Jewish, instead of Muslime, but was, in fact, illiterate. Although the stories themselves might have been derived from her own oral storytelling, Roland Tabet actually penned the novels attributed to her.

12. I have not been able to establish a definitive list of films that were commissioned through the Film Colonial initiative other than René Le Somptier's *La Marche vers le soleil*. However, press clippings indicate that several films were produced that address the terms of the initiative outlined by Tony Jourdan in the memo previously cited. A tentative list would include Gaston Vincke's documentary *Vers l'Eldorado* (Toward Eldorado), which was associated with an expedition organized through the Musée d'Ethnographie du Trocadéro as part of the Monteux expedition that focused on gold prospecting in Guyana; Alfred Chaumel's *Au Cameroun* (To Cameroon), adapted from *Le Réveil d'un race au Cameroun* (The awakening of a race in Cameroon, 1928); Charles Barrois's *Visions de la grande île* (Visions of a great island), about Madagascar; and J.-K. Raymond-Millet's *Le*

Périple de J.-K. Raymond-Millet: A travers l'AOF (J.-K. Raymond Millet's voyage through French West Africa), which was a compilation film analogous to Millet's *Promenade en AEF* (A walk through French Equatorial Africa) and was also produced for the exhibition. Two of the more relevant press clippings include P. H. P., "Le Cinéma au secours de nos colonies," *Ciné-comoedia* (December 14, 1930): n.p.; Nino Frank, "Un excellent documentaire: Notre oeuvre au Cameroun," *Pour vous* 80 (May 29, 1930): 8–9 (a discussion of Chaumel's film *Au Cameroon*); and G. B., "Propagande coloniale par le film," *Le Courrier-cinéma* 11 (February 1933): n.p.

13. Coissac, "Le Cinéma au service de la civilisation et de la propagande," 78. Some of Lyautey's celebrated essays include "Le Rôle social de l'officier," *La Revue des deux mondes* 114, no. 4 (March–April 1891): 443–59, and "Du rôle colonial du l'armée," *La Revue des deux mondes* 157 (January 15, 1900): 316–17.

14. Jean Locquin, "Le cinématographe et les questions coloniales," *Les Annales coloniales* (October 4, 1924): n.p.

15. Ministère des Colonies, *Exposition coloniale internationale et des pays d'outre-mer, Paris 1931* (Rapport Général présenté par le Gouverneur Général [Marcel] Olivier), vol. 1, *Conception et organisation* (Paris: Impr. Nationale, 1932), 237.

16. "Chez les buveurs du sang," *Cinémonde* 163 (December 3, 1931): 779; Odile D. Cambier, "En parlant avec le baron Gourgaud du *Vrai visage de l'Afrique*," *Cinémonde* 166 (December 24, 1931): 852.

17. Jean Vigaud, "Notre opinion à l'exposition," *Ciné-miroir* 326 (1931): 427.

18. Dudley Andrew and Steven Ungar, *Popular Front Paris and the Poetics of Culture* (Cambridge, Mass.: Belknap Press of Harvard University Press, 2005), 301.

19. Hodeir and Pierre, *L'Exposition coloniale*, 104.

20. Daniel R. Headrick, *The Tentacles of Progress: Technology Transfer in the Age of Imperialism, 1850–1940* (Oxford: Oxford University Press, 1988), 136.

21. Marcel Oms, "Un cinéaste des années 20: René Le Somptier," *Cahiers de la Cinémathèque* 33–34 (Autumn 1981): 212 (207–13).

22. Daniel Bertin, "Une grande manifestation coloniale," *La Presse coloniale* 2368 (January 29, 1930): 3. *La Marche vers le soleil* is presently unavailable for screening, although fragments of the original negative exist at the Archives du Film.

23. Although *La Marche vers le soleil* has not been restored, 123 advance publicity photographs are available at the Bibliothèque du Film in Paris. See their Web site (http://www.bifi.fr/) for further information.

24. Marquisette de Bosky, "Une blanche parmi les noirs: Le Voyage de Marquisette Bosky en Afrique," *Ciné-miroir* 198 (January 18, 1929): 38. See also the following numbers of Marquisette de Bosky's chronicle of the production, published under the same title: *Ciné-miroir* 195 (December 28, 1928): 836; *Ciné-miroir* 196 (January 4, 1929): 5; *Ciné-miroir* 197 (January 11, 1929): 23; *Ciné-miroir* 198 (January 18, 1929): 38; and *Ciné-miroir* 199 (January 25, 1929): 52.

25. Eric Le Roy, "Le Somptier, René," in "Dictionnaire du cinéma français des années vingt," special issue, *1895* 33 (June 2001): 252 (251–53).

26. Kristin Thompson, "The Rise and Fall of Film Europe," in *"Film Europe" and "Film America": Cinema, Commerce, and Cultural Exchange, 1920–1939*, ed. Andrew Higson and Richard Maltby (Exeter, England: Exeter University Press, 1999), 56–81.

27. Le Somptier served as secretary general of the Ministry of Physical Education in 1929, and Henry Paté held a position in the early period of this ministry, from 1920 to 1921 during the Aristide Briand government. See Coissac, "Le Cinéma au service de la civilisation et de la propagande," 63; see also Oms, "Un cinéaste des années 20," 212, and

the anonymous piece "Un film sur les colonies françaises," *Cinéma spectacles* 454 (February 5–11, 1928): 4.

28. Bertin, "Une grande manifestation coloniale," 3. Extensive passages from Frédéric François-Marsal's speech are excerpted in this article.

29. Jean Marguet, "La France, puissance coloniale, possède-t-elle un cinéma colonial?" *Cinémonde* 95 (August 14, 1930): 519.

30. Eric Le Roy, "Le Somptier, René," 251.

31. Louis Delluc, "Photogénie (1921)," in *Ecrits cinématographiques 1*, ed. Pierre Lherminier (Paris: La Cinémathèque Française, 1985), 31–77.

32. *Le Fils du soleil* (dir. René Le Somptier, cinéroman in eight chapters, screenplay Pierre Mercourt, prod. L'Echo de Paris, Film de la Société des Cinéromans, 1924).

33. Oms, "Un cinéaste des années 20," 212. The Société des Cinéromans was commissioned to produce Jean Renoir's film *Le Bled* for the 1930 Algerian Centennial in Algiers.

34. David Henry Slavin, "The French Left and the Rif War, 1924–25: Racism and the Limits of Internationalism," *Journal of Contemporary History* 26 (1991): 5 (5–32).

35. CAOM, Gouvernement générale de l'Indochine to Monsieur le Commisaire de l'Indochine à l'Exposition Coloniale Internationale de Paris, Hanoi, July 10, 1930, in Agence FOM (Indochina) documents, carton 530, dossier 41, no. 875 SPT. See Nguyen Van Ky, *La Société vietnamienne face à la modernité: Le Tonkin de la fin du XIXe siècle à la seconde guerre mondiale* (Paris: L'Harmattan, 1995), 385–89. This section of Ky's book includes a list of films held at the Agences Économiques de l'Indochine in 1935.

36. *Gabriel Veyre, opérateur lumière, autour du monde avec le cinématographe, correspondences, 1896–1900,* ed. Pierre Jacquier and Marion Pranal (Lyon: Insitut Lumière and Actes Sud, 1996). See *La Production cinématographique des Frères Lumière,* ed. Michèlle Aubert and Jean-Claude Seguin (Paris: Editions Mémoires de Cinéma, 1996), 310–19. See also Panivong Norindr, "'La Trace Lumière': Early Cinema and Colonial Propaganda in French Indochina," in *The Cinema: A New Technology for the 20th Century,* ed. André Gaudréault, Catherine Russell, and Pierre Véronneau (Lausanne: Éditions Payot, 2004), 329–39, and Panivong Norindr, "Vietnam," in *Encyclopedia of Early Cinema,* ed. Richard Abel (London: Routledge, 2005), 678–79.

37. Panivong Norindr, "Representing Indochina: the French colonial phantasmatic and the Exposition Coloniale de Paris," *French Cultural Studies* 6, part 1, no. 16 (February 1995): 39 (35–60). Norindr also includes a number of useful etymological references as to the origin of "Indo-Chine" (39, n. 3). See also Norindr's *Phantasmatic Indochina: French Colonial Ideology in Architecture, Film, and Literature* (Durham, N.C.: Duke University Press, 1996).

38. Nicola Cooper, *France in Indochina: Colonial Encounters* (Oxford, England: Berg, 2001).

39. For more about the historical rediscovery of Chinese science and technology, see Joseph Needham's comprehensive seven-volume encyclopedic exploration, which was continued by his research assistants and collaborators after his death. Joseph Needham, *Science and Civilization in China* (Cambridge: Cambridge University Press, 1954–98), vol. 4, part 3, 487–535. Cited from Robert Findlay, "China, the West, and World History in Joseph Needham's *Science and Civilisation in China,*" *Journal of World History* 11, no. 2 (2000): 265–303.

40. Octave Homberg, *La France des cinq parties du monde* (Paris: Les Petits-Fils de Plon et Nourrit, 1927). Homberg combats this idea of decentralization zealously in this Vichy-esque treatise, which is saturated with metaphors of cleansing, visions of purity, and images of imperial grandeur.

41. Gail Paradise Kelly, "Schooling and National Integration: The Case of Interwar Vietnam," *Comparative Education* 18, no. 2 (1982): 175–95.

42. Gail Paradise Kelly, "Colonial Schools in Vietnam: Policy and Practice," in *Education and Colonialism,* ed. Philip G. Altbach and Gail Paradise Kelly (New York: Longman Press, 1978), 97.

43. Ibid., 98. See also Trinh Van Thao, *L'École française en Indochine* (Paris: Karthala, 1995).

44. Pierre Brocheux and Daniel Hémery, *Indochine: La Colonisation ambiguë* (Paris: La Découverte, 1995), 220.

45. CAOM, Politique du film (Gouverneur Général de l'Indochine) documents, series L81, dossier 60025, "Chef Local du service de l'Enseignement Supérieur en Cochinchine," June 25, 1932.

46. Clarence J. North, *The Chinese Motion Picture Market,* U.S. Bureau of Foreign and Domestic Commerce, Trade Information Bulletin 467 (Washington, D.C.: Government Printing Office, 1927).

47. "Kim Van Kieu," *Courrier d'Haiphong* (March 16, 1924), n.p. According to this article, the film was produced by E. A. Famechon with Paul Thierry and was made by Indochine Films in association with Maison de la Pommeraye.

48. L. Bonnatout, "Kim Van Kieu," *Avenir du Tonkin,* March 7, 1924, n.p., CAOM press clippings file, Agence FOM, carton 248, dossier 363.

49. For the most authoritative account of early French colonial cinema in Vietnam, see Donald Dean Wilson Jr., "Colonial Việt Nam on Film: 1896 to 1926," 2 vols. (Ph.D. diss., City University of New York, 2007).

50. The Cinémathèque Nationale du Ministère du Travail et de l'Hygiène was established with the Comité National de Défense contre la Tuberculose under the Office National d'Hygiène Sociale. The beginnings of the anti-tuberculosis campaign in France were largely financed by the Rockefeller Foundation, and that, in turn, led to the establishment of the Office National d'Hygiène Sociale.

51. For further discussion of La Cinémathèque de la Ville de Paris, see Béatrice De Pastre–Robert and Emmanuelle Devos, "La Cinémathèque de la Ville de Paris," *1895* 18 (Summer 1995): 107–21; and Béatrice de Pastre, "Cinéma éducateur et propagande coloniale à Paris au début des années 1930," *Revue d'histoire moderne et contemporaine* 51, no. 4 (2004); 135–51.

52. "Au Musée Pédagogique: Règlement du service de location des films," *Le Cinéopse* 37 (September 1, 1921): n.p. Among the seven different categories defined, the first, "Voyages," included a number of films from the colonies, including Africa, Asia, and Oceania.

53. Raymond Borde and Charles Perrin, *Les Offices du cinéma éducateur: Et la survivance du muet, 1925–1940* (Lyon: Presses Universitaire de Lyon, 1992), 8. Thanks to Dana Polan for this source.

54. Auguste Bessou, *Rapport Général sur l'emploi du cinématographe dans les différentes branches de l'enseignement* (Paris: Impr. Nationale, 1920).

55. Georges-Michel Coissac, *Histoire du cinématographe: De ses origines à nos jours* (Paris: Éditions du Cinéopse, 1925), 518.

56. Raoul Girardet, *L'idée coloniale en France de 1871 à 1962* (Paris: Hachette, 1972), 137–38.

57. Bessou, *Rapport Général,* 4.

58. Ibid., 22.

59. Eugène Reboul, *Le Cinéma scolaire et éducateur* (Paris: Presses Universitaires de France, 1926), 4.

60. "Rapport de M. Pessemesse sur la Propagande scolaire," in *Congrès National d'Action et de Propagande Coloniales*, 30 (29–38).

61. Guy Olivio, "Aux origines du spectacle cinématographique en France: Le Cinéma Forain; L'Exemple des villes du Midi Méditerranéen," *Revue d'histoire moderne et contemporaine* 33 (April–June 1986): 225 (210–28).

62. Notably, the Société pour l'Organisation de la Propagande Coloniale par le Cinématographe was involved in this effort, which was presided over by Léon Riotor, conseiller municipal and président de la Commission du Cinématographe Scolaire de la Ville de Paris.

63. Georges-Michel Coissac, "Un cinéma colonial gratuit," *Le Cinéopse* 43 (March 1923): 255.

64. *Indochine Française: Part I Annam* (Paris: Publications du Gouvernement Général de l'Indochine in association with G. de Malherbe et Cie Imprimeurs, 1919).

65. See "La Mise en valeur des colonies," 1920. It was presented to the French senate on February 27, 1920. Charles-Robert Ageron, "Les Colonies devant l'opinion publique française (1919–1939)," in *Cahiers de l'Institut d'Histoire de la Presse et de l'Opinion* (Tours: Institut d'Histoire de la Presse et de l'Opinion, 1972–73) 1: 1–37.

66. "Discours prononcé par M. Albert Sarraut à l'ouverture des cours de l'Ecole Colonial," speech presented at the opening of the École Colonial, Impr. du Palais, Paris, November 5, 1923.

67. Correspondence from M. Garnier, Agence Économique de l'Indochine, to M. le Gouverneur Général de l'Indochine, in CAOM, Agence FOM, carton 248, dossier 363, no. 251-A, March 14, 1927.

68. Emile Roux-Parassac, "Les Enquêtes du cinéopse: L'Agence Économique de l'Indo-Chine, Office du Gouvernement Général de l'Indo-Chine Française," *Le Cinéopse* 68 (April 1925): 263–65.

69. On April 15, 1924, a five-year contract was approved by the French Official Government Council in Indochina between the governor general and Indochine Films. CAOM press clippings file, Agence FOM, carton 248, dossier 363. See the article, "La Transformation du service cinématographique," in *France–Indochine: Le Reveil Saïgonnais,* April 20, 1924, n.p.

70. Antoine Borrel, "Proposition de loi: Tendant à la création d'un 'Office national du Cinématographe,'" in *Chambre des Députés, Treizième Législature, Session Extraordinaire de 1927* 5030, 24.

71. Gérard Madieu, "Introduction," *Pathé-mensuel* 1 (October 1921): 1.

72. Octave-Jacques Gérin and C. Espinadel, *La Publicité suggestive: Théorie et technique* (Paris: Dunod, 1927), viii.

73. For example, at the 1914 International Exhibition, held in Lyons alongside yet another reconstructed Senegalese village, a number of documentary film shorts were commissioned for an exhibition on various techniques of silk production in Italy, Japan, and Cambodia. Pathé camera operators were commissioned by the Lyons Chamber of Commerce to bring back edited moving images. Although the initial assignment was to make an epic on the world history of silk manufacture throughout the ages in five parts, a more modest approach was finally adopted. Current techniques of silk production around the world were showcased, and the final product was a wearable commodity made by Parisian designers and exhibited by French models. Several scenes of the film were hand painted to highlight the silk garments. See "A l'Exposition de Lyon: Le cinéma du soie," *L'Echo du film* 23 (July 18, 1914): 12.

74. Gérin and Espinadel, *La Publicité suggestive,* 45.

75. J. Arren, *Sa majesté, la publicité* (Tours: A. Mame et fils, 1914), 91–92.

76. Jean Martin, *Lexique de la colonisation française* (Paris: Dalloz, 1988), 163. See also the preface to Jules Ferry, *Le Tonkin et la mère-patrie* (Paris: Harvard, 1890), which opens with a July 29, 1885, speech synthesizing Ferry's colonial doctrine.

77. Jehane de Vimbelle, "Chronique du cinéma éducateur," *Le Cinéopse* 48 (August 1923): n.p.

78. "Rapport de M. Leroi, 'Trains-Exposition sur les Foires-Exposition Coloniales,'" in *Congrès National d'Action et de Propagande Coloniale*, 62–68.

79. Ibid., 61.

80. *Comment propager nos idées: Par la presse, par le tract et l'affiche, par le livre, par les conferences, par le théâtre, par le cinéma, par la radiodiffusion, par le phonographe, par la chanson; Manuel pratique à l'usage des hommes d'action* (Paris: Bloud et Gay, 1932), 3.

81. Arren, *Sa majesté, la publicité*, 16.

82. Paul Leglise, "Les Institutions cinématographiques des années vingt," *Cahiers de la Cinémathèque* 33–34 (Autumn 1981): 56 (46–56).

83. A more extensive article appears in *Comment propager nos idées*, 391–421, and in an earlier article that outlines some of the meetings of the Congrès Catholique Internationale du Cinématographe, "Les Catholiques et le cinématographe," *Revue internationale du cinéma éducateur* 2 (August 1929): 190–96.

84. Gabriel Tarde, *L'Opinion et la foule* (Paris: Félix Alcan, 1901).

85. Gabriel Tarde, *Les Lois de l'imitation* (Paris: Editions Kimé, 1993 [1890]), 4. See in particular chapter 1, "La Repétition universelle," from which this discussion of natural history is excerpted in Alfred Espinas, *Des Sociétés animals* (Paris: Librarie Félix Alcan, 1924 [1878]).

86. Tarde, *Les Lois de l'imitation*, 84.

87. Scipio Sighele, *La Foule criminelle*, trans. Paul Vigny (Paris: Félix Alcan, 1892), 57. This was originally published in Italian under the title *La folla delinquente* (Torino: Fratelli Boca, 1891).

88. Gustave Le Bon, *Psychologie des foules* (Paris: Quadridge, 1995 [1895]), 17.

89. "Les Cinémas aux colonies," *Les Annales coloniales*, August 2, 1926, n.p. See CAOM press clippings file, Agence FOM, carton 248, dossier 363.

90. The number of movie theaters in the colonies is somewhat unclear, partially due to unreliable statistics concerning second- and third-run theaters, which usually served the native populations and were located either in working-class neighborhoods or outside the city.

91. Aimé-François Legendre, *La Crise mondiale: L'Asie contre l'Europe* (Paris: Librairie Plon, 1932), 287. See in particular the chapter titled "Le Cinéma et le prestige de la race blanche en Asie," 268–91.

92. William Marston Seabury, *Motion Picture Problems* (New York: Arno Press, 1978 [1929]), 320.

93. Ibid., 289.

94. See the short article by Father Louis Jalabert, "Le Film corrupteur," *Etudes: Action populaire* 68 (October 5, 1921): n.p. This article primarily criticizes individual French films but is also heavily dosed with anti-Semitic remarks leveled against the Benoît-Lévy cinema holdings.

95. Maurice Rouvroy, "Pour l'enfance et l'adolescence," *Revue internationale du cinéma éducateur* 2 (August 1929): 159–66.

96. Dr. F. Humbert, "The Effect of the Cinematograph on the Mental and Physical Well-Being of Children," in Seabury, *Motion Picture Problems*, 265–355.

97. Ibid., 337.

98. For further information on the development of crowd psychology, see Susana Barrows, *Distorting Mirrors: Visions of the Crowd in Late Nineteenth-Century France* (New Haven, Conn.: Yale University Press, 1981). See also Andreas Huyssen, *After the Great Divide* (Bloomington: Indiana University Press, 1986), 44–62.

99. Etienne Dennery, *Foules d'Asie* (Paris: Armand Colin, 1930), 241. The research for this book was funded by none other than Albert Kahn through the scholarship program Autour du Monde, which was directed by Henri Bergson.

100. Of the numerous articles I have read, only one article specifies some of the gunfighting westerns that were thought to have dangerous effects. The short films starring Tom Mix, Buck Jones, Art Accord, W. S. Hart, Eddie Polo, and Richard Talmadge, as well as the Charlie Chaplin comedies, are cited in an article by Paul Saffar, "Comment les Arabes aiment le cinéma," *Pour vous* 143 (August 13, 1931): 4. Paul Saffar was one of the most knowledgeable critics of North African cinema during the interwar period. He wrote a regular column concerning production news in North Africa in the weekly journal *Cinéma et spéctacles,* based in Marseilles.

101. It has been noted that both Woodrow Wilson and Lenin both took a deep interest in John A. Hobson's important book *Imperialism: A Study* (London: A. Constable, 1905). Hobson analyzed an expression that was to be the key to Cecil Rhodes's policy in South Africa, "To combine the commercial with the imaginative," as a revealing conjugation of imperial expansion.

102. Sir Hesketh Bell, *Foreign Colonial Administration in the Far East* (London: E. Arnold, 1928), 121–23. Cited by A. J. W. Harloff, "L'Influence pernicieuse du cinéma sur les peuples de l'Orient" (1934), 1–2, in CAOM clippings file, dossier 64384, Fonds du Gouvernement général de l'Indochine.

103. *Cinéma et spectacles: Organe officiel de la cinématographie du Midi de la France et de l'Afrique du Nord.* See articles by Raymond Huguenard, "Cinéma colonial," *Cinéma et spectacles* 493 (November 4–10, 1928): 1; Emile Flavin, "Le Cinéma en Afrique du Nord," *Cinéma et spectacles* 494 (November 11–17, 1928); 1; Raymond Huguenard, "Cinéma colonial," *Cinéma et spectacles* 500 (December 23, 1928–January 3, 1929): 1; and G. Moulan, "Et nos colonies?" *Cinéma et spectacles* 508 (February 28–March 2, 1929): 1. See also Myrima Rex, "Le Cinéma et les coloniaux," *Cinégraph* (October 1931): 17. In this last short article, written following the 1931 Colonial Exhibition, Rex's major concern was to determine the influence of cinema on the indigenous peoples from the colonies.

104. Huguenard, "Cinéma colonial," *Cinéma et spectacles* 493: 1.

105. Jens Ulff-Møller, "Hollywood's 'Foreign War': The Effect of National Commercial Policy on the Emergence of the American Film Hegemony in France, 1920–1929," in *"Film Europe" and "Film America,"* ed. Higson and Maltby, 194.

106. Emile Flavin, "Le Cinéma en Afrique du Nord," *Cinéma et spectacles* 494 (November 11–17, 1928). However, the cinema houses in Algeria and Tunisia were already quite well developed and served as outlets for French films.

107. A series of comparisons were developed by Vidi, who visited California for an extended period, followed by a response from Fernand Laborde, who claimed that the economic model of development used in California was not relevant to the North African situation. For more detail see Vidi (pseud.), "L'Exemple de la Californie," *Revue politique et parlementaire* 144, no. 430 (September 10, 1930): 422–31; Fernand Laborde, "La Colonisation Nord-Africaine: L'Exemple de la Californie," *L'Afrique Française: Renseignements coloniaux et documents publiés par le Comité de l'Afrique française* 39 (1930): 659–62.

108. Gérard Talon, "Cinéma français: La Crise de 1928," in *Synchronismes: L'Année 1928,* ed. Henri Agel et al. (Paris: Editions du Signe, 1975), 104–16. Throughout this essay Talon argues that the French film industry was the harbinger of multinational cooperation, so the French film industry was hardly affected by domestic economic currents.

109. Moulan, "Et nos colonies?" 1.

110. CAOM, Politique du film, Gouvernement générale de l'Indochine, series L81, dossier 42049.

111. "Le cinéma en Indochine," *La Depêche coloniale,* March 1922, n.p., in CAOM clippings file, Agence FOM, carton 248, dossier 363: Indochine Cinéma 1921–1953. This is a press clipping that describes the genesis of censorship restrictions in Indochina and recounts some of the problems.

112. François Chevaldonné, "Le Cinéma colonial en Afrique du Nord: Naissance et fonctionnement d'un code," *Revue Algerienne des sciences juridiques économiques et politiques* 14, no. 3 (September 1977): 529–48.

113. These films were actually censored at the time of their release in France. See ". . . de nos correspondents . . . en Tunisie," *Cinémonde* 2 (November 2, 1928): 119.

114. Pierre Boulanger, *Le Cinéma colonial* (Paris: Seghers, 1976), 74.

6. Humanitarian Visions and Colonial Imperatives

1. Jean Jamin, "Les Objets ethnographiques sont-ils des choses perdues?" in *Temps perdu, temps retrouvé: Voir les choses du passé au present,* ed. Jacques Hainard and Roland Kaehr (Neuchâtel, Switzerland: Musée d'ethnographie, 1985), 68 (51–74). Jamin coins the term *idéogramme matériel,* which I have adapted as "material ideograms."

2. See my own earlier article "La Poterie, la chronophotographie, et les archives coloniales françaises," *Xoana: Images et sciences sociales* 2 (May 1994): 7–24.

3. Fatimah Tobing Rony, *The Third Eye: Race, Cinema, and Ethnographic Spectacle* (Durham, N.C.: Duke University Press, 1996). Tobing Rony's earlier article details the work of Regnault in "Those Who Sit and Those Who Squat: The 1895 Films of Félix-Louis Regnault," *Camera Obscura* 28 (1992): 263–89. She has also made a short film about this subject titled *On Cannibalism* (1994, 6', distributed by Women Make Movies). See also Félix-Louis Regnault, "Le Langage par les gestes," *La Nature* 1324 (October 15, 1898): 315 (315–17). The notion of Neolithic man as on the verge of human civilization and represented by Senegalese subjects refers to Gabriel de Mortillet's work "Promenades préhistoriques à l'Exposition universelle," *Matériaux pour l'histoire positive et philosophique de l'homme* 3 (1867): 21, 241, 368 (181–283, 285–368), as cited by Michael Hammond, "Anthropology as a Weapon of Social Combat in Late-Nineteenth-Century France," *Journal of the History of the Behavioral Sciences* 16 (1980): 120 (118–32).

4. Timothy Mitchell, "Orientalism and the Exhibitionary Order," in *Colonialism and Culture,* ed. Nicholas B. Dirks (Ann Arbor: University of Michigan Press, 1992), 293–95.

5. William H. Schneider. *An Empire for the Masses: The French Popular Image of Africa, 1870–1900* (Westport, Conn.: Greenwood Press, 1982), 128. For an announcement of this event see H. A. Mazard, "Jardin d'Acclimatation de Paris—Les Nubiens," *Matériaux pour l'histoire primitive et naturelle de l'homme: Revue illustrée* 12, no. 8 (1877): 342–44.

6. The journal was known as *Bulletins et Mémoires de la Société d'Anthropologie de Paris.* The *Société d'Anthropologie de Paris* was originally founded in 1859 by Paul Broca and quickly became the dominant voice of anthropology in France, displacing the *Société Ethnologique de Paris,* which had been founded in 1839, with a strong basis in Saint-Simonian and republican ideology. For more on an interpretation of the positivistic faith

in numbers, see Ian Hacking, "Biopower and the Avalanche of Printed Numbers," *Humanities and Society* 5, no. 3–4 (Summer–Fall 1982): 279–95.

7. George W. Stocking Jr., *Race, Culture, and Evolution: Essays in the History of Anthropology* (Chicago: University of Chicago Press, 1982), 58.

8. Joseph Deniker and Louis Laloy, "Mémoires originaux: Les Races exotiques à l'Exposition Universelle de 1889," *L'Anthropologie* 1 (1890): 257–94. In 1900, *Les Races et peuples de la terre: Éléments d'anthropologie et d'ethnographie* was simultaneously published in English under the title *The Races of Man: An Outline of Anthropology and Ethnography* and became the benchmark publication concerning the specificity of racial types and ethnic groups. For a sampling of Deniker's work translated into English, see *This Is Race,* ed. Earl W. Count (New York: Henry Schuman, 1950), 207–21. See also Sylviane Leprun, *Le Théâtre des colonies: Scénographie, acteurs, et discours de l'imaginaire dans les expositions, 1855–1937* (Paris: L'Harmattan, 1986), and Catherine Hodeir, "Decentering the Gaze at the French Colonial Exhibitions," in *Images and Empire: Visuality in Colonial and Postcolonial Africa,* ed. Paul S. Landau and Deborah D. Kaspin (Berkeley: University of California Press, 2002), 233–52.

9. Ernest-Théodore Hamy, "Les Expositions de l'état au Champ-de-Mars et à la Esplanade des Invalides," in *Exposition Universelle de 1889 à Paris,* ed. Alfred Picard (Paris: Impr. des Journaux Officiels, 1890), 173.

10. Jean-François de Bourgoing, *Tableau de l'Espagne moderne* (Paris: Chez G. Dufour et Éditions d'Ocagne, 1806 [1789]), 1: 271. De Bourgoing also noted that a Russian nobleman, de Czernichew, who read the first edition of this text, proposed such an idea to Catherine II of Russia, who was known to receive and act on ideas of such extravagance. De Bourgoing did not know whether the proposal was well received by the empress.

11. Dominique Lajard and Félix-Louis Regnault, "Poterie crue et origine du tour," *Bulletins et Mémoires de la Société d'Anthropologie de Paris* 6, fourth series (December 19, 1895): 734–39.

12. Alain Nicholas, "An Interview with Jean Rouch," in *Cinema Kino 1: Premier Contact–Premier Regard,* ed. Pierre-Louis Jordan (Marseilles: Images en Manoeuvres Editions, 1992), 294–95. The centrality of Regnault's chronophotographs to visual anthropology has been established by Emilie de Brigard, "The History of Ethnographic Film," in *Principles of Visual Anthropology,* ed. Paul Hockings (The Hague: Mouton De Gruyer, 1975), 13–44; Anthony R. Michaelis, *Research Films in Biology, Anthropology, Psychology, and Medicine* (New York: Academic Press, 1955); Martin Tuareg, "The Development of Standards for Scientific Films in German Ethnography," *Studies in Visual Communication* 9 (Winter 1983): 19–29; Tobing Rony, *The Third Eye;* and Thierry Lefebvre, "Ethnographie," in *Une encyclopédie du court métrage français,* ed. Jacky Evrard and Jacques Kermabon (Liège, Belgium: Éditions Yellow Now, 2004), 152–55.

13. Johannes Fabian, *Time and the Other: How Anthropology Makes Its Object* (New York: Columbia University Press, 1983).

14. The Musée de l'Ethnographie at Trocadéro became attached to the Muséum National d'Histoire Naturelle on the grounds of the Palais du Trocadéro in 1928, and the initial building was constructed for the 1878 Universal Exhibtion. The Palais was then occupied by the Musée d'Ethnographie in 1879, rebuilt in 1937, and renamed the Musée de l'Homme by 1938. See Paul Rivet and Georges Henri Rivière, "La Réorganisation du Musée d'Ethnographie du Trocadéro," *Bulletin du Musée d'Ethnographie du Trocadéro* 1 (January 1931): 2–11; see also Nélia Dias, *Le Musée d'Ethnographie du Trocadéro (1878–1908): Anthropologie et muséologie en France* (Paris: CNRS Éditions, 1991). The collections held by the Musée de l'Homme (along with the now closed Musée National des Arts d'Afrique et d'Océanie) have been moved to its successor, the Musée du Quai Branly, opened in 2006.

15. Sander Gilman, "Black Bodies, White Bodies," in *Race, Writing, and Difference,* ed. Henry Louis Gates Jr. (Chicago: University of Chicago Press, 1985), 232. Gilman also cites several issues of the autopsy report in German, as well as other such reports. See also Mathias Georg Guenther, "From 'Brutal Savages' to 'Harmless People': Notes on the Changing Western Image of the Bushman," *Paideuma* 26 (1980): 123–40, and M. van Wyk Smith, "'The Most Wretched of the Human Race': The Iconography of the Khoikhoin (Hottentots) 1500–1800," *History and Anthropology* 5, nos. 3–4 (1992): 285–330.

16. Stephen Jay Gould, "This View of Life: The Hottentot Venus," *Natural History* 91, no. 10 (October 1982): 20.

17. *The Return of Sara Baartman* (dir. Zola Maseko, 2005, 55', First Run Icarus); *The Life and Times of Sara Baartman* (dir. Zola Maseko, 1998, 52', First Run Icarus). See also Cris McGreal, "Homeward Bound," *Manchester Guardian Weekly,* February 28–March 6, 2002, 26, and Rachel L. Swarns, "Mocked in Europe of Old, African Is Embraced at Home at Last," *New York Times,* May 4, 2002, A3.

18. Claude Blanckaert, "The Origins of French Ethnology," in *Bones, Bodies, Behavior: Essays on Biological Anthropology,* ed. George W. Stocking Jr. (Madison: University of Wisconsin Press, 1988), 49 (18–55).

19. Toby A. Appel, *The Cuvier–Geoffroy Debate: French Biology in the Decades before Darwin* (Oxford: Oxford University Press, 1987). The debate between Georges Cuvier and Etienne Geoffroy Saint-Hilaire concerned the relative significance of a functional reading of human anatomy related to Cuvier's theory of four *embranchements*. In opposition, Saint-Hilaire's "unity of composition" foregrounded a structural approach to evolutionary adaptation related to the marginalized Transformist approach of Lamarck.

20. Stocking, *Race, Culture, and Evolution,* 56. Nélia Dias outlines in great detail the founding of the Société de l'Anthropologie de Paris and its relationship with other organizations of the same period, including La Société d'Ethnographie, in *Le Musée d'Ethnographie du Trocadéro.*

21. Paul Broca, "La Linguistique et l'anthropologie," *Bulletins et Mémoires de la Société d'Anthropologie,* series 3 (1862): 264.

22. Thomas G. August, "Nineteenth-Century Exoticism in France: The Formation of French Colonial Attitudes," *Historicus* 1 (Spring 1979): 95 (84–96).

23. Alice L. Conklin, "Civil Society, Science, and Empire in Late Republican France: The Foundation of Paris's Museum of Man," "Science and Civil Society," ed. Lynn K. Nyhart and Thomas H. Broman, special issue, *Osiris* 17 (2002): 263 (255–90).

24. As Michael Hammond has described, these strands were not mutually exclusive and represented political attitudes related to state power. See his essay "Anthropology as a Weapon of Social Combat in Late-Nineteenth-Century France," 118–32.

25. Krzysztof Pomian, "Entre l'invisible et le visible: La Collection," *Libre: Politique–anthropologie–philosophie* 340, no. 3 (1978): 38.

26. See Jennifer Michael Hecht's discussion of the Society of Mutual Autopsy for further discussion of atheism and the brain autopsy pact among medical doctors and physical anthropologists in *The End of the Soul: Scientific Modernity, Atheism, and Anthropology in France* (New York: Columbia University Press, 2003).

27. Félix-Louis Regnault, "Objets offerts: La Chronophotographie dans l'ethnographie," *Bulletins et Mémoires de la Société d'Anthropologie de Paris* 1, no. 4 (October 1900): 422.

28. Félix-Louis Regnault, "Les Musées de films," *Biologica: Revue scientifique du médecine* 16 (1912): 20.

29. Félix-Louis Regnault, "L'Histoire du cinéma: Son rôle en anthropologie," *Bulletins et Mémoires de la Société d'Anthropologie de Paris* 3, no. 7 (July 6, 1922): 65 (61–65).

30. Sally Price, *Primitive Art in Civilized Places* (Chicago: University of Chicago Press, 1989).

31. Pomian, "Entre l'invisible et le visible," 38.

32. Aimé Césaire, *Aimé Césaire: The Collected Poetry,* trans. Clayton Eshleman and Annette Smith (Berkeley: University of California Press, 1983), 59. I have altered the published translation.

33. Ibid., 83–85. ". . . le soir / nos multicolores puretés / et lie, lie-moi sans remords / lie moi à tes vastes bras à l'argile lumineuse, / lie ma noire vibration au nombril même du monde / lie, lie-moi, fraternité âpre. / Puis, m'étranglant de son lasso d'étoiles."

34. Claude Blanckaert, "The Origins of French Ethnology," 43.

35. Jean Brunhes' (1869–1930) *La Géographie humaine* was initially published as an 843-page volume with numerous plates by the Paris-based scientific press Félix Alcan in 1910. It was translated and expanded and remained a major work in the history of geography.

36. Lucien Febvre, *La Terre et l'évolution humaine: Introduction géographique à l'histoire* (Paris: La Renaissance du Livre, 1924 [1922]), as cited in Marie-Claire Robic, "La Géographie dans le mouvement scientifique," in *Jean Brunhes: Autour du monde, regards d'un géographe, regards de la géographie* (Paris: Conseil général Hauts-de-Seine, Musée Albert Kahn, Vilo, 1993), 63. See also Paul Vidal de la Blache, *Atlas général historique et géographique* (Paris: Armand Colin, 1894).

37. Teresa Castro, "Les Archives de la Planète: A Cinematographic Atlas," *Jump Cut: A Review of Contemporary Media* 4 (Winter 2006): 2 (9 pages); Christian Jacob, *L'Empire des cartes: Approche théorique de la cartographie à travers l'histoire* (Paris: Albin Michel, 1992), 97. Jacob's book has been translated as *The Sovereign Map: Theoretical Approaches in Cartography throughout History,* ed. Edward H. Dahl, trans. Tom Conley (Chicago: University of Chicago Press, 2006).

38. Jordana Mendelson, "Contested Territory: The Politics of Geography in Luis Buñuel's *Las Hurdes: Tierra sin pan,*" *Locus Amoenus* 2 (1996): 233 (229–42).

39. Thanks to Barbette Mangolte (professor of visual arts, University of California–San Diego) for pointing me toward the exhibition context for this film.

40. James F. Lastra, "Why Is This Absurd Picture Here? Ethnology/Equivocation/Buñuel," *October* 89 (Summer 1999): 52 (51–68). Thanks to Steve Ungar for this important reference.

41. Jean Jamin, "Objets trouvés des paradis perdus: A propos de la Mission Dakar–Djibouti," in *Collections Passion,* ed. Jacques Hainard and Roland Kaehr (Neuchâtel, Switzerland: Musée d'Ethnographie, 1982), 89 (69–100).

42. Mendelson, "Contested Territory," 237.

43. Paul Rivet and Georges-Henri Rivière, "La Mission ethnographique et linguistique Dakar-Djibouti," in "Mission Dakar–Djibouti, 1931–1933," special issue, *Le Minotaure* 2 (1933): 3 (3–6).

44. Lefebvre, "Ethnographie," 153.

45. Anne Doquet, *Les Masques dogon: Ethnologie savante et ethnologie autochtone* (Paris: Karthala, 1999), 7.

46. Georges Henri Rivière and Paul Rivet, "La Réorganisation du Musée d'Ethnographie du Trocadéro," *Bulletin du Muséum,* second series, 2, no. 5 (1930): 1–10.

47. James Clifford, *The Predicament of Culture: Twentieth-Century Ethnography, Literature, and Art* (Cambridge, Mass.: Harvard University Press, 1988).

48. Jeanne Beausoleil, "Albert Kahn, une utopie pour demain?" in *Albert Kahn: Réalités d'une utopie,* ed. Jeanne Beausoleil and Pascal Ory (Boulogne: Musée Albert Kahn, 1995), 20.

49. Eric LeRoy, "Le Fonds cinématographique colonial aux Archives du film et du dépôt légal du CNC (France)," *Journal of Film Preservation* 93 (October 2001): 55–59. This collection is also referred to as Les Archives du Film at the Bois D'Arcy, which is also the seat of the Centre National du Cinématographie (CNC). For a description of the Albert Kahn collection, see "La Photothèque—Cinémathèque Albert Kahn," in *Au-delà d'un jardin . . . Albert Kahn* (Boulogne: Musée d'Albert Kahn, 1986), 12. This is a sixteen-page, large-format pamphlet for an exhibition held from February 5 to April 27, 1986, at the Musée Albert Kahn. Note that 170,000 meters of film is roughly 557,740 feet of film, equivalent to one hundred hours of screening time based on a calculation of 35 mm film run at 24 frames per second, or two hundred hours given the longer (sixteen frames per second) running speeds of the period.

50. Jean Brunhes, "Ethnographie et géographie humaine," *L'Ethnographie* 1 (October 15, 1913): 38 (29–40).

51. For a more detailed discussion of how Albert Kahn made his fortune, see Gilles Baud Berthier, "Les Origines de la fortune d'Albert Kahn" and "Le Métier de la banque," in *Albert Kahn: Réalités d'une utopie,* ed. Beausoleil and Ory.

52. The Bourses de Voyage Autour du Monde grant program was established in 1898. It followed by two years the establishment of Cecil Rhodes's Oxford scholarship program, which was to enable young British subjects who grew up in the colonies to spend a year at Oxford. Kahn's scholarship program was of a different nature and yet was clearly influenced by his encounter with Rhodes in South Africa. For further documentation on this matter, see Alain Petit, "Le Premier élève de Bergson: Un précurseur alsacien de l'UNESCO," *Hommes et mondes* 40 (November 1949): 413–35.

53. Jean-Jacques Renoliet, "La Paix, un nouveau cadre de références," in *Albert Kahn: Réalités d'une utopie,* ed. Beausoleil and Ory, 258.

54. Marcel Mauss, "The Problem of Nationality," *Proceedings of the Aristotelian Society* 20 (1920): 242–52.

55. Ibid., 247.

56. See the following two chapters in *Jean Brunhes: Autour du monde, regards d'un géographe, regards de la géographie* (Paris: Conseil Général Hauts-de-Seine, Musée Albert Kahn, Vilo, 1993). The first includes course notes presented at the Collège de France and is titled "La Bosnie–Herzégovie: Extraits du cours de Jean Brunhes au Collège de France, décembre 1912–février 1913," 239–61; the second is a short descriptive essay about Brunhes' work in the region by Michel Sivignon, "Jean Brunhes et les Balkans," 262–64.

57. "Les Archives de la Planète" and "La Photothèque—Cinémathèque Albert Kahn," in *Au-delà d'un jardin . . . Albert Kahn,* 9–12. See Paula Amad's article "Cinema's 'Sanctuary': From Pre-documentary to Documentary Film in Albert Kahn's Archives de la Planète (1908–1931)," *Film History* 13 (2001): 138–59. Amad lists the cameramen and photographers who worked for Kahn in an appendix to this article, which translates and condenses many of the descriptions in the pamphlet. See also Amad, "Between the 'Familiar Text' and the 'Book of the World,'" in *Virtual Voyages: Cinema and Travel,* ed. Jeffrey Ruoff (Durham, N.C.: Duke University Press, 2006), 99–116.

58. Flore Hervé, "Les Archives de la Planète, 1909–1931," in *Albert Kahn: Réalités d'une utopie,* ed. Beausoleil and Ory, 197.

59. It was not a coincidence that Michel Clemenceau is the son of Georges Clemenceau, the French prime minister from 1906 to 1909 and 1917 to 1920, who negotiated the Treaty of Versailles. Georges Clemenceau was a frequent guest at Kahn's villa and part of Kahn's extended circle of politicians and decision makers. The project in Afghanistan was commissioned by King Amanullah to study a railway link that would pass through

Afghanistan. See Claudie de Guillebon, Jacques Ostier, and Philippe Gentile, eds., *L'Espace Albert Kahn,* trans. V. Spencer (Paris: MUSEES 2000, 1991), 45.

60. Martine Balard, "Le Reverend Père Aupais (1877–1945), artisan d'une reconnaissance africaine," in *Pour une reconnaissance africaine: Dahomey 1930: Des Images au service d'une idée,* ed. Jeanne Beausoleil (Paris: Conseil Général Hauts-de-Seine, Musée Albert Kahn, Vilo, 1996), 66–76 (51–78).

61. Latour, *The Pasteurization of France,* 60.

62. Albert Kahn, *Des Droits et devoirs des gouvernements* (Paris: Impr. de Vaugirard, 1918), 2.

63. Sophie Couëtoux, "De la Société Autour du Monde à la Coopération Intellectuelle," in *Albert Kahn: Réalités d'une utopie,* ed. Beausoleil and Ory, 285–96.

64. André Bazin, "The Ontology of the Photographic Image," in *What Is Cinema?* ed. and trans. Hugh Gray (Berkeley: University of California Press, 1967 [1945]), 1: 9–16.

65. Richard Maltby, "The Cinema and the League of Nations," in *"Film Europe" and "Film America": Cinema, Commerce, and Cultural Exchange, 1920–1939,* ed. Andrew Higson and Richard Maltby (Exeter, England: University of Exeter Press, 1999), 96 (82–116). With regard to this point, Maltby cites Harold L. Smith, "Formation of a French Motion Picture Control Commission," memorandum, February 20, 1928, NARA microfilm 560, roll 46, frame 975. The search aid for the International Educational Film Institute at UNESCO explains that a French Film Committee was set up on May 20, 1930, as a branch of the Italian International Institute for Film Education. See "Archives du Comité Français de l'Institut International du Cinéma Éducatif," reference no. 1.811, Correspondence Section, Archives for the Institute for Intellectual Cooperation, UNESCO, Paris.

66. For more detail concerning the founding of the Committee for Intellectual Cooperation under the League of Nations, see F. P. Walters, *A History of the League of Nations* (London: Oxford University Press, 1952), 1: 190–94.

67. Rose-Marie Mossé-Bastide, *Bergson éducateur* (Paris: Presses Universitaires de France, 1955), 119.

68. Jean-Jacques Renoliet, *L'Unesco oubliée: La Société des Nations et la cooperation intellectuelle, 1919–1946* (Paris: Publications de la Sorbonne, 1999).

69. Henri Bergson, *Mélanges,* ed. André Robinet with Marie-Rose Mossé-Bastide, Martine Robinet, and Michel Gauthier (Paris: Presses Universitaires de France, 1972), 1350.

70. Henri Bergson, *Essai sur les données immédiates de la conscience* (Paris: Félix Alcan, 1914 [1889]).

71. Henri Bergson, *Matter and Memory,* ed. and trans. Nancy Margaret Paul and W. Scott Palmer (New York: Zone Books, 1991 [1896]), 154.

72. For more on the philosophical debates between association and assimilation as it applied to a theory of mind, see James Ward, "Assimilation and Association," *Mind* 2, no. 5 (January 1893): 347–62.

73. Henri Bergson, "Appendice III: Le 'Temps propre' et la 'ligne d'Univers,'" in *Durée et simultanéité* (Paris: Presses Universitaires de France, 1992), 208.

74. Peter L. Galison, "Einstein's Clocks: The Place of Time," *Critical Inquiry* 26 (Winter 2000), 386 (355–89). For a fuller elaboration on Galison's arguments see his *Einstein's Clocks, Poincaré's Maps* (New York: W. W. Norton, 2003).

75. Galison, "Einstein's Clocks: The Place of Time," 385.

76. Jimena Canales, "Einstein, Bergson, and the Experiment That Failed: Intellectual Cooperation at the League of Nations," *MLN* 120 (2005): 1168 (1168–91). Thanks to Suzanne Guerlac for this reference.

77. Michael Biezunski, "Einstein's Reception in Paris in 1922," in *The Comparative Reception of Relativity,* ed. Thomas F. Glick (Boston: D. Reidel, 1983), 169–88.

78. "Discussion avec Einstein, April 6, 1922," in *Mélanges,* ed. Robinet et al., 1340 (1340–47). See the partial English translation of this interchange (154–59) and a supplementary essay by Robin Durie titled "From Absolute to Relative Time," in *Duration and Simultaneity: Bergson and the Einsteinian Universe,* ed. Robin Durie (Manchester, England: Clinamen Press, 1999), 202–8.

79. Canales, "Einstein, Bergson, and the Experiment that Failed," 1168; Canales cites Alan Sokal and Jean Bricmont, "Un regard sur l'histoire des rapports entre science et philosophie: Bergson et ses successeurs," in *Impostures intellectuelles* (Paris: Odile Jacob, 1997), 165–84.

80. Robinet et al., "Discussion avec Einstein," 1341.

81. Ibid., 1346.

82. Albert Einstein, letter to the Anti-Imperialist League, September 6, 1929, in *Albert Einstein: Oeuvres choisies 6, écrits politiques,* ed. Jean-Philippe Mathieu (Paris: Editions du Seuil and Éditions du CNRS, 1991), 77–78. See also Philippe Dewitte, *Les Mouvements nègres en France, 1919–1939* (Paris: L'Harmattan, 1985), 47.

83. Albert Einstein, letter to Gilbert Murray, president of the Executive Committee at the League of Nations, July 13, 1922, in *Albert Einstein,* ed. Mathieu, 53.

84. Albert Einstein, letter to Gilbert Murray, May 30, 1924, in ibid., 60–61.

85. Bergson, *Durée et simultanéité,* 59 (emphasis in original).

86. Henri Bergson, *Creative Evolution,* trans. Arthur Mitchell (Lanham, Md.: University Press of America, 1983 [1906]), 306.

87. One of the critiques of Bergson's notion of the Cinematograph as mind, a notion that had little to do with cinema as an emerging art form, was journalist Paul Souday's "Bergsonisme et Cinéma," published in the magazine *Le Film: Hebdomadaire Illustré* 83 (October 15, 1917): 9–10.

88. Bergson, *Creative Evolution,* 306.

89. William Marston Seabury, ed., *Motion Picture Problems: The Cinema and the League of Nations* (New York: Avondale Press, 1929), 235–64.

90. Seabury, *Motion Picture Problems,* 237–38. See also Maltby, "The Cinema and the League of Nations," 93–94.

91. "Résolutions adoptées à l'unaminité par le Congrès International du Cinématographe, Paris, 27 September–3 October 1926," in Seabury, *Motion Picture Problems,* 361.

92. Christel Taillibert, *L'Institut International du Cinématographie Éducatif: Regards sur le rôle du cinéma éducatif dans la politique internationale du facisme italien* (Paris: L'Harmattan, 1999), 99.

93. As cited by Seabury, *Motion Picture Problems,* 163. From *League of Nations Journal of the 8th Ordinary Session of the Assembly,* Geneva, September 7, 1927, 24.

94. Seabury, *Motion Picture Problems,* 164.

95. League of Nations Archives, Geneva (LNA), "Comité Executif de l'Insitut du Cinématographe Éducatif: Cinquième session, tenue à Rome les 23 au 24 janvier 1930," reference code ICE/C.E.P./5e Session/P.V.2.: 2.

96. Maltby, "The Cinema and the League of Nations," 106.

97. LNA, "Société des Nations: Insitut du Cinématographe Éducatif: Conseil Administration: 5ième session: 1ère séance, tenue à Rome le 26 octobre 1932 à 10 heures," reference code ICE/C.A./5e Session/P.V.1.: 15.

98. LNA, "Intellectual Co-operation Organisation: International Educational Cinematographic Institute: Permanent Executive Committee: 19th Session: Item 7 of the Agenda," January 28, 1935, reference code ICE/C.E.P./23.: 1.

99. "Economic Conference on the Freedom of Trade and Tariff Restrictions, May 1927 and October–November 1927: Proceedings of the League of Nations," in Seabury, *Motion Picture Problems,* 142.

100. Ernest Renan, "What Is a Nation?" in *Becoming National: A Reader,* ed. Geoff Eley and Ronald Grigor Suny (Oxford, England: Oxford University Press, 1996), 42–55. The original French version, titled "Qu'est-ce qu'une nation?" was presented as a lecture at the Sorbonne on March 11, 1882.

101. Dr. Humbert's report was presented to the Child Welfare Committee, Geneva, in May and reproduced in Seabury, *Motion Picture Problems,* 265. It was commissioned by Dr. Longeuil, delegate of the International Institute for Intellectual Cooperation.

102. Maurice Rouvroy, "Pour l'enfance et l'adolescence," *Revue internationale du cinéma éducateur* 2 (August 1929): 159–66; emphasis in original. See also M.-J. Janvier, "Névrose cinématographique: Enfants adolescents; Ravages causés par l'abus du cinema; Le bien que le cinéma pourrait faire," *Revue de l'Oeuvre Nationale de l'Enfance* 5, no. 6 (March 1924): 349–65. For further discussion of Maurice Rouvroy's work, see Mark D'hoker, "Contributions de Maurice Rouvroy (1879–1954) aux soins en résidence de la jeunesse à problèmes psycho-sociaux pendant l'entre-deux-guerres," in "Beyond the Pale, Behind Bars: Marginalization and Institutionalization from the 18th to 20th Century," special issue, *Paedagogica Historica* 26, no. 2 (1990): 211–46. Thanks to Mark D'hoker for specifying the reference to Janvier's "Névrose cinématographique."

103. UNESCO League of Nations Archive, Paris. Within the Archives de la Commission Internationale de la Coopération Intellectuelle, see Archives du Comité Français de l'Institut International du Cinéma Éducatif, series 13/7, enquêtes divers, series 8/10. For a list of the questions, see Taillibert, *L'Institut International du Cinématographie Éducatif,* 172–74.

104. The French version of the journal, *Revue internationale du cinéma éducateur* (1929–35), has served as my primary source of reference. The journal was published monthly during this period and often featured a series of special issues on questions of hygiene and the uses of cinema in the workplace. It was later reorganized on a smaller scale in 1935 and renamed *Interciné,* but also became associated with the more popular Italian film magazine *Cinema* in 1936. See Taillibert, *L'Institut International du Cinématographie Éducatif,* 316–22. Once the Italians left the league in 1938 due to the invasion and occupation of Ethiopia, all activities of the ICE ceased.

105. *Revue internationale du cinéma éducateur* 1 (July 1929): 8. See the first editorial statement of the journal's goals (7–11).

106. Ibid., 11.

107. Félix Lampe, "L'Enseignement de la géographie par le film," *Revue internationale du cinéma éducateur* 4 (April 1932): 295–308.

108. Ernst Jünger, "Total Mobilization," in *The Heidegger Controversy: A Critical Reader,* ed. Richard Wolin, trans. Joel Golb and Richard Wolin (Cambridge, Mass.: MIT Press, 1993), 122–39.

109. Jamin, "Objets trouvés des paradis perdus," 82, 84–89.

110. Lampe, "L'Enseignement de la géographie par le film," 302.

111. See the following articles from the ICE journal: Jean Comandon, "L'Évolution de la microcinématographie," *Revue Internationale du Cinéma Éducateur* 6 (June 1932): 487–94; "Les grands documentaires: 'Pori,'" *Revue internationale du cinéma éducateur* 2 (February 1931): 195–99 (*Pori* is a UFA production filmed during the course of an expedition led by von Gontard and Herbert Kluge in Sudan, depicting the Masai, along with other ethnic groups and animals); "Les grands documentaires: 'Trader Horn,'" *Revue*

internationale du cinéma éducateur 10 (October 1931): 1044–45; "Les grands documentaires: 'Au pays du scalp,'" *Revue internationale du cinéma éducateur* 6 (June 1931): 650 (this film was edited from footage shot by Alberto Cavalvanti for la Compagnie Universelle Cinématagraphique, based in Paris, following a four-year expedition to South America led by the Marquis de Wavrin); and "'Le Vrai visage de l'Afrique' présenté à l'I.C.E.," *Revue internationale du cinéma éducateur* 6 (June 1932): 554.

112. Martin Heidegger, "The Age of the World Picture," in *The Question concerning Technology and Other Essays,* ed. and trans. William Lovitt (New York: Harper and Row, 1977), 133 (115–54).

113. Ibid., 128, 134. See Heidegger's discussion of *Weltbild* as "a conception of the world" and of *Gebilt* as a "structured image."

CONCLUSION

1. The dynamometer was developed by a mechanical engineer, Edme Régnier (1751–1825), as part of a series of inventions related to public safety, such as a hand-cranked fire ladder and the rifle safety. Weights and measures was a significant domain of Régnier's work and was closely associated with an eighteenth-century emphasis on mechanical inventions developing in the shadow of Newtonian physics. Régnier's invention of a mechanism that measured the strength of gunpowder *(l'éprouvette portative),* won him the admiration and respect of numerous scientific luminaries of the day and locates his work within the context of a historically determined niche coterminous with the French Revolution. In fact, the dynamometer was later customized to measure human capacities following Régnier's development of the combination lock, the padlock, and a vision-corrected viewfinder for the near-sighted artilleryman. Régnier adapted recent inventions to the operational needs of a human agent rather than simply using machines to imitate human functionality. He also transformed a number of his devices so that they could be used in conducting on-site observations (as he did with his portable meteorological devices), such as the anemometer, used to measure wind speed, and the potamometer, used to measure the force of river currents. For a complete list of Régnier's inventions, see Edme Régnier, *Note des inventions du Cen Régnier, conservateur du Dépôt Central de l'Artillerie, membre de l'Athénée de Arts, de la Société d'Encouragement pour l'Industrie Nationale . . .* (Paris: Impr. de Prault, n.d., ca. 1801).

2. Christian Pociello, *La science en mouvements: Étienne Marey et Georges Demenÿ, 1870–1920* (Paris: Presses Universitaires de France, 1999), 56; Francisco Amoros y Ondeano, *Nouveau manuel d'education physique, gymnastique, et morale* (Paris: Roret, 1830).

3. Michel Foucault, *Discipline and Punish,* trans. Alan Sheridan (New York: Vintage Books, 1979), 103; Georges Vigarello, *Histoire du viol: XVIe–XXe siècle* (Paris: Seuil, 1998), 104–9.

4. Jean-Pierre Yahi, "Duel, savate, et boxe française: Une nouvelle destinée des coups," in "Aimez-vous les stades?" ed. Alain Ehrenberg, special issue, *Recherches* 43 (April 1980): 125, 116–18, 121–22 (113–32).

5. Jacques Ulmann, *De la gymnastique aux sports modernes: Histoire des doctrines de l'éducation physique* (Paris: Presses Universitaires de France, 1965), 287.

6. Pociello, *La Science en mouvements,* 52.

7. Alain Ehrenberg, *Le corps militaire: Politique et pédagogie en démocratie* (Paris: Auber Montainge, 1983), 111.

8. Georges Hébert, "A propos d'un pieux anniversaire . . . une infamie," in Pociello, *La Science en mouvements,* 321.

9. Georges Hébert, *La Culture virile et les devoirs physiques de l'officier combattant* (Paris: G. Codinet Cie, 1913), x–xi, 8; Jacques Defrance, "La Signification culturelle de l'hébertisme," *Revue des sciences et techniques des activités physiques et sportives* 31 (May 1933): 60 (47–63). See also Jean-Michel Delaplace, "Culture et nature dans la 'méthode naturelle' de Georges Hébert (1875–1957)," in *Le Sport français dans l'entre-deux-guerres,* ed. Jean-Philippe Saint-Martin and Thierry Terret (Paris: L'Harmattan, 2000), 239–58.

10. Georges Hébert, *L'Éducation physique, virile, et morale par la méthode naturelle,* 6th ed. (Paris: Librairie Vuibert, 1936), vol. 1, plate 1. Hébert described the scene as an attempt by the artist to reproduce the sculptural beauty of young men and women with the same studied exactitude as the aging queen, the tropical flora, and the clothing worn by a member of the expedition.

11. Ulmann, *De la gymnastique aux sports modernes,* 358–59.

12. André Rauch, "Violence et maîtrise de soi en boxe," in "Le Gouvernement du corps," special issue, *Communications* 56 (1993): 139–54.

13. Ed Cunningham, "Siki Denies Coming from Jungle; Admits Double Crossing Carpentier," *Ring Magazine,* August 1925, 28.

14. Gerald Early, "Battling Siki, the Boxer as Natural Man," in *The Culture of Bruising* (Hopewell, N.J.: Ecco Press, 1994), 70.

15. Timothée Jobert, *Champions noirs, racisme blanc: La Metropole et les sportifs noirs en contexte colonial, 1901–1944* (Grenoble: Presses Universitaires de Grenoble, 2006), 115–56.

16. Peter Benson, *Battling Siki: A Tale of Ring Fixes, Race, and Murder in the 1920s* (Fayetteville: University of Arkansas Press, 2006), 95.

17. Paul Eaton Reeve, "Homage to Battling Siki," *View* 3 (1942): 21 (emphasis in original). Thanks to Peter Wollen for this reference.

18. *New York World,* December 16, 1925, 4, as cited by Benson, *Battling Siki,* 269.

19. British American Scientific International Commercial (BASIC) English. See Charles K. Ogden, *Basic English: A General Introduction with Rules and Grammar* (London: K. Paul, Trench, Trubner, 1930).

20. *Siki* (dir. Niek Koppen, 1992, Holland, 62').

21. Eduardo Arroyo, *Panama Al Brown* (Paris: Bernard Grasset, 1998), 34.

22. James Clifford, *The Predicament of Culture: Twentieth-Century Ethnography, Literature, and Art* (Cambridge, Mass.: Harvard University Press, 1998), 137.

23. Jean Jamin, "Objets trouvés des paradis perdus: A propos de la Mission Dakar–Djibouti," in *Collections Passion,* ed. Jacques Hainard and Roland Kasehr (Neuchâtel, Switzerland: Musée d'Ethnographie, 1982), 78.

24. From the program "Grand Gala de la Boxe," April 15, 1931, Cirque d'Hiver. Photothèque, Musée du quai Branly.

25. *Le Minotaure* 2 (1933): 1.

26. This is my own description after viewing a film of a twelve-round nontitle fight between Brown and Teddy Baldock held on May 21, 1931, in London.

27. Arroyo, *Panama Al Brown,* 211–12.

28. Francis Steegmuller, *Cocteau: A Biography* (Boston: Atlantic Monthly Press, 1970), 434.

29. E. E. Cummings, "47 [ondumonde]" (from the 1935 manuscript *No Thanks*), in *Complete Poems, 1904–1962,* ed. George James Firmage (New York: Liveright, 1994), 430.

30. Guy Laborde, "Danses pour Barbette—Al Brown à Médrano," *Le Temps* (under the rubric "Spectacles"), May 3, 1938, n.p.

31. David Lewis Hammarstrom, *Behind the Big Top* (South Brunswick, N.J.: A. S. Barnes, 1980), 34.

32. Jean Cocteau, "Le Numéro Barbette," *La Nouvelle revue Française* 18, no. 154 (July 1, 1926): 263 (257–63).

33. Hovey Burgess, "The Classification of Circus Techniques," *Drama Review: TDR* 18, no. 1 (March 1974): 65–70.

34. Richard Broome, "The Australian Reaction to Jack Johnson, Black Pugilist, 1907–9," in *Sport in History: The Making of Modern Sporting History,* ed. Richard Cashman and Michael McKernan (St. Lucia, Australia: University of Queensland Press, 1979), 358 (343–63).

35. Geoffrey C. Ward, *Unforgivable Blackness: The Rise and Fall of Jack Johnson* (New York: Knopf, 2004), 132. Ward also mentions that Burns later accused Jack London of being a strong advocate for racial equality who belittled him in every way. This was in spite of London's powerful race-baiting exhortation against Johnson's golden smile upon winning the fight: "But one thing remains. Jeffries must emerge from his alfalfa farm and remove that smile from Johnson's face. Jeff, it's up to you" (133).

36. For a discussion of early boxing film culture in the United States see Dan Streible, "A History of the Boxing Film, 1894–1915: Social Control and Social Reform in the Progressive Era," *Film History* 2 (1989): 235–57.

37. Eldridge Cleaver, *Soul on Ice* (New York: McGraw-Hill, 1968), as cited by Al-Tony Gilmore, *Bad Nigger! The National Impact of Jack Johnson* (Port Washington, N.Y.: Kennikat Press, 1975), 25.

38. Johnson was initially charged with abduction, but that charge was transformed into a violation of the White Slave Traffic Act, better known as the Mann Act, by the Bureau of Investigation (the predecessor of the FBI). See Randy Roberts, *Papa Jack: Jack Johnson and the Era of White Hopes* (New York: Free Press, 1983), 144.

39. Jack Johnson, *Mes Combats* (Paris: P. Lafitte, 1914). See also two articles by Jack Johnson that appeared in *La Boxe et les boxeurs: Revue hebdomadaire illustrée des sports de défense* (December 1909–1925): "La Lutte pour les haricots," vol. 414 (April 11, 1923): 15–17, and "Le Boxeur, homme du monde," vol. 418 (May 9, 1923): 15–16.

40. Robert A. Nye, "Degeneration, Neurasthenia, and the Culture of Sport in *Belle Époque* France," *Journal of Contemporary History* 17 (1982): 59–62 (51–68).

41. See [Marshall Walter] Major Taylor, *The Fastest Bicycle Rider in the World: An Autobiography* (Worcester, Mass.: Wormley, 1928); and Jobert, *Champions noirs, racisme blanc,* 17–49. The Jules Beau Photographic Collection at the Bibliothèque Nationale Print Collection has a series of images (R36608–36614) depicting Major Taylor dating from May 27, 1901. For more on the origins of the Olympic Games as an expression of the internationalist European spirit, see John J. MacAloon, *This Great Symbol: Pierre de Coubertin and the Origins of the Modern Olympic Games* (Chicago: University of Chicago Press, 1981). See also Fabrice Auger, "L'Idée coloniale chez Pierre de Coubertin," in *À l'école de l'aventure: Practiques sportives de plein air et idéologie de la conquête du monde,* ed. Christian Pociello and Daniel Denis (Voiron, France: Presses Universitaires du Sport, 2000), 55–70.

42. Jody Blake, *Le Tumulte Noir: Modernist Art and Popular Entertainment in Jazz-Age Paris, 1900–1930* (University Park: Pennsylvania State University Press, 1999), 15–16.

43. Gallerie 1900–2000, *Arthur Cravan: Poète et boxeur* (Paris: Terrain Vague, 1992).

44. Claude Meunier, *Ring noir: Quand Apollinaire, Cendrars, et Picabia découvraient les boxeurs nègres* (Paris: Plon, 1992), 75–76.

INDEX

Created by Eileen Quam

PETER J. BLOOM is associate professor of film and media studies at the University of California–Santa Barbara.